EASY PIANO

ISBN 0-634-04584-9

7777 W. BLUEMOUND RD. P.O. BOX 13819 MILWAUKEE, WI 53213

For all works contained herein:
Unauthorized copying, arranging, adapting, recording or public performance is an infringement of copyright.
Infringers are liable under the law.

Visit Hal Leonard Online at
www.halleonard.com

Contents

100	If You Leave Me Now	CHICAGO	1976
108	It's Impossible (Somos Novios)	PERRY COMO	1971
105	It's Too Late	CAROLE KING	1971
112	Joy to the World	THREE DOG NIGHT	1971
120	Looks Like We Made It	BARRY MANILOW	1977
115	Make It With You	BREAD	1970
124	Nadia's Theme	FROM "THE YOUNG AND THE RESTLESS"	1976
127	Night Fever	BEE GEES	1978
132	One Less Bell to Answer	THE 5TH DIMENSION	1970
136	Our House	CROSBY, STILLS, NASH & YOUNG	1970
143	Oye Como Va	SANTANA	1971
148	Precious and Few	CLIMAX	1972
158	Rainy Days and Mondays	CARPENTERS	1971
153	Ready to Take a Chance Again (Love Theme)	FROM "FOUL PLAY"	1978
162	She's Always a Woman	BILLY JOEL	1978
172	So Far Away	CAROLE KING	1971
176	Speak Softly, Love (Love Theme)	ANDY WILLIAMS	1972
167	Summer Nights	FROM "GREASE"	1972
178	Teach Your Children	CROSBY, STILLS, NASH & YOUNG	1970
183	Three Times a Lady	THE COMMODORES	1978
188	Top of the World	CARPENTERS	1973
198	The Way We Were	BARBRA STREISAND	1974
202	We've Only Just Begun	CARPENTERS	1970
206	When Will I Be Loved	LINDA RONSTADT	1975
208	Where Do I Begin (Love Theme)	ANDY WILLIAMS	1971
193	Yesterday Once More	CARPENTERS	1973
212	You and Me Against the World	HELEN REDDY	1974
218	You've Got a Friend	JAMES TAYLOR	1971

ANNIE'S SONG

Words and Music by
JOHN DENVER

Copyright © 1974 Cherry Lane Music Publishing Company, Inc. (ASCAP) and DreamWorks Songs (ASCAP)
Worldwide Rights for DreamWorks Songs Administered by Cherry Lane Music Publishing Company, Inc.
International Copyright Secured All Rights Reserved

G
rain.
arms.
Like a storm in the
Let me lay down be -
2
5

F G Am F
des - ert,
side you,
like a sleep - y blue
let me al - ways be

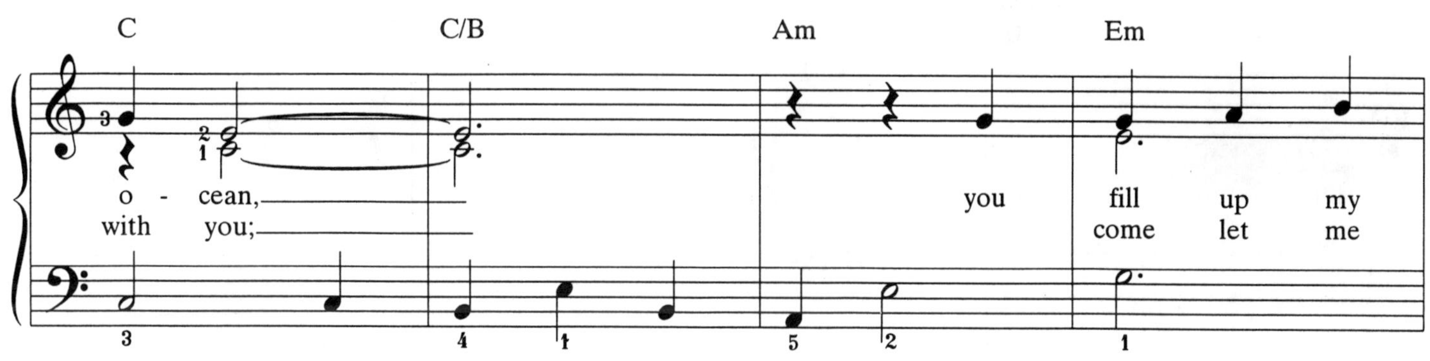
C C/B Am Em
o - cean,
with you;
you fill up my
come let me

To Coda
F Em Dm G7
sens - es,
love you,
come fill me a -
come love me a -

1.
C
Csus4
C
gain.
Come let me
2.
C
Csus4
C
gain.
You
D.S. (lyric 1) al Coda
fill up my
Coda
C
Csus4
gain.
C
Csus4
C

BLESS THE BEASTS AND CHILDREN

Words and Music by BARRY DeVORZON
and PERRY BOTKIN, JR.

© 1971 (Renewed 1999) SCREEN GEMS-EMI MUSIC INC.
All Rights Reserved International Copyright Secured Used by Permission

Fm/A♭
G7♯5
Cm
chil - dren,
for the world
can nev - er be
Fsus
F
B♭
Gsus
G
the
world
they see.
E♭
E♭maj7
D♭/E♭
mf
Light their
way
when the
dark - ness
sur -
Fm/E♭ E♭
F
C♭/G♭
G♭
rounds them;
Give them
love
let it

D♭/F
E♭/F
F
shine all a - round ___ them.
B♭
Fm/A♭
G7
mp
Bless the beasts and the chil - dren;
Give them shel - ter
Cm
Fsus
F
B♭
from a storm; ___
Keep them safe; ___
Gsus
G
C
8va
Keep them warm.
rit.
p

BABY WHAT A BIG SURPRISE

Words and Music by
PETER CETERA

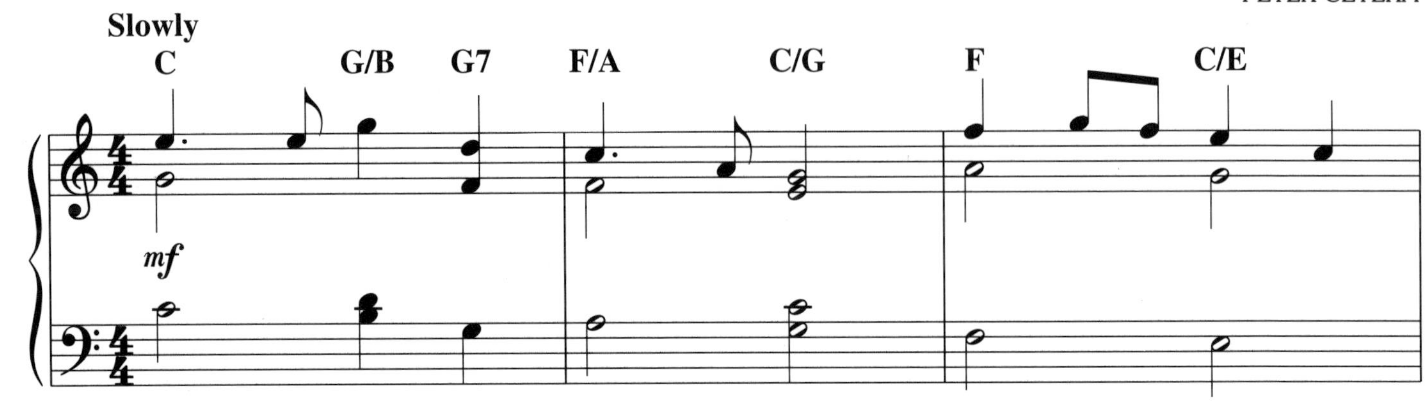

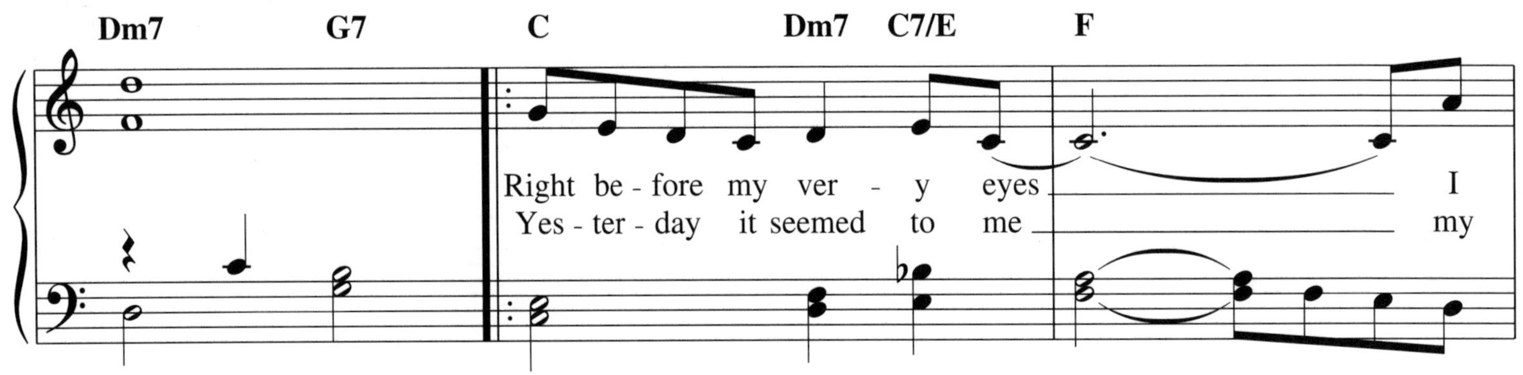

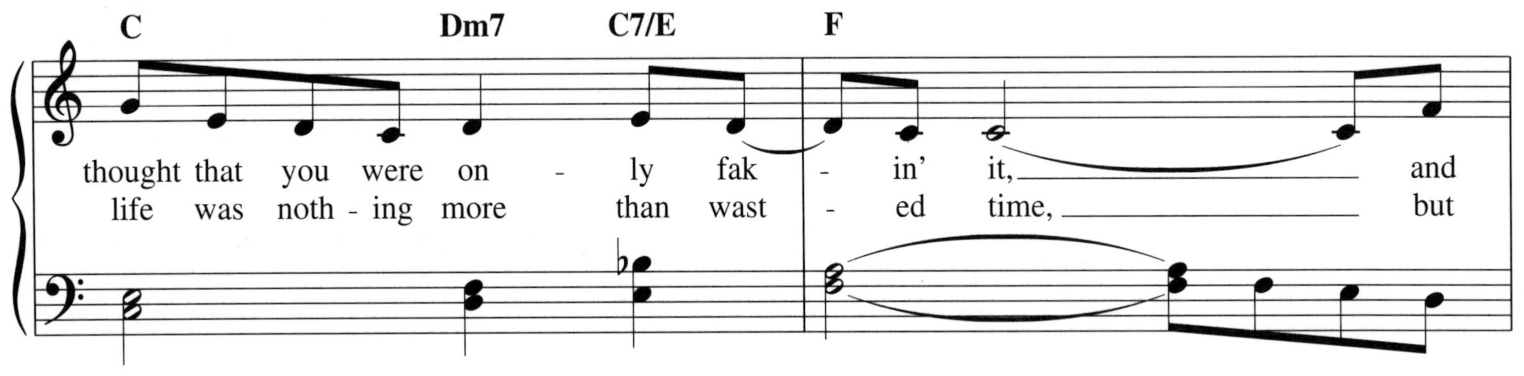

Copyright © 1977 by BMG Songs, Inc.
International Copyright Secured All Rights Reserved

F
C/E
Dm7
B♭
C
F
prise;
right be-fore my ver - y eyes, oh, oh,
1.
E♭
B♭
2.
C/E
E♭
oh, oh.
oh, oh,
B♭
Am
oh.
Just to be a - lone was a
G
C
Am
G
lit - tle more than I could take,
then you came to stay.

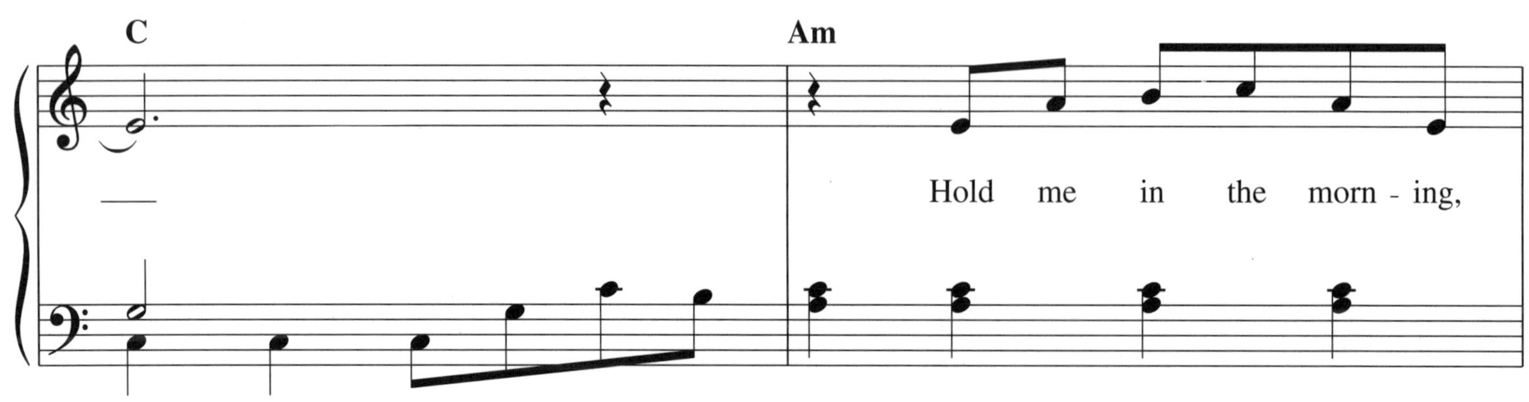
C
Am
Hold me in the morn - ing,

G
C
Am
G
love me in the af - ter - noon.
Help me find my way,

B♭
G/B
C
Dm7
C7/E
hey,
yeah.
Now and then just like be - fore

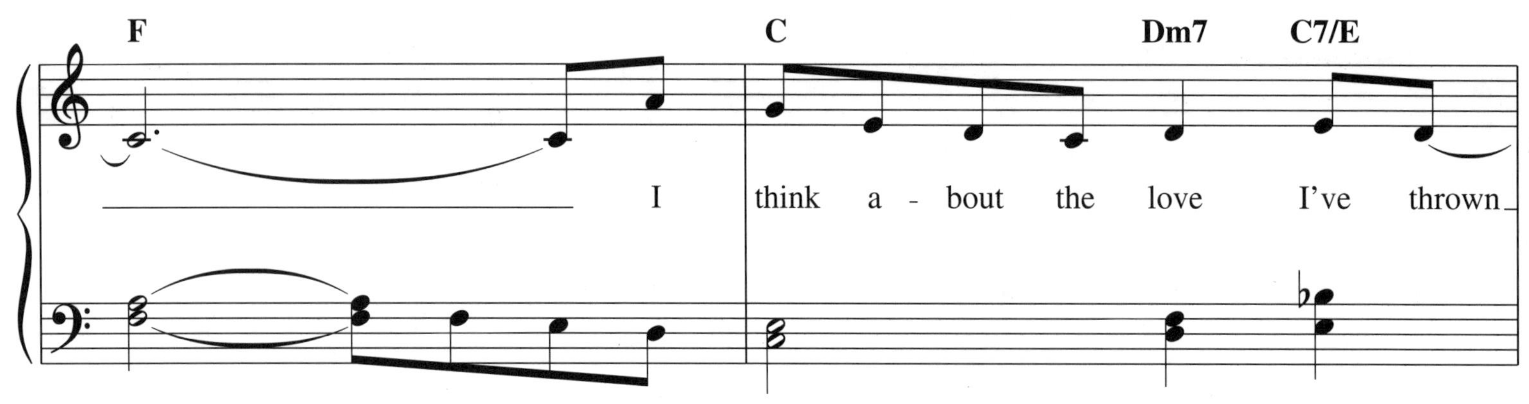
F
C
Dm7
C7/E
I
think a - bout the love I've thrown

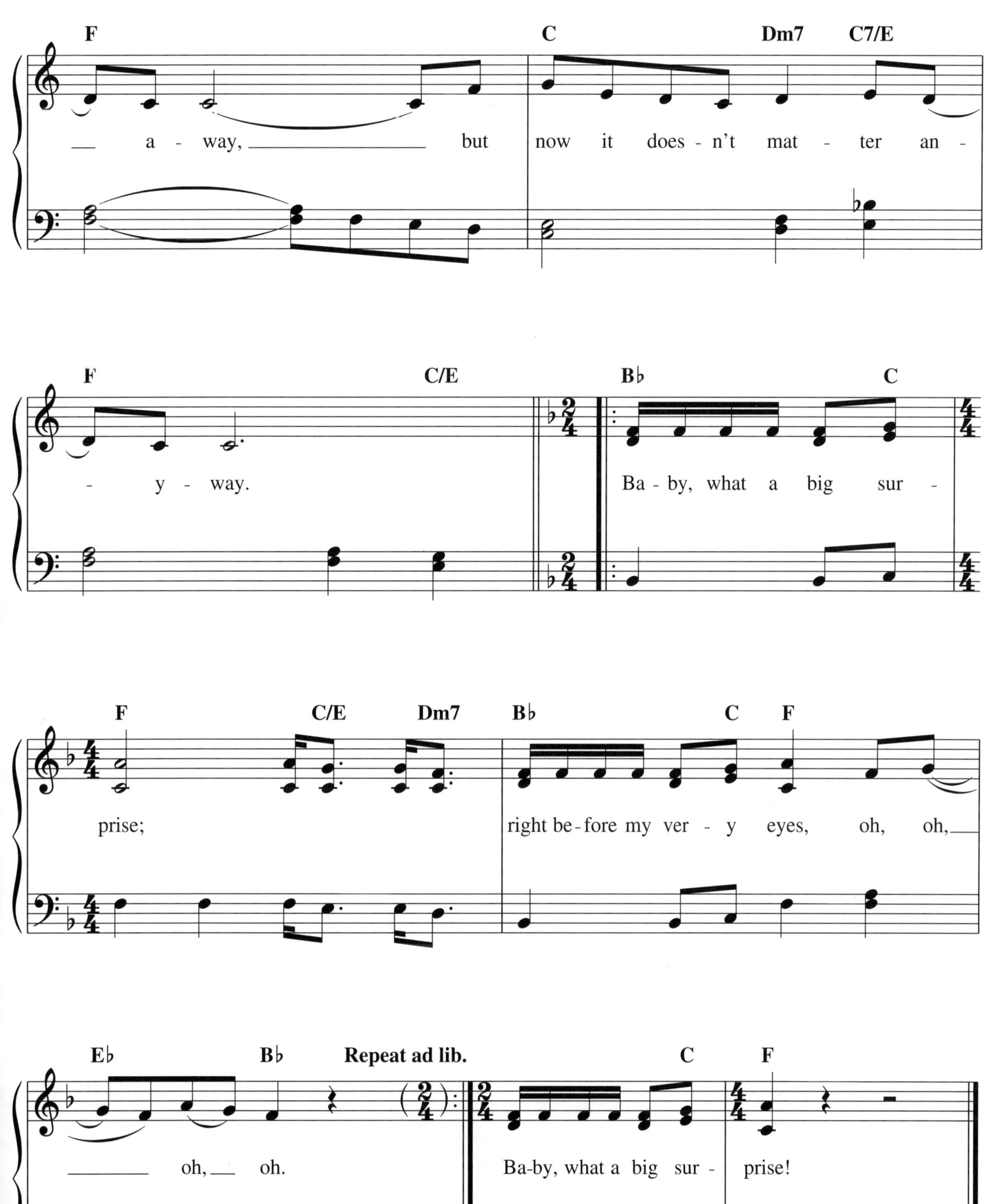
F
C
Dm7
C7/E
a - way,
but
now it does - n't mat - ter an -
F
C/E
B♭
C
- y - way.
Ba - by, what a big sur -
F
C/E
Dm7
B♭
C
F
prise;
right be - fore my ver - y eyes, oh, oh,
E♭
B♭
Repeat ad lib.
C
F
oh, oh.
Ba-by, what a big sur - prise!

BABY, I'M-A WANT YOU

Words and Music by
DAVID GATES

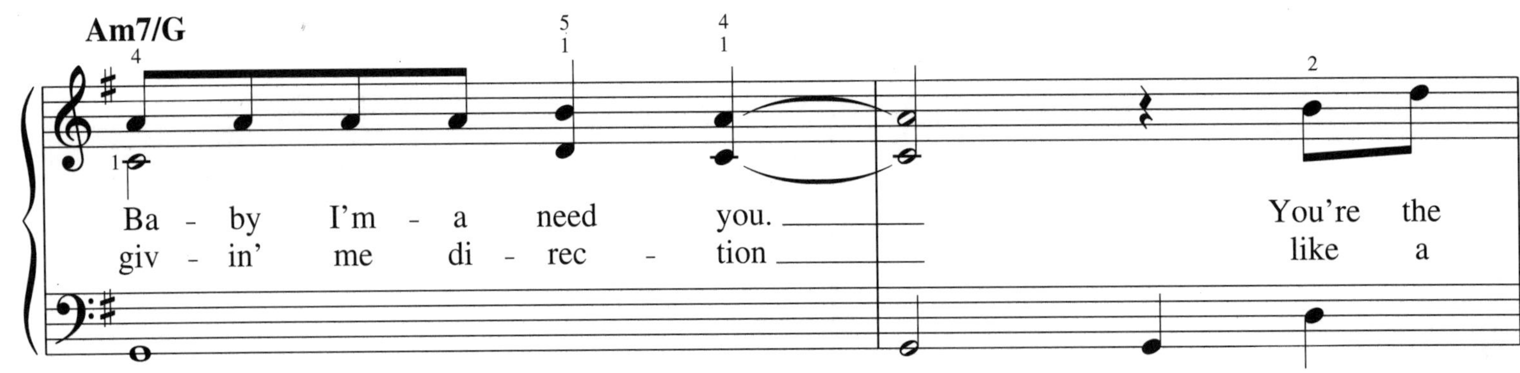

Copyright © 1971 Sony/ATV Tunes LLC
Copyright Renewed
All Rights Administered by Sony/ATV Music Publishing, 8 Music Sqaure West, Nashville, TN 37203
International Copyright Secured All Rights Reserved

Gmaj7
4 2 2
on - ly one I care e - nough to hurt
guid - ing light to help me through my dark -

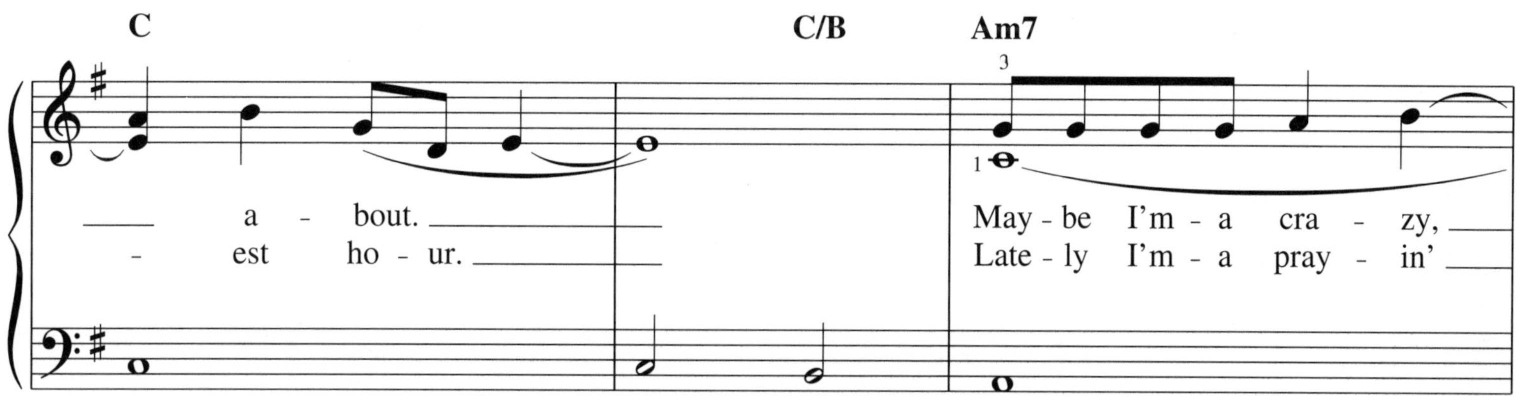
C
C/B
Am7
3
1
a - bout.
- est ho - ur.
May - be I'm - a cra - zy,
Late - ly I'm - a pray - in'

3
1.
C/D
but I just can't live with - out your
that you'll

2.
C/D
4 4
al - ways be a - stay - in' be - side

G
Bm7
me.
Used to be my life was

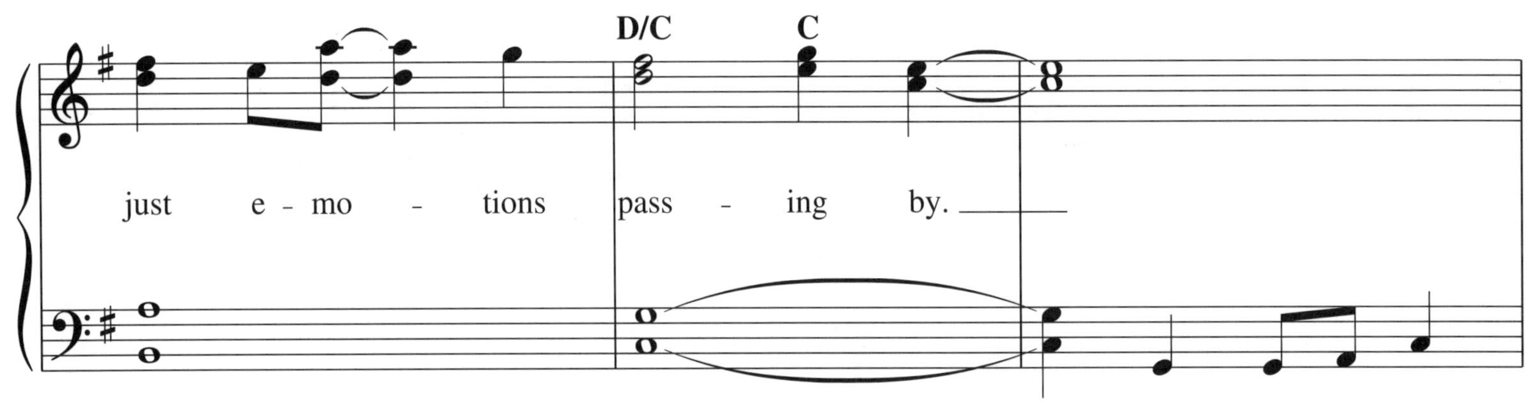
D/C
C
just e - mo - tions pass - ing by.

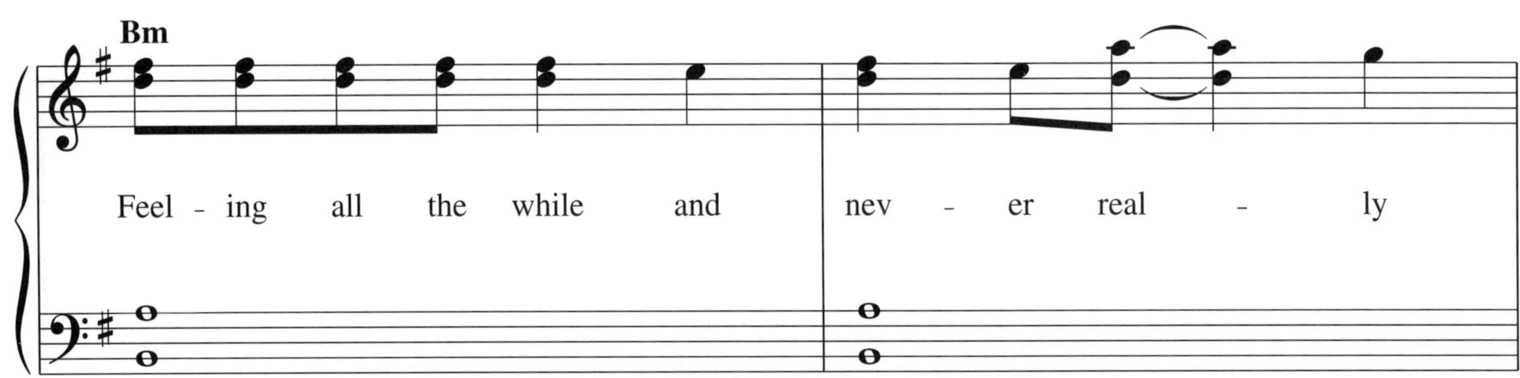
Bm
Feel - ing all the while and nev - er real - ly

D/C
C
G
know - ing why.
Instrumental solo

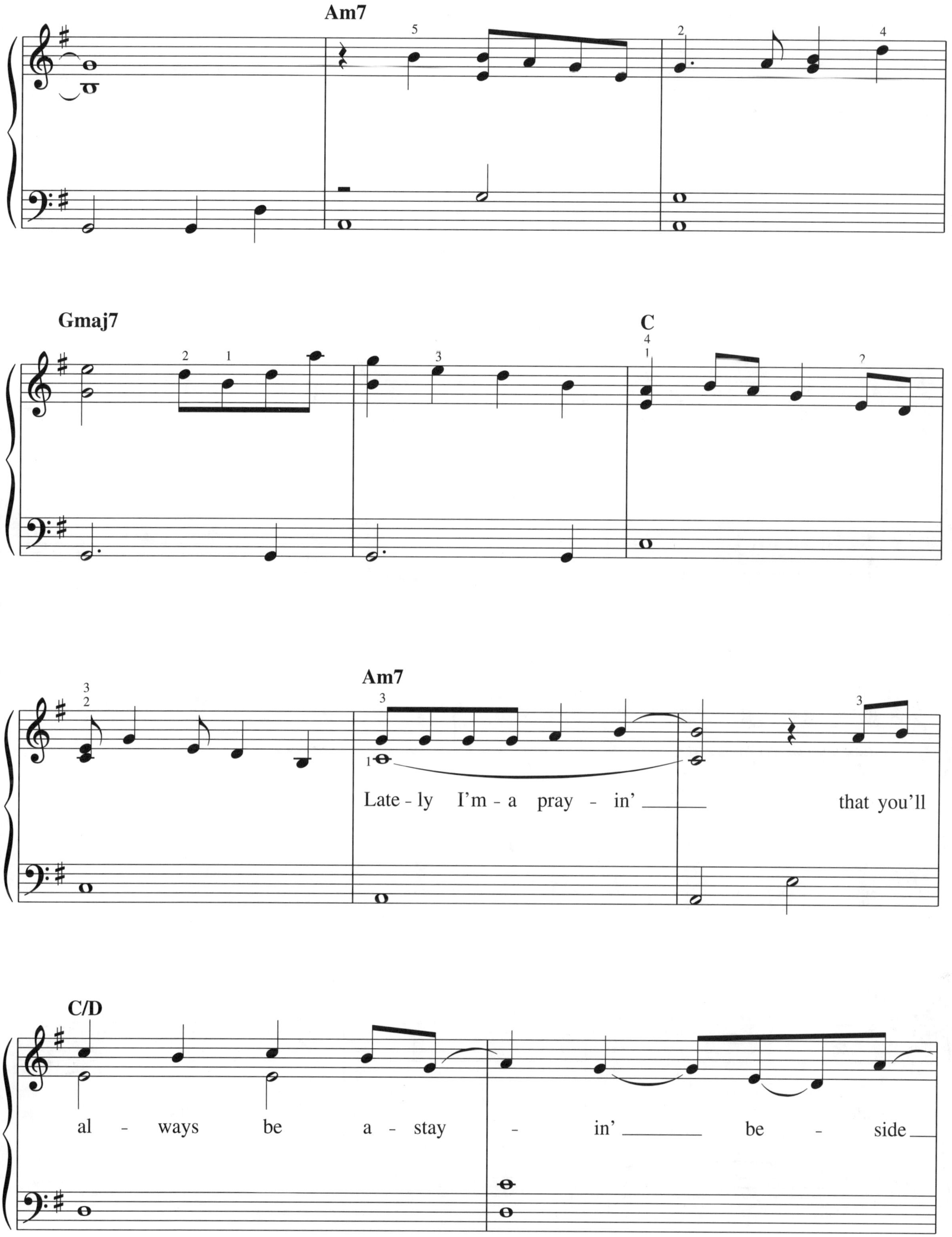

Am7

Gmaj7

C

Am7

Late - ly I'm - a pray - in' that you'll

G
Bm7
3
1
me.
Used to be my life was

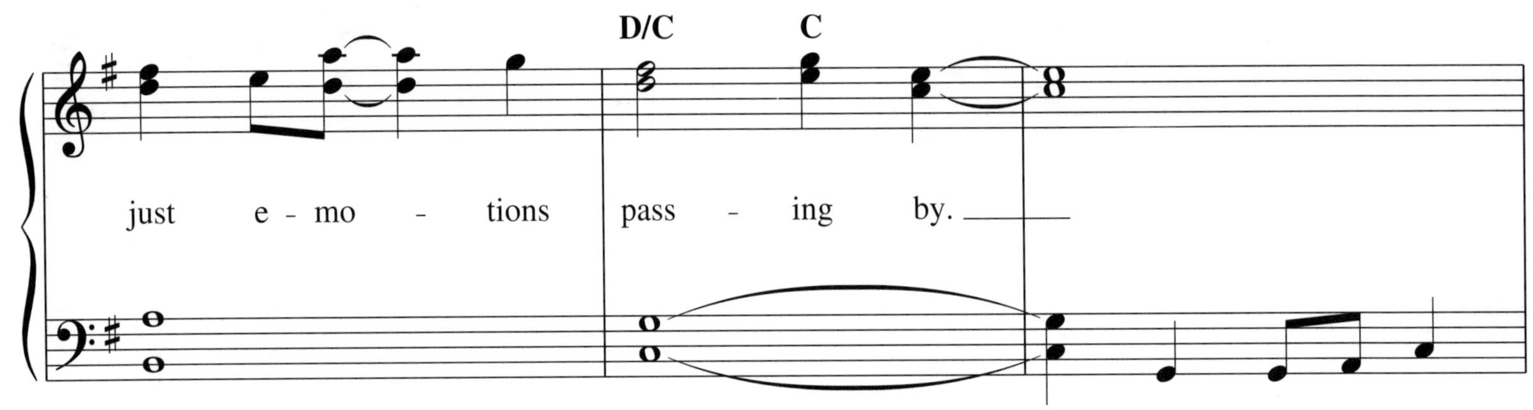
D/C
C
just e - mo - tions pass - ing by.

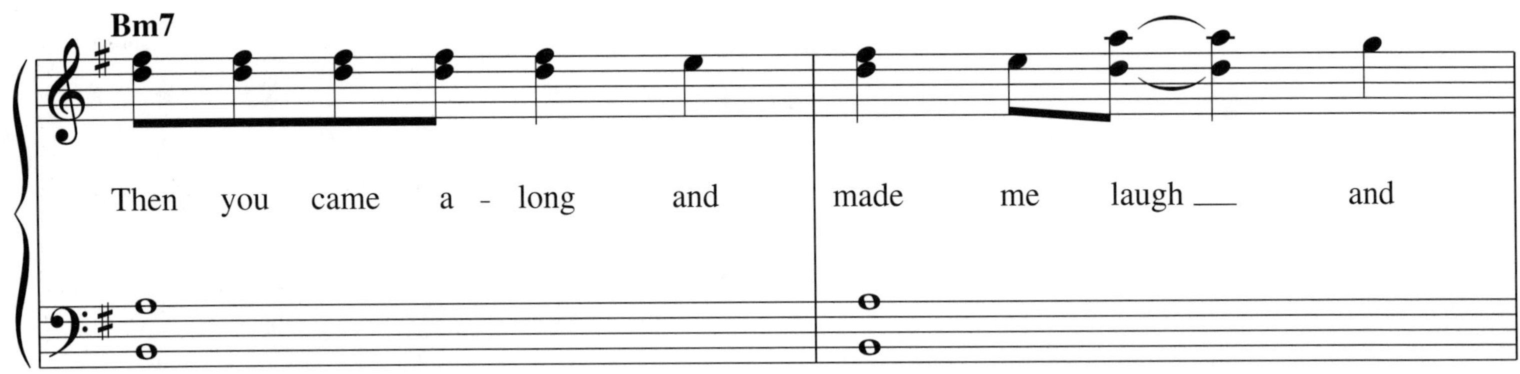
Bm7
Then you came a - long and made me laugh and

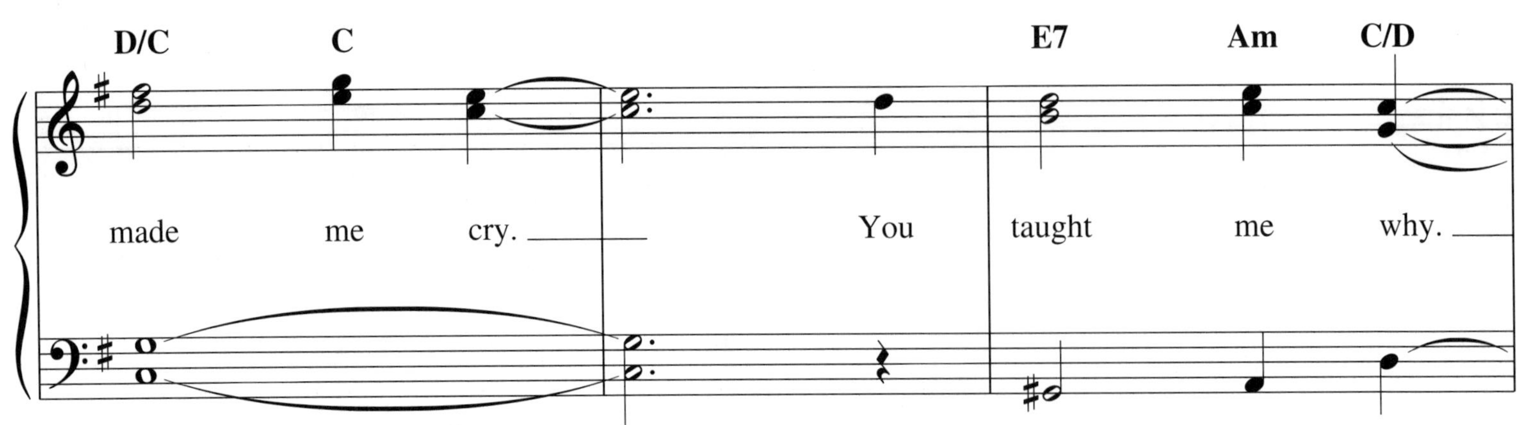
D/C
C
E7
Am
C/D
made me cry. You taught me why.

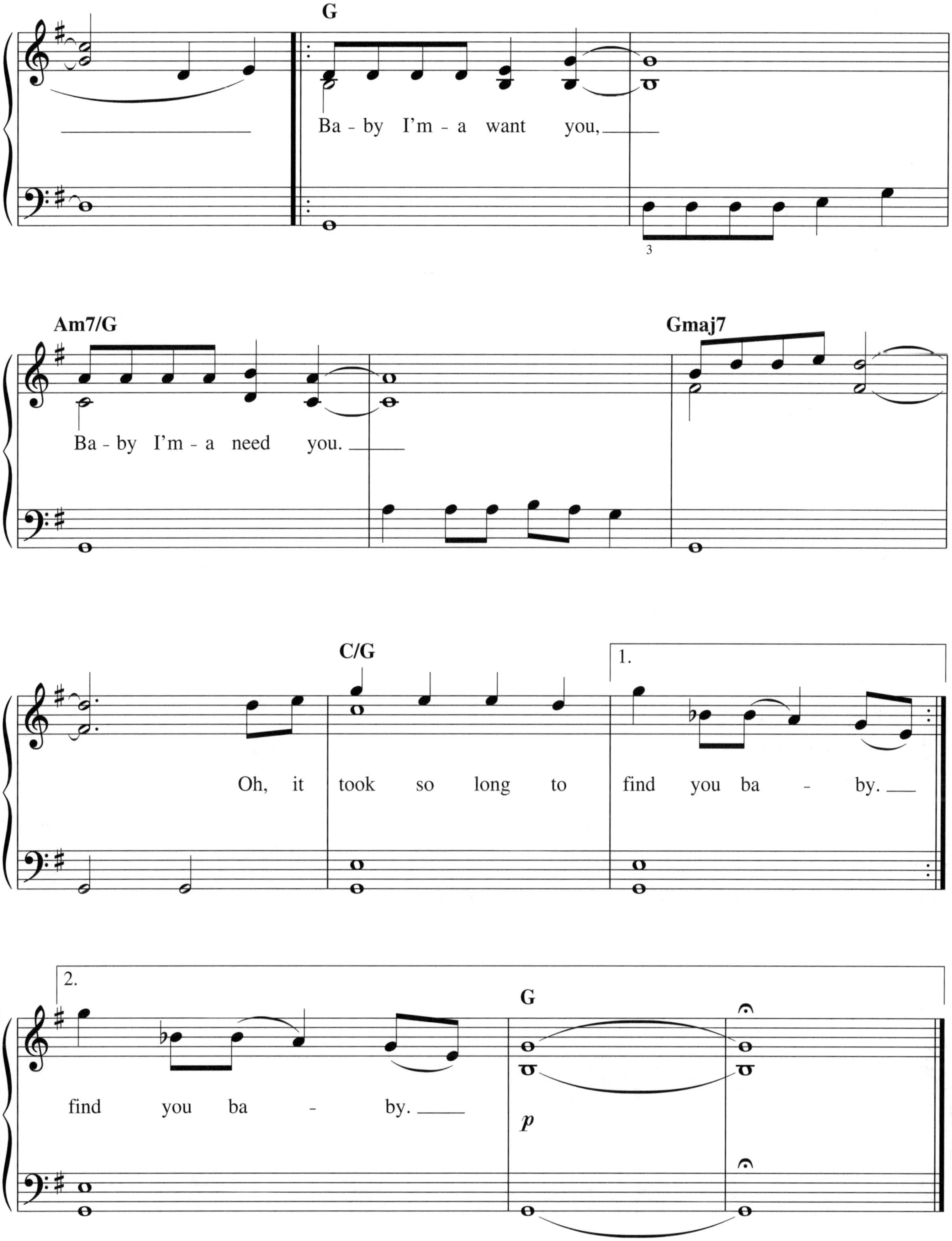

G

Ba - by I'm - a want you,

Am7/G Gmaj7

Ba - by I'm - a need you.

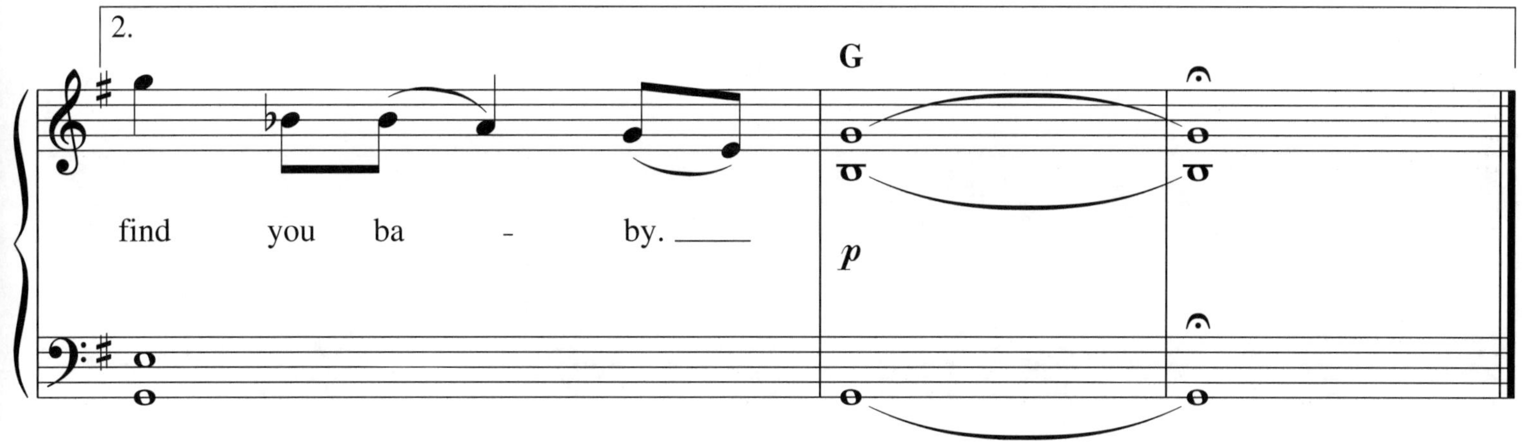

BEAST OF BURDEN

Words and Music by MICK JAGGER
and KEITH RICHARDS

© 1978 EMI MUSIC PUBLISHING LTD.
All Rights for the U.S. and Canada Controlled and Administered by COLGEMS-EMI MUSIC INC.
All Rights Reserved International Copyright Secured Used by Permission

B♭
B♭maj7
B♭
F/A
Am I hard e - nough_ am I rough e - nough_ am I
B♭
F/A
B♭ C
To Coda
rich e - nough_ I'm not too blind_ to see.___
F
C/E Dm
B♭
F
C/E Dm
I'll nev - er be your beast___ of bur - den.
So let's go home______
B♭
F
Dm
B♭
___ and draw the cur-tains.
Mu-sic on the ra - di - o.
Come on ba - by make sweet love to

D.S. al Coda
CODA
F
C/E
Dm
B♭
C
me.
Am I
Oh little sister
F
Dm
B♭
F
C/E
Dm
pretty, pretty,
pretty, pretty girl.
B♭
C
F
C/E
Dm
B♭
F
C/E
Dm
B♭
F
F/A
You're a
pretty, pretty, pretty, pretty,

B♭maj7
F
F/A
B♭maj7
pret-ty, pret-ty, girl, __
pret-ty, pret-ty, pret-ty, pret-ty,
pret-ty, pret-ty girl. __
F
F/A
B♭
F
F/A
Come on ba - by
please, __ please, __
please. ________
B♭
F
C/E Dm
B♭
(Spoken:) I'll tell ya
you can put me out __
on the street, _
F
C/E Dm
B♭
F
put me out with no __
shoes on my feet. _ (Sung): But
put me out put me out

Dm
B♭
F
C/E Dm
B♭
F
C/E Dm
put me out of mi - se - ry.
All your sick-ness I can
B♭
F
Dm
B♭
suck it up
Throw it all at me, I can
shrug it off.
F
Dm
B♭
F
F/A
There's one thing that
I don't un - der-stand.
You keep on tell-ing me I
B♭
F
C/E
Dm
B♭
ain't your kind of man. Ain't I
rough e - nough.
Oh!
Ain't I

F C/E Dm B♭ F C/E Dm
tough e-nough, ain't I rich e-nough, in love e - nough,
B♭ F C/E Dm B♭ F F/A B♭
Ooh ooh please.
I'll nev-er be your beast
I'll nev-er be your beast
I won't need no beast
F F/A B♭
of bur - den, I'll nev - er be your beast of bur - den,
of bur - den, I've walked for miles and my feet are hurt - ing,
of bur - den, I need no fuss - ing I need no nurs - ing,
Repeat and Fade
F C/E Dm B♭ F C/E Dm B♭ B♭/C
nev-er, nev-er, nev-er, nev-er nev-er, nev-er, nev - er be.
all I want is you to make love to me.
nev-er, nev-er, nev-er, nev-er, nev-er, nev-er, nev - er be.

BLUE BAYOU

Words and Music by ROY ORBISON
and JOE MELSON

Copyright © 1961 (Renewed 1989) by Acuff-Rose Music, Inc., Barbara Orbison Music Company, Orbi-Lee Music and R-Key Darkus Music
All Rights Reserved Used by Permission

C7
sav - ing dimes; work - ing 'til the sun don't shine;
sav - ing dimes; work - ing 'til the sun don't shine;

F
look - ing for - ward to hap - pi - er times on Blue Bay - ou.
look - ing for - ward to hap - pi - er times on Blue Bay - ou.

E♭ F
I'm go - ing back some day, come what may to
I'm go - ing back some day, gon - na stay on

C7
Blue Bay - ou, where you sleep all day and the
Blue Bay - ou, where the folks are fine and the

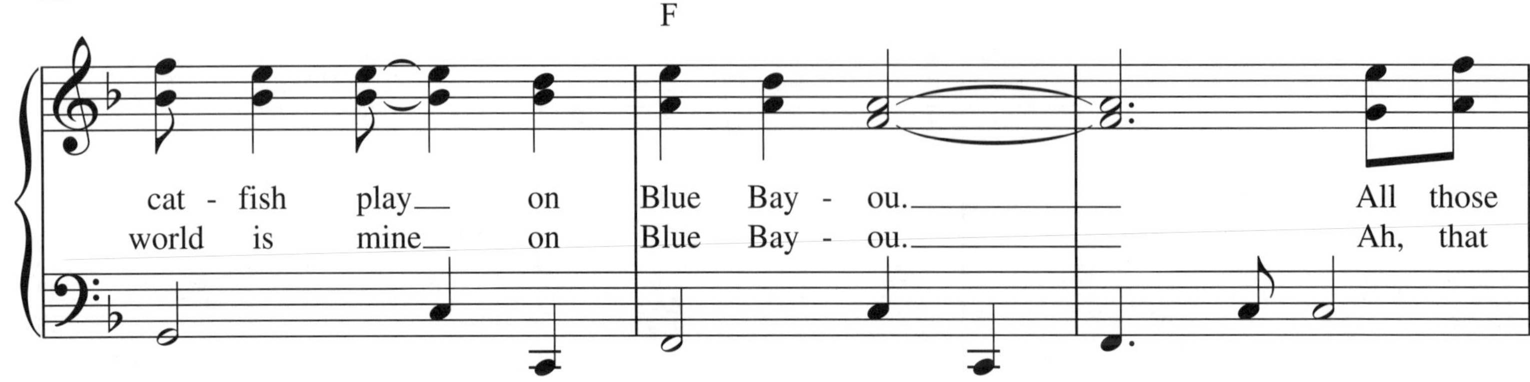
F
cat - fish play on Blue Bay - ou. All those
world is mine on Blue Bay - ou. Ah, that

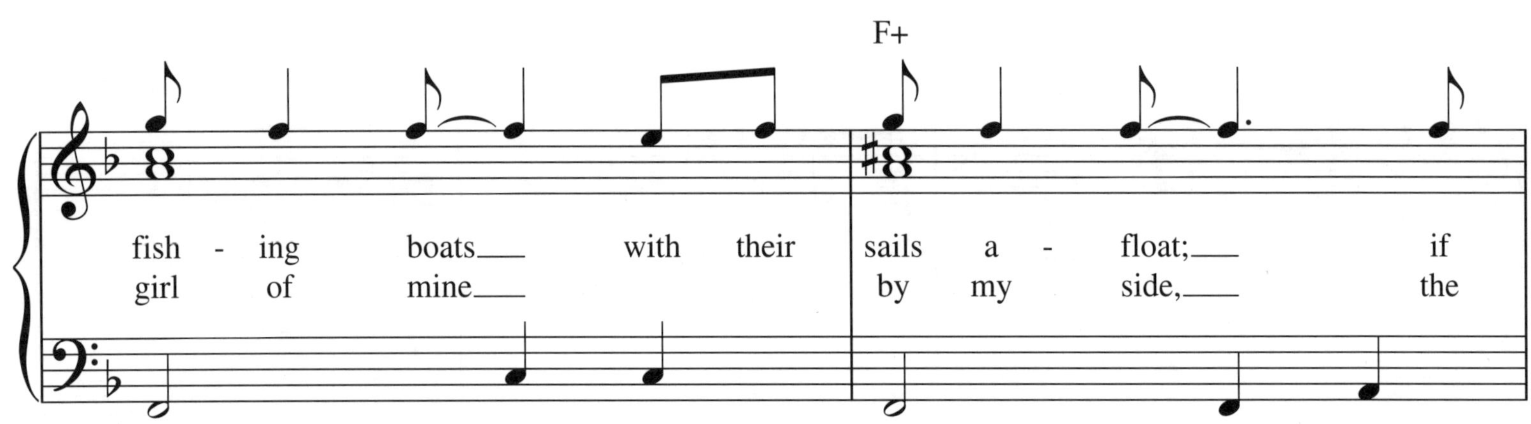
F+
fish - ing boats with their sails a - float; if
girl of mine by my side, the

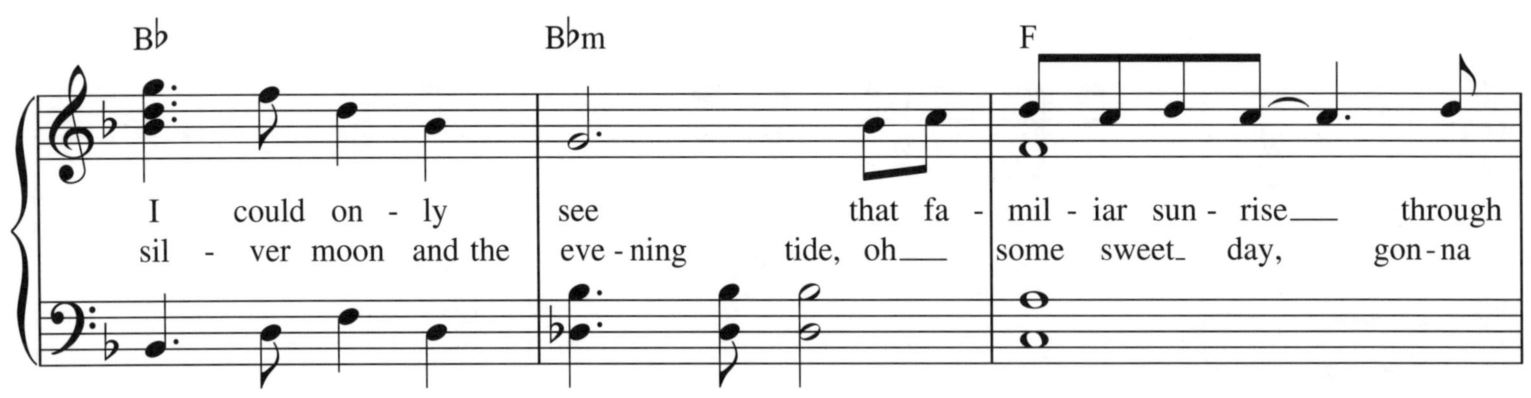
B♭
B♭m
F
I could on - ly see that fa - mil - iar sun - rise through
sil - ver moon and the eve - ning tide, oh some sweet day, gon - na

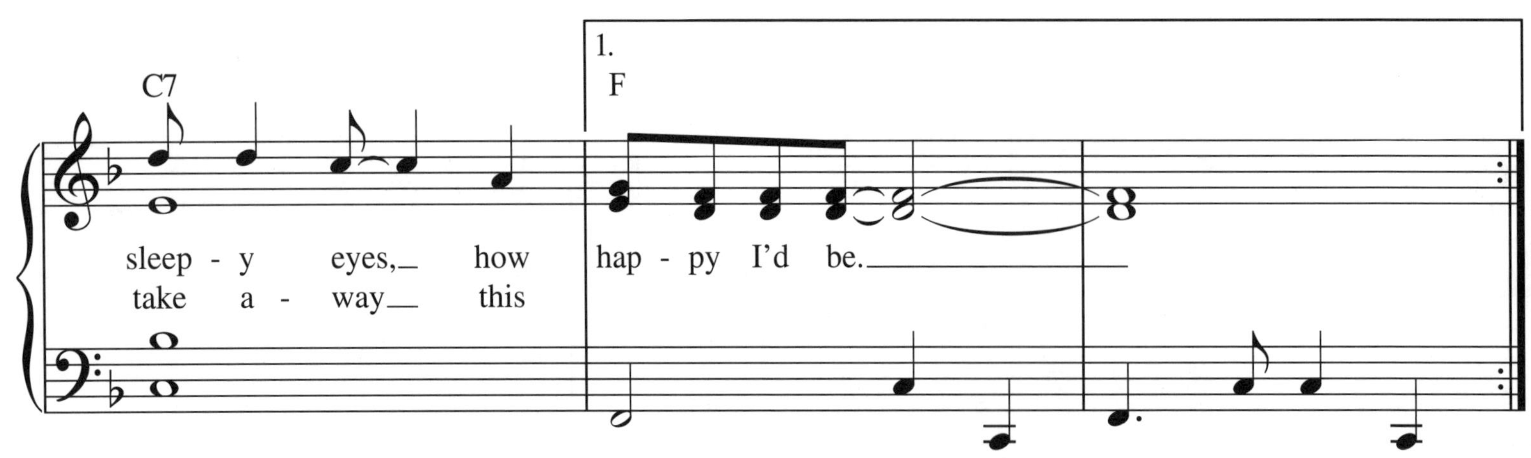
C7
1.
F
sleep - y eyes, how hap - py I'd be.
take a - way this

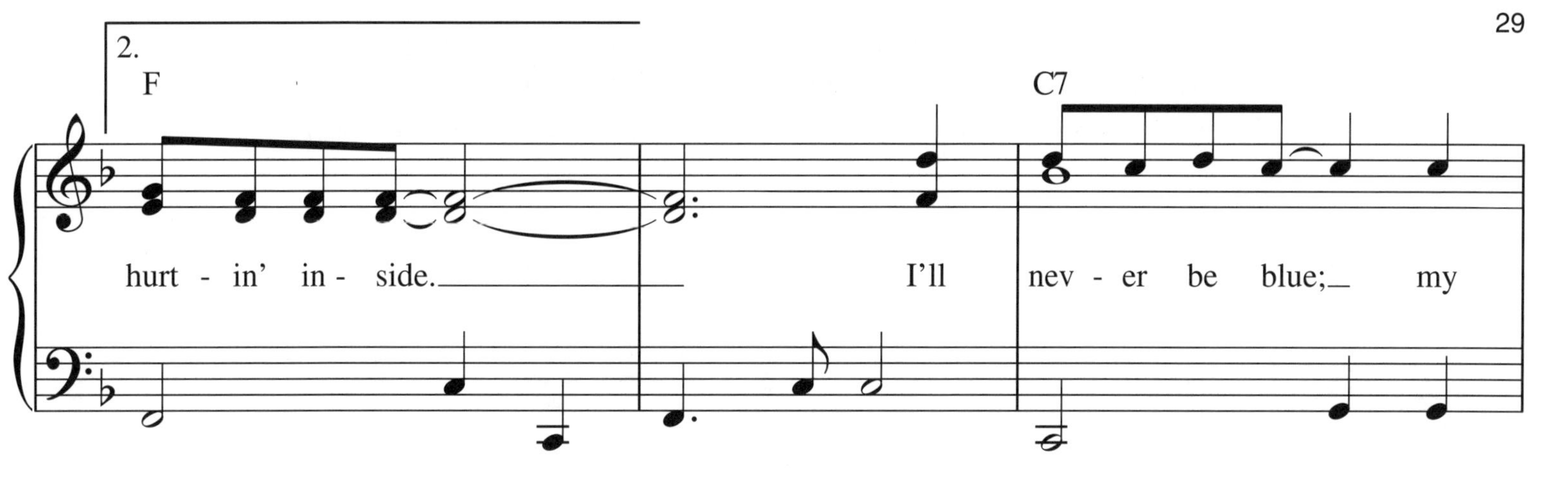
2.
F
C7
hurt - in' in - side.
I'll
nev - er be blue; my

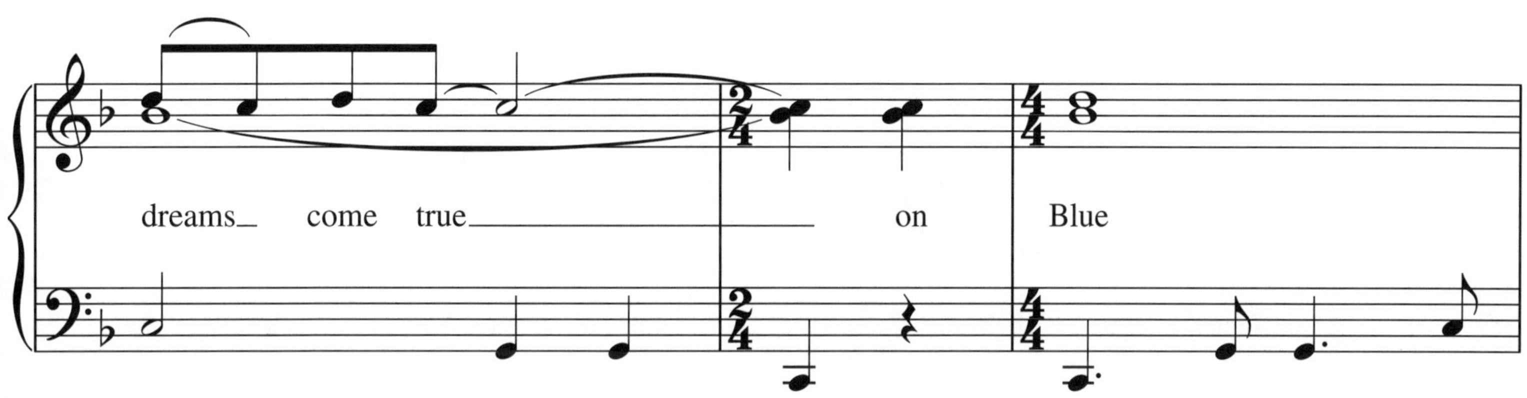
dreams come true
on
Blue

F
Bay - ou.

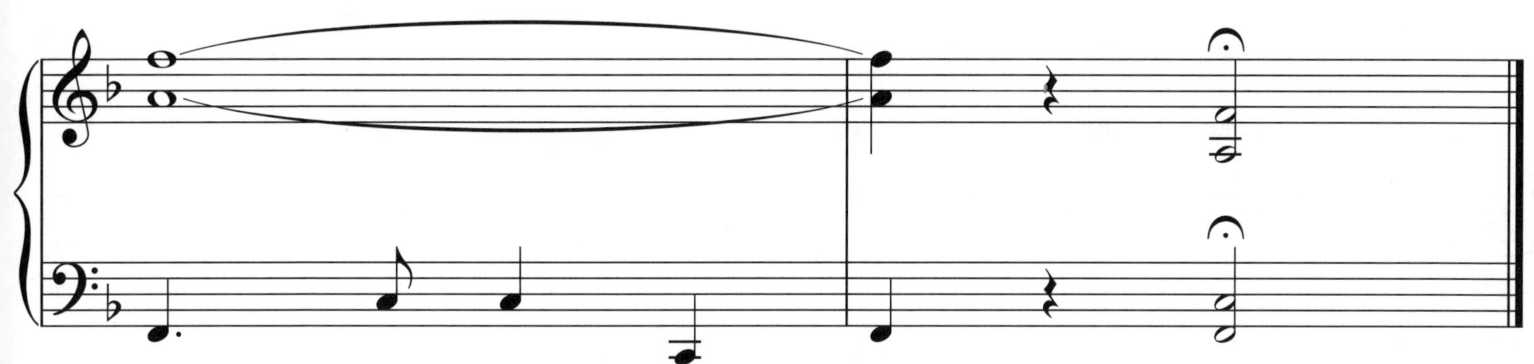

THE BRADY BUNCH

Theme from the Paramount Television Series THE BRADY BUNCH

Words and Music by SHERWOOD SCHWARTZ
and FRANK DEVOL

Moderately fast, in 2

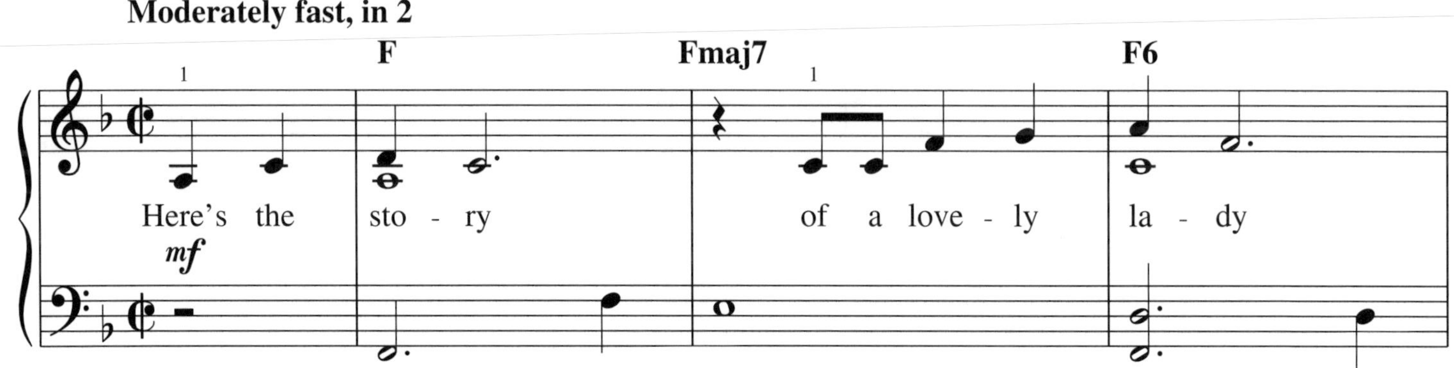

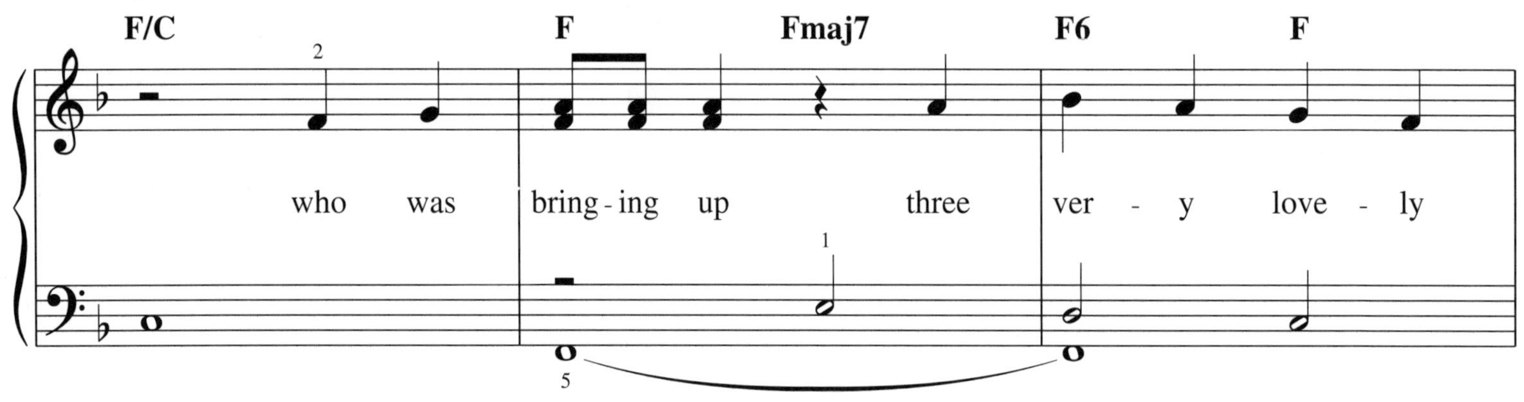

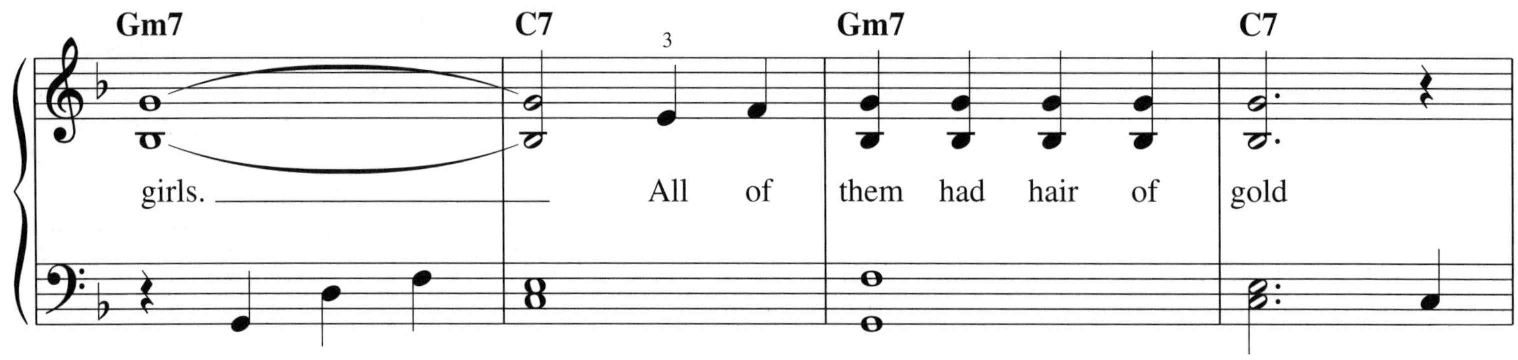

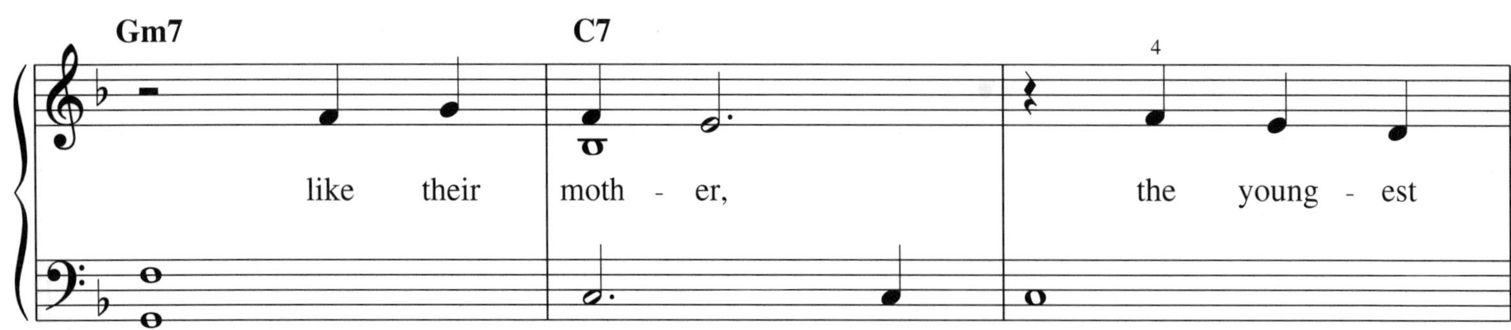

Copyright © 1969 (Renewed 1997) by Addax Music Company, Inc.
International Copyright Secured All Rights Reserved

F
1
2
1
one in curls. It's the sto - ry

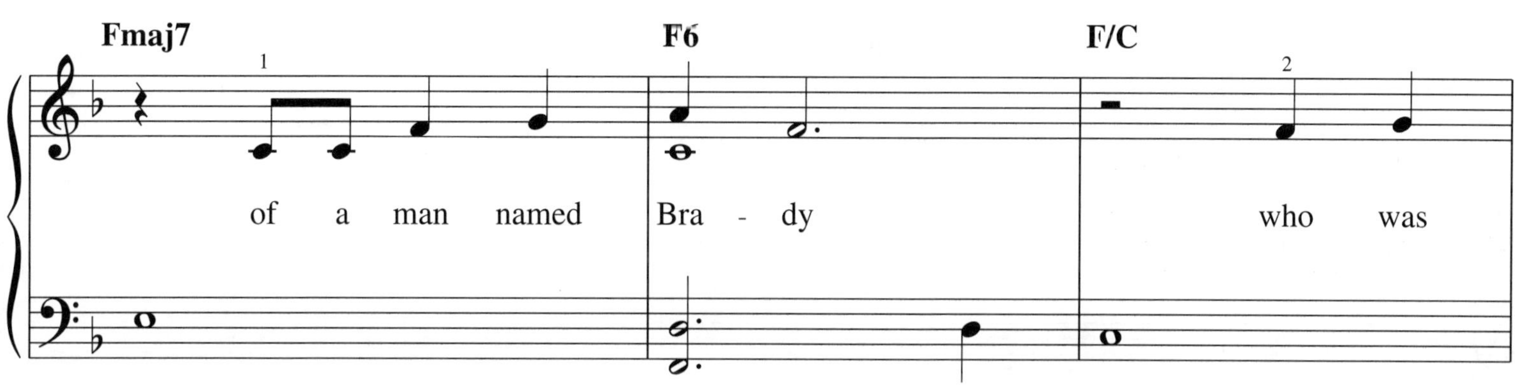
Fmaj7
F6
F/C
1
2
of a man named Bra - dy who was

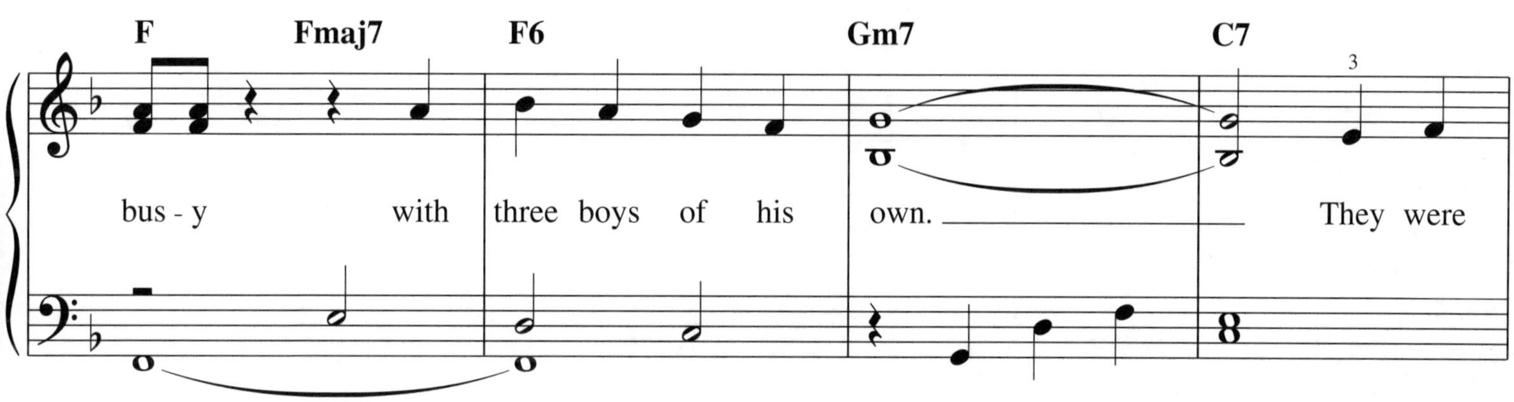
F
Fmaj7
F6
Gm7
C7
3
bus - y with three boys of his own. They were

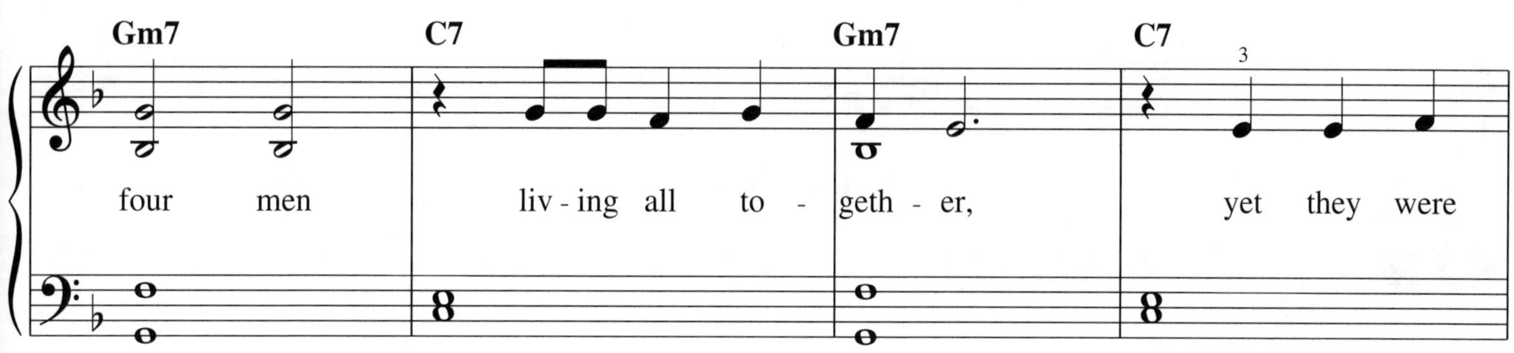
Gm7
C7
Gm7
C7
3
four men liv - ing all to - geth - er, yet they were

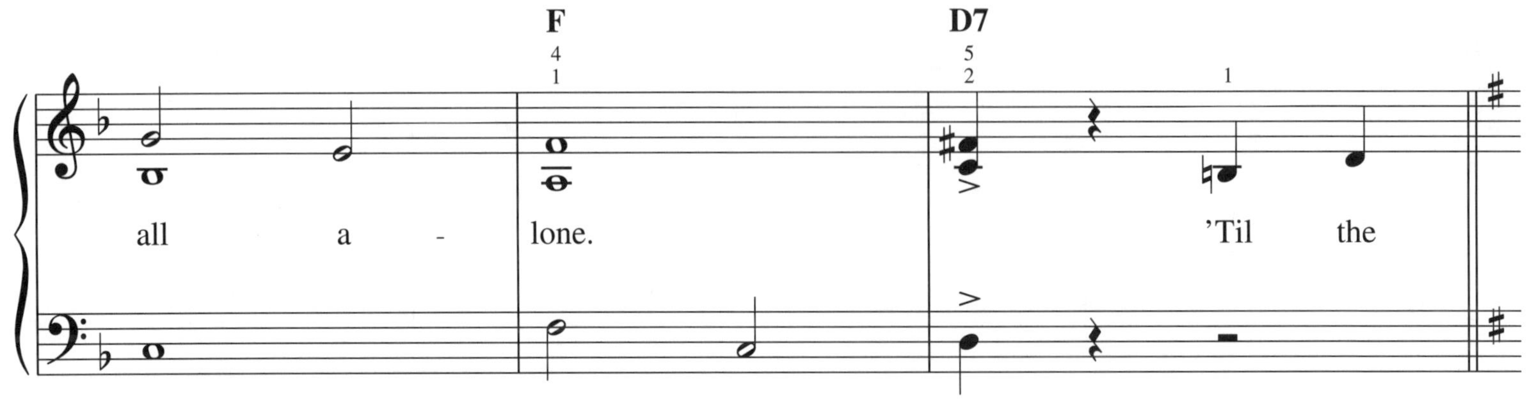
F
D7
4
1
5
2
1
all a - lone. 'Til the

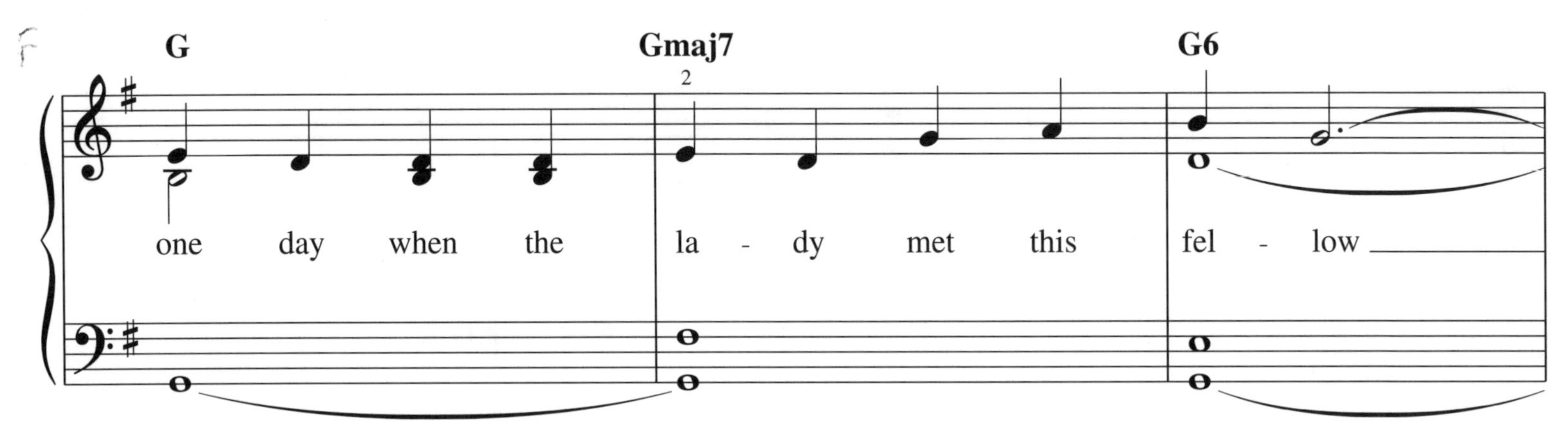
G
Gmaj7
G6
2
one day when the la - dy met this fel - low

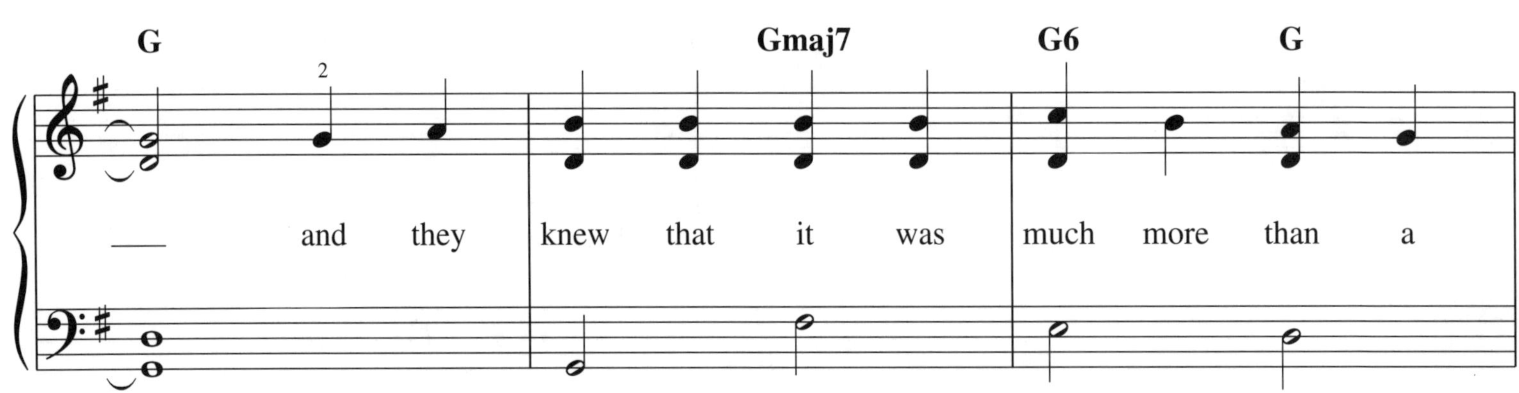
G
Gmaj7
G6
G
2
and they knew that it was much more than a

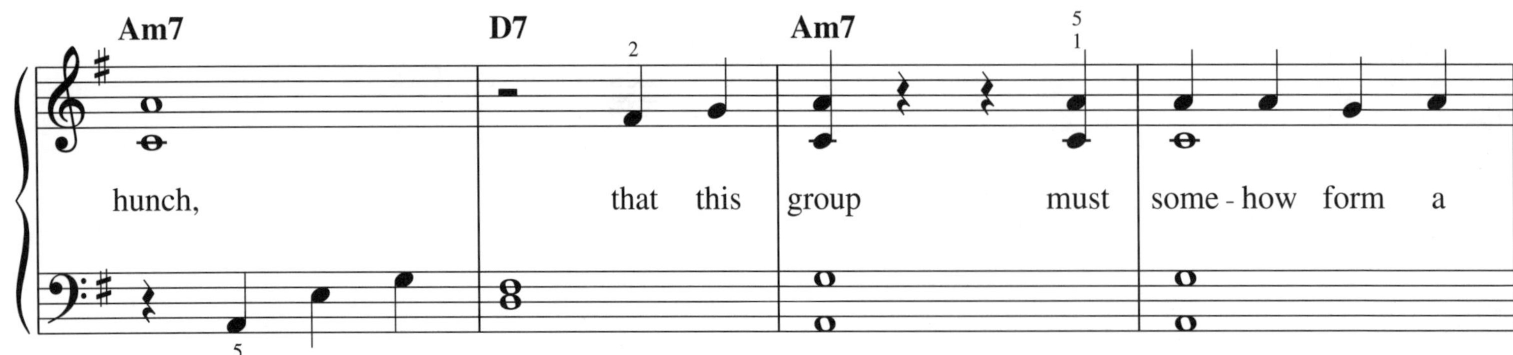
Am7
D7
Am7
2
5
1
5
hunch, that this group must some - how form a

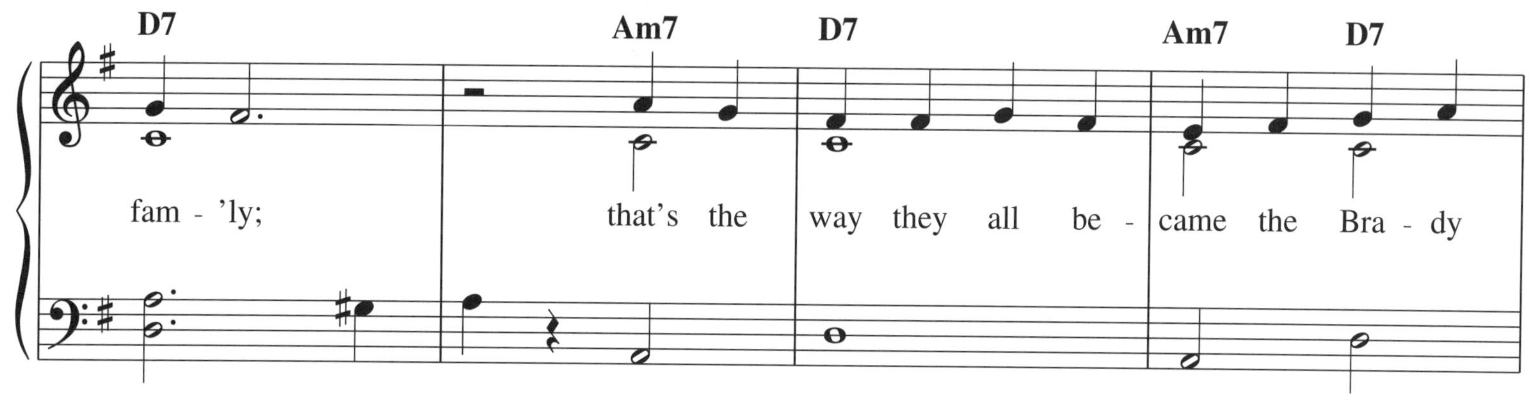
D7
Am7
D7
Am7
D7
fam - 'ly; that's the way they all be - came the Bra - dy

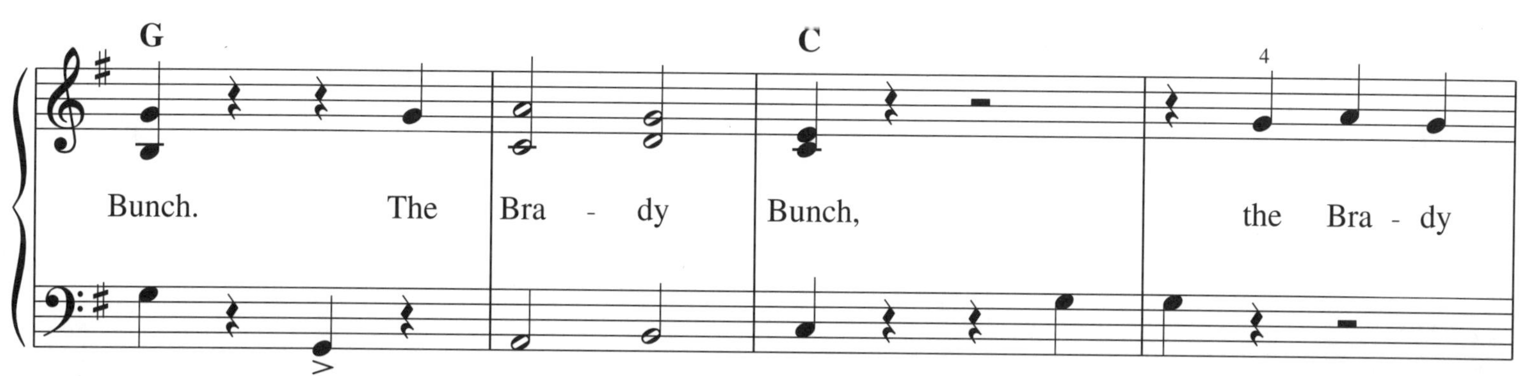
G
C
4
Bunch. The Bra - dy Bunch, the Bra - dy

G
2
A7
Bunch. That's the way they be -
cresc.

Am7
D7
G
came the Bra - dy Bunch.
f

(They Long to Be)
CLOSE TO YOU

Lyric by HAL DAVID
Music by BURT BACHARACH

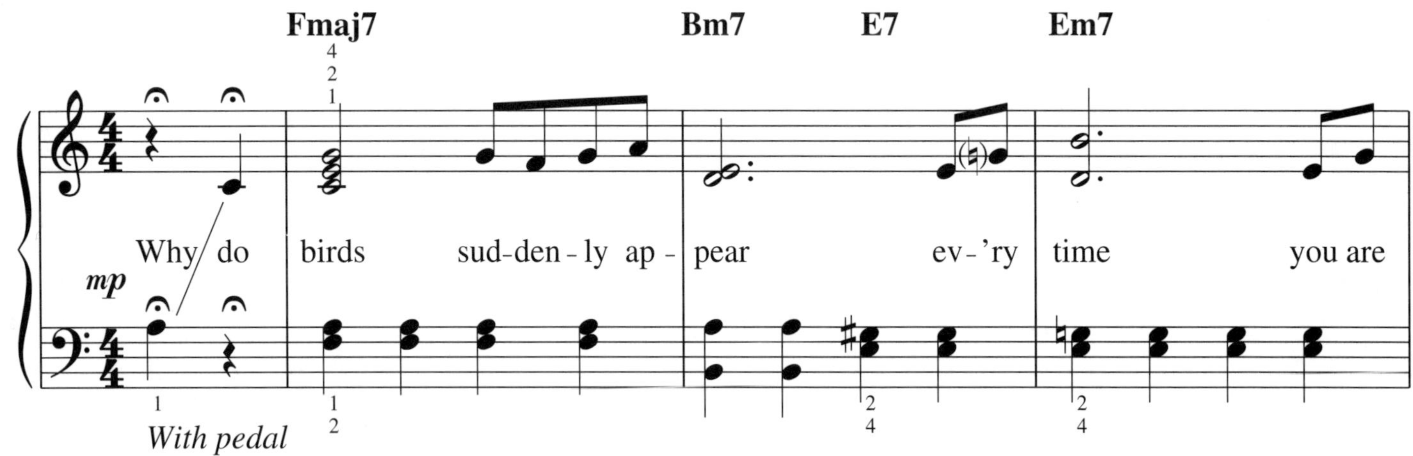

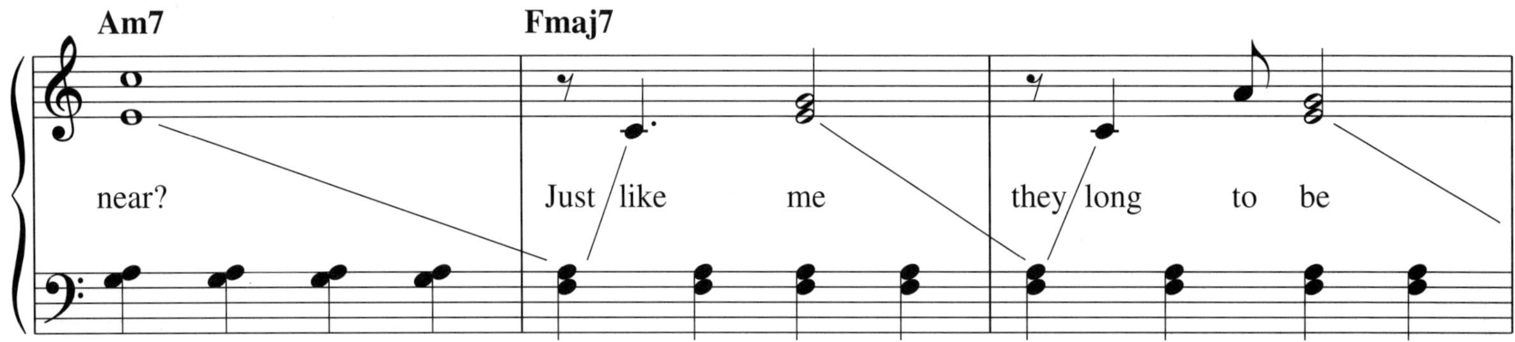

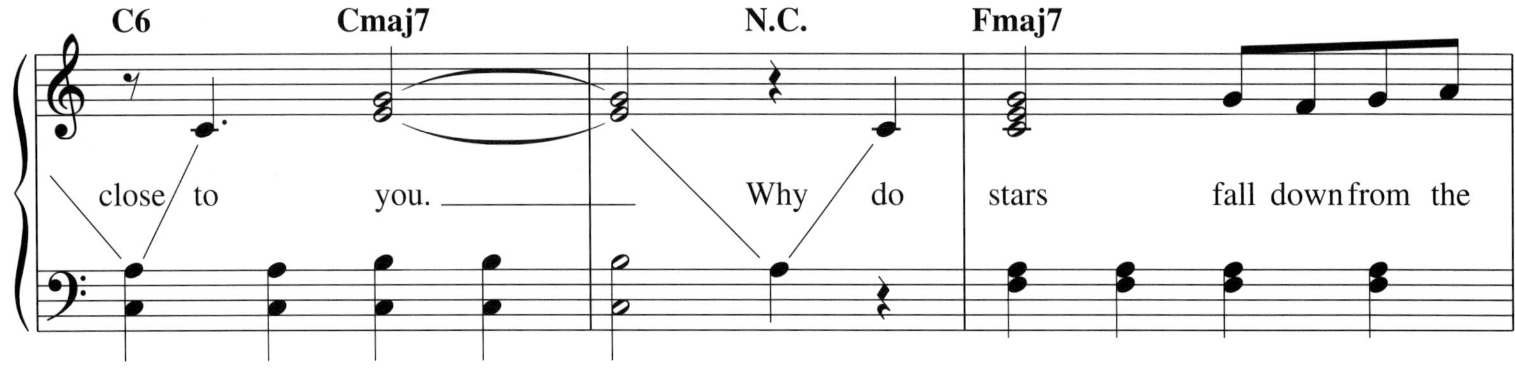

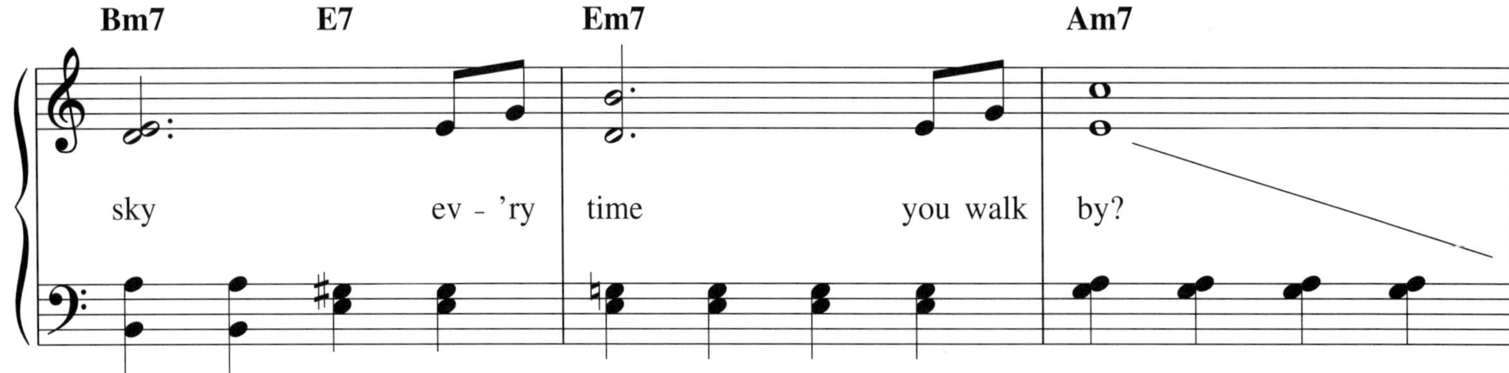

Copyright © 1963 (Renewed) Casa David and New Hidden Valley Music
International Copyright Secured All Rights Reserved

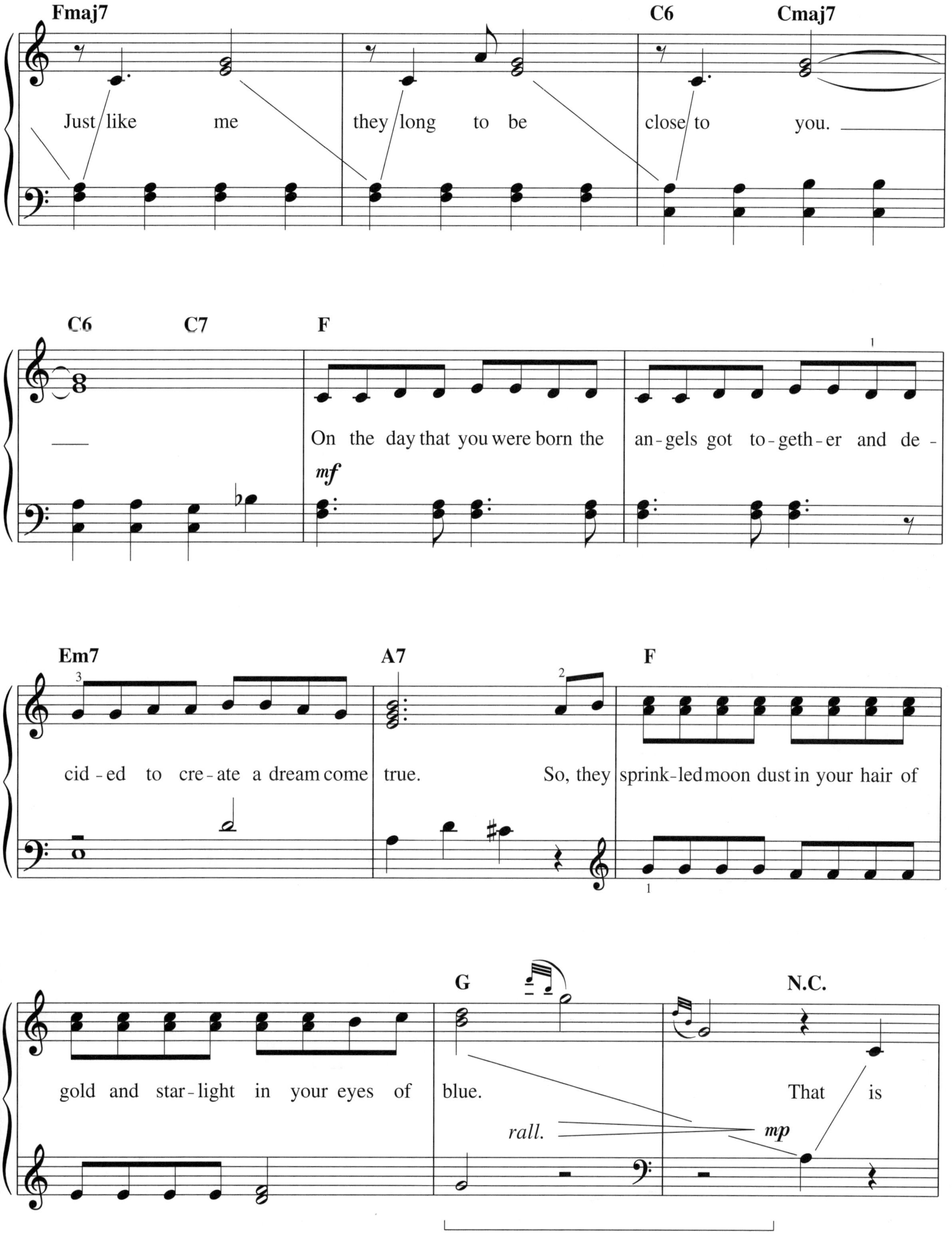

Fmaj7
C6
Cmaj7
Just like me they long to be close to you.
C6
C7
F
On the day that you were born the angels got together and decided to create a dream come true.
mf
Em7
A7
F
So, they sprinkled moon dust in your hair of gold and starlight in your eyes of blue.
G
N.C.
That is
rall.
mp

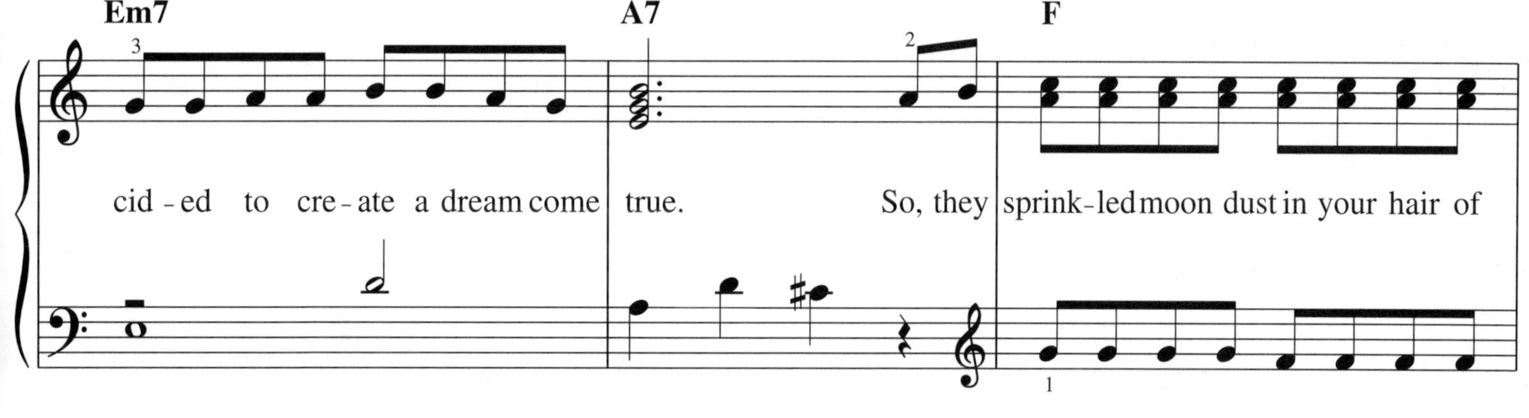

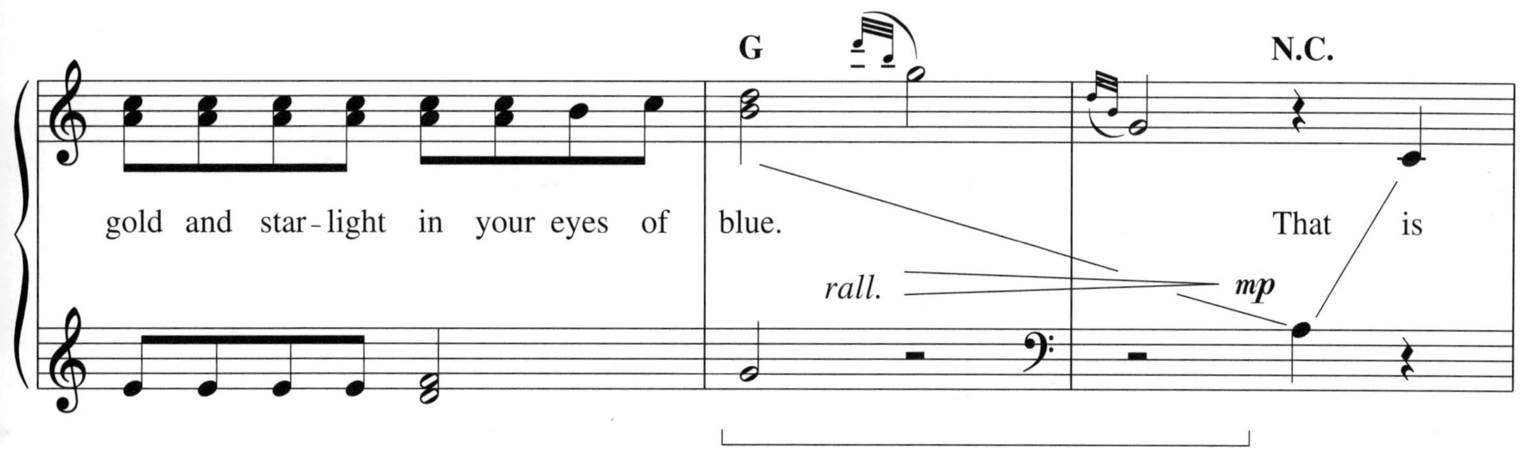

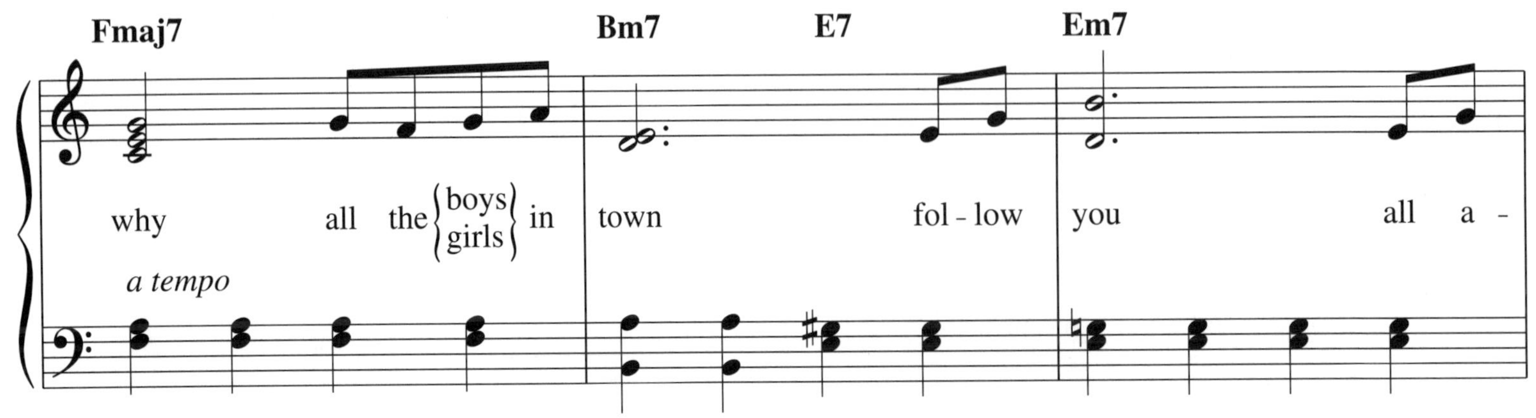
Fmaj7
Bm7
E7
Em7
why all the {boys girls} in town fol - low you all a -
a tempo

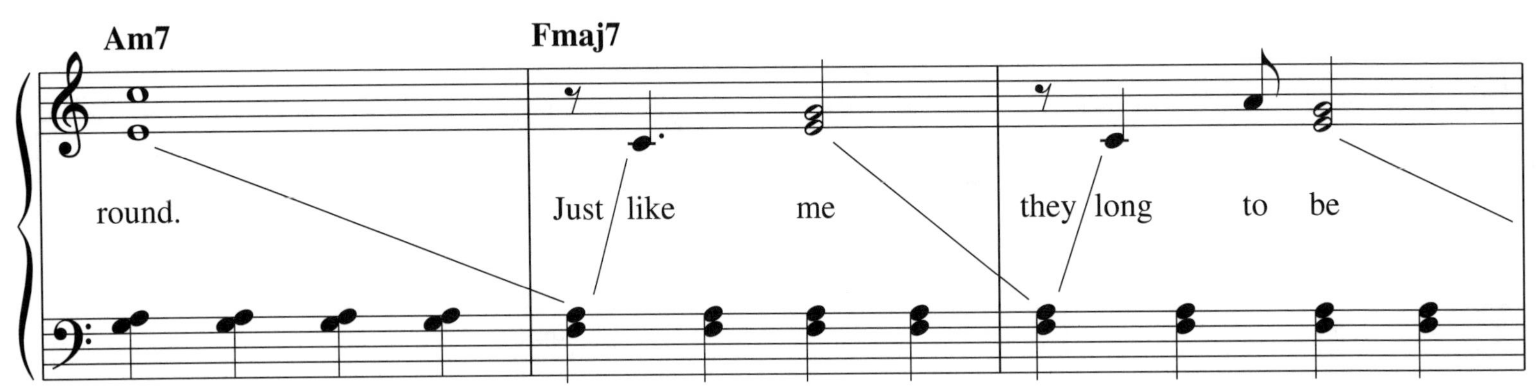
Am7
Fmaj7
round. Just like me they long to be

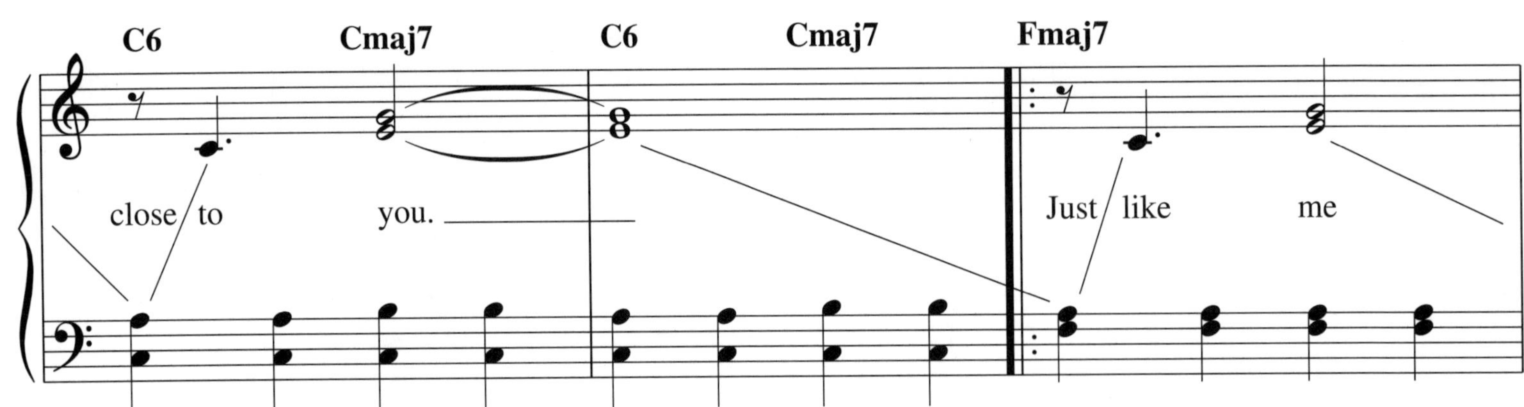
C6
Cmaj7
C6
Cmaj7
Fmaj7
close to you.
Just like me

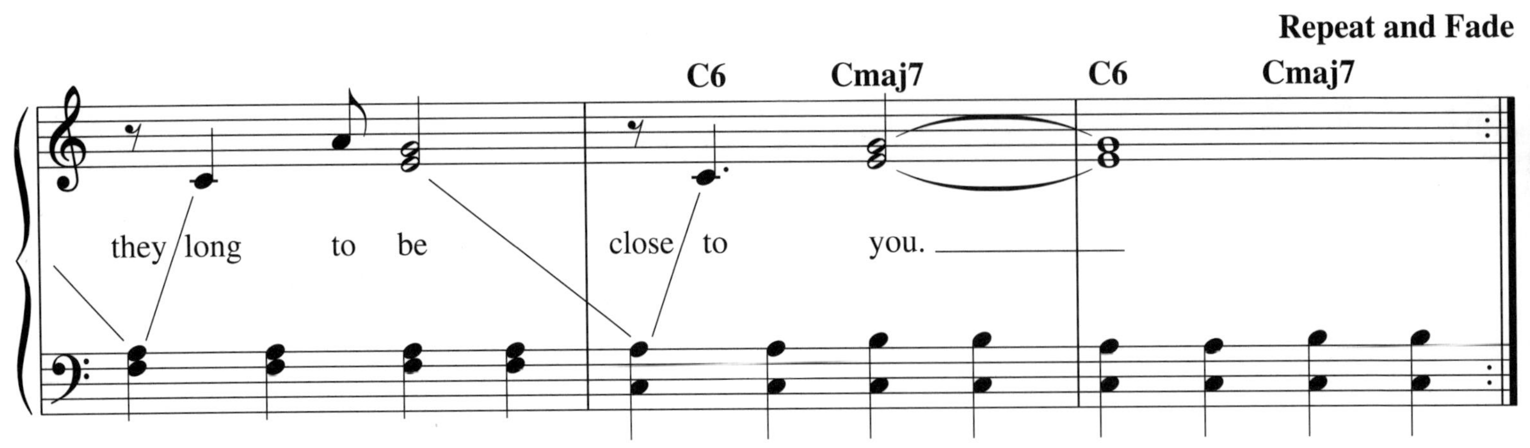
Repeat and Fade
C6
Cmaj7
C6
Cmaj7
they long to be close to you.

COPACABANA
(At the Copa)

Music by BARRY MANILOW
Lyric by BRUCE SUSSMAN and JACK FELDMAN

Moderately, with a Latin "feel"

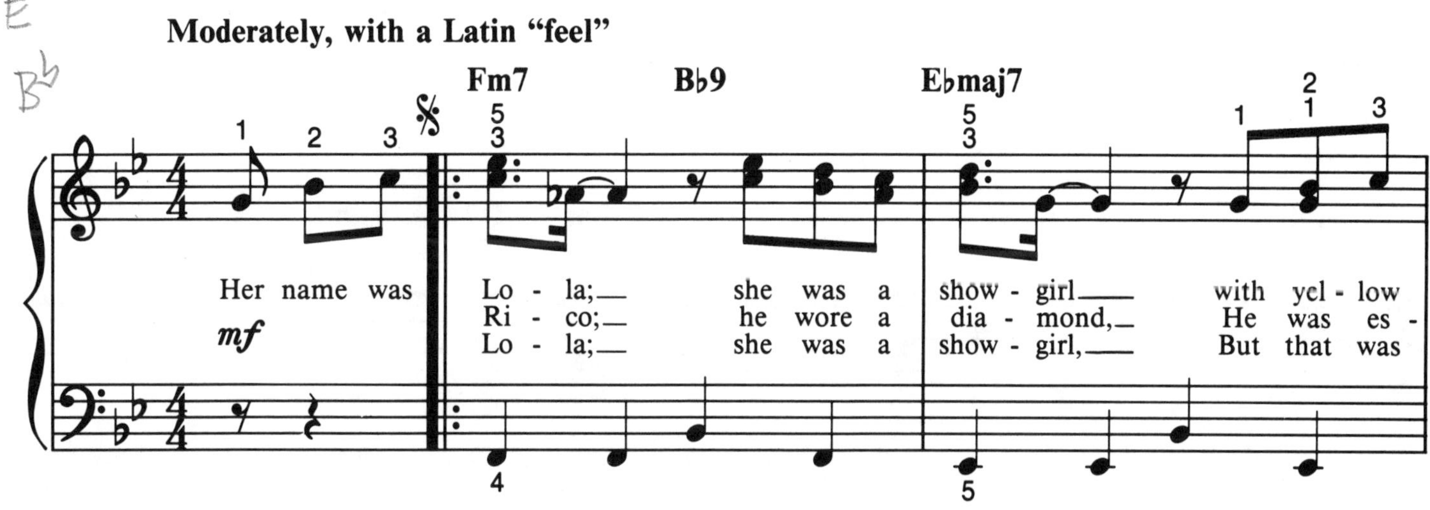

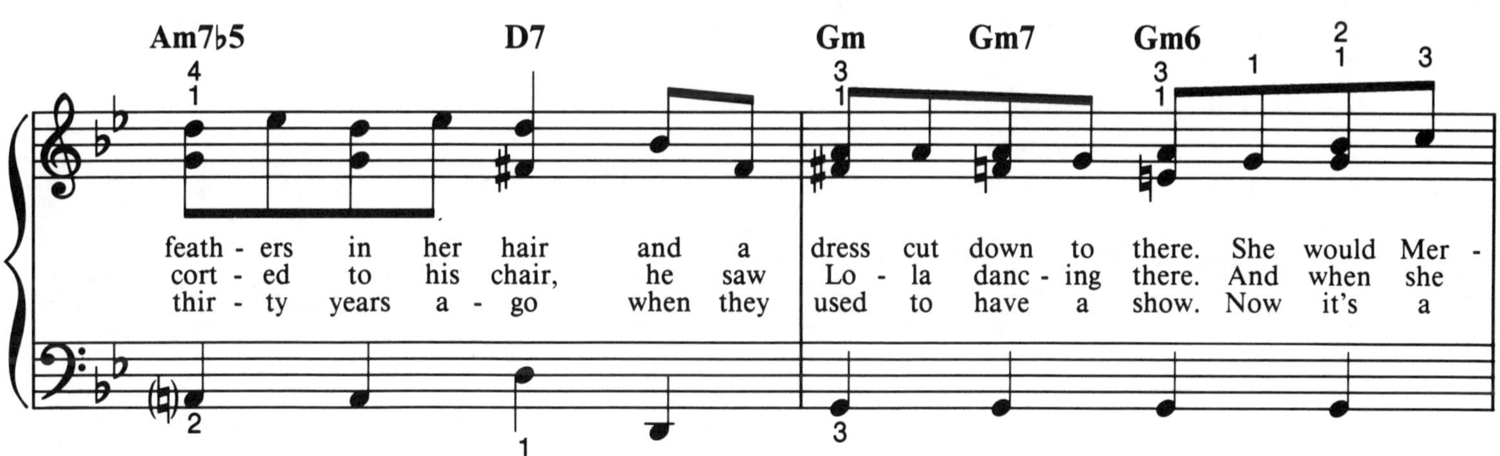

Copyright © 1978 by Careers-BMG Music Publishing, Inc., Appoggiatura Music and Camp Songs
All Rights Administered by Careers-BMG Music Publishing, Inc.
International Copyright Secured All Rights Reserved

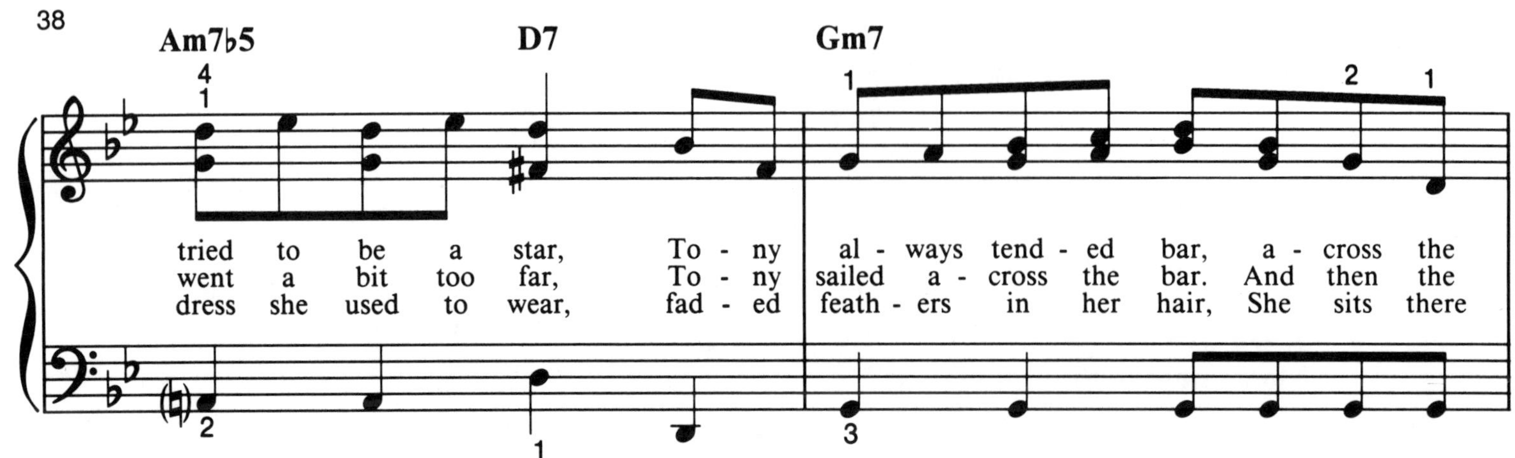
Am7♭5
D7
Gm7
tried to be a star, To - ny al - ways tend - ed bar, a - cross the
went a bit too far, To - ny sailed a - cross the bar. And then the
dress she used to wear, fad - ed feath - ers in her hair, She sits there

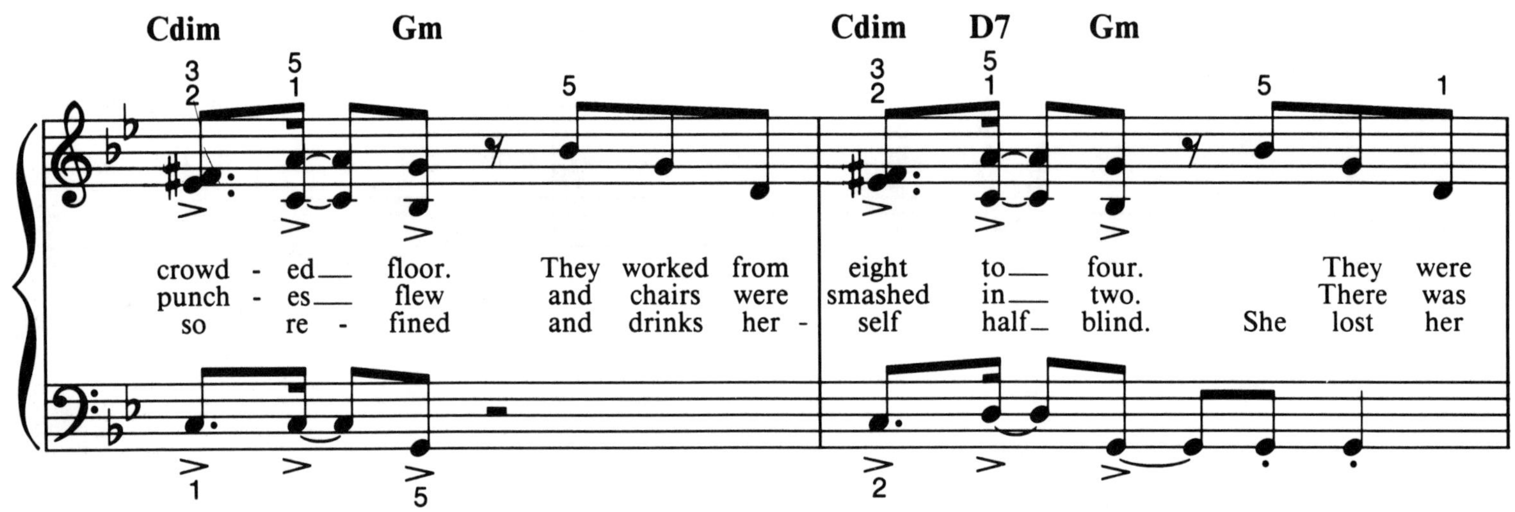
Cdim
Gm
Cdim
D7
Gm
crowd - ed floor. They worked from eight to four. They were
punch - es flew and chairs were smashed in two. There was
so re - fined and drinks her - self half blind. She lost her

Cm7
D7
Gm
D7/F♯
B♭7/F
young and they had each oth - er, who could ask for more?
blood and a sin - gle gun-shot, but just who shot who?
youth and she lost her To - ny, now she's lost her mind!
At the

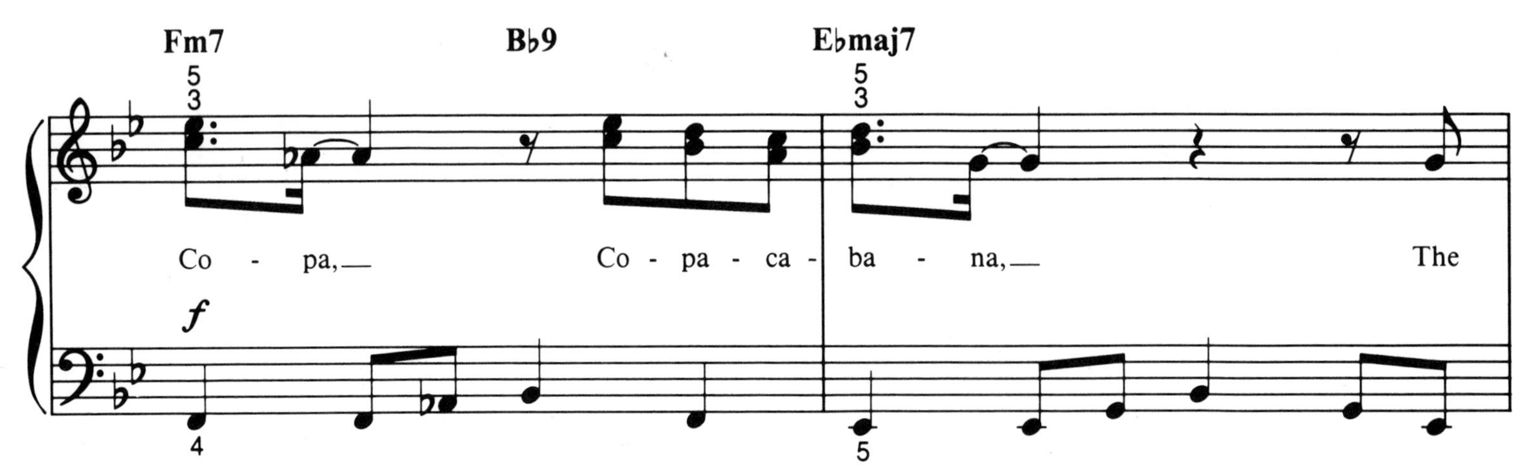
Fm7
B♭9
E♭maj7
Co - pa, Co - pa - ca - ba - na, The
f

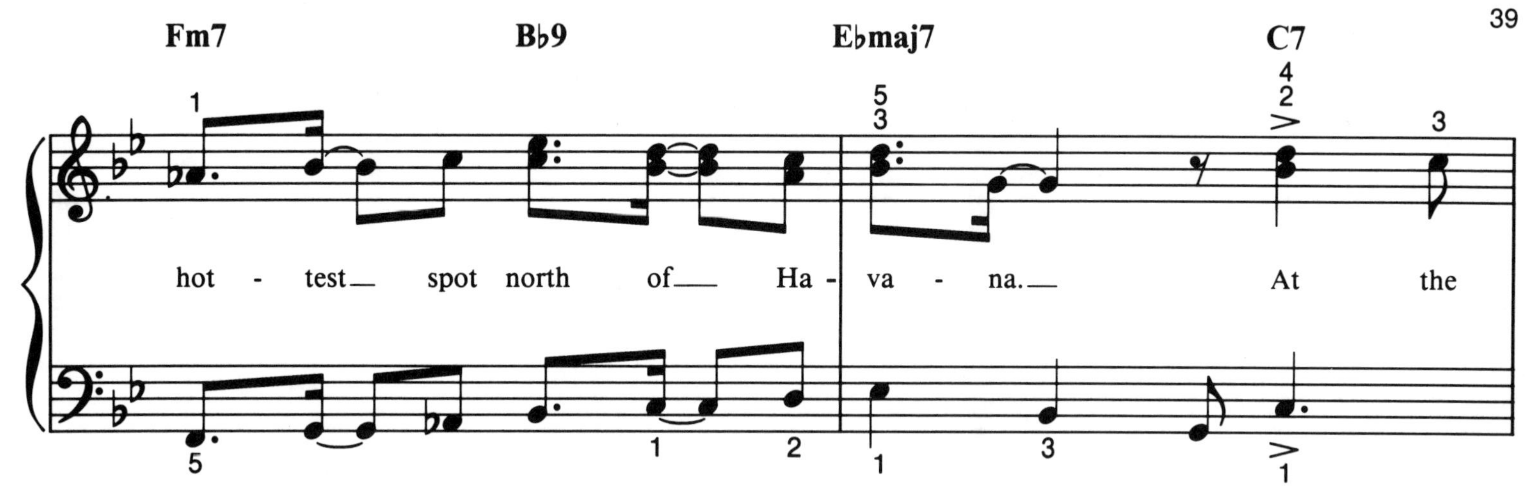
Fm7
B♭9
E♭maj7
C7
hot - test spot north of Ha - va - na. At the

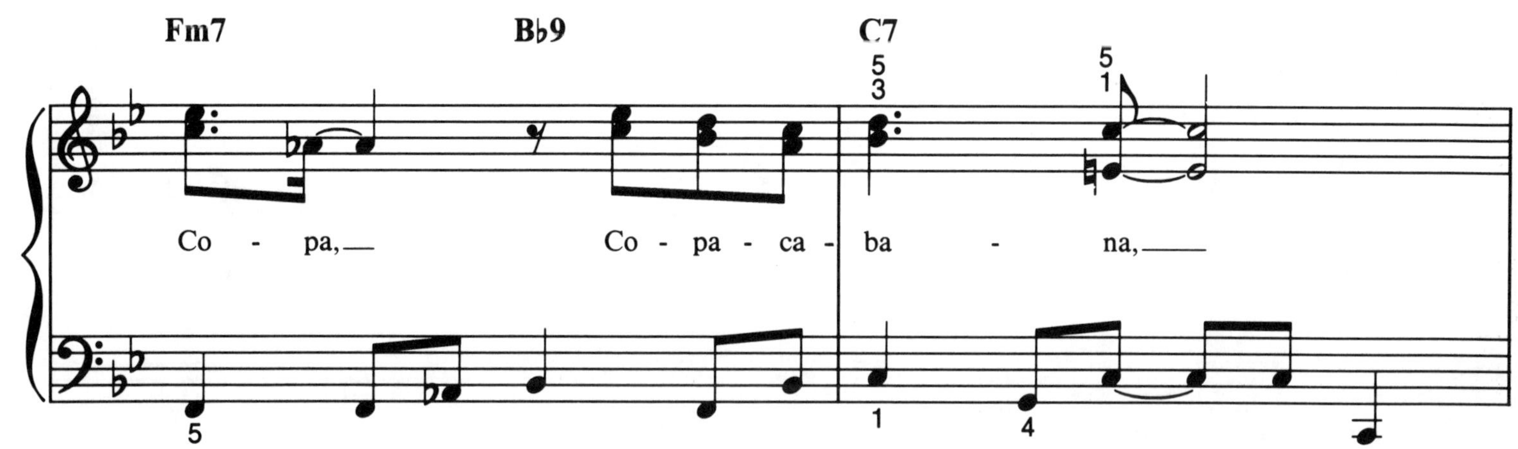
Fm7
B♭9
C7
Co - pa, Co - pa - ca - ba - na,

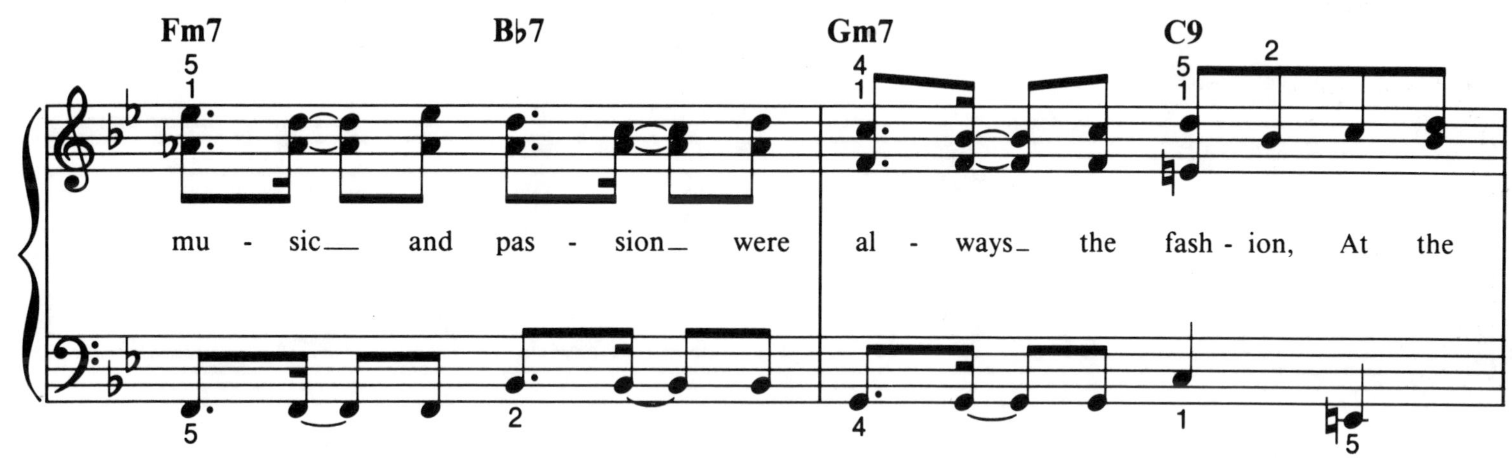
Fm7
B♭7
Gm7
C9
mu - sic and pas - sion were al - ways the fash - ion, At the

Fm7
To Coda
D7♭9
Gm9
F♯m9
Co - pa
they fell in love.
she lost her love.
mf

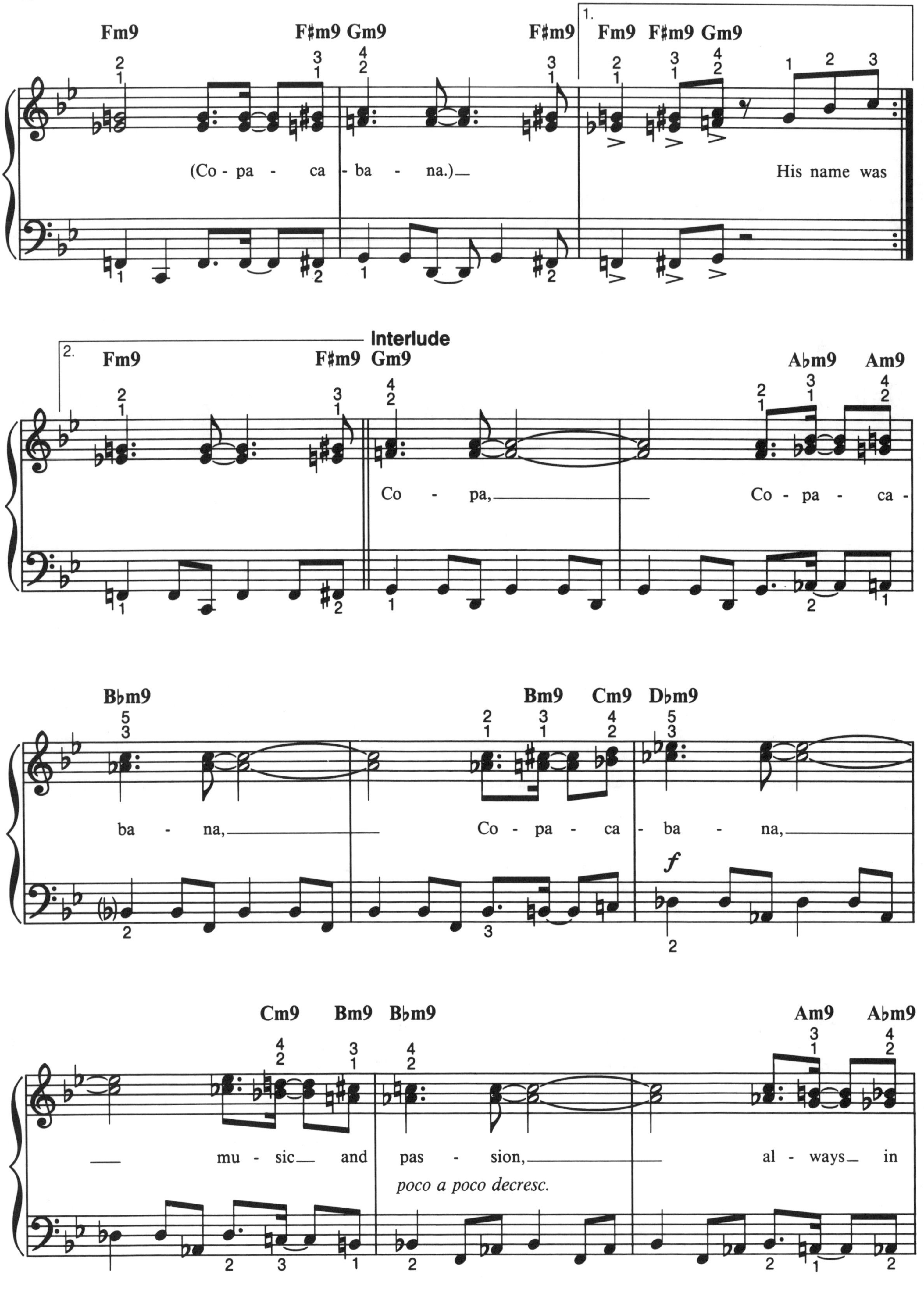
1.
Fm9 F♯m9 Gm9 F♯m9 Fm9 F♯m9 Gm9
(Co - pa - ca - ba - na.)
His name was
2.
Interlude
Fm9 F♯m9 Gm9 A♭m9 Am9
Co - pa, Co - pa - ca -
B♭m9 Bm9 Cm9 D♭m9
ba - na, Co - pa - ca - ba - na,
f
Cm9 Bm9 B♭m9 Am9 A♭m9
mu - sic and pas - sion, al - ways in
poco a poco decresc.

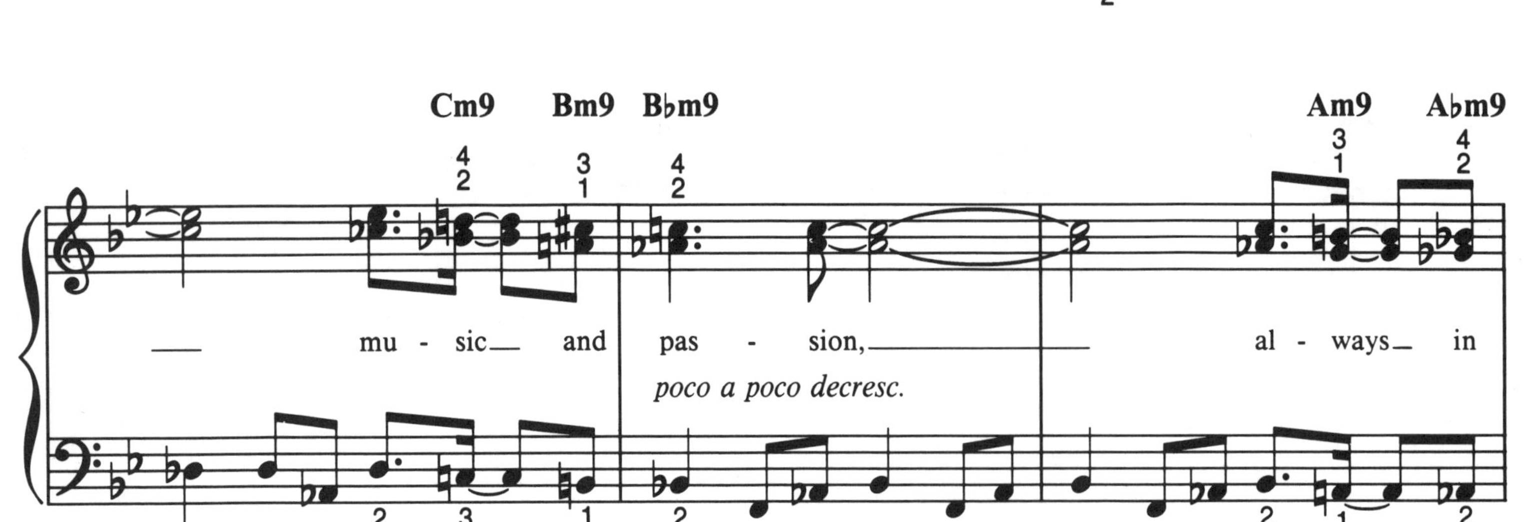

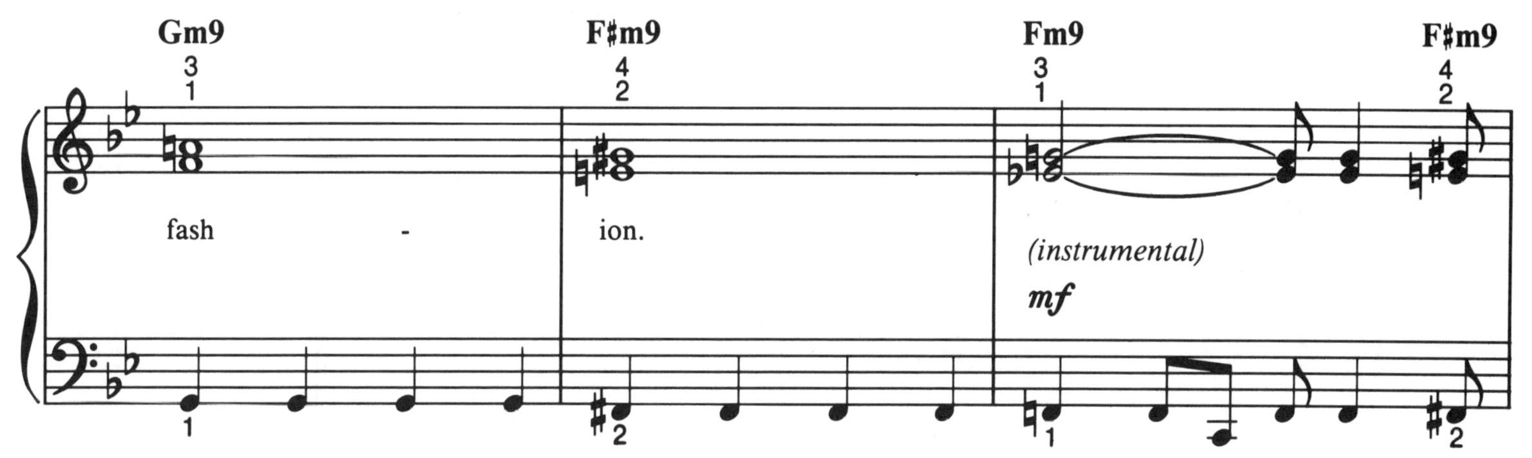
Gm9
F♯m9
Fm9
F♯m9
fash - ion.
(instrumental)
mf

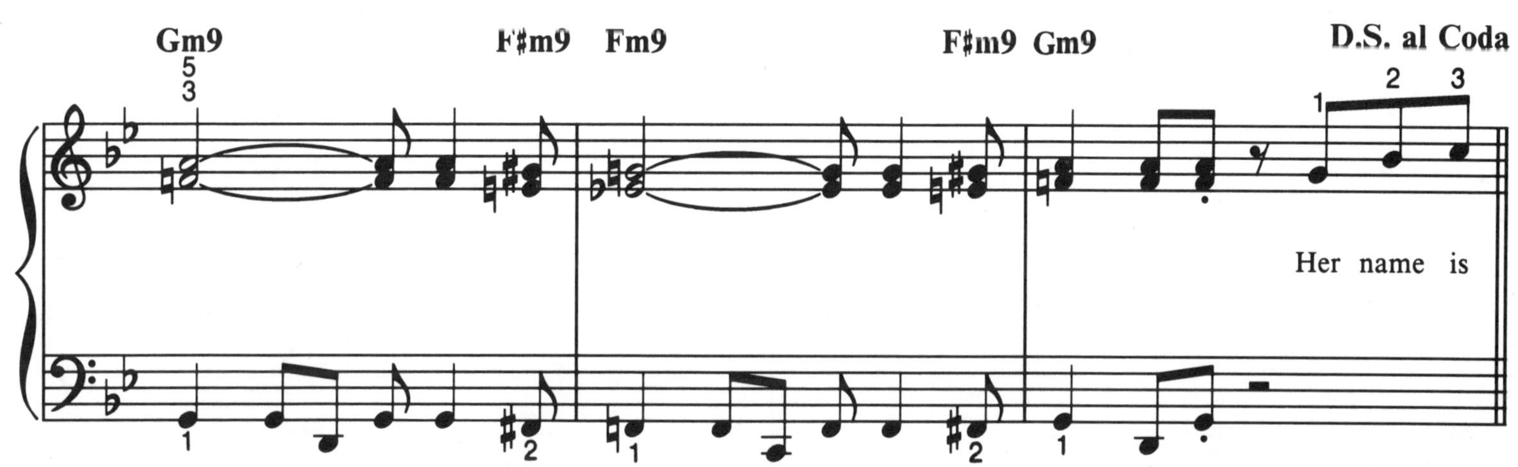
Gm9
F♯m9
Fm9
F♯m9
Gm9
D.S. al Coda
Her name is

CODA
D7♭9
Gm
F♯m
Fm
F♯m
don't fall in
love,
mf
don't fall in

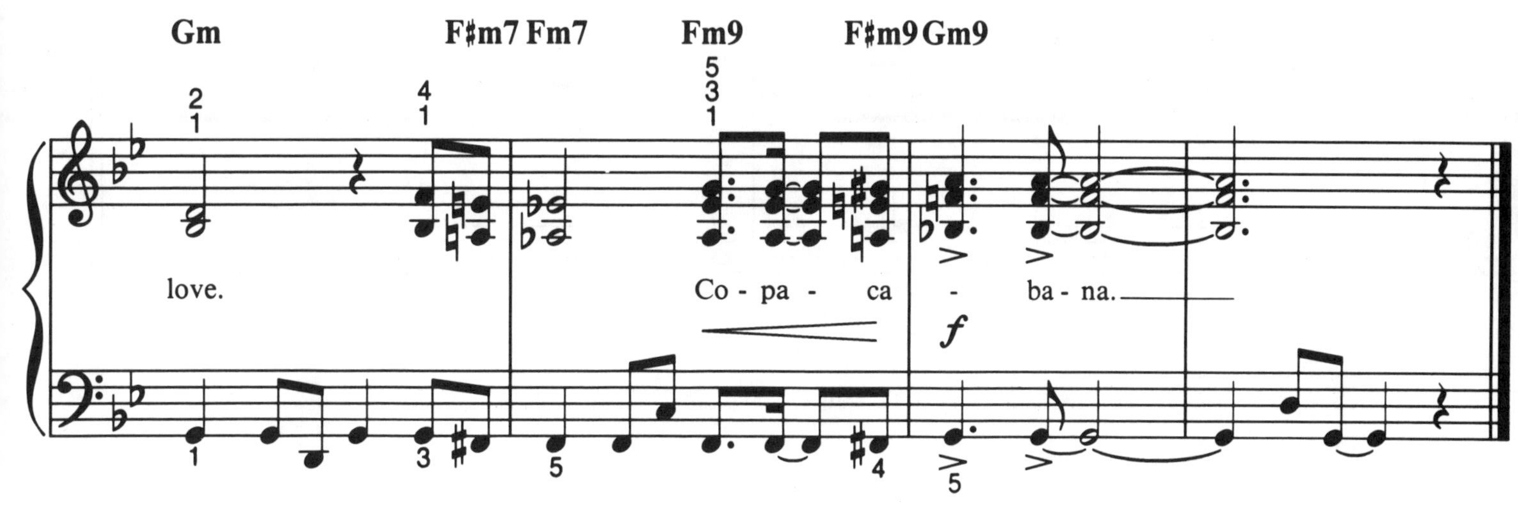
Gm
F♯m7 Fm7
Fm9
F♯m9 Gm9
love.
Co - pa - ca - ba - na.
f

COULD IT BE MAGIC

Words and Music by BARRY MANILOW
and ADRIENNE ANDERSON

Moderately, with motion

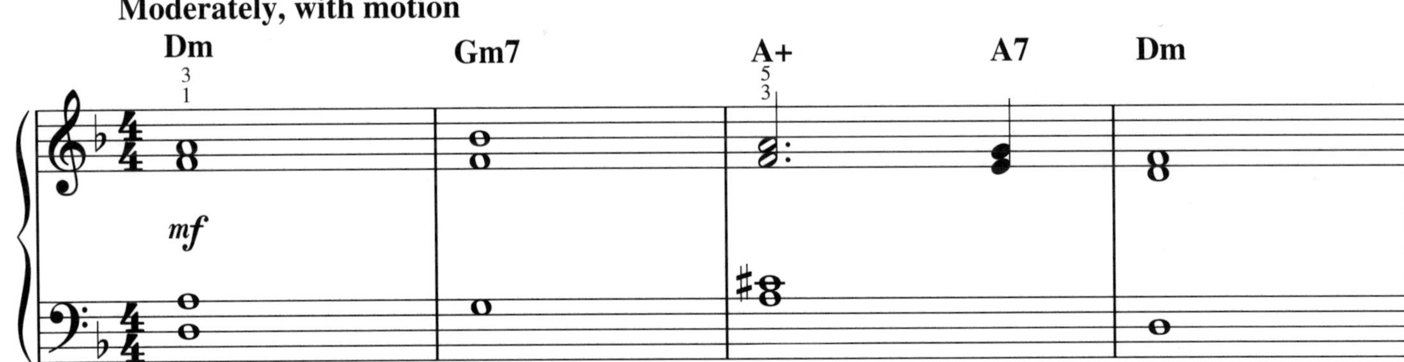

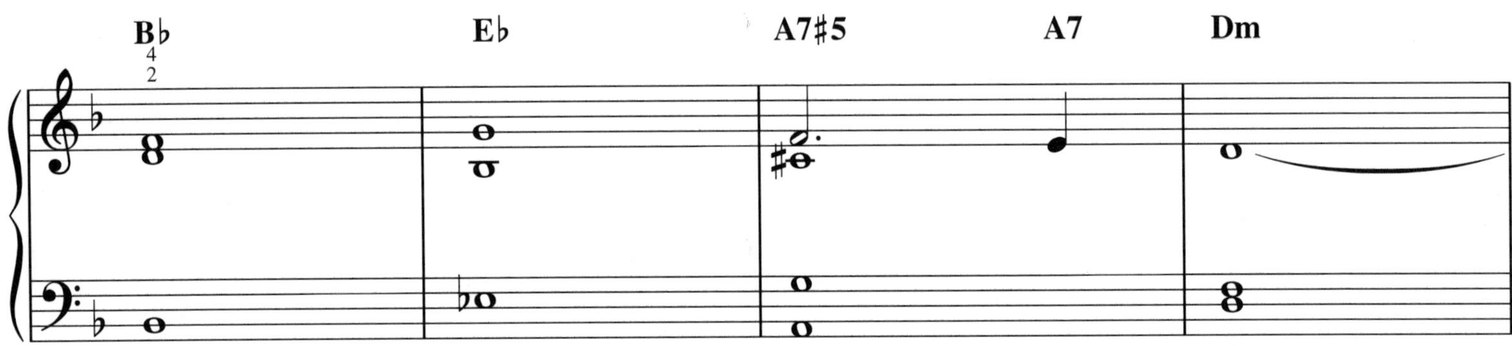

Copyright © 1973 by Careers-BMG Music Publishing, Inc. and EMI Longitude Music
Copyright Renewed
International Copyright Secured All Rights Reserved

Dsus
D
E
Fmaj7
2
Spir - it, move ___ me ev - 'ry time ___ I'm
La - dy, take ___ me high up - on ___ a

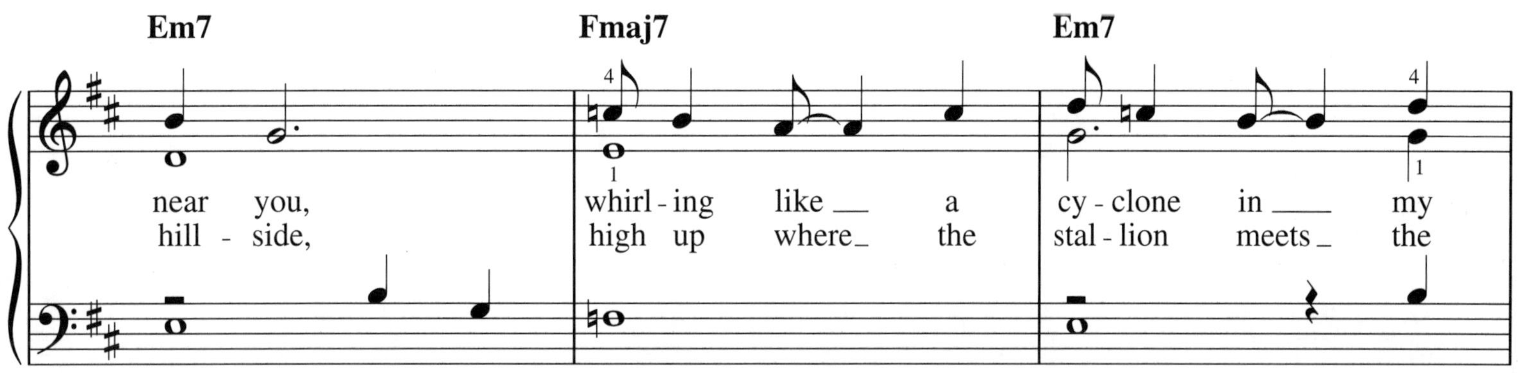
Em7
Fmaj7
Em7
4
1
4
1
near you, whirl - ing like ___ a cy - clone in ___ my
hill - side, high up where ___ the stal - lion meets ___ the

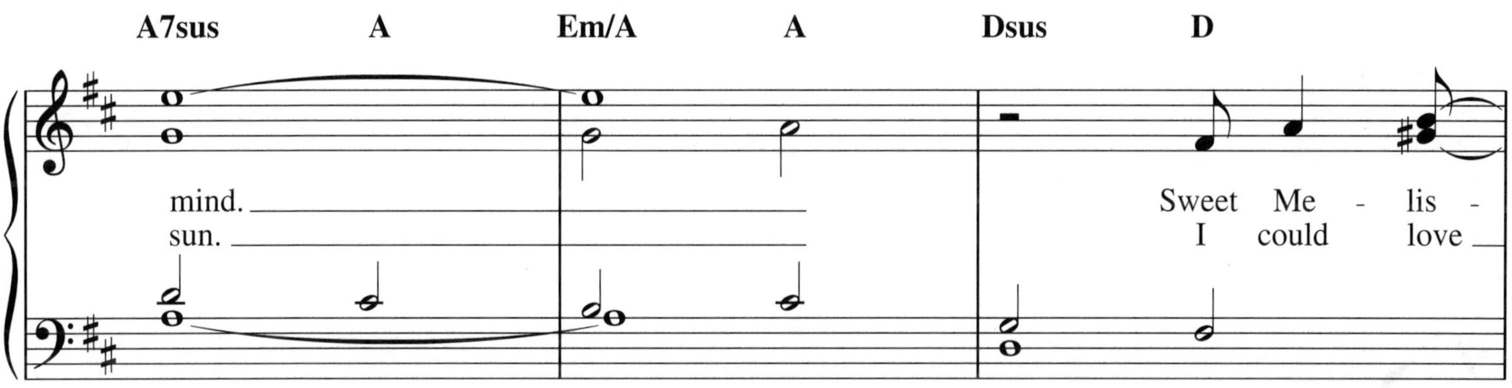
A7sus
A
Em/A
A
Dsus
D
mind. ___ Sweet Me - lis -
sun. ___ I could love ___

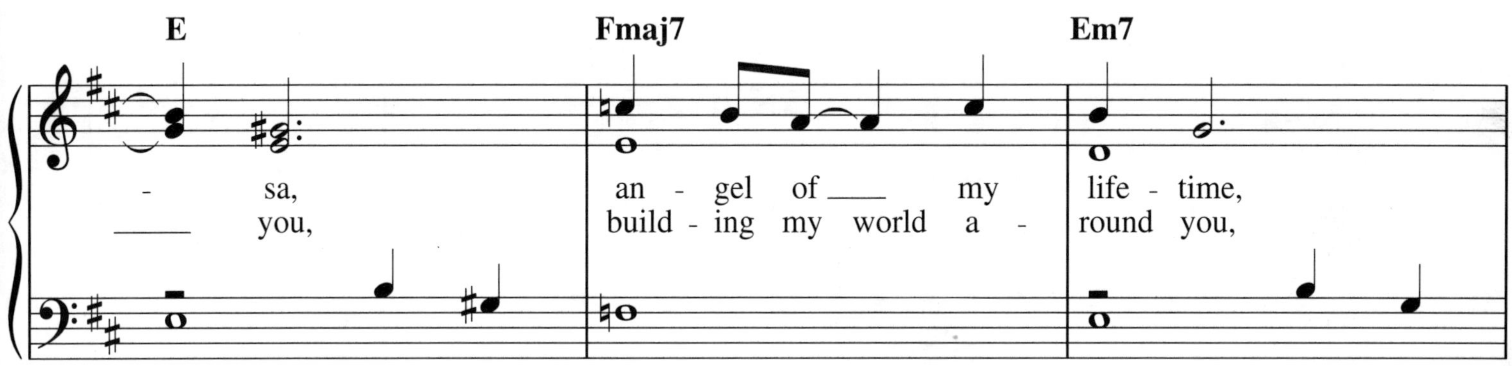
E
Fmaj7
Em7
- sa, an - gel of ___ my life - time,
___ you, build - ing my world a - round you,

Fmaj7
Em7
A7sus
A
A7/G
Dm/F
A/E
an - swer to all an - swers I can find. Ba-by, I love you.
nev - er leave you till my life is done. Ba-by, I love you.

Dm
B♭/D
A/C♯
Come, come, come in - to my
now, now, now and hold on

Cmaj7
Am/C
Bm7
B♭7
Last time
To Coda
arms. Let me know the won - der of
fast. Could this be the mag - ic at

1.,3.
2.
A7
A7/G
Dm/F
A/E
A7
Em
all of you. Ba-by, I want you
last?

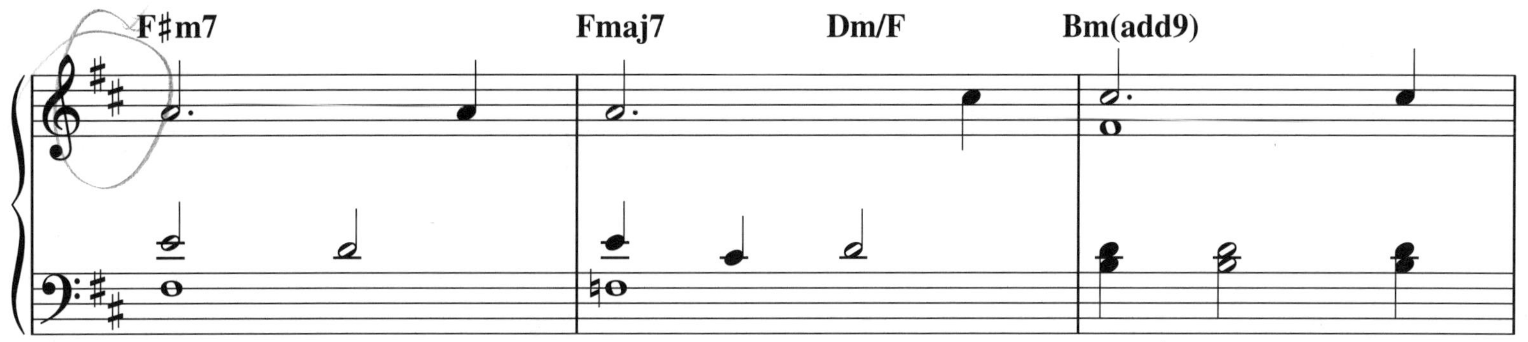
F♯m7
Fmaj7
Dm/F
Bm(add9)

F♯m11

Bm(add9)
2
1
3
1
F♯m11

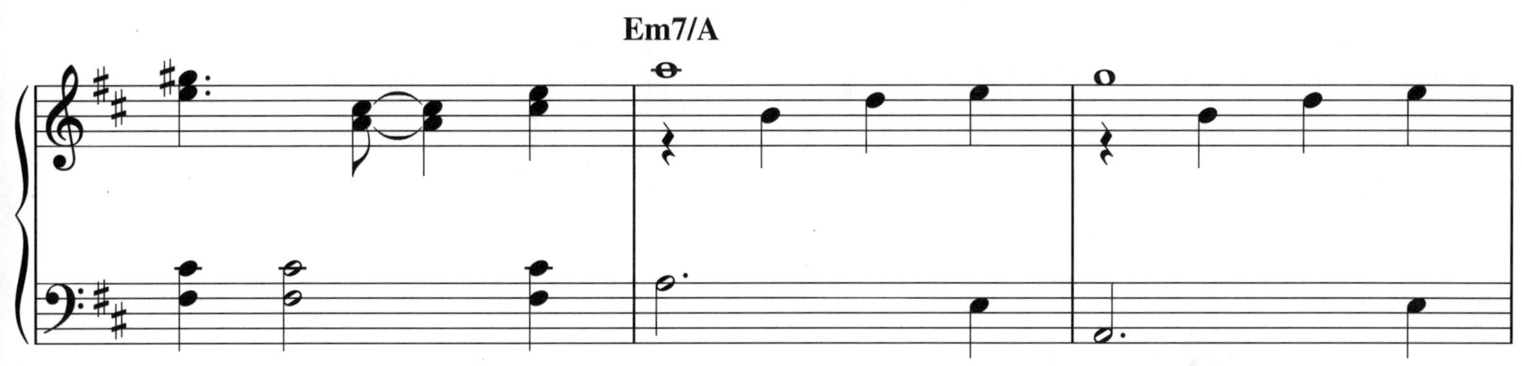
Em7/A

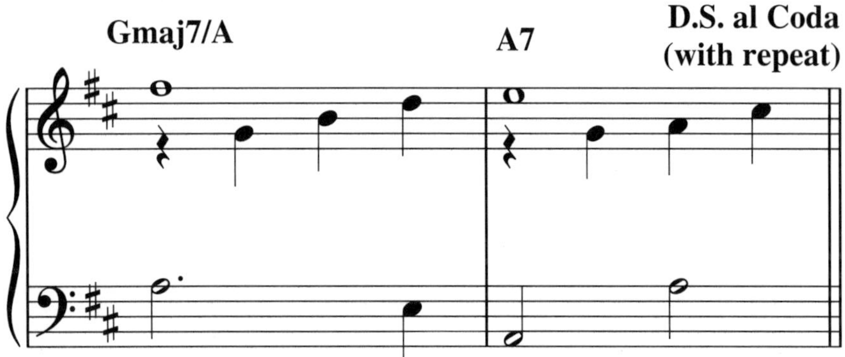
Gmaj7/A
A7
D.S. al Coda
(with repeat)

CODA
A7
last?

A7/G
DM/F
A/E
Dm
B♭/D
Could it be mag - ic?
Come,
now,
Come,
come,
now,
come,

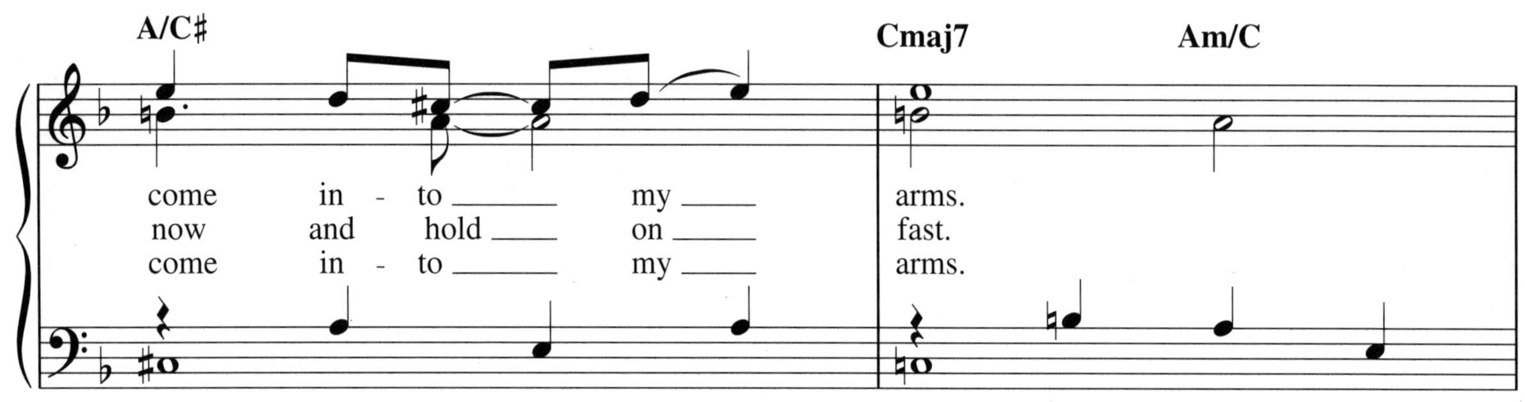
A/C♯
Cmaj7
Am/C
come in - to my arms.
now and hold on fast.
come in - to my arms.

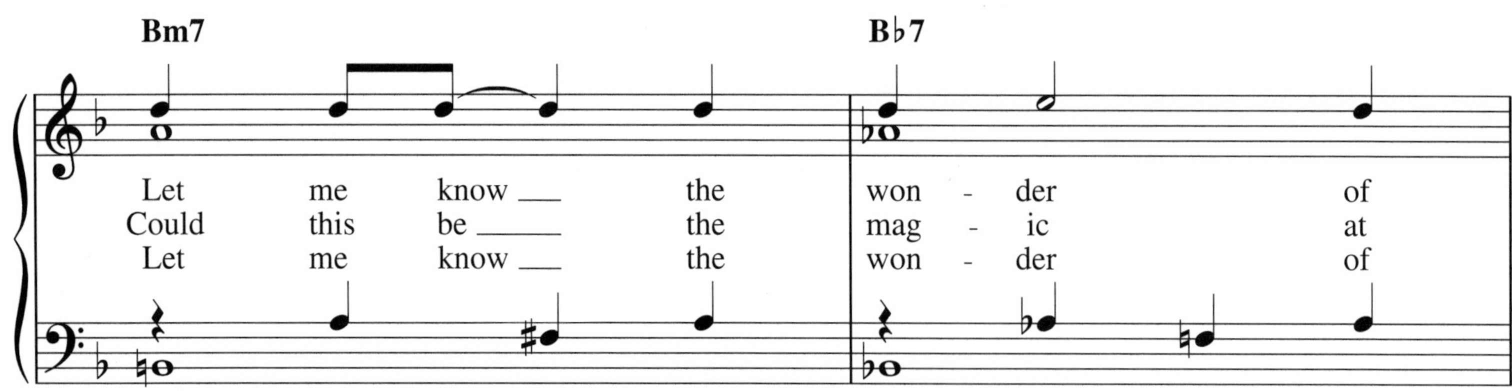
Bm7
B♭7
Let me know the won - der of
Could this be the mag - ic at
Let me know the won - der of

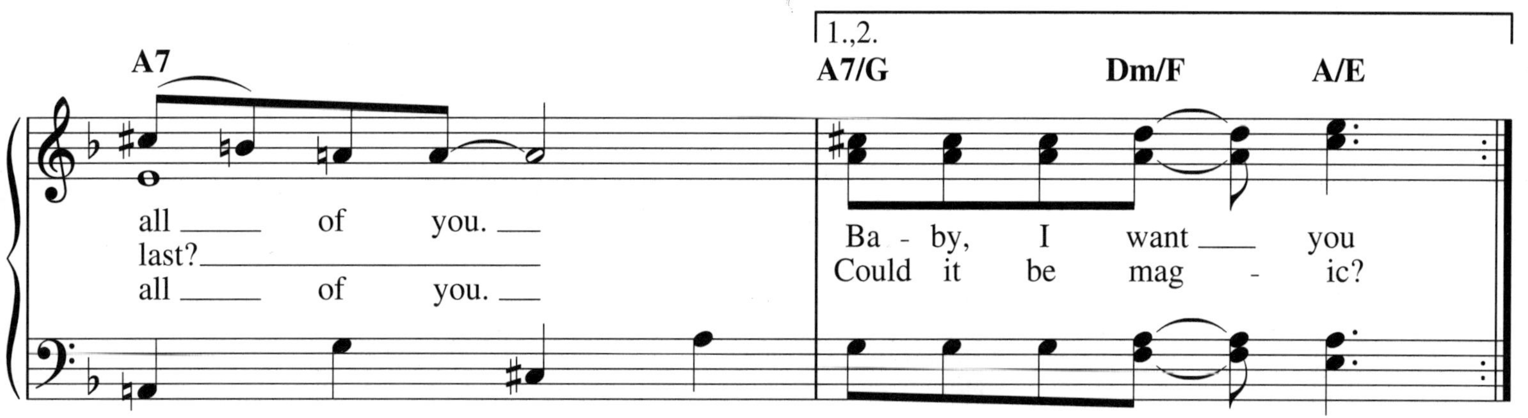
1.,2.
A7
A7/G
Dm/F
A/E
all of you.
last?
all of you.
Ba - by, I want you
Could it be mag - ic?

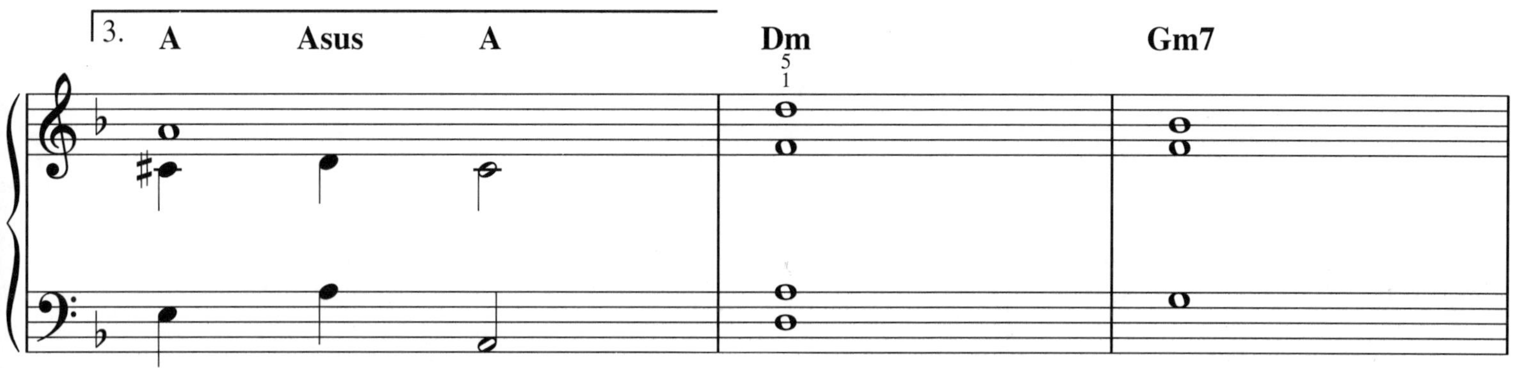
3.
A
Asus
A
Dm
Gm7

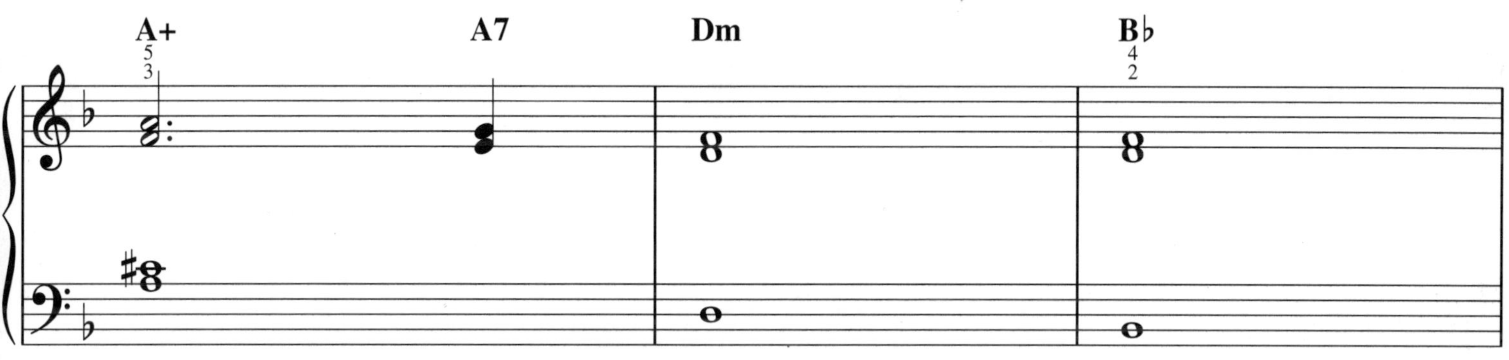
A+
A7
Dm
B♭

E♭ A7♯5 A7 Dm

DEJA VU

Lyrics by ADRIENNE ANDERSON
Music by ISAAC HAYES

Copyright © 1979 by Rightsong Music Inc. and Careers-BMG Music Publishing, Inc.
International Copyright Secured All Rights Reserved

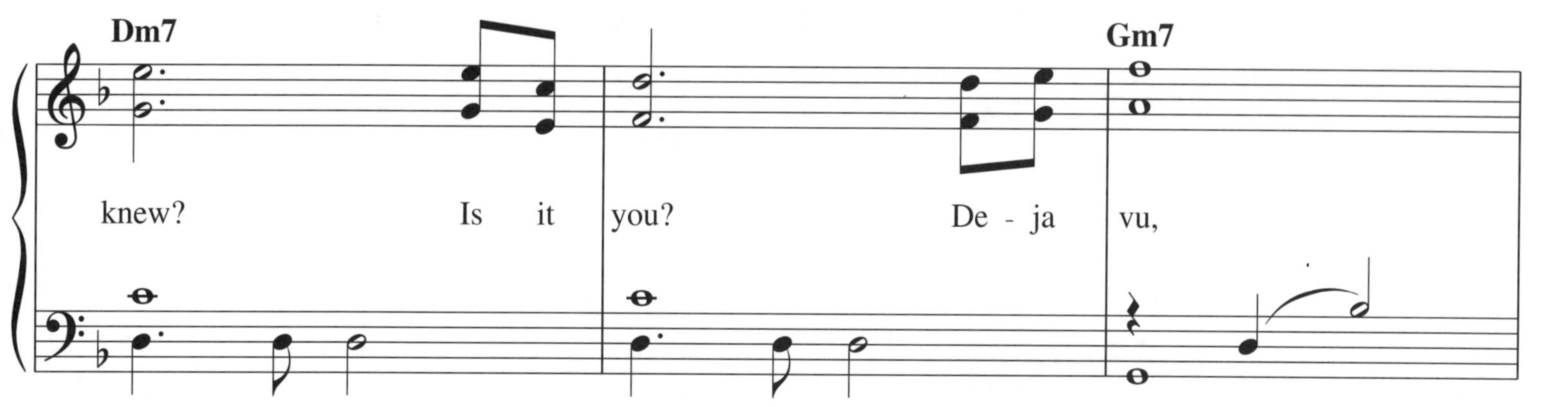
Dm7
Gm7
knew? Is it you? De - ja vu,

Dm7
could you be the dream that might come true, Shin-ing through? I keep re-

Am7
Gm7
Dm
To Coda
C♭/D♭
mem-ber-ing me, I keep re-mem-ber-ing you, De - ja vu

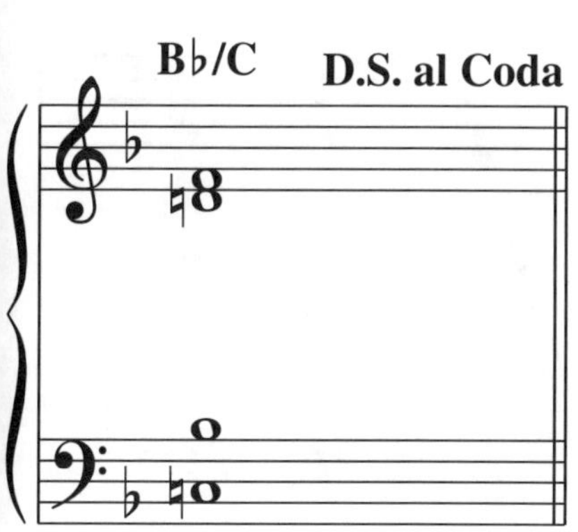
B♭/C
D.S. al Coda

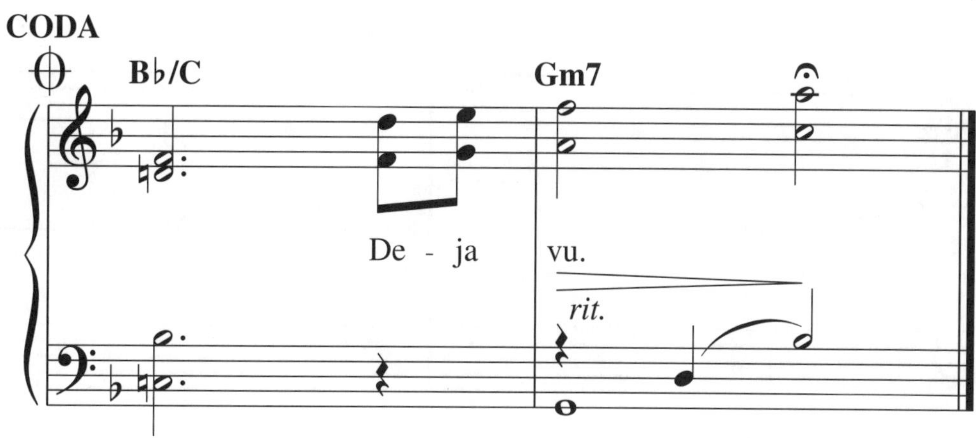
CODA
B♭/C
Gm7
De - ja vu.
rit.

DO YOU KNOW WHERE YOU'RE GOING TO?

Theme from MAHOGANY

Words by GERRY GOFFIN
Music by MIKE MASSER

© 1973 (Renewed 2001) SCREEN GEMS-EMI MUSIC INC. and JOBETE MUSIC CO., INC.
All Rights for JOBETE MUSIC CO., INC. Controlled and Administered by EMI APRIL MUSIC INC.
All Rights Reserved International Copyright Secured Used by Permission

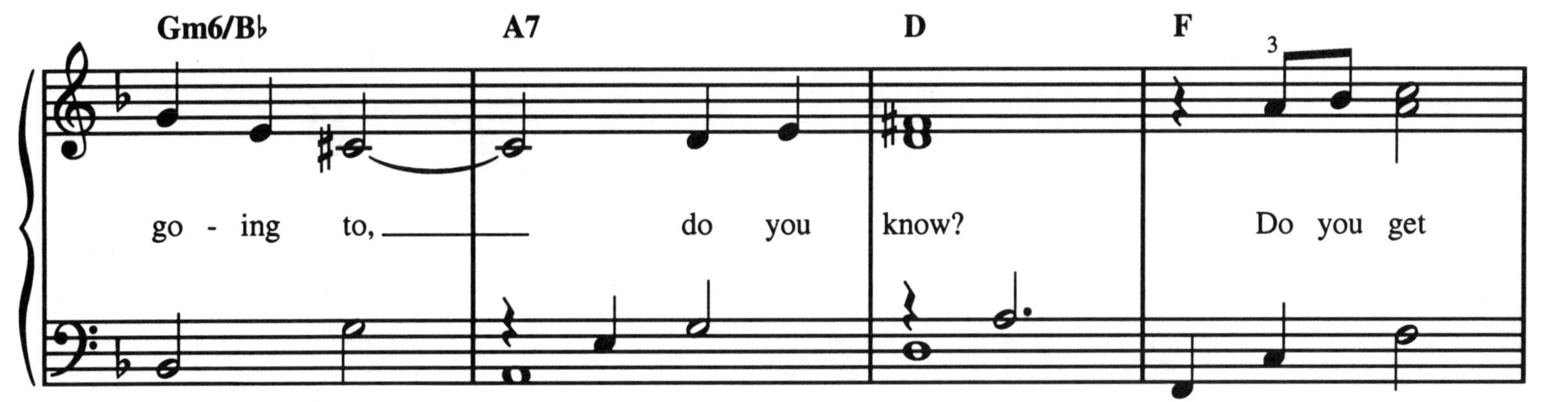
Gm6/B♭
A7
D
F
3
go - ing to, do you know? Do you get

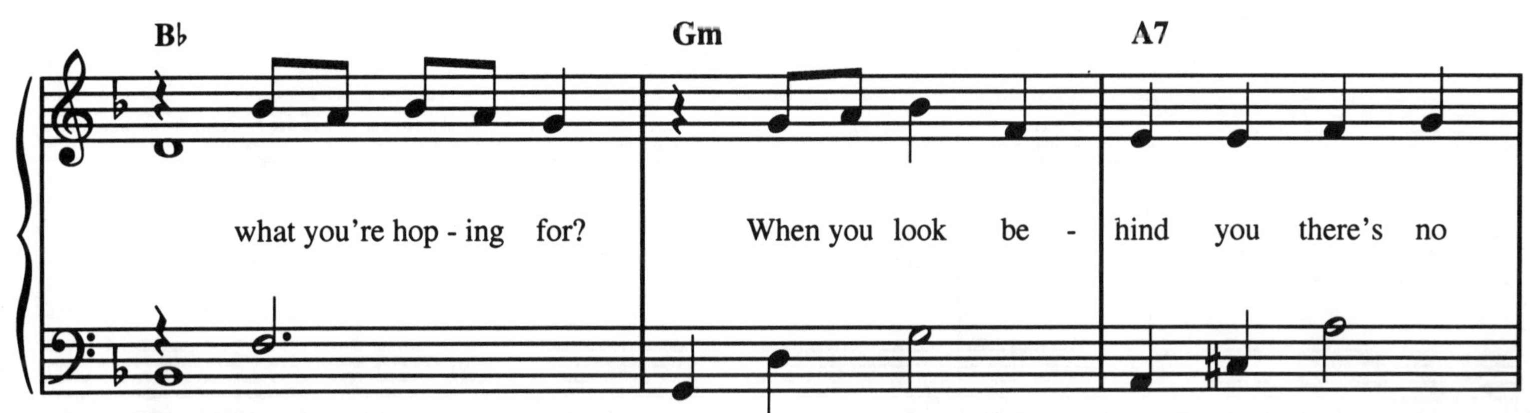
B♭
Gm
A7
what you're hop - ing for? When you look be - hind you there's no

Dm
Gm6/B♭
o - pen door. What are you hop - ing for,

A7
To Coda
D
E/D
2
do you know? Once we were stand - ing

A/C♯
A
B
Em7
still in time, chas - ing the fan -
G/A
D
G
D
- ta - sies that filled our minds. And you
E/D
C♯m7
knew how I loved you but my spir - it was
F♯m7
Bm7
D/E
free, laugh-ing at the ques - tions that you

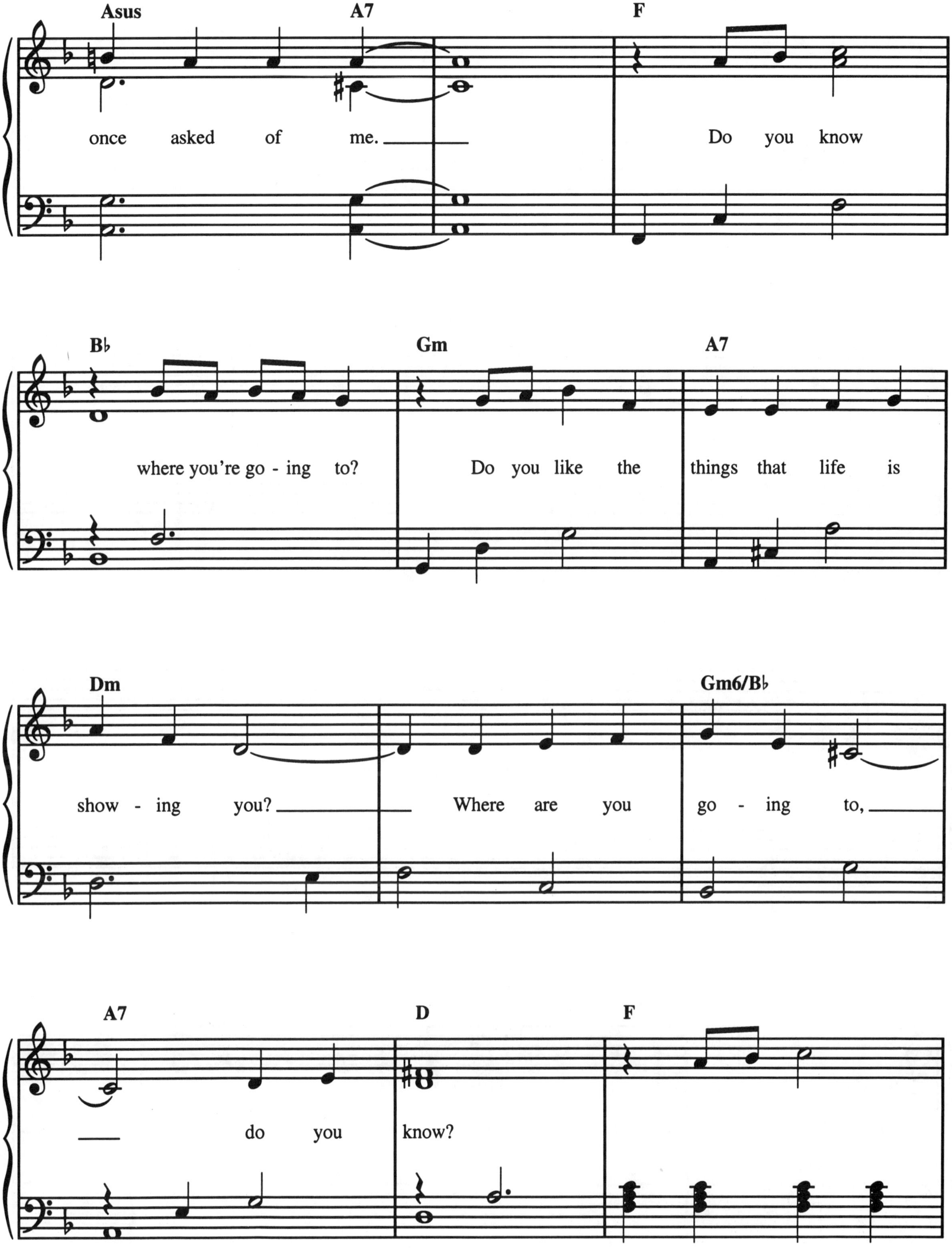

Asus A7 F

once asked of me. Do you know

B♭ Gm A7

where you're go - ing to? Do you like the things that life is

Dm Gm6/B♭

show - ing you? Where are you go - ing to,

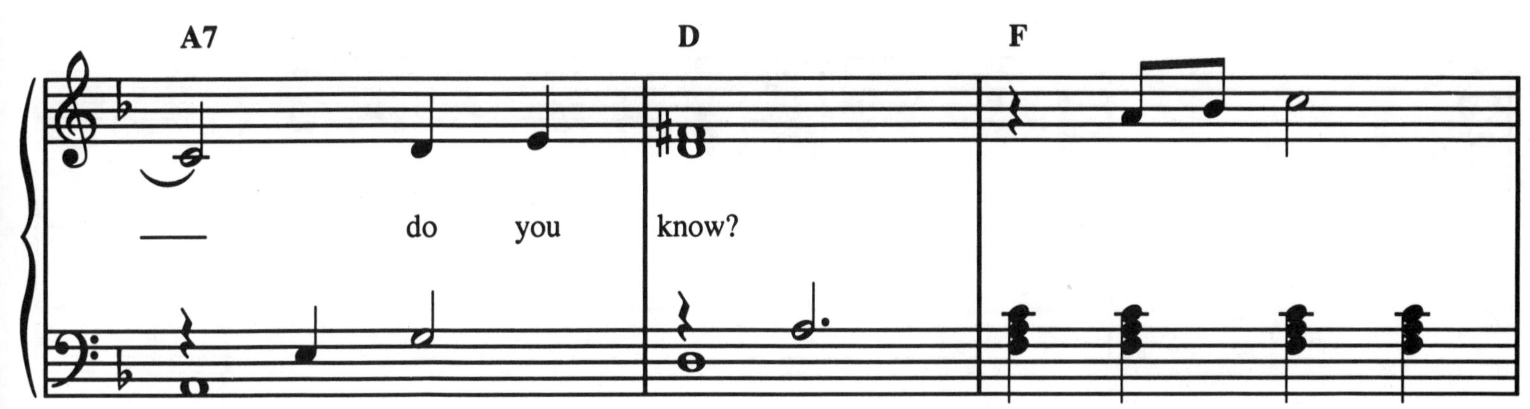

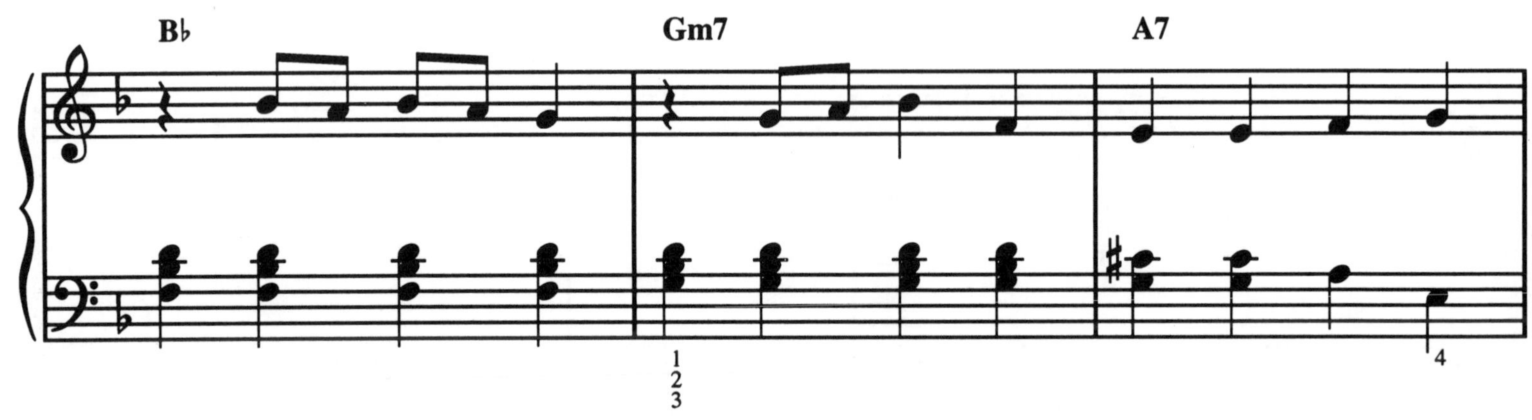
B♭
Gm7
A7
1
2
3
4

Dm
Gm6/B♭
A7

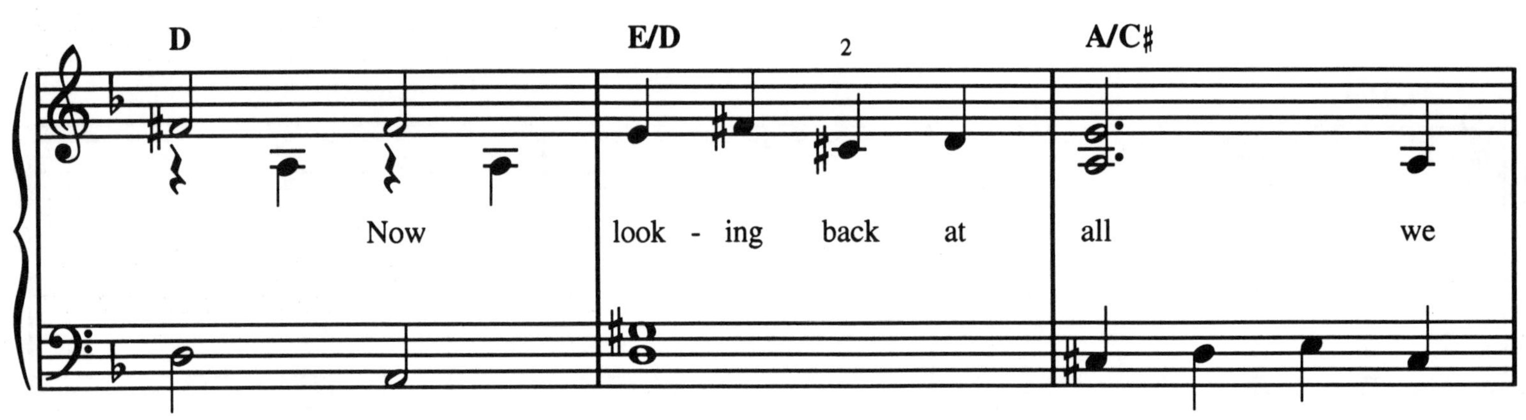
D
E/D
2
A/C♯
Now
look - ing back at
all we

A
4
G/E
A7sus
D G D
planned,
we let so man- - y dreams just
slip through our hands.
1

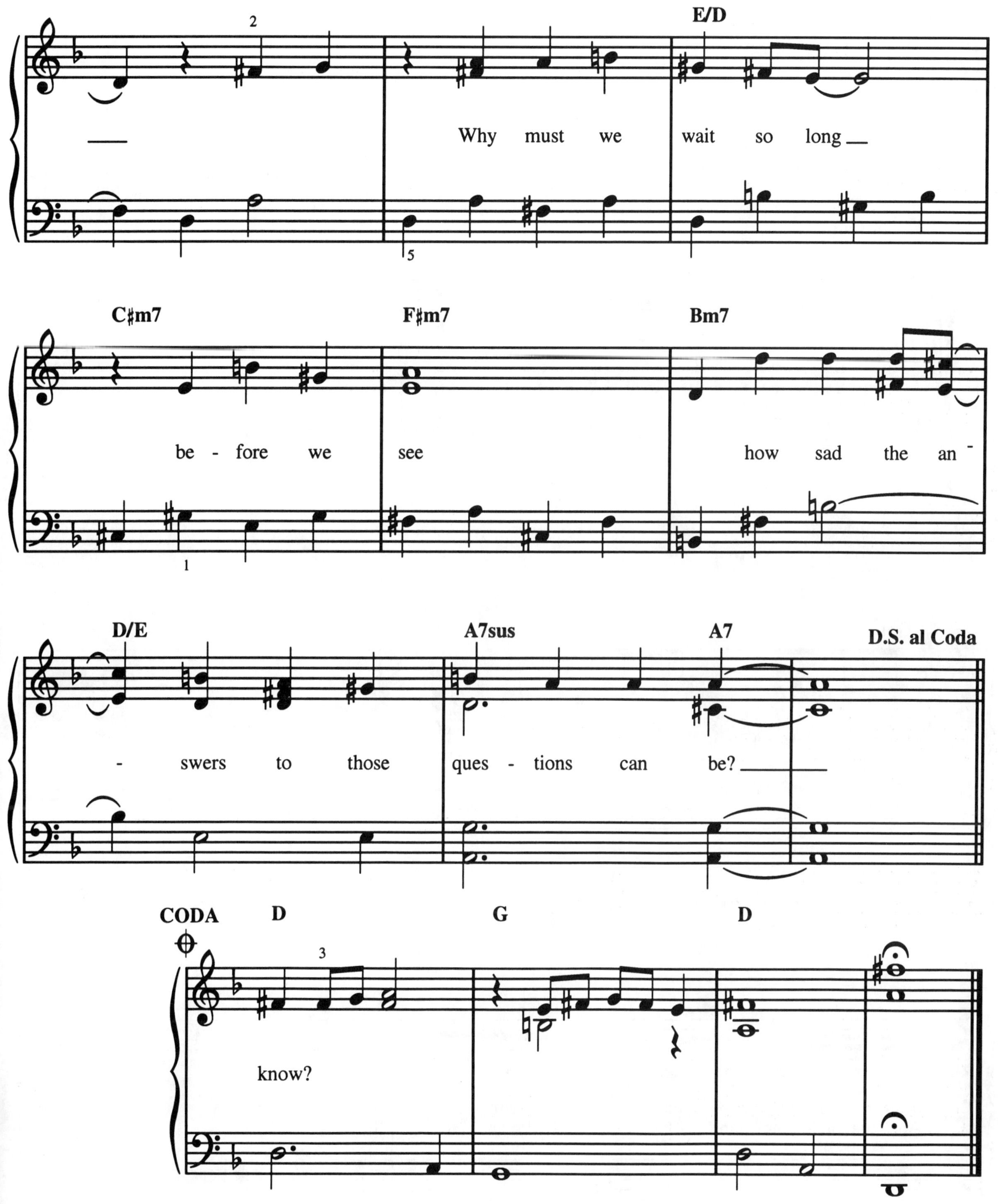

2
E/D
Why must we wait so long
5
C♯m7
F♯m7
Bm7
be - fore we see how sad the an -
1
D/E
A7sus
A7
D.S. al Coda
- swers to those ques - tions can be?
CODA
D
G
D
3
know?

DON'T CRY OUT LOUD

Words and Music by CAROLE BAYER SAGER
and PETER ALLEN

Slowly

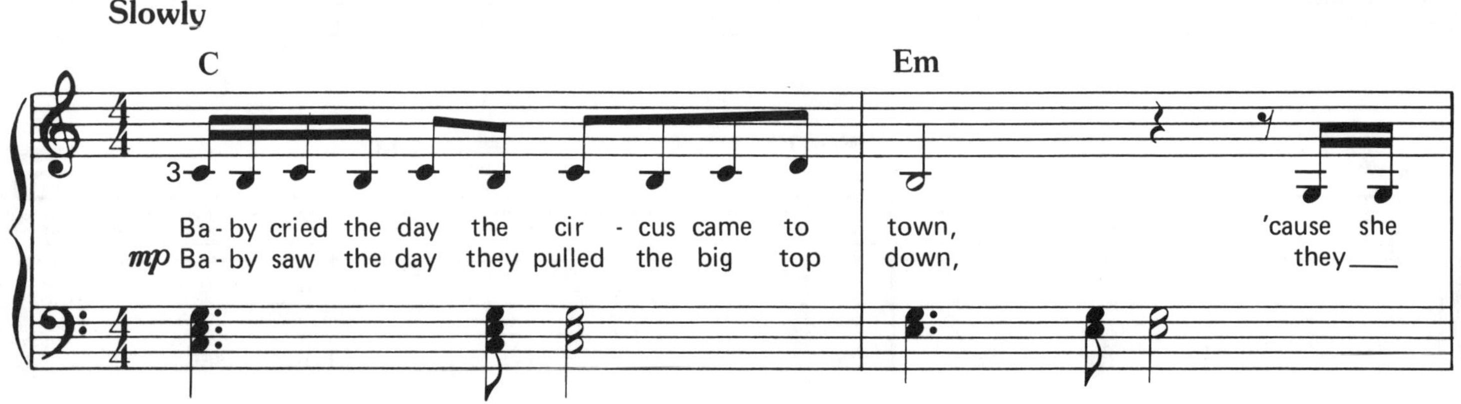

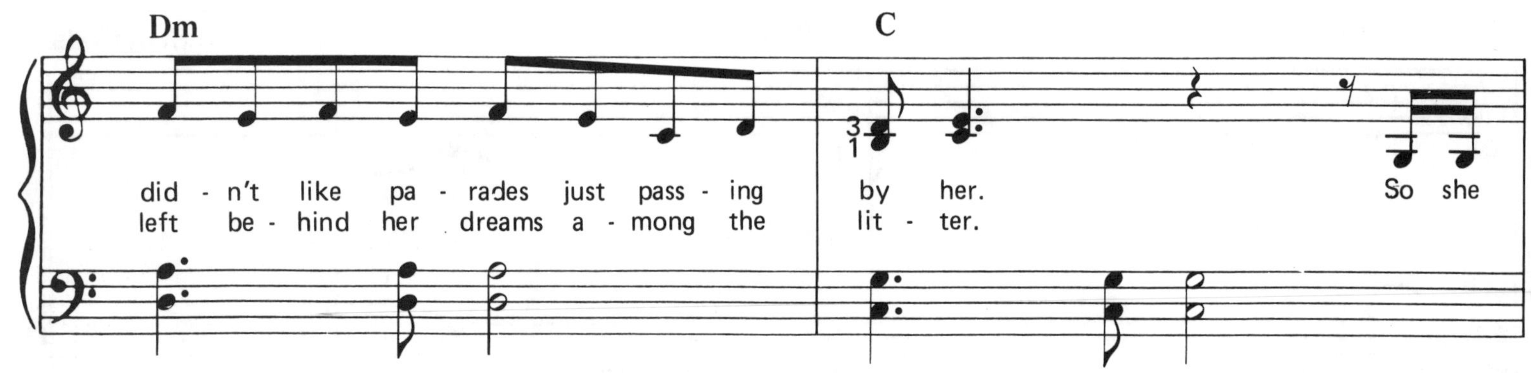

Copyright © 1976, 1978 by Unichappell Music Inc., Begonia Melodies, Inc., Irving Music, Inc. and Woolnough Music, Inc.
All Rights for Begonia Melodies, Inc. Administered by Unichappell Music Inc.
All Rights for Woolnough Music, Inc. Administered by Irving Music, Inc.
International Copyright Secured All Rights Reserved

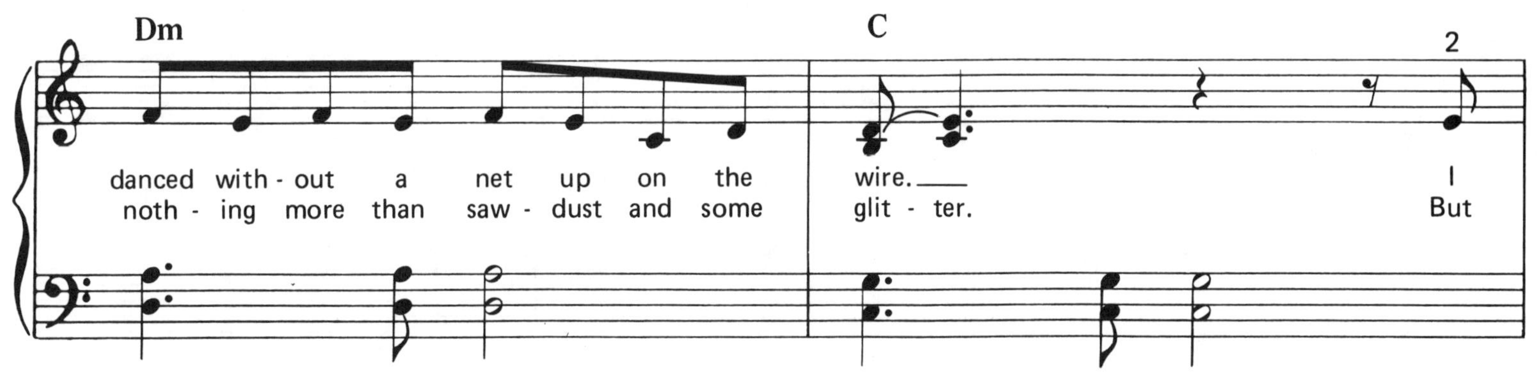
Dm
C
2
danced with - out a net up on the
wire.
I
noth - ing more than saw - dust and some
glit - ter.
But

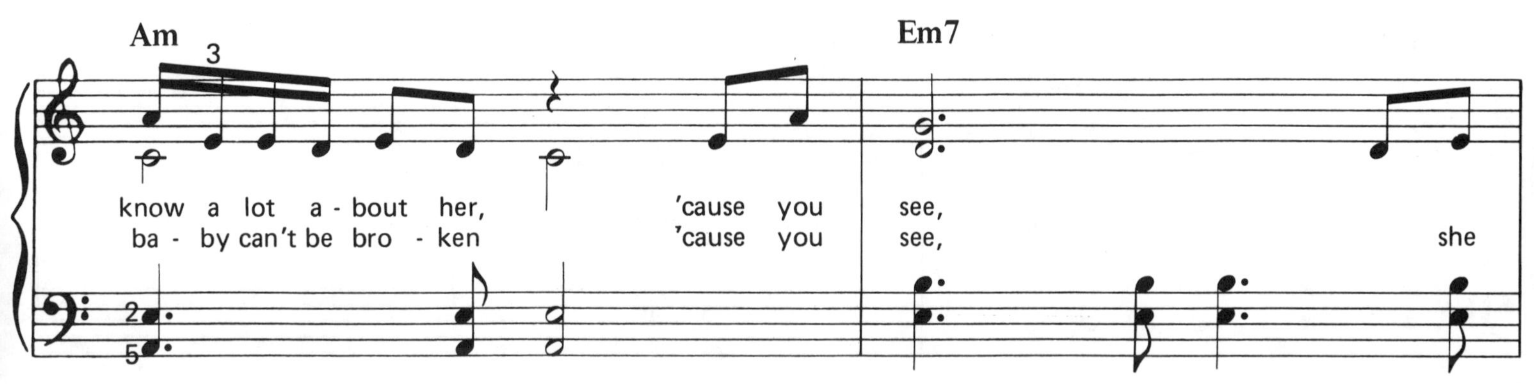
Am
3
Em7
know a lot a - bout her, 'cause you
see,
ba - by can't be bro - ken 'cause you
see,
she
2
5

Am7
D7
Gsus
G7
1
5
ba - by is an aw - ful lot like
me.
had the fin - est teach - er that's
me.
I told her,
2

C
G/B
4
Am
5
Dm
Don't cry out
loud, Just keep it in -
side, learn how to
1
2
1
3

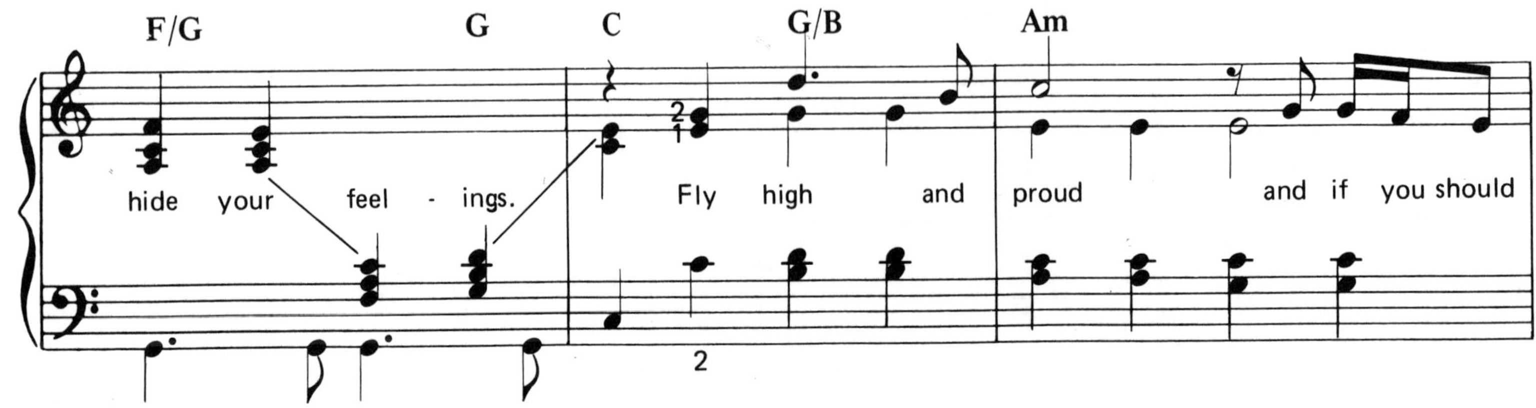
F/G
G
C
G/B
Am
hide your feel - ings. Fly high and proud and if you should
2

Dm7
To Coda
1
Gsus
A
fall, re - mem - ber you al - most had it all.

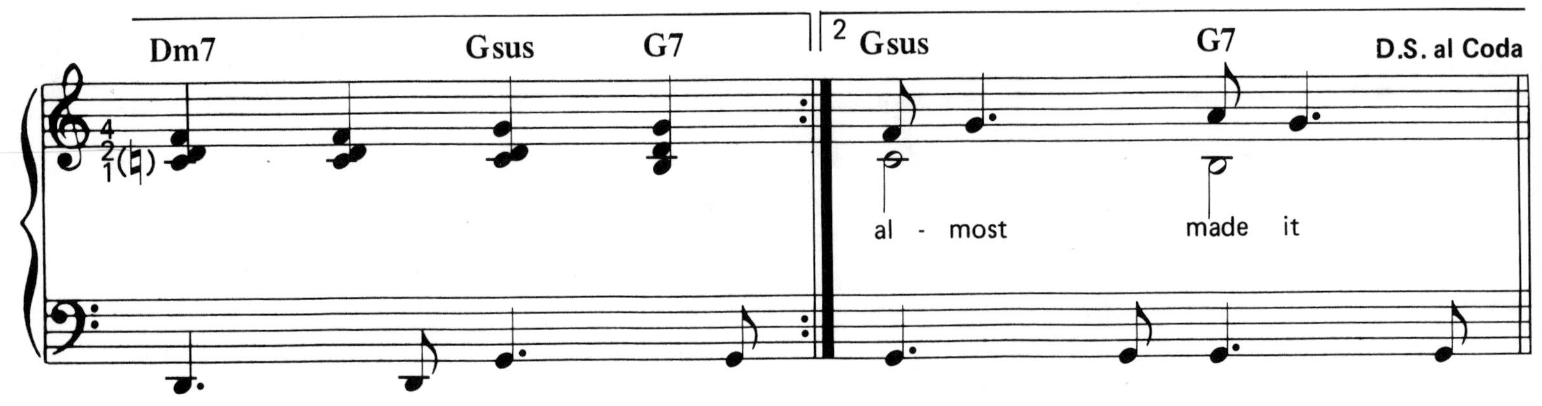
Dm7
Gsus
G7
2
Gsus
G7
D.S. al Coda
al - most made it

CODA
Gsus
G7
C
al - most had it all.
1

GOODBYE TO LOVE

Words and Music by RICHARD CARPENTER
and JOHN BETTIS

Copyright © 1972 HAMMER AND NAILS MUSIC and ALMO MUSIC CORP.
Copyright Renewed
All Rights Administered by ALMO MUSIC CORP.
All Rights Reserved Used by Permission

C G/C Csus G/C
live or die, time and time a - gain the chance for
heart of mine, sure - ly time will lose these bit - ter

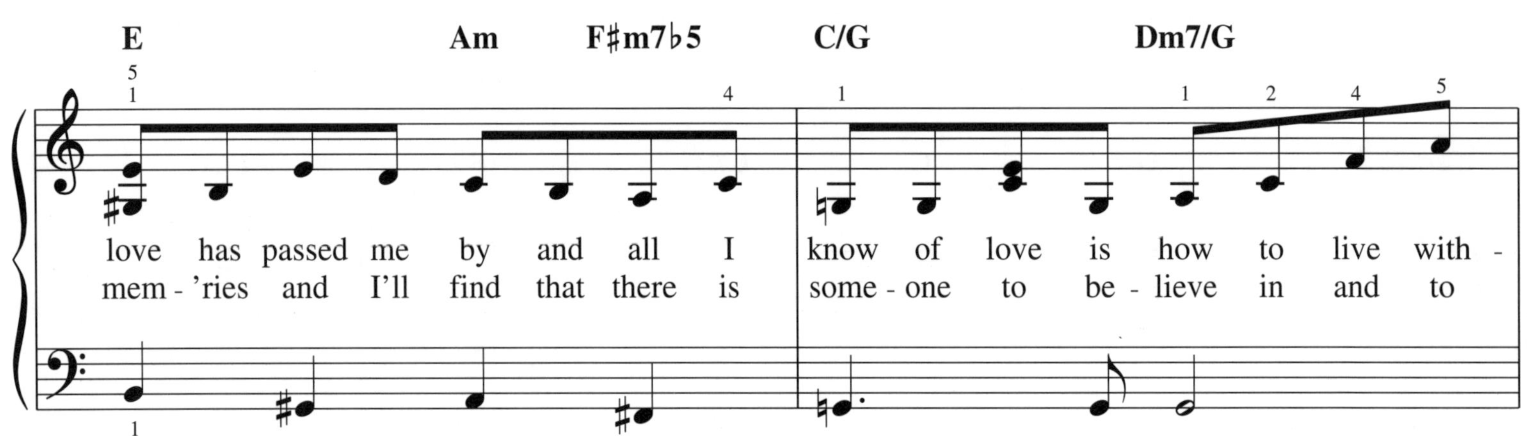
E Am F♯m7♭5 C/G Dm7/G
love has passed me by and all I know of love is how to live with -
mem - 'ries and I'll find that there is some - one to be - lieve in and to

Em7/G E/G♯ Am F♯m7♭5
out it. I just can't seem to find it.
live for, some - thing I could live for.
(End instrumental)

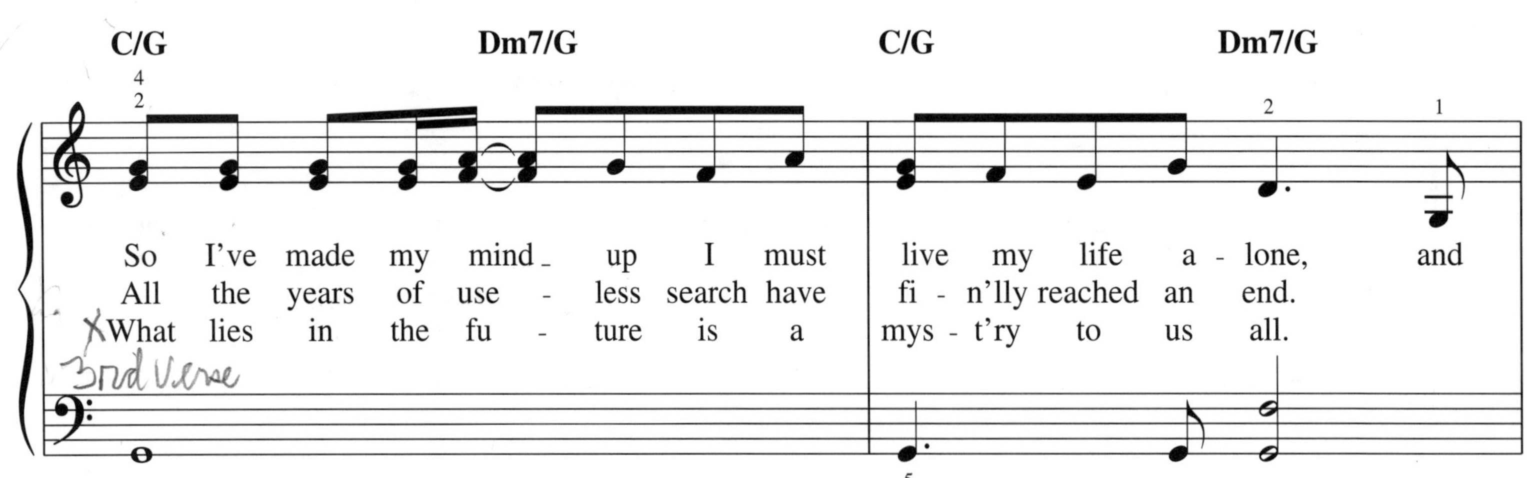
C/G Dm7/G C/G Dm7/G
So I've made my mind up I must live my life a - lone, and
All the years of use - less search have fi - n'lly reached an end.
What lies in the fu - ture is a mys - t'ry to us all.
3rd Verse

To Coda
1.
C/G
Dm7/G
though it's not the eas - y way I
Lone - li - ness and emp - ty days will
No one can pre - dict the wheel of
guess I've al - ways known I'd say good -
2.
be my on - ly friend. From this
Em7
A7
day love is for - got - ten, I'll go
Dm7♭5
on as best I
Gsus
G
D.S. al Coda
can.
CODA
for - tune as it falls.
Dmaj7/A
Em7/A
There may come a time when I will

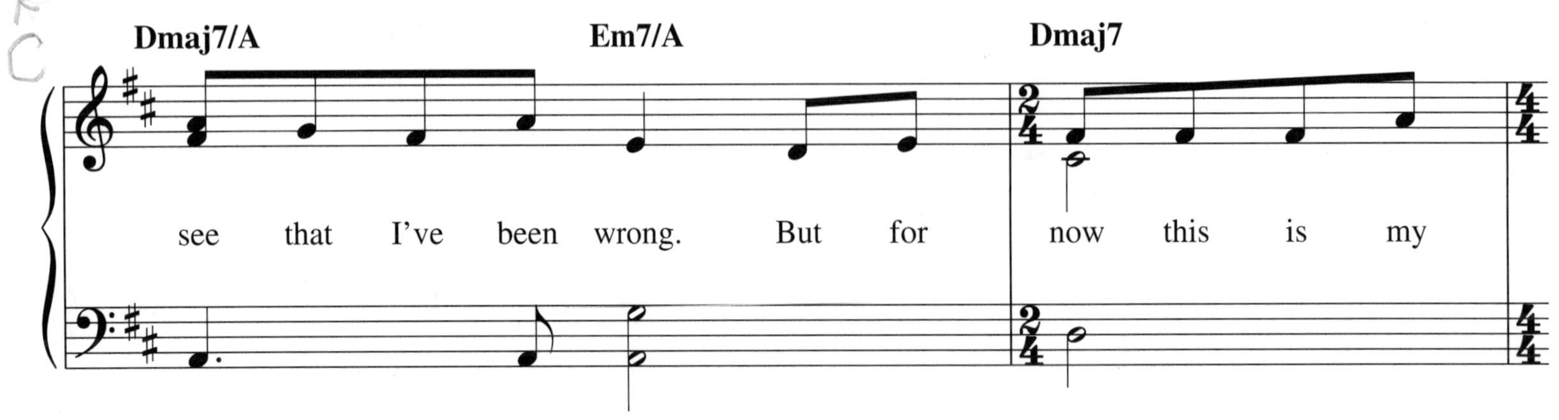
Dmaj7/A
Em7/A
Dmaj7
see that I've been wrong. But for
now this is my

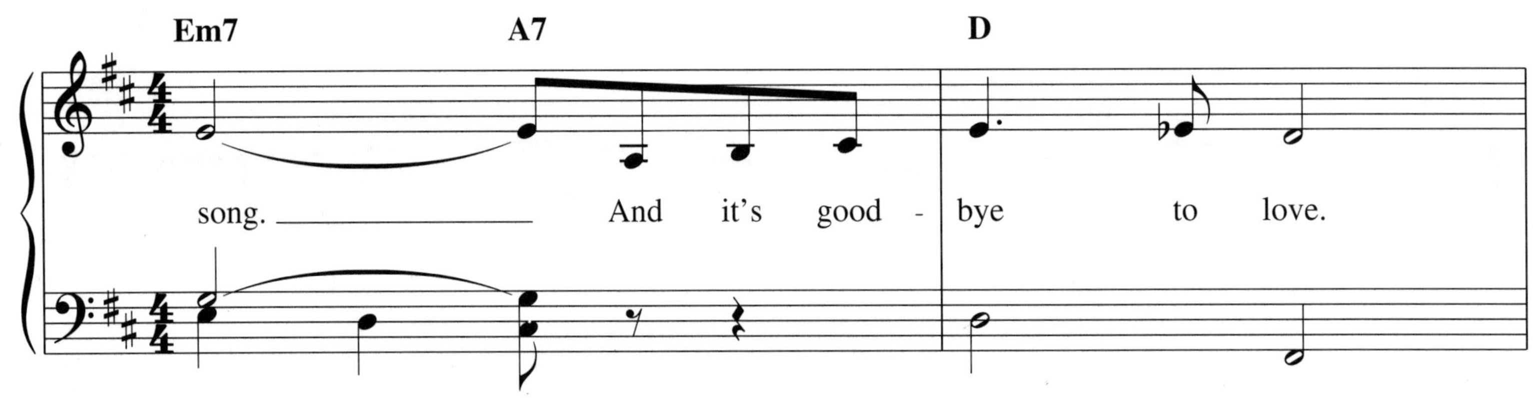
Em7
A7
D
song. And it's good - bye to love.

G/A
D
I'll say good - bye to love.

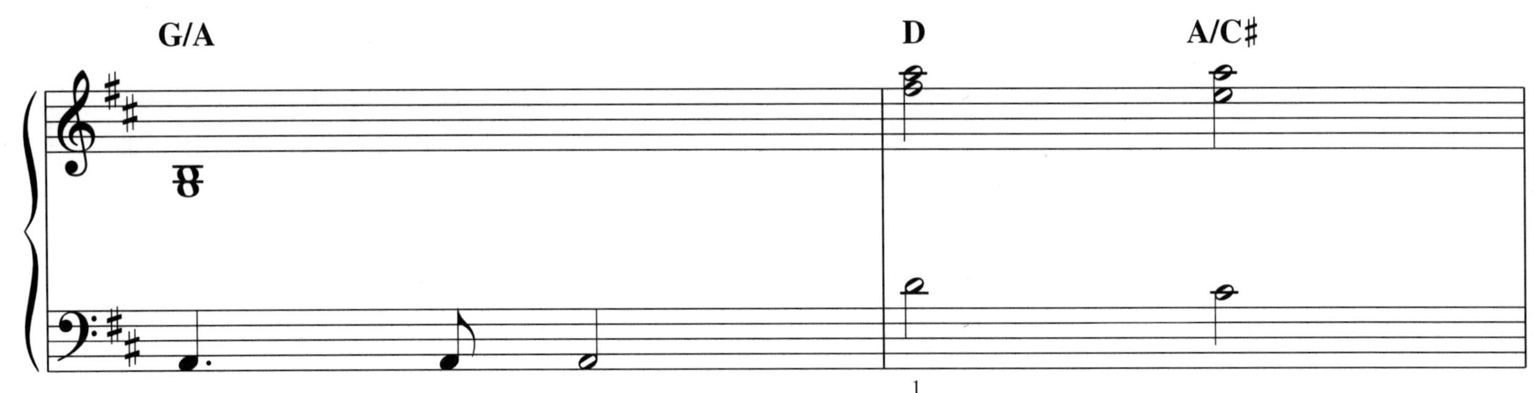
G/A
D
A/C♯
1

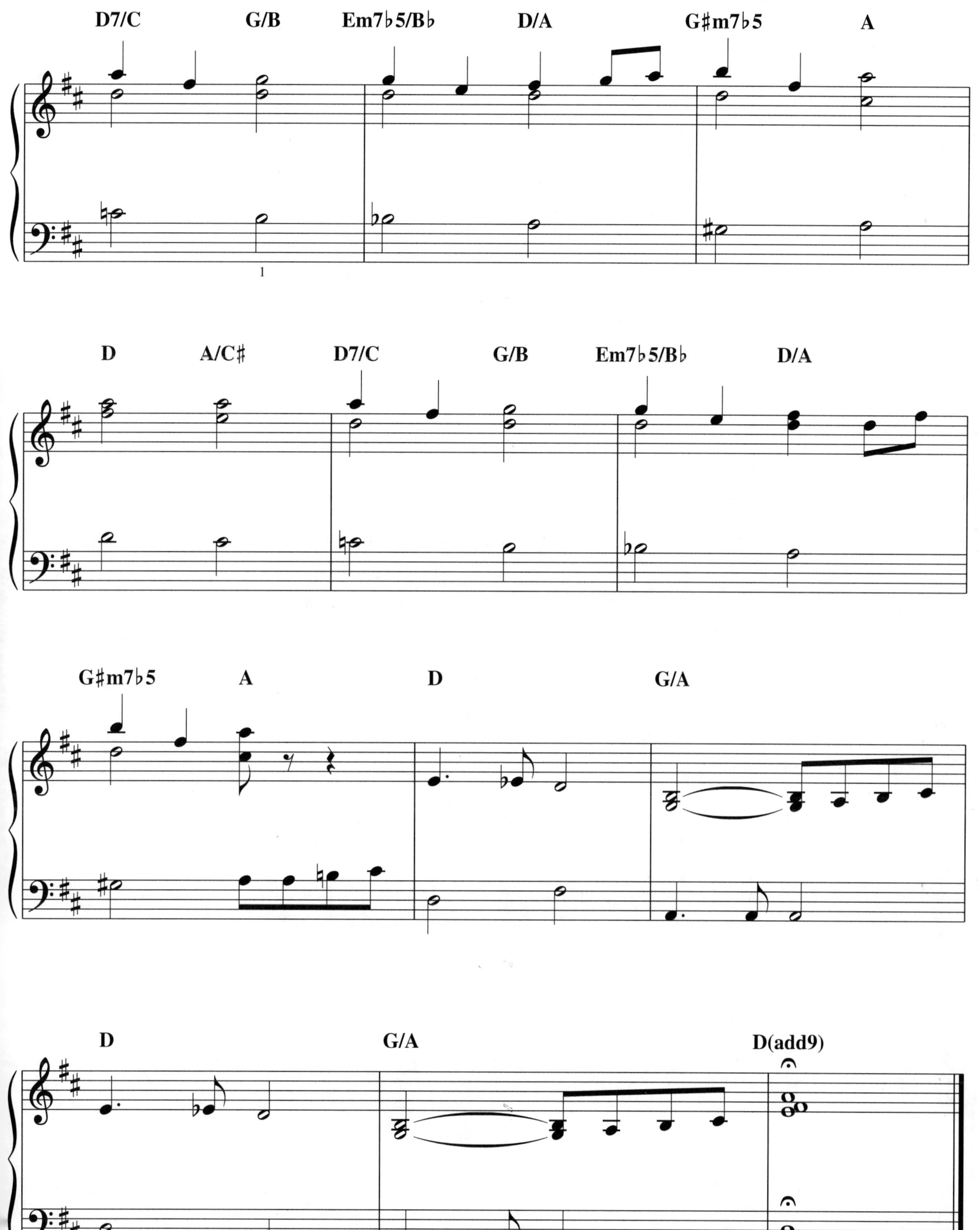
D7/C
G/B
Em7♭5/B♭
D/A
G♯m7♭5
A
1
D
A/C♯
D7/C
G/B
Em7♭5/B♭
D/A
G♯m7♭5
A
D
G/A
D
G/A
D(add9)

HANDS OF TIME

Theme from the Screen Gems Television Production BRIAN'S SONG

Words by ALAN BERGMAN and MARILYN BERGMAN
Music by MICHEL LEGRAND

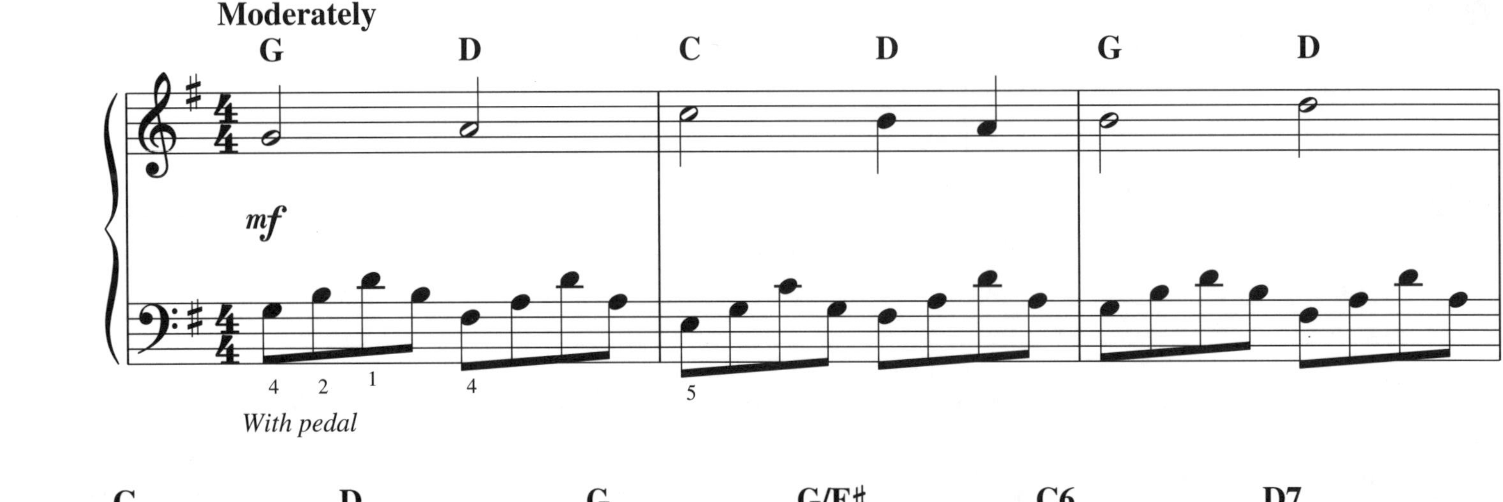

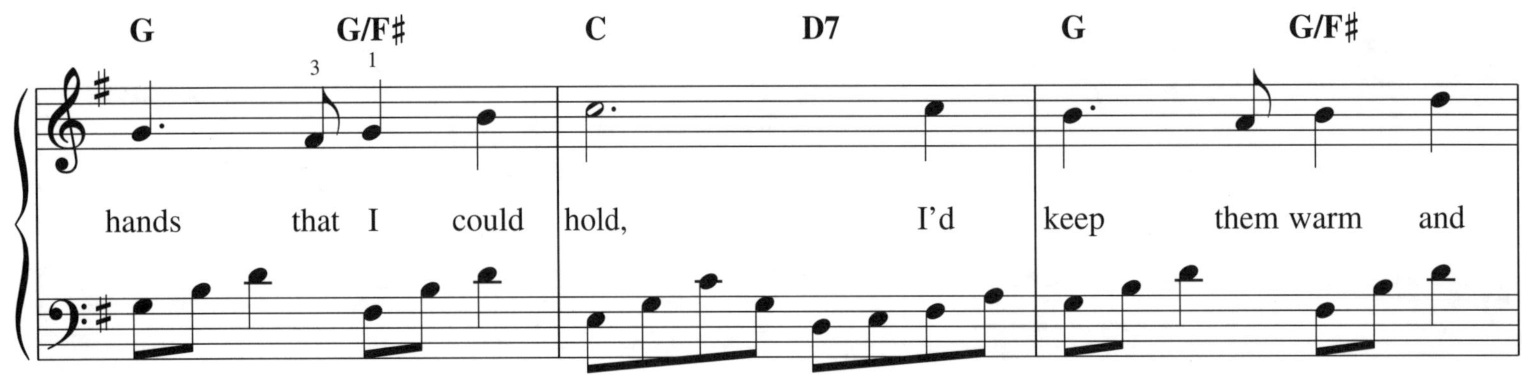

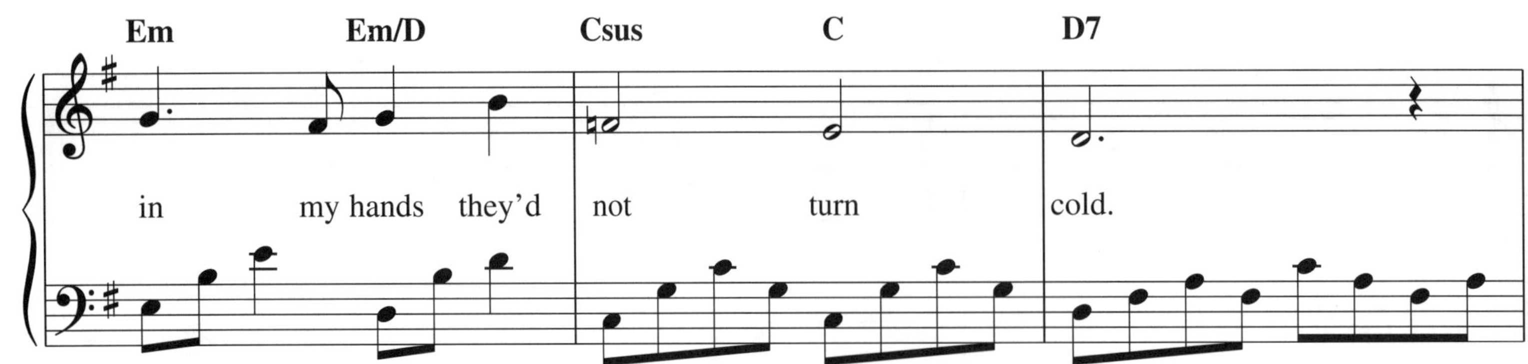

© 1972 (Renewed 2000) COLGEMS-EMI MUSIC INC.
All Rights Reserved International Copyright Secured Used by Permission

G G/F♯ C6 D7 G G/F♯
Hand in hand we'd choose the mo - ments that should
Em6 Bm Em
last; the love - ly mo - ments that should have no
A7 D Dm7
fu - ture and no past. The sum-mer from the top of the
D Dm7 Am7
swing, the com-fort in the sound of a lul - la - by, the

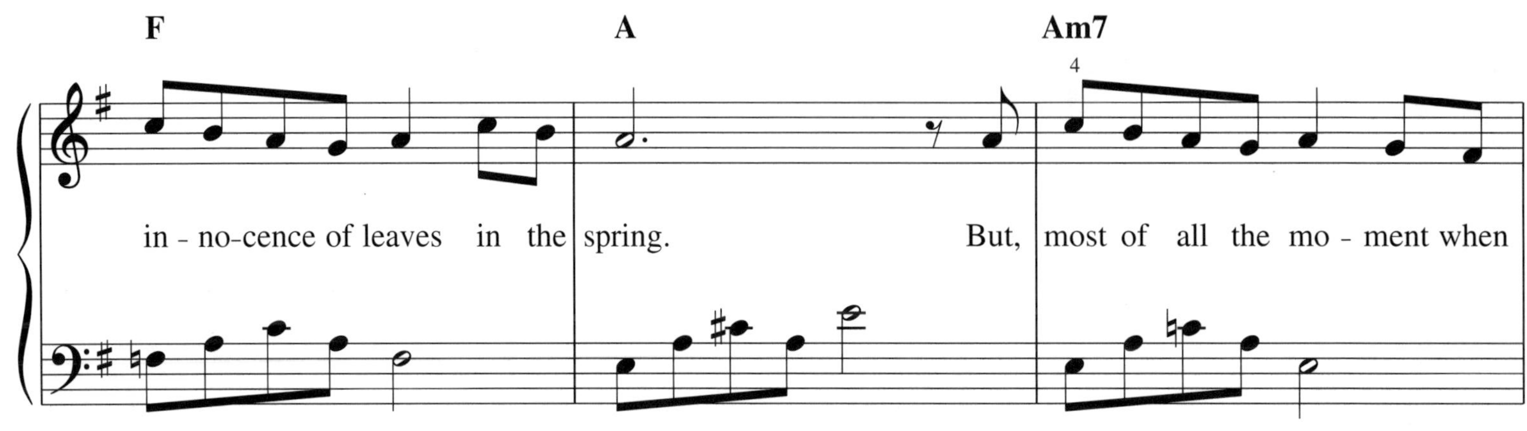
F
A
Am7
4
in - no-cence of leaves in the spring.
But, most of all the mo - ment when

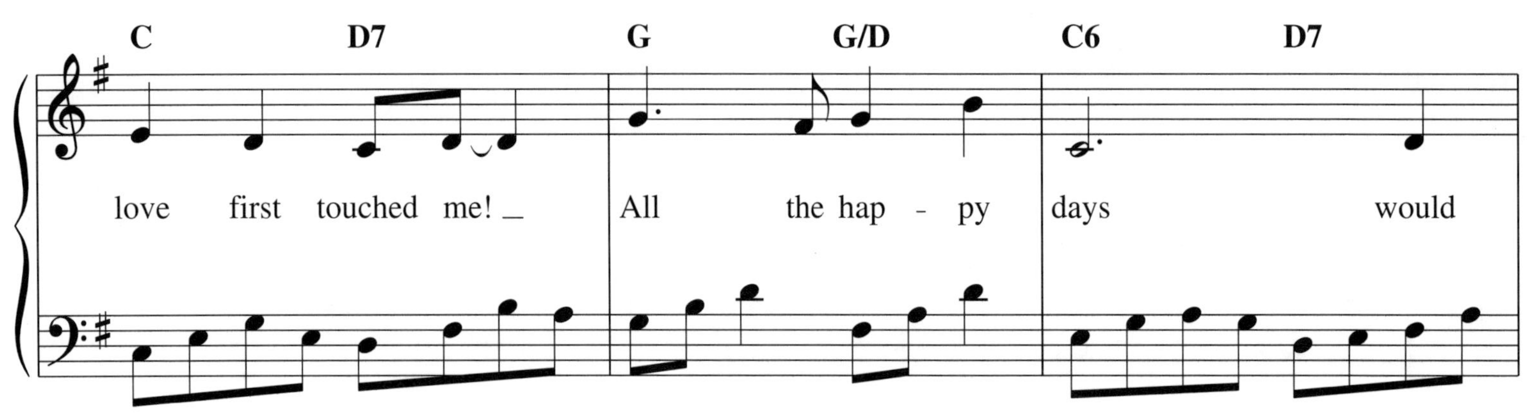
C
D7
G
G/D
C6
D7
love first touched me! _
All the hap - py
days would

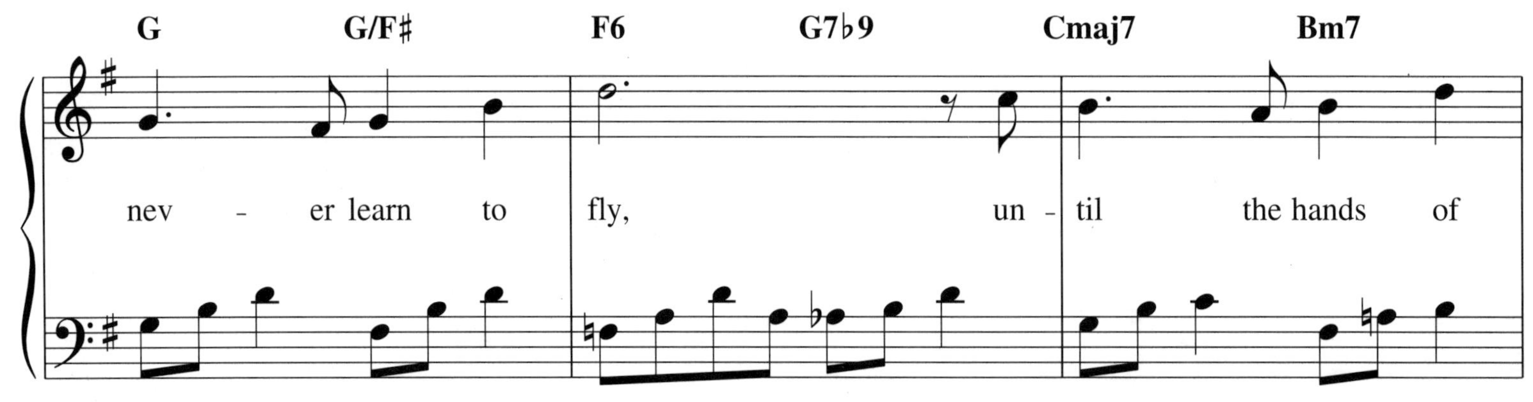
G
G/F♯
F6
G7♭9
Cmaj7
Bm7
nev - er learn to
fly,
un - til the hands of

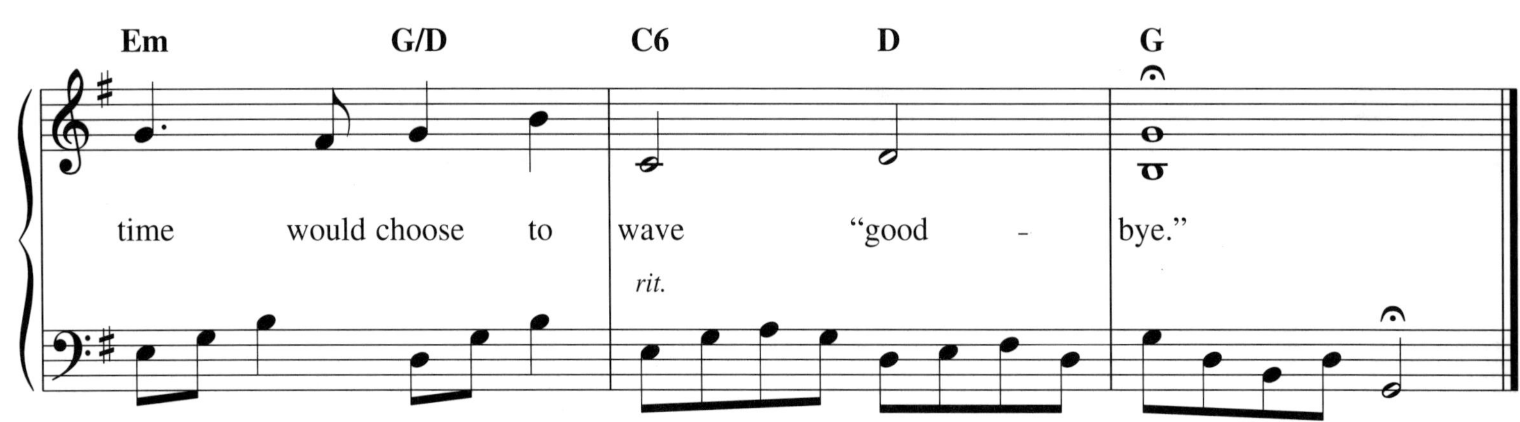
Em
G/D
C6
D
G
time would choose to
wave "good - bye."
rit.

HAPPY DAYS

Theme from the Paramount Television Series HAPPY DAYS

Words by NORMAN GIMBEL
Music by CHARLES FOX

Copyright © 1974 by Bruin Music Company
International Copyright Secured All Rights Reserved

C
Am
F
This day is ours.
Oh, please be mine.

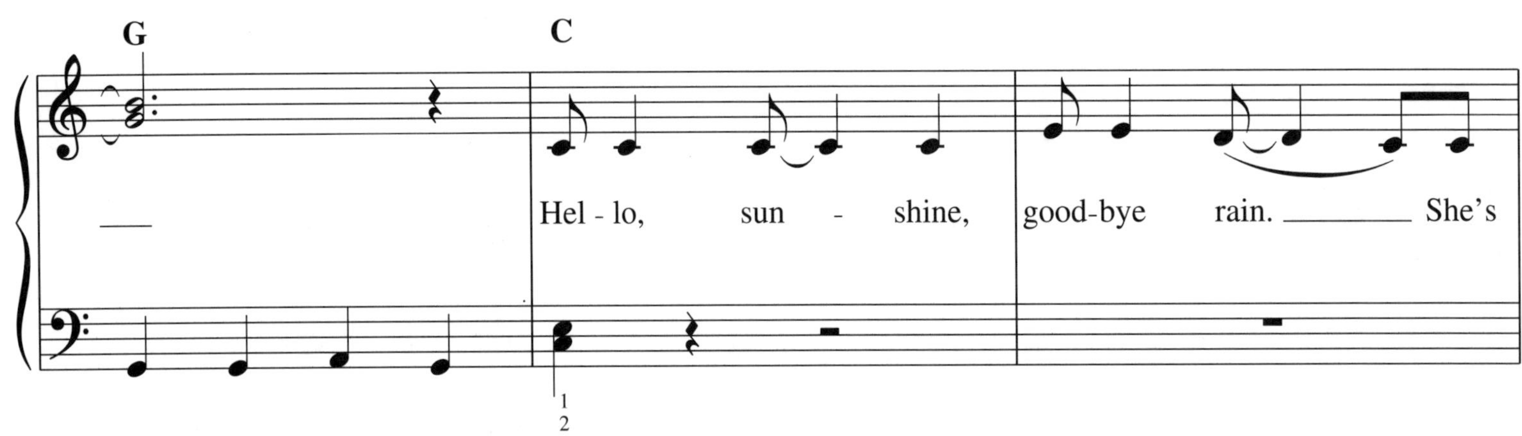
G
C
Hel - lo, sun - shine, good-bye rain. She's

F
D
wear-ing my school ring on a chain.
She's my stead - y

G
I'm her man.
I'm gon - na love her all I can.

C
Am
F
G
This day is ours.
Won't you be mine?
2
C
Am
F
This day is ours.
Oh, please be mine.
G
C
Am
These hap - py days are yours and
F
G
F
F/G
C
mine. These hap - py days are yours and mine, hap - py days!

I AM WOMAN

Words by HELEN REDDY
Music by RAY BURTON

Moderate Rock

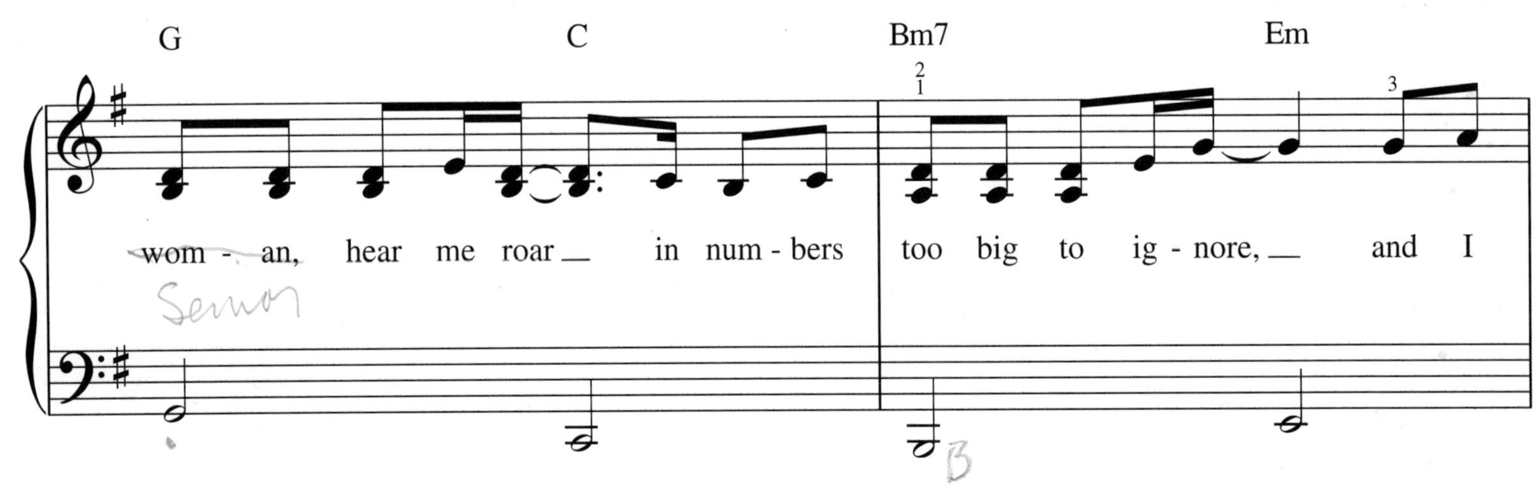

Copyright © 1971 IRVING MUSIC, INC. and BUGGERLUGS MUSIC CO.
Copyright Renewed
All Rights Administered by IRVING MUSIC, INC.
All Rights Reserved Used by Permission

G
C
G
C
heard it all be - fore and I've been
down there on the floor, no one's

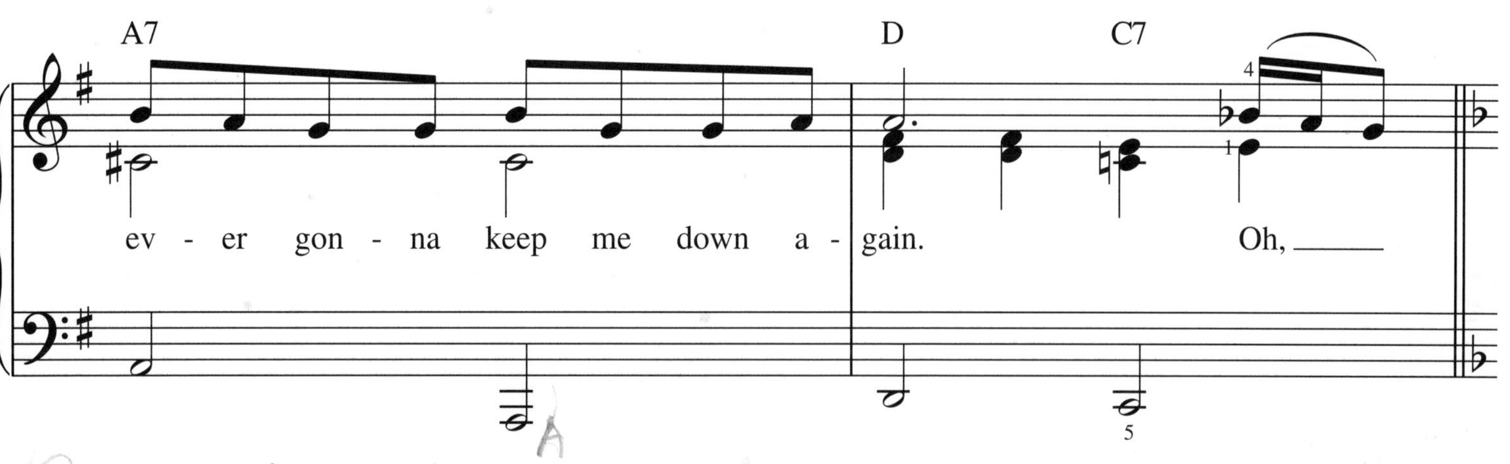
A7
D
C7
ev - er gon - na keep me down a - gain.
Oh,

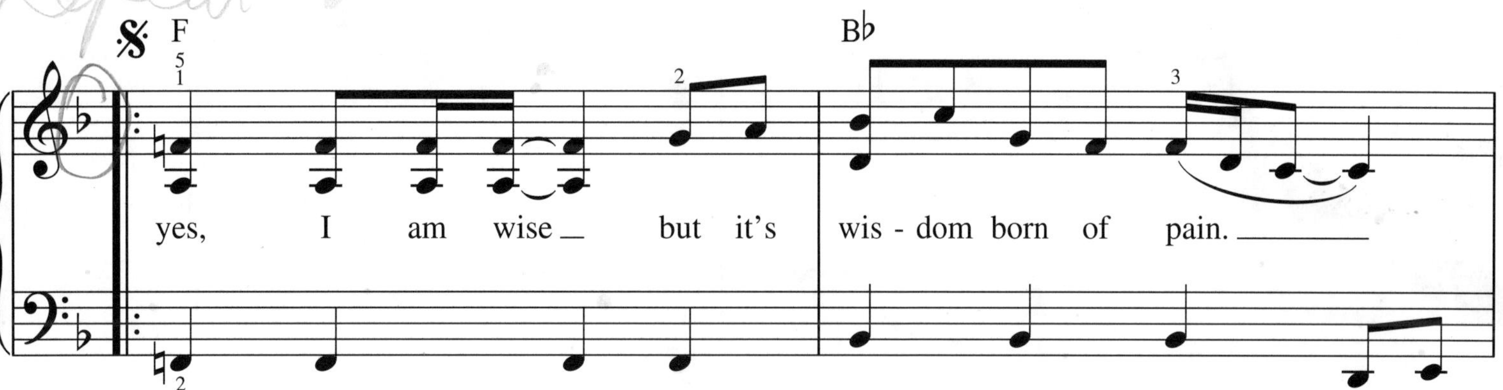
Repeat
F
B♭
yes, I am wise but it's
wis - dom born of pain.

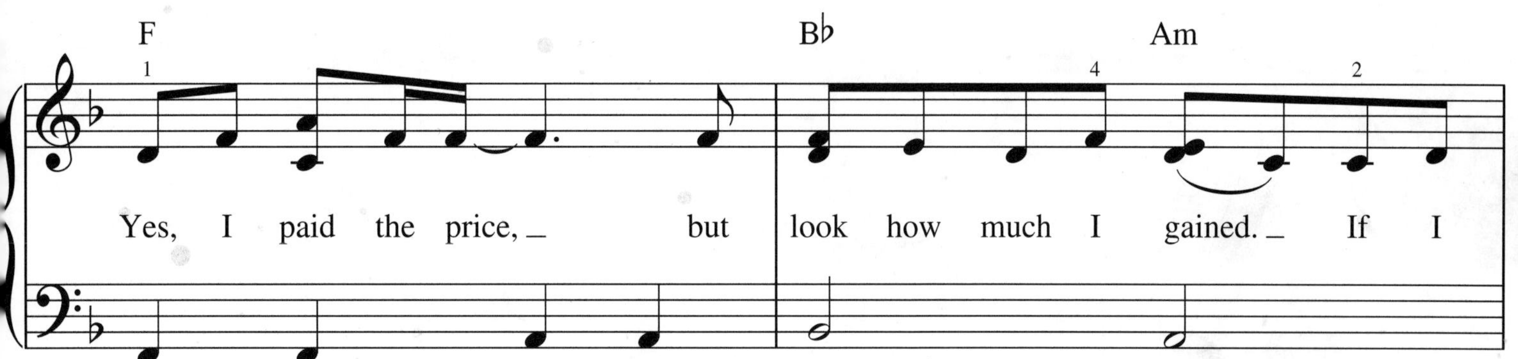
F
B♭
Am
Yes, I paid the price, but
look how much I gained. If I

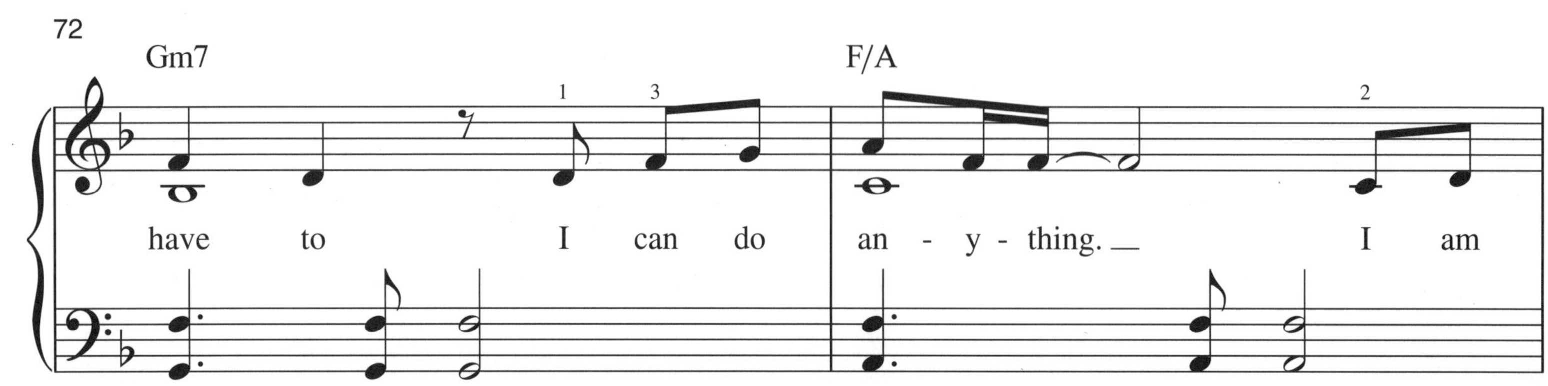
Gm7
F/A
have to I can do
an - y - thing.
I am

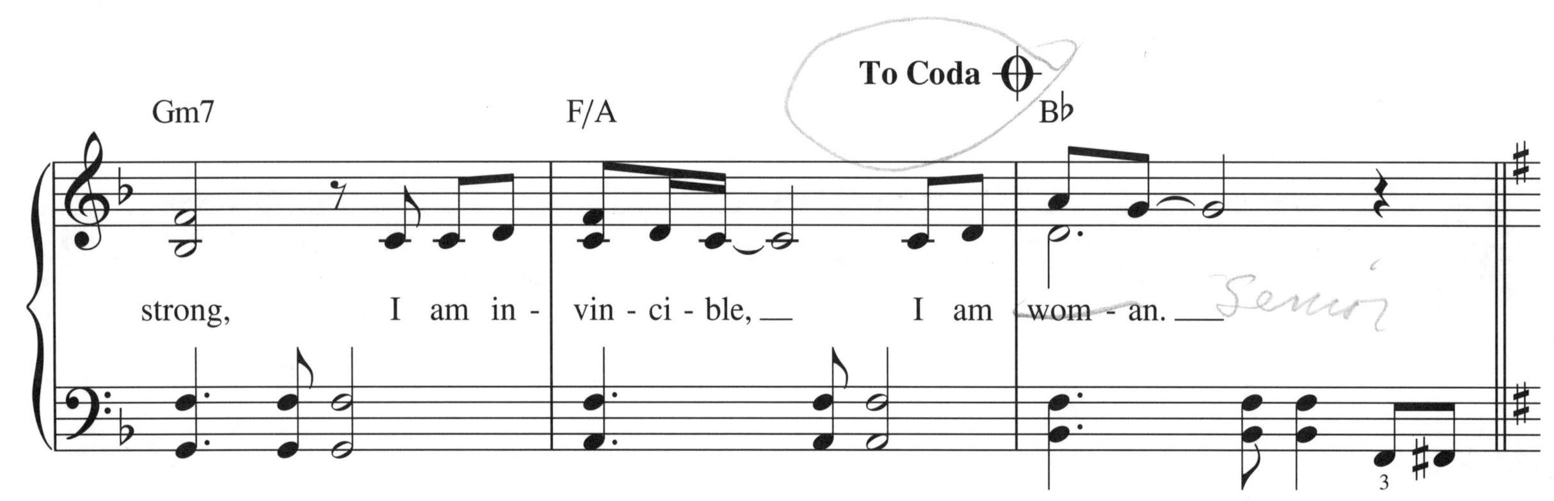
To Coda
Gm7
F/A
B♭
strong, I am in -
vin - ci - ble,
I am
wom - an.

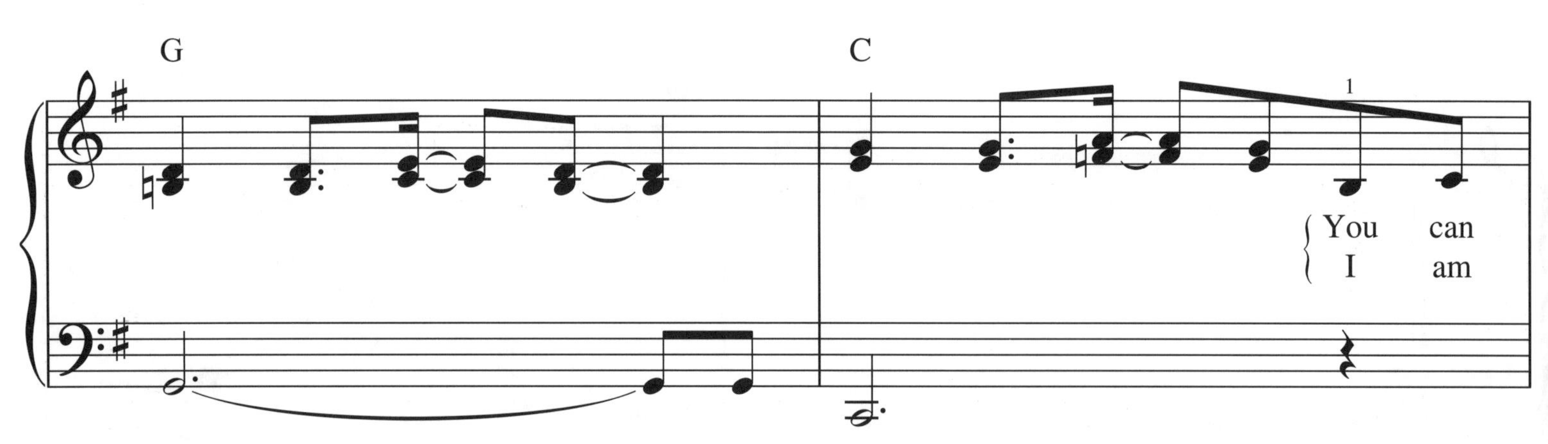
G
C
You can
I am

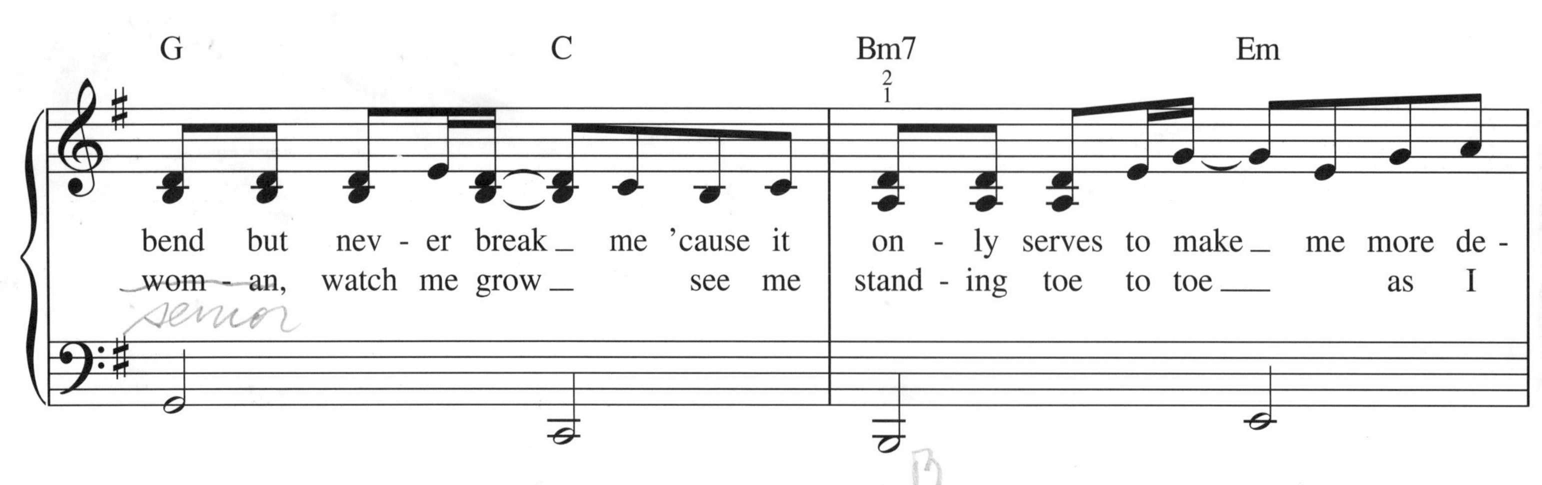
G
C
Bm7
Em
bend but nev - er break me 'cause it
on - ly serves to make me more de -
wom - an, watch me grow see me
stand - ing toe to toe as I

C
Dsus
D
ter - mined to a - chieve my fi - nal goal. And I
spread my lov - in' arms a - cross the land. But I'm
G
C
G
C
come back e - ven strong - er, not a nov - ice an - y long - er, 'cause you've
still an em - bry - o with a long, long way to go un -
A7
1.
D
C7
deep - ened the con - vic - tion in my soul. Oh,
til I make my broth - er un - der -
2.
D
C7
D.S. al Coda
stand. Oh,
CODA
B♭maj9
B♭6
F
wom - an!

I HONESTLY LOVE YOU

Words and Music by PETER ALLEN
and JEFF BARRY

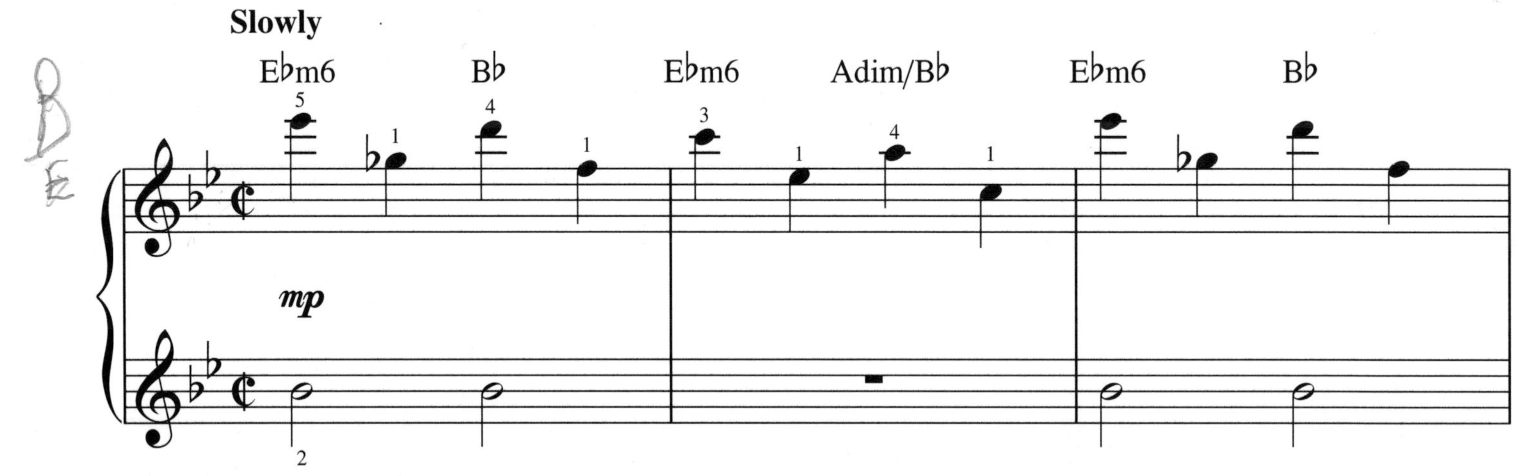

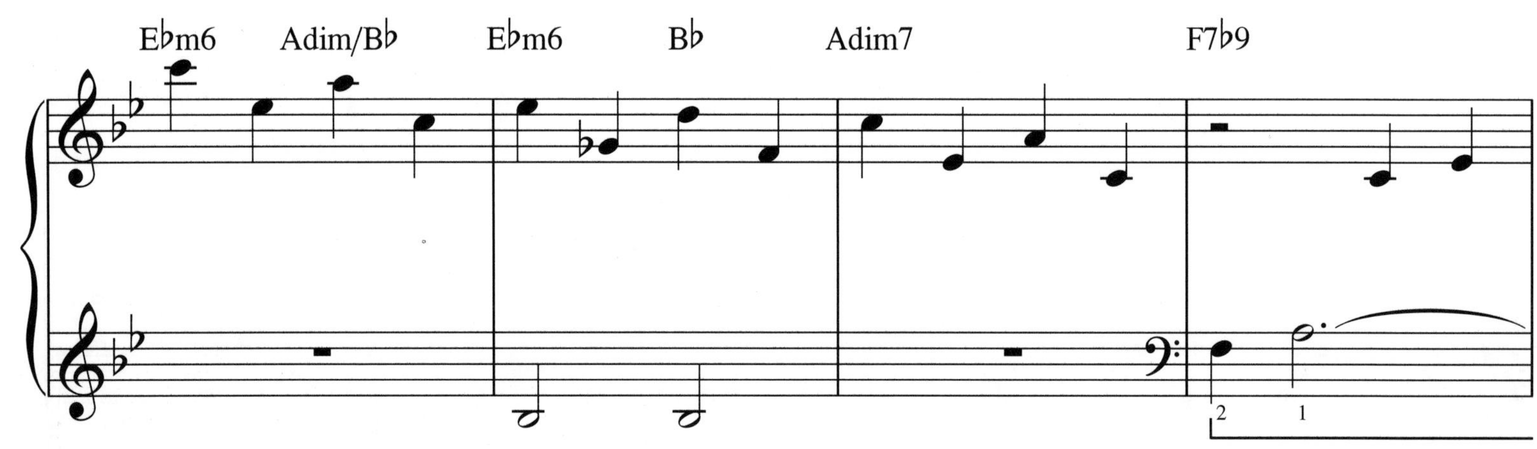

Copyright © 1974 IRVING MUSIC, INC., WOOLNOUGH MUSIC and JEFF BARRY INTERNATIONAL
All Rights Administered by IRVING MUSIC, INC.
All Rights Reserved Used by Permission

F/B♭
A♭/B♭
lit - tle more than I should.
We both know I got some -
see it in your eyes.
May - be it was bet -

E♭
B♭/F
- where else to go.
But I got some - thin' to tell
- ter left un - said.
But this is pure and sim -

C7
you that I nev - er thought I would,
but
- ple and you must re - a - lize
that it's

E♭
B♭/D
Cm7
F7
I be - lieve you real - ly ought to know.
com - in' from my heart and not my head.

B♭
F/B♭
E♭/B♭
I love you.
I hon - est - ly love

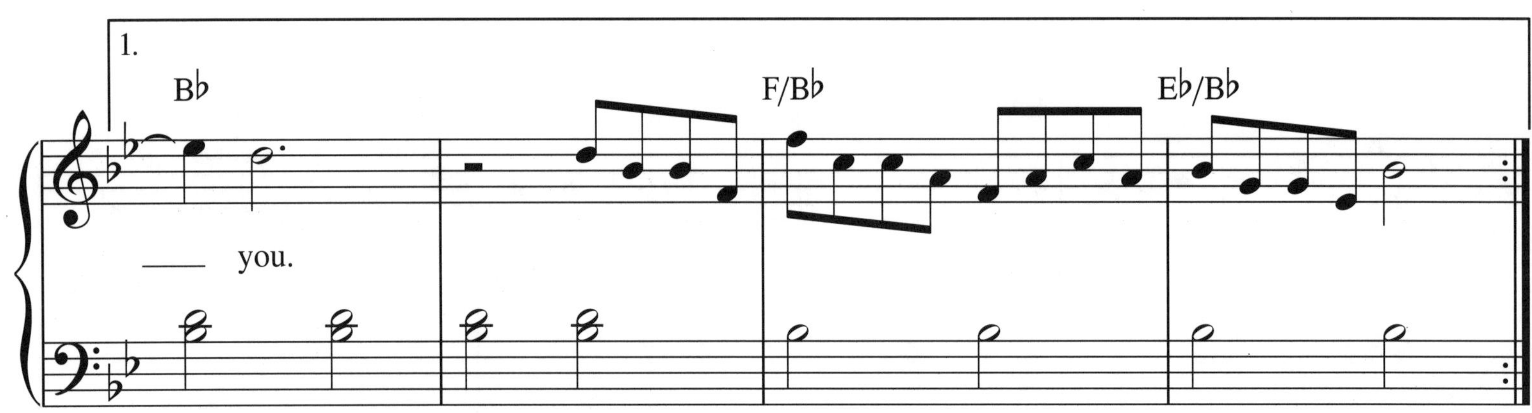
1.
B♭
F/B♭
E♭/B♭
you.

2.
B♭
F/B♭
A♭/B♭
B♭
you.

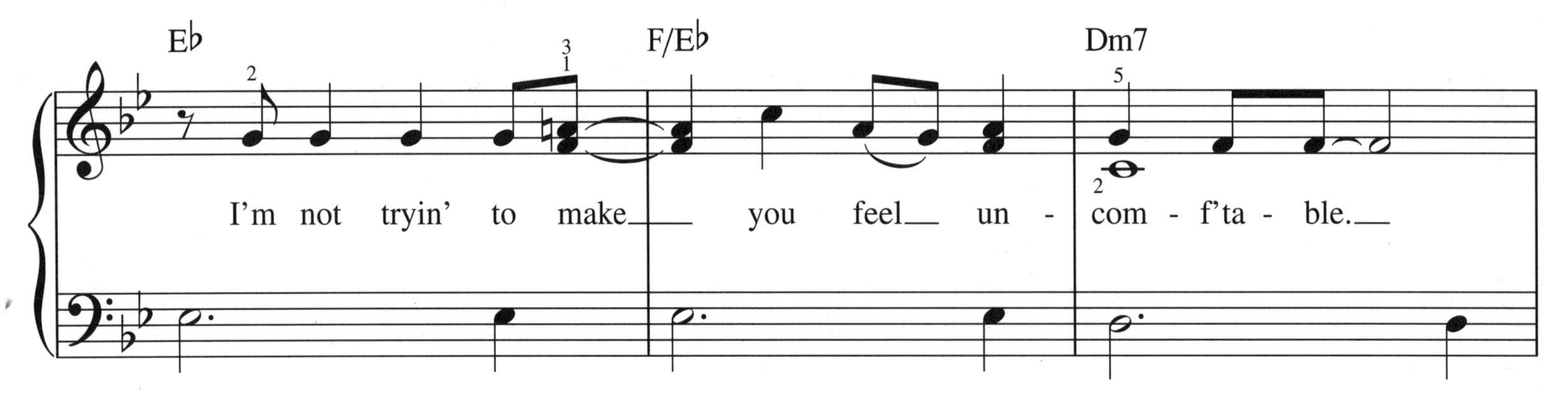
E♭
F/E♭
Dm7
I'm not tryin' to make you feel un - com - f'ta - ble.

Gm7
Cm7
F7
I'm
not tryin' to make you
an - y - thing at

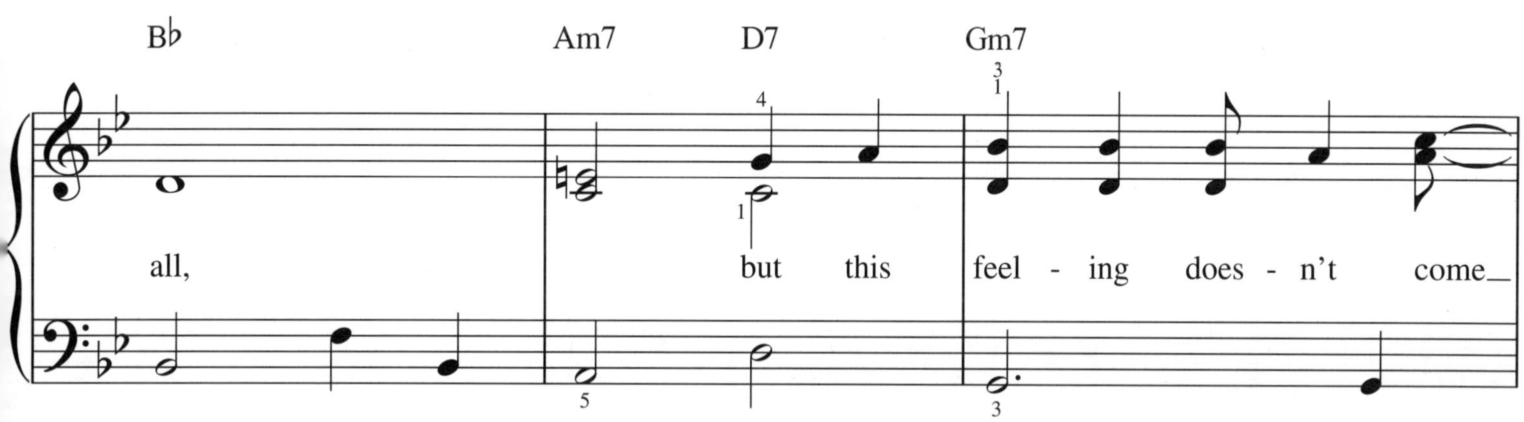
B♭
Am7
D7
Gm7
all,
but this
feel - ing does - n't come

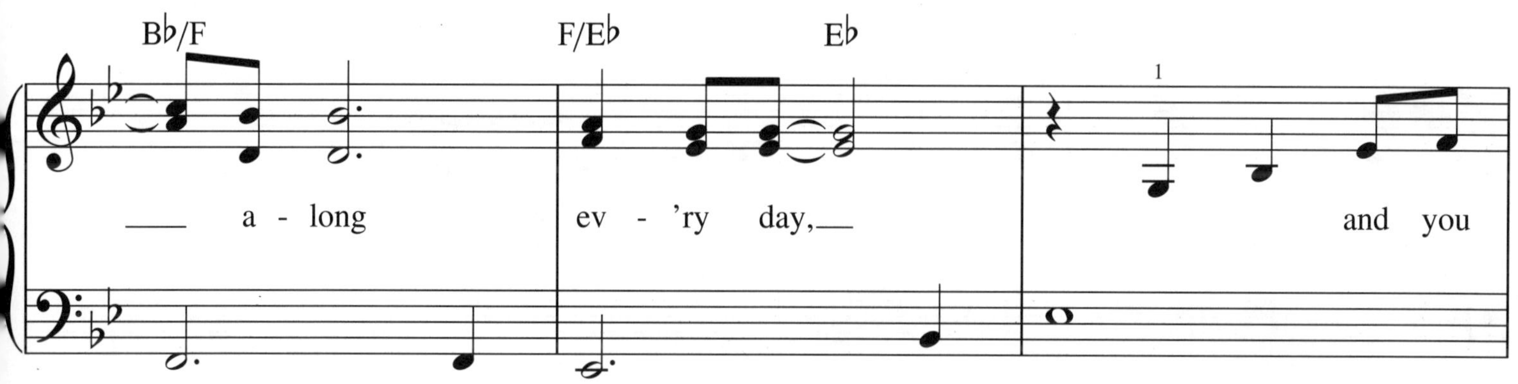
B♭/F
F/E♭
E♭
a - long
ev - 'ry day,
and you

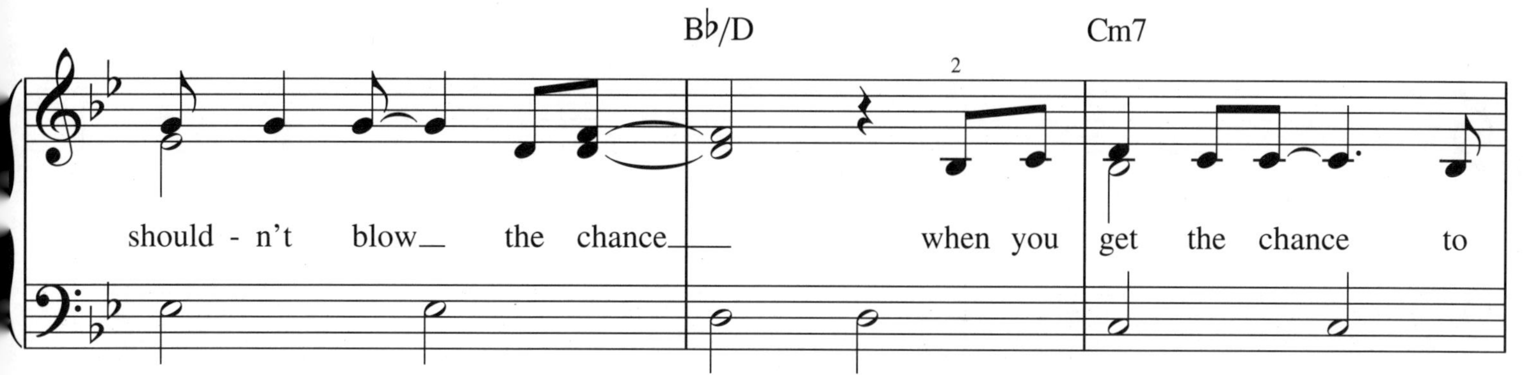
B♭/D
Cm7
should - n't blow the chance
when you
get the chance to

Cm7/F
B♭
2
say;
I
love
you.

F/B♭
E♭/B♭
Spoken: I love you.
5

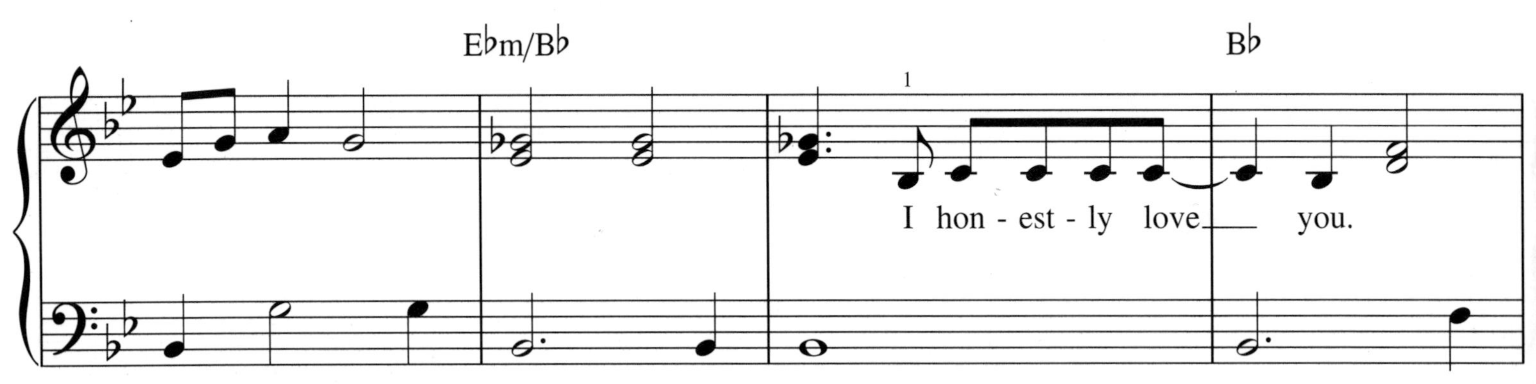
E♭m/B♭
1
B♭
I hon - est - ly love you.

F/G

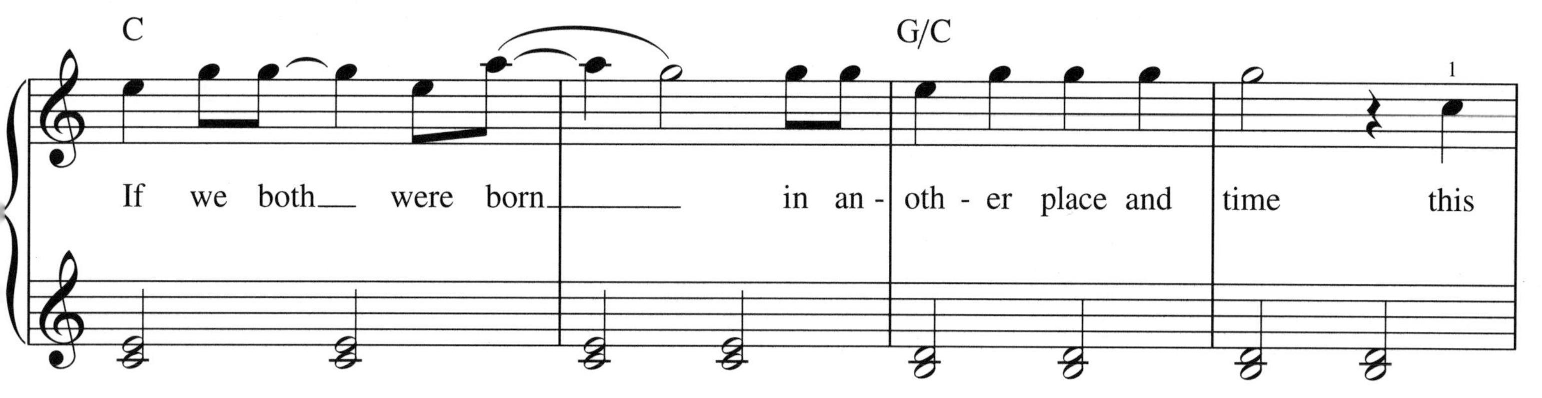
C
G/C
If we both were born in an - oth - er place and time this

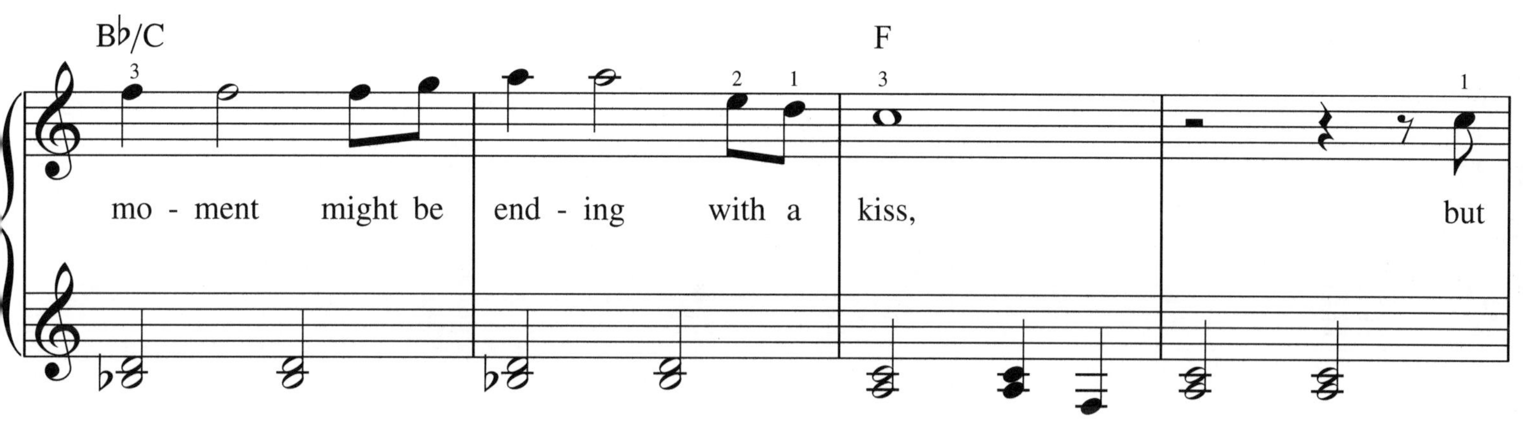
B♭/C
F
mo - ment might be end - ing with a kiss, but

C/G
D7
there you are with yours and here I am with mine, so I

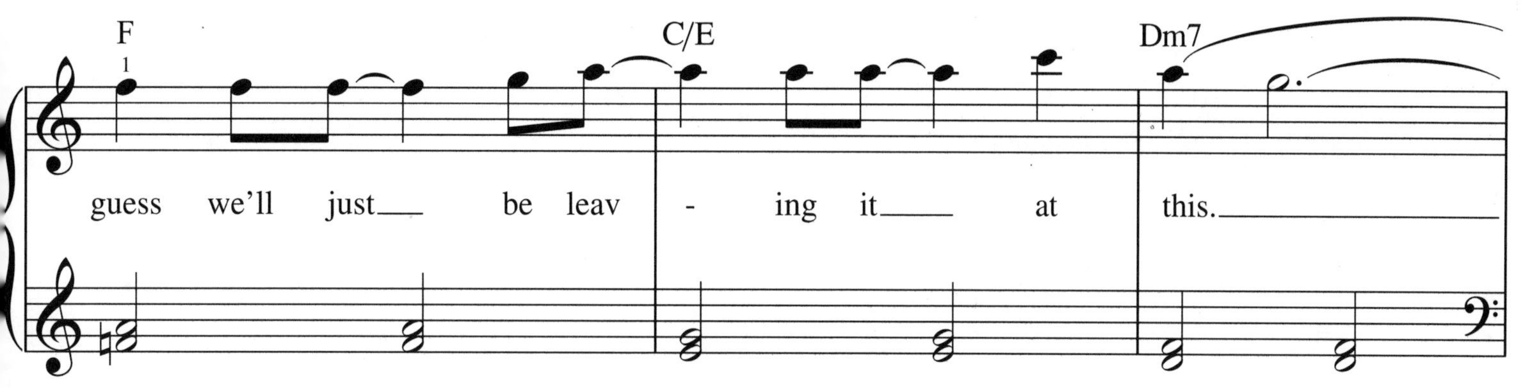
F
C/E
Dm7
guess we'll just be leav - ing it at this.

Dm7/G
C
G/C
2
I love you.

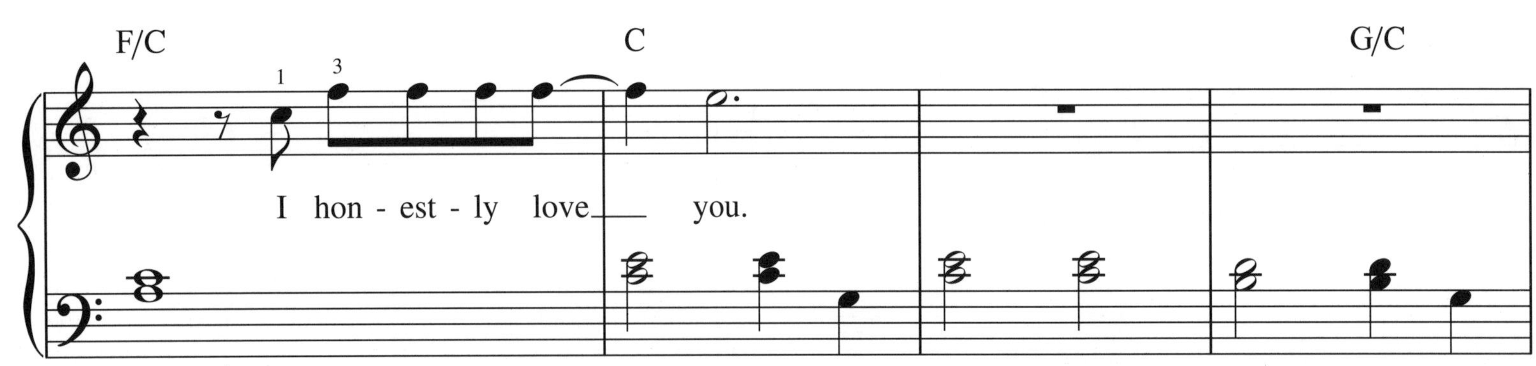
F/C
C
G/C
1 3
I hon - est - ly love you.

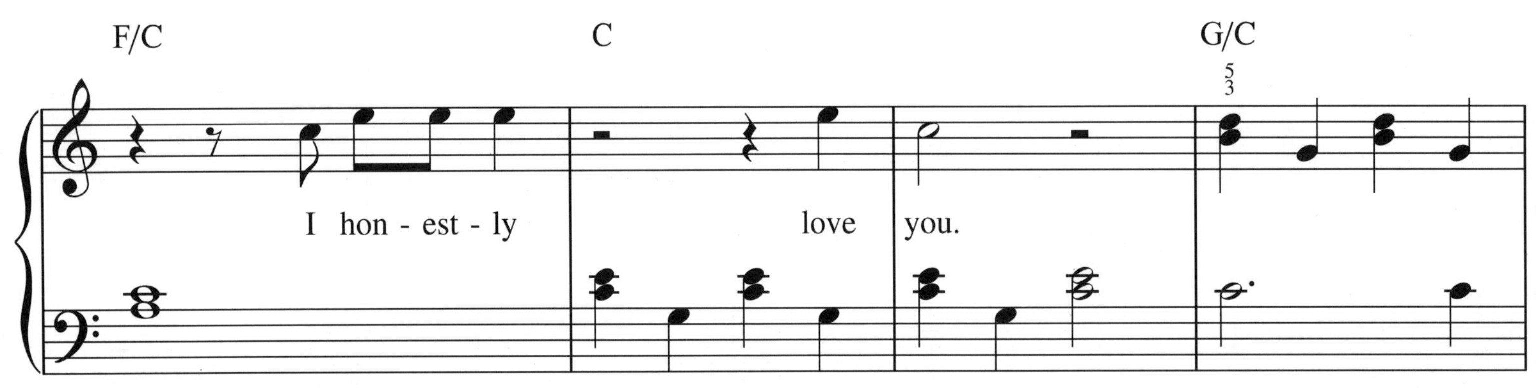
F/C
C
G/C
5
3
I hon - est - ly love you.

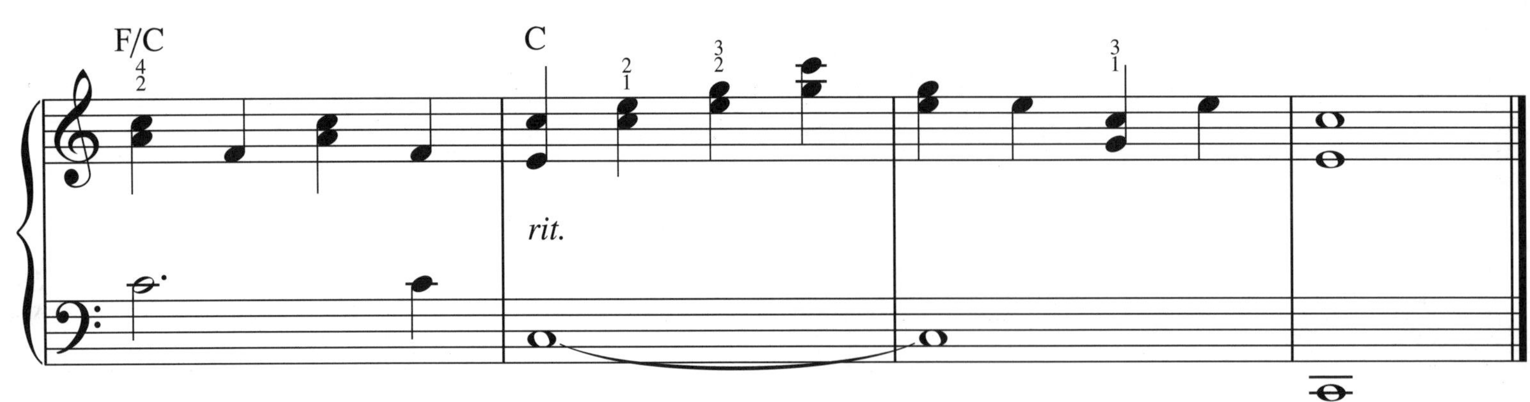
F/C
C
4
2
2
1
3
2
3
1
rit.

IF

Words and Music by
DAVID GATES

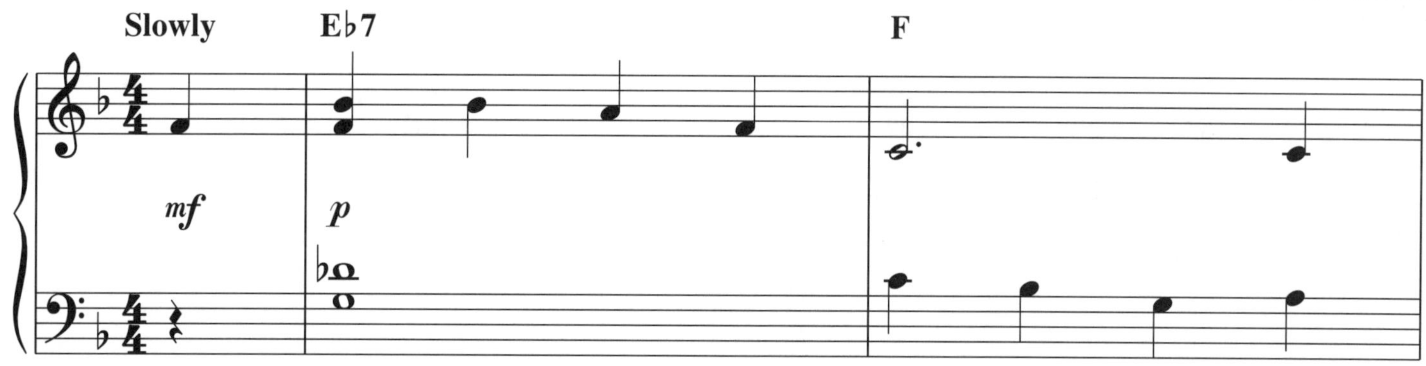

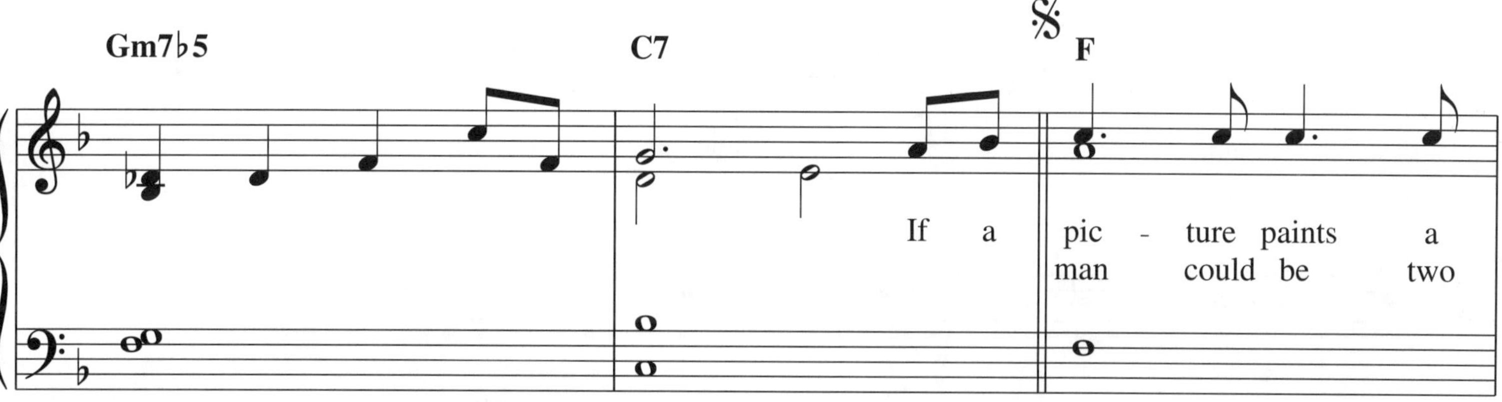

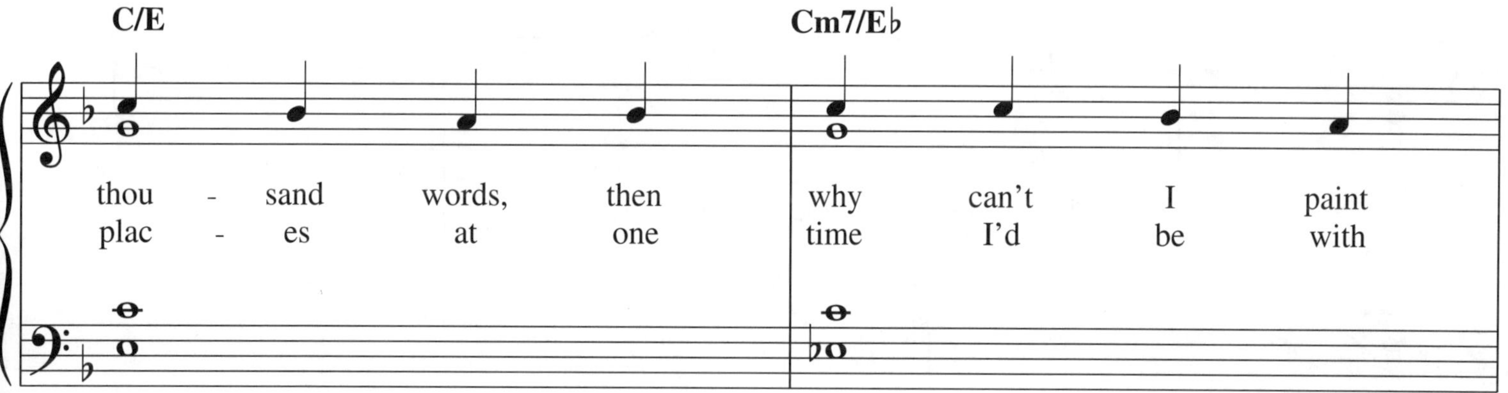

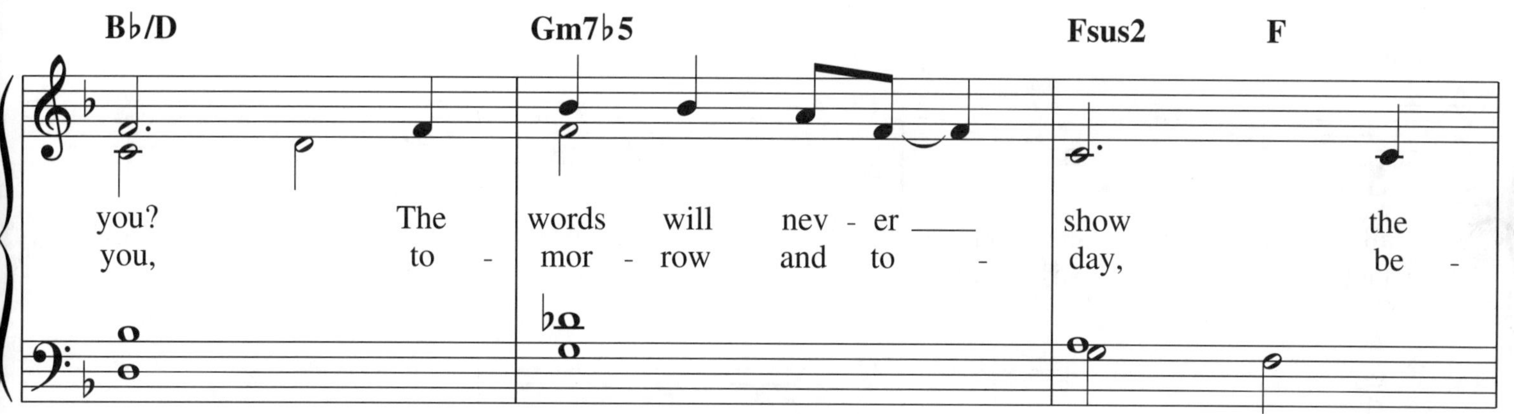

Copyright © 1971 Sony/ATV Tunes LLC
Copyright Renewed
All Rights Administered by Sony/ATV Music Publishing, 8 Music Square West, Nashville, TN 37203
International Copyright Secured All Rights Reserved

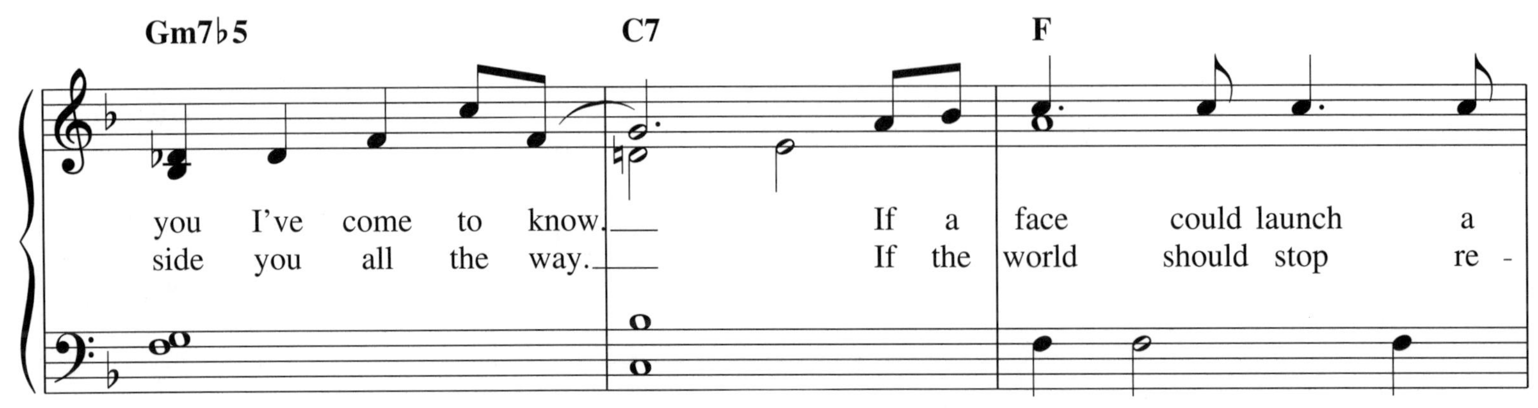
Gm7♭5
C7
F
you I've come to know. If a face could launch a
side you all the way. If the world should stop re -

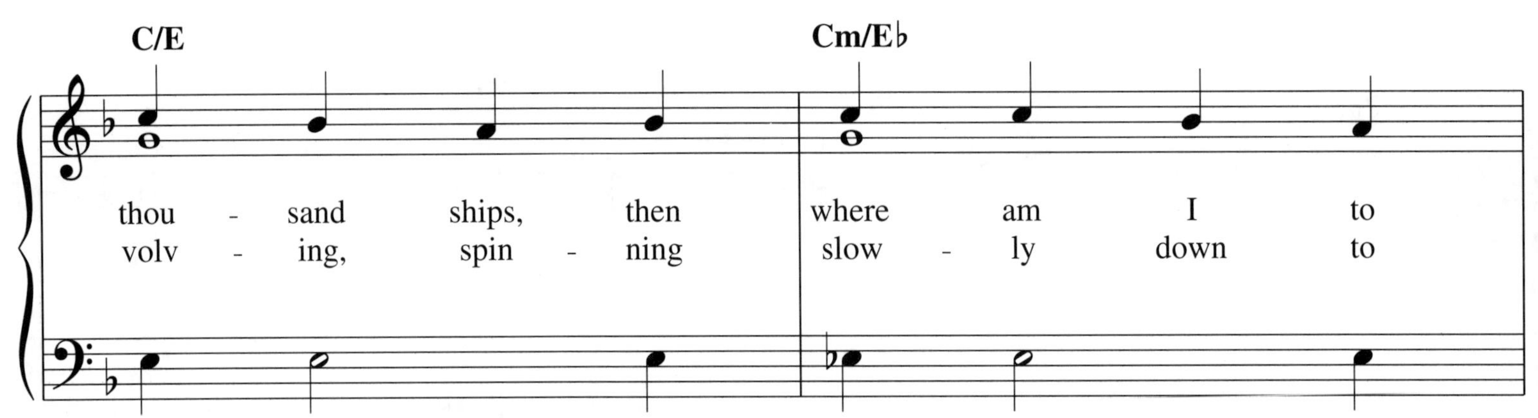
C/E
Cm/E♭
thou - sand ships, then where am I to
volv - ing, spin - ning slow - ly down to

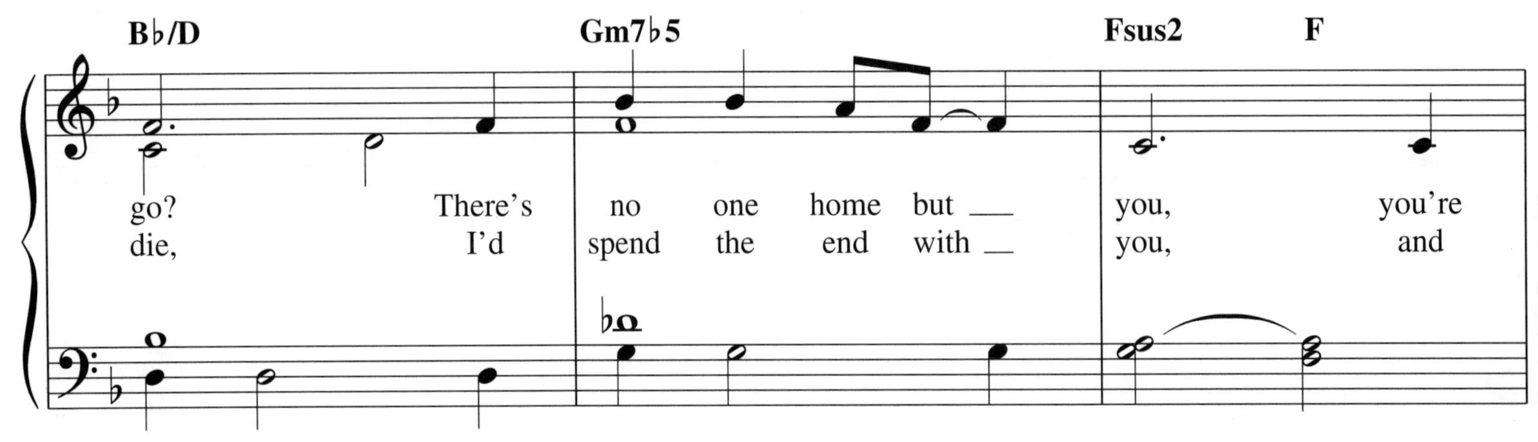
B♭/D
Gm7♭5
Fsus2
F
go? There's no one home but you, you're
die, I'd spend the end with you, and

Gm7♭5
C7
Dm
all that's left me too. And when my
when the world was through. Then one by

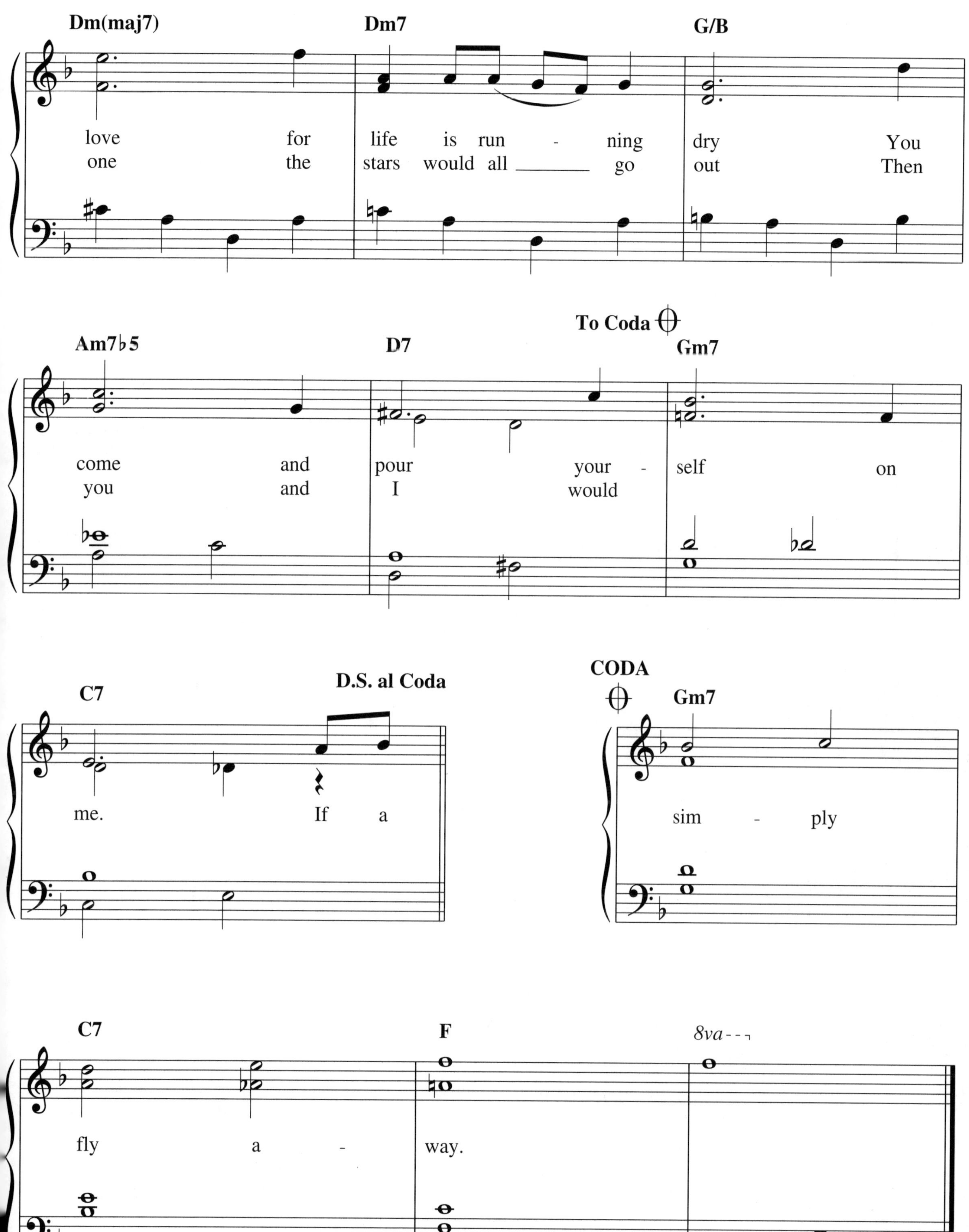
Dm(maj7)
Dm7
G/B
love for life is run - ning dry You
one the stars would all go out Then
Am7♭5
D7
To Coda
Gm7
come and pour your - self on
you and I would
C7
D.S. al Coda
me. If a
CODA
Gm7
sim - ply
C7
F
8va
fly a - way.

I WON'T LAST A DAY WITHOUT YOU

Words and Music by PAUL WILLIAMS
and ROGER NICHOLS

Copyright © 1972 ALMO MUSIC CORP.
Copyright Renewed
All Rights Reserved Used by Permission

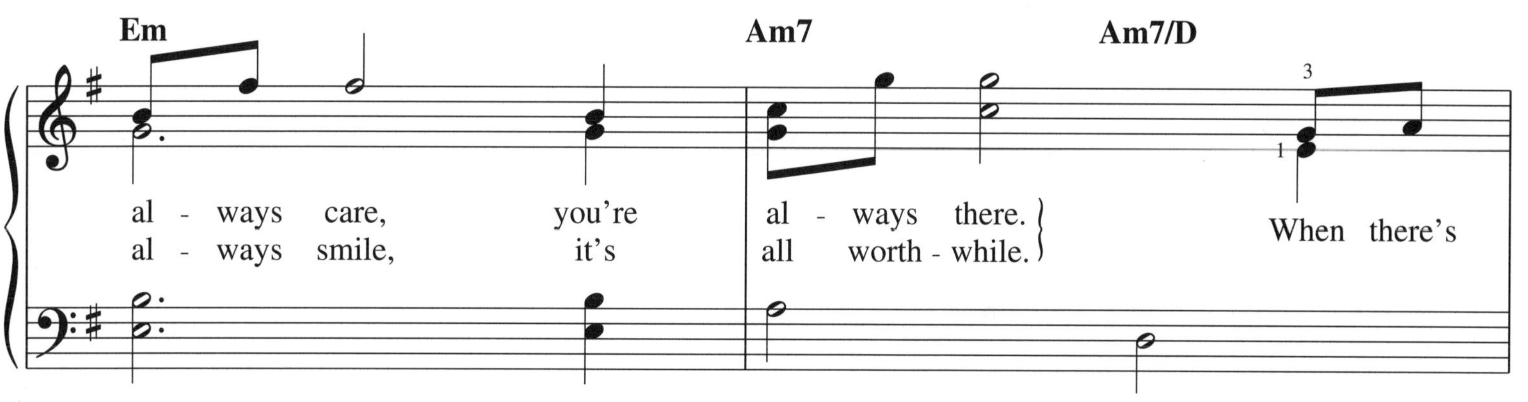
Em
Am7
Am7/D
al - ways care, you're al - ways there. When there's
al - ways smile, it's all worth - while.

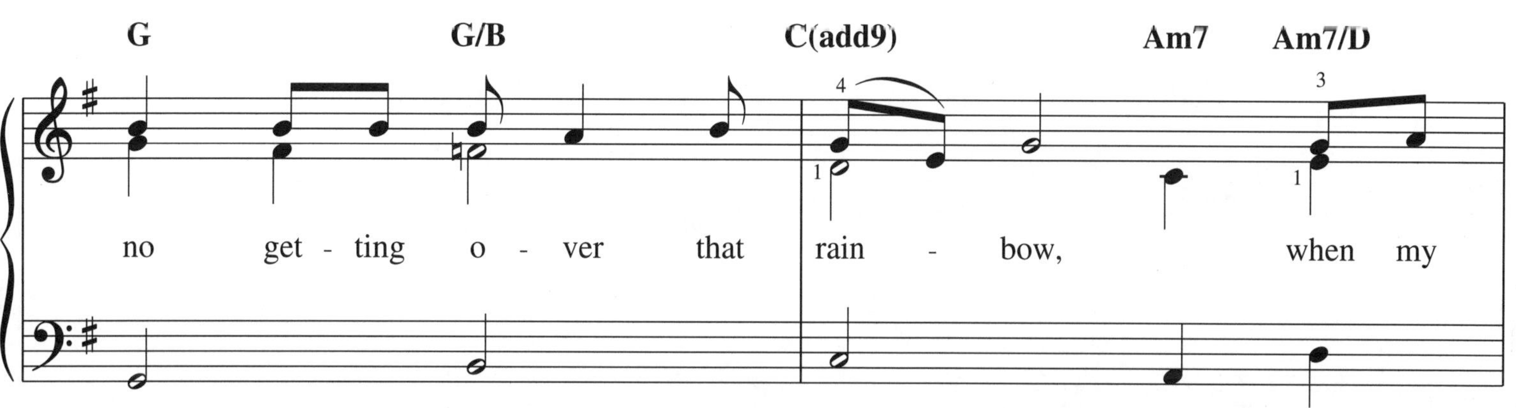
G
G/B
C(add9)
Am7
Am7/D
no get - ting o - ver that rain - bow, when my

G
G/B
C
Am7
Am7/D
small - est of dreams won't come true, I can

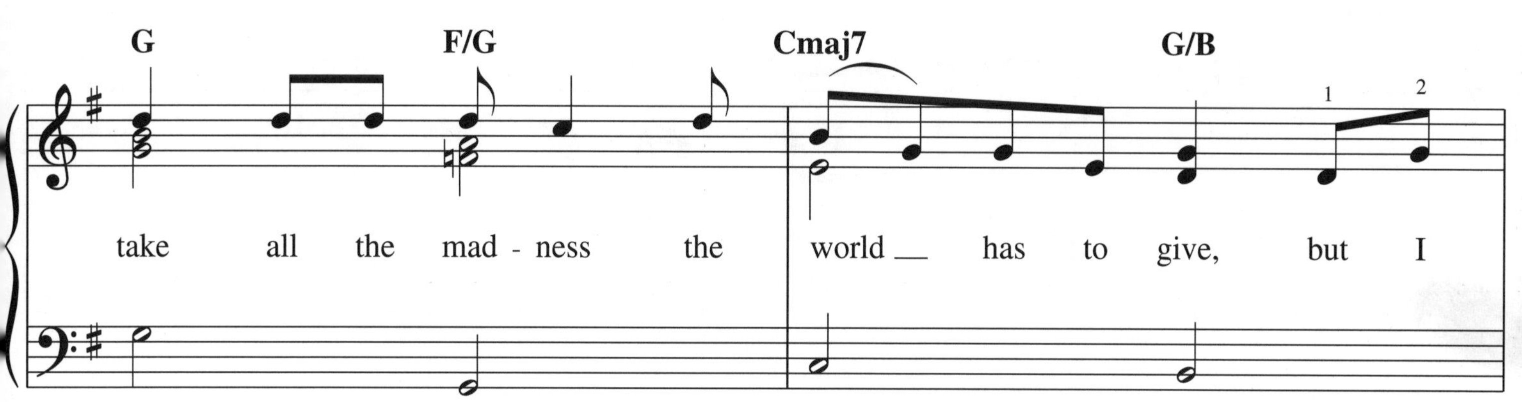
G
F/G
Cmaj7
G/B
take all the mad - ness the world __ has to give, but I

1.
2.
Am7
D7
G
G/B
C
D7
won't last a day with - out you.
G
G(add9)
Em7
A7
Dmaj7
you.
Touch me and I end up sing - ing,
Em7
A7
B7sus
B7
trou - bles seem to up and dis - ap - pear,
you
C♯m7
F♯7
Bmaj7
touch me with the love you're bring - ing,

G♯m7
Amaj7
B7sus
B7
I can't real - ly lose when you're near. When you're
Am7
D7
G
Bm7
near my love, if all my friends have for -
C
C/D
Em
got - ten half their prom - is - es they're not un - kind, just
Am7
C/D
G
Bm7
hard to find. One look at you and I

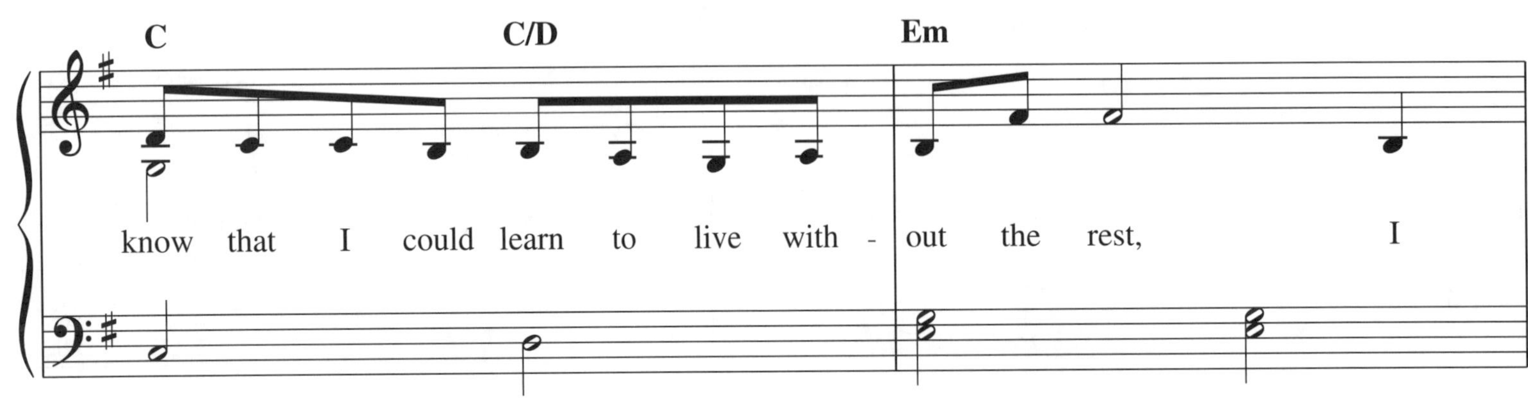
C
C/D
Em
know that I could learn to live with - out the rest, I

Am7
Am7/D
G
G/B
found the best. When there's no get - ting o - ver that

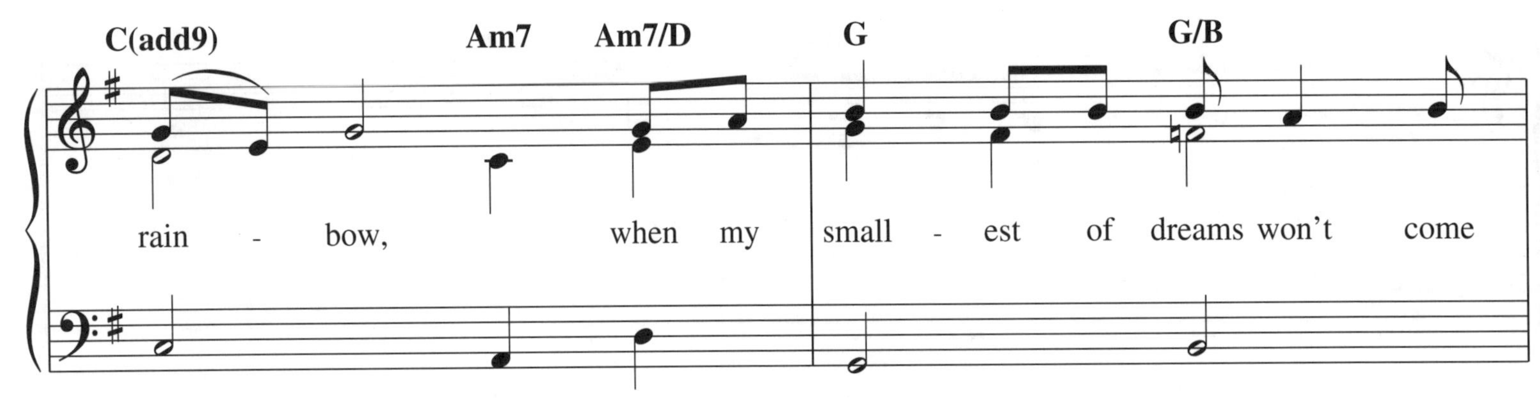
C(add9)
Am7
Am7/D
G
G/B
rain - bow, when my small - est of dreams won't come

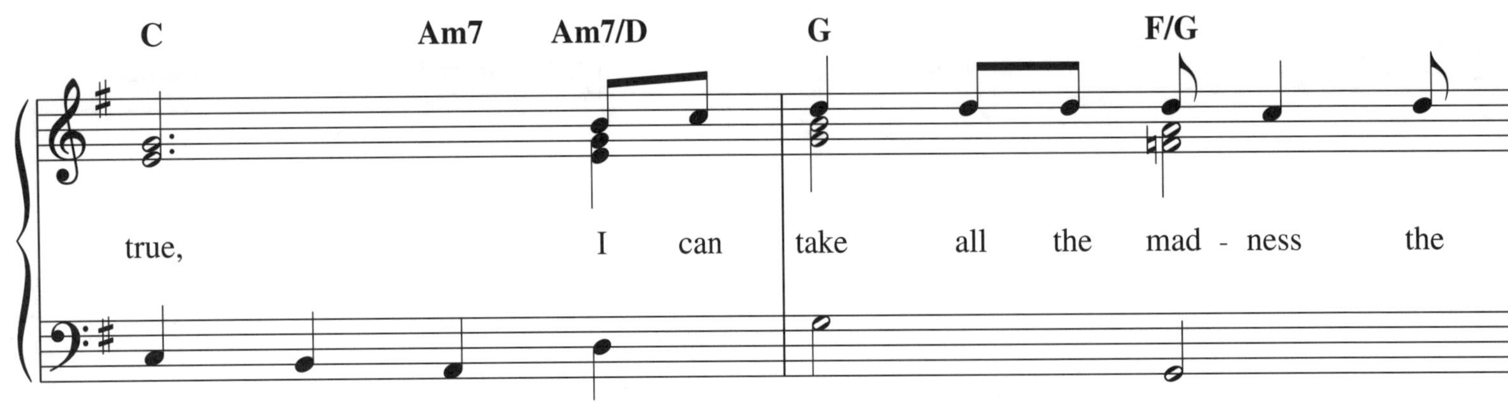
C
Am7
Am7/D
G
F/G
true, I can take all the mad - ness the

Cmaj7
G/B
1.
Am7
D7
world _ has to give, but I
won't last a day with - out
G
Am7/D
2.
Am7
D7sus
D7
you. When there's
won't last a day ___ with - out
G
G/B
C
D7
G
G/B
you.
C
D7
G(add9)

I WRITE THE SONGS

Words and Music by
BRUCE JOHNSTON

Copyright © 1970 by Artists Music, Inc.
Copyright Renewed
All Rights Administered by BMG Songs, Inc.
International Copyright Secured All Rights Reserved

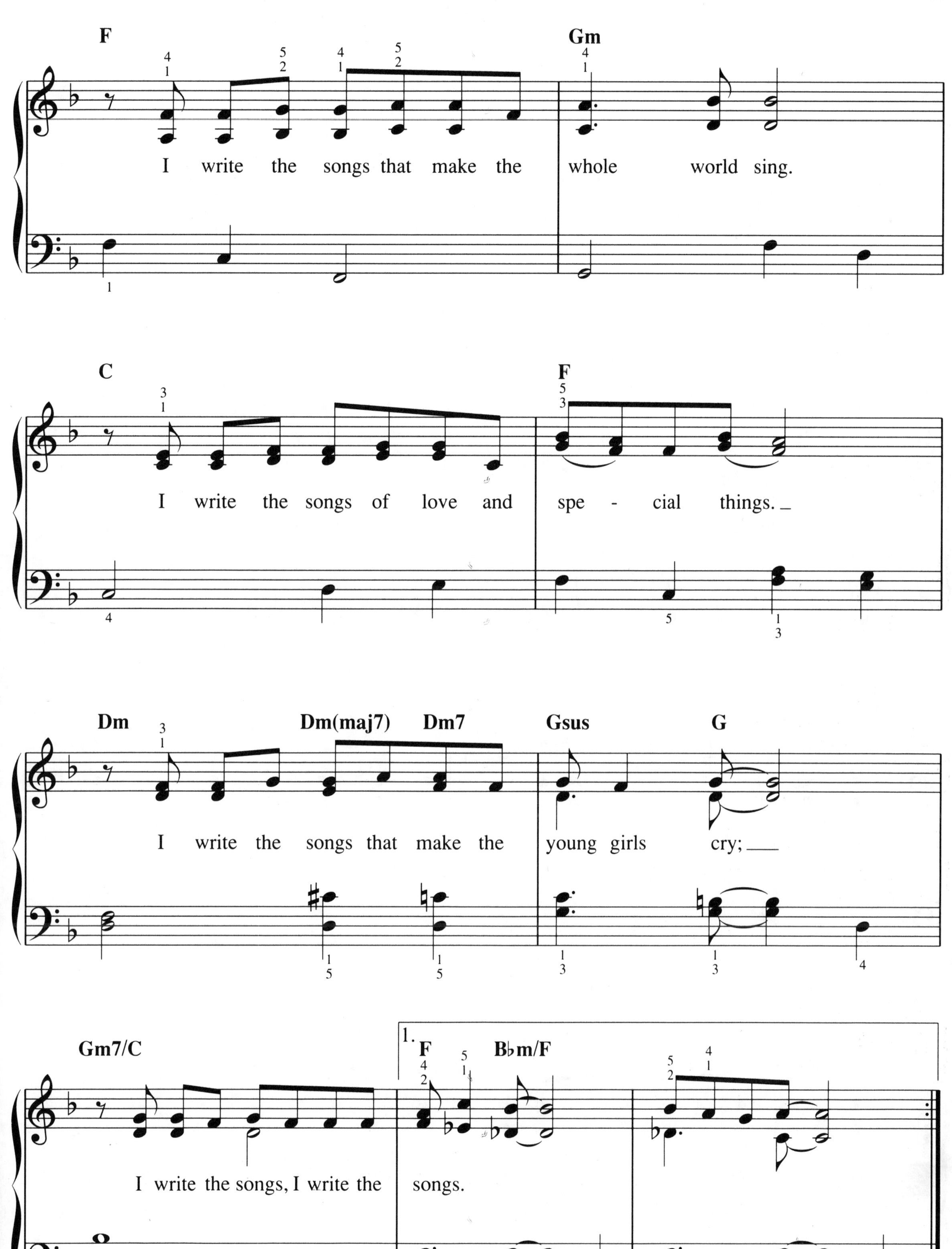
F
Gm
I write the songs that make the whole world sing.
C
F
I write the songs of love and special things.
Dm
Dm(maj7)
Dm7
Gsus
G
I write the songs that make the young girls cry;
Gm7/C
1.
F
B♭m/F
I write the songs, I write the songs.

2.

F E7sus E7

songs. Oh, my mu - sic makes you dance ___ and gives you

Em7 E7 A A/G♯ F♯m A/E

spir-it to take a chance, and I wrote some rock-'n' roll so you _ can move. ___

G7sus G7 G7sus G7

Mu - sic fills your heart, ___ well, that's a real fine place to start. It's from

C7sus C7 C7sus C7 C7sus C7 C7sus C

me, it's for you, it's from you, it's for me, it's a world _ wide sym-pho-ny.

A
Bm7
E
I write the songs that make the whole world sing. _
I write the songs of love and
A
F♯m
F♯m(maj7) F♯m7
B7sus
B
spe - cial things. _
I write the songs that make the young girls cry; _
Bm7/E
F♯m
F♯m(maj7) F♯m7
A/B
B
I write the songs, I write the songs.
I am
Bm7/E
A
Dm/A
A
mu - sic, and I write the songs.
rit.

I'LL NEVER LOVE THIS WAY AGAIN

Words and Music by RICHARD KERR
and WILL JENNINGS

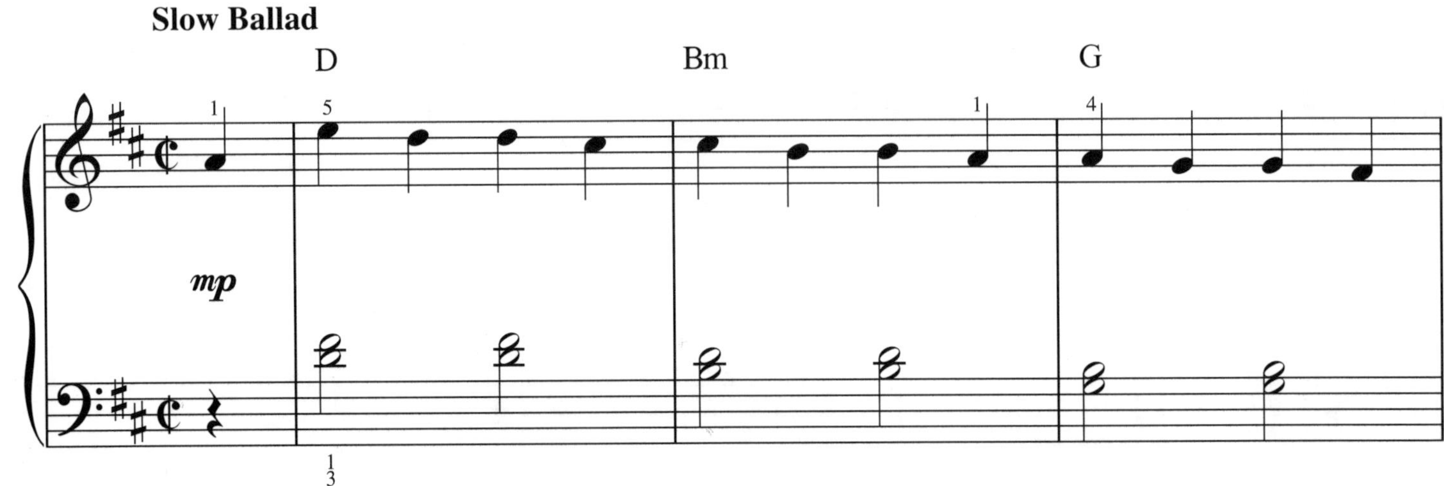

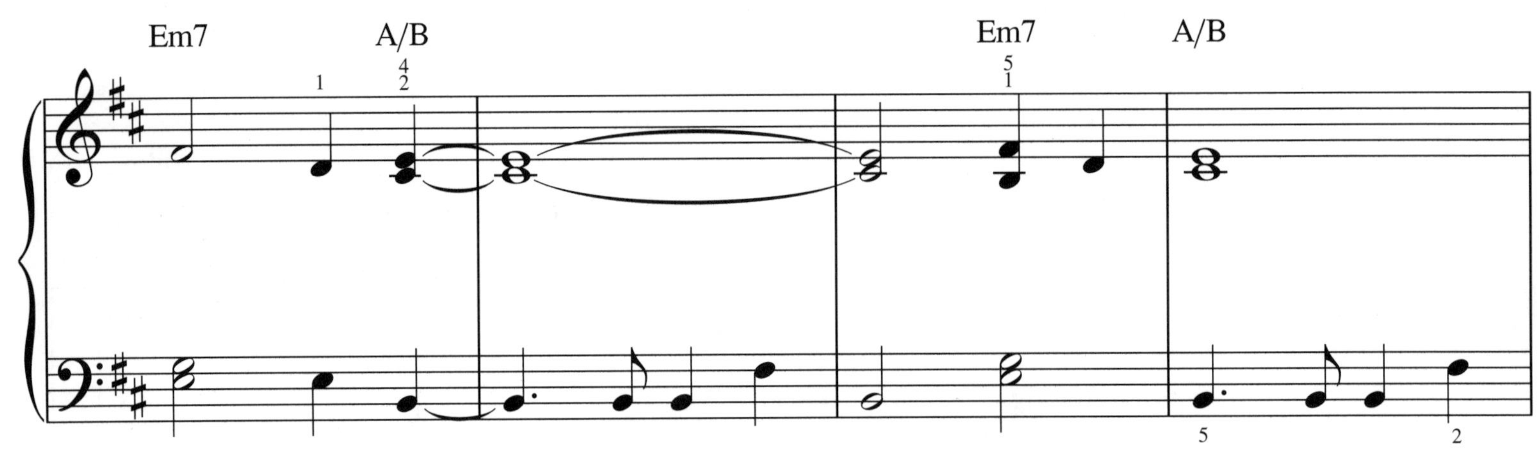

Copyright © 1977 IRVING MUSIC, INC.
All Rights Reserved Used by Permission

G
D/F♯
Gmaj7
made each one come true, something no one
back for yes - ter - day; I won't turn my head

F♯m7
Bm7
else had ev - er found a way to do. I've
in sor - row if you should go a - way. I'll

Em7
F♯m7
Gmaj7
kept the mem - 'ries one by one, since you took me in;
stand here and re - mem - ber just how good it's been,

G6
A7sus
and I know I'll nev - er love this way a - gain.

D/A
D(add2)
I know I'll nev -
Bm7
Em7
F♯7/A♯
- er love this way a - gain, so I keep
Bm7
Bm7/E
E7
A7
hold - in' on be - fore the good is gone.
D(add2)
Bm7
I know I'll nev - er love

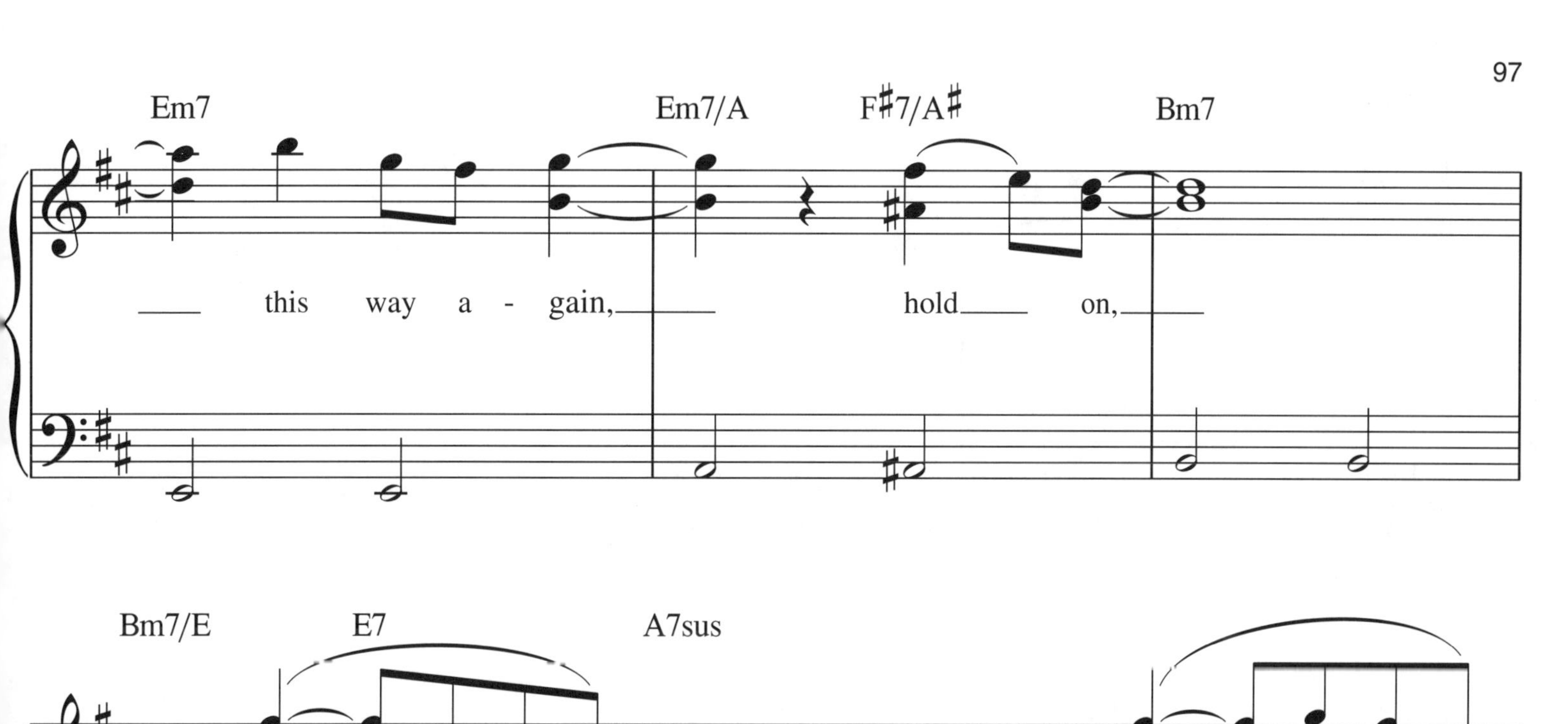
Em7
Em7/A
F♯7/A♯
Bm7
this way a - gain,
hold on,

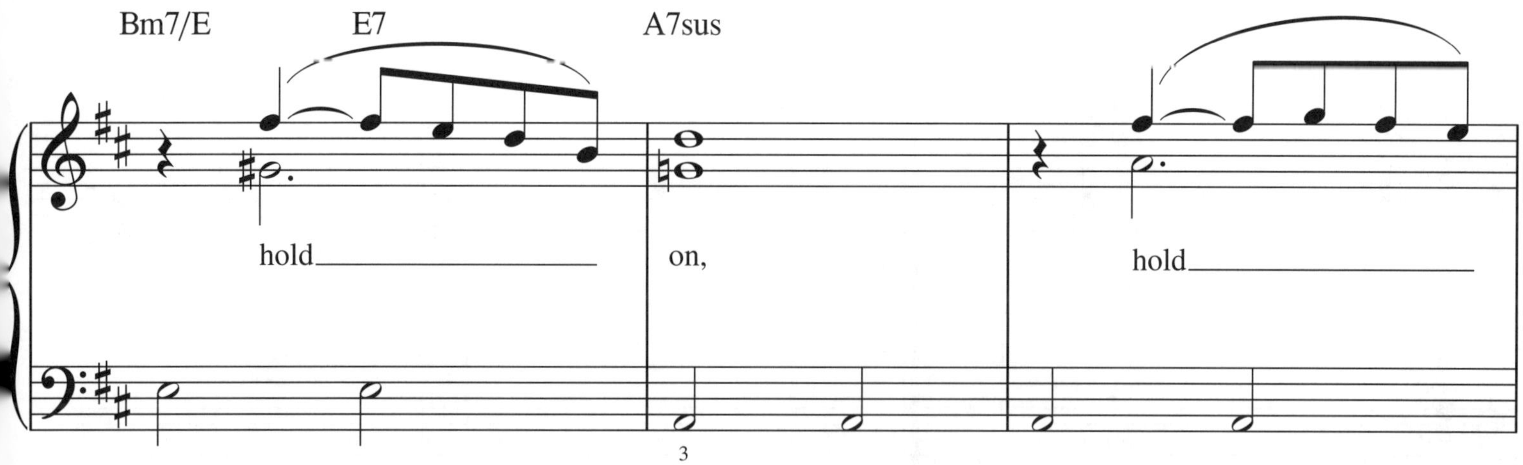
Bm7/E
E7
A7sus
hold
on,
hold

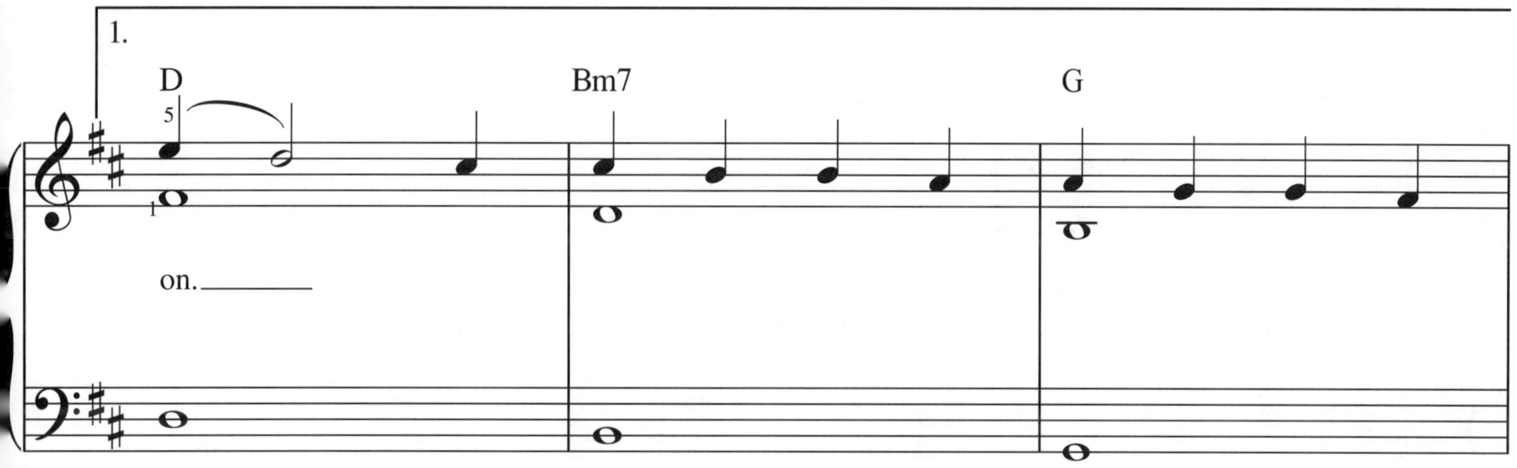
1.
D
Bm7
G
on.

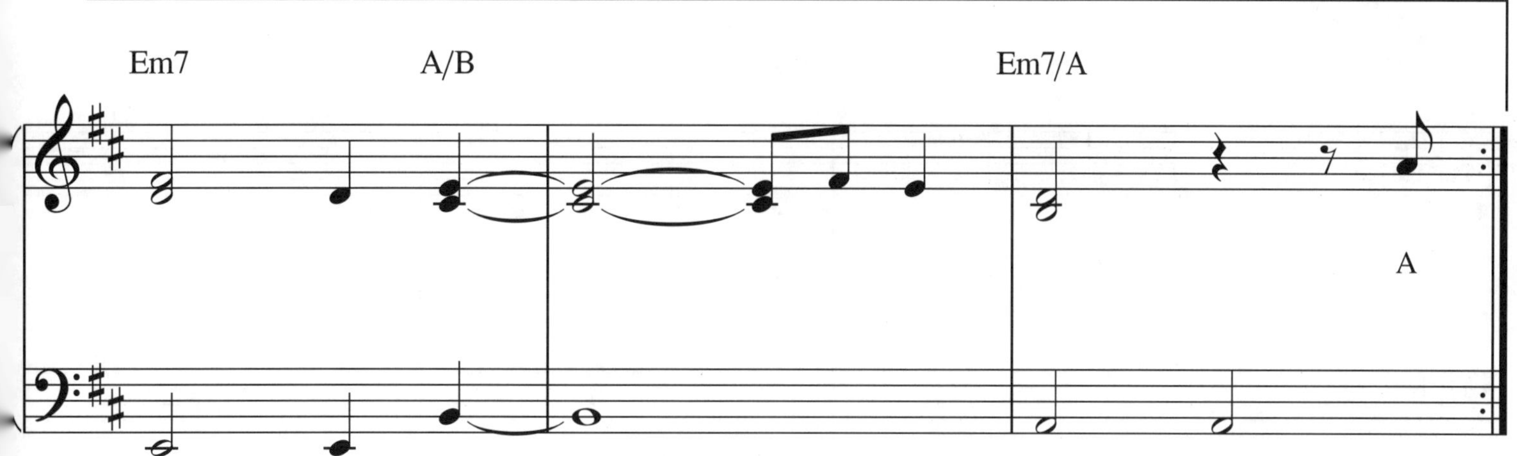
Em7
A/B
Em7/A
A

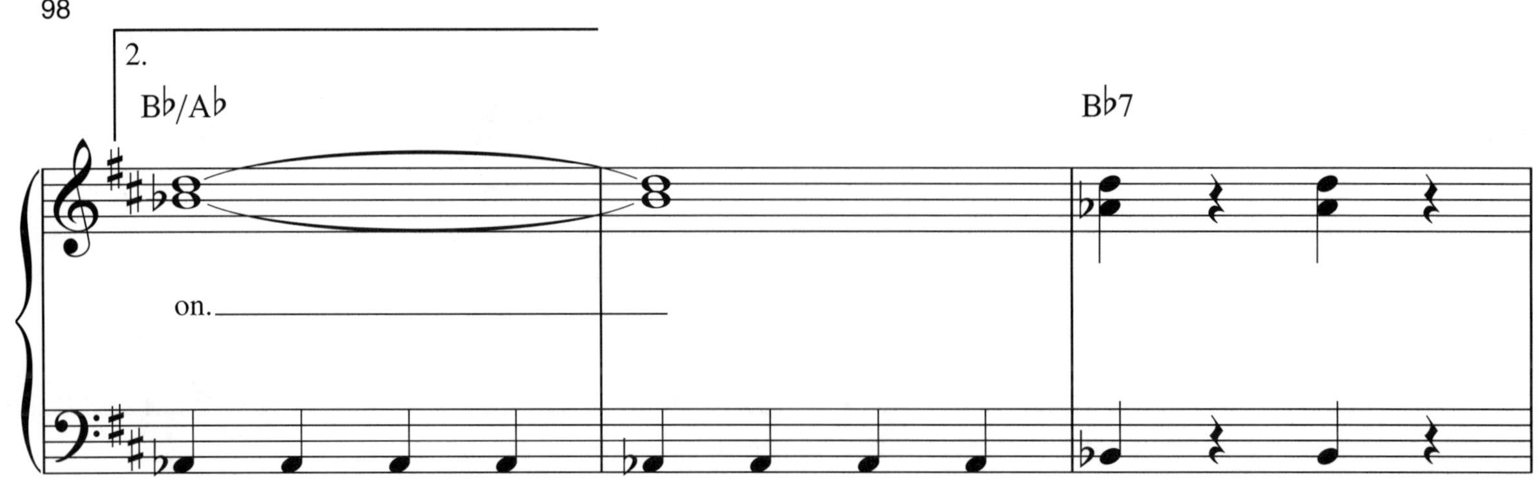
2.
B♭/A♭
B♭7
on.

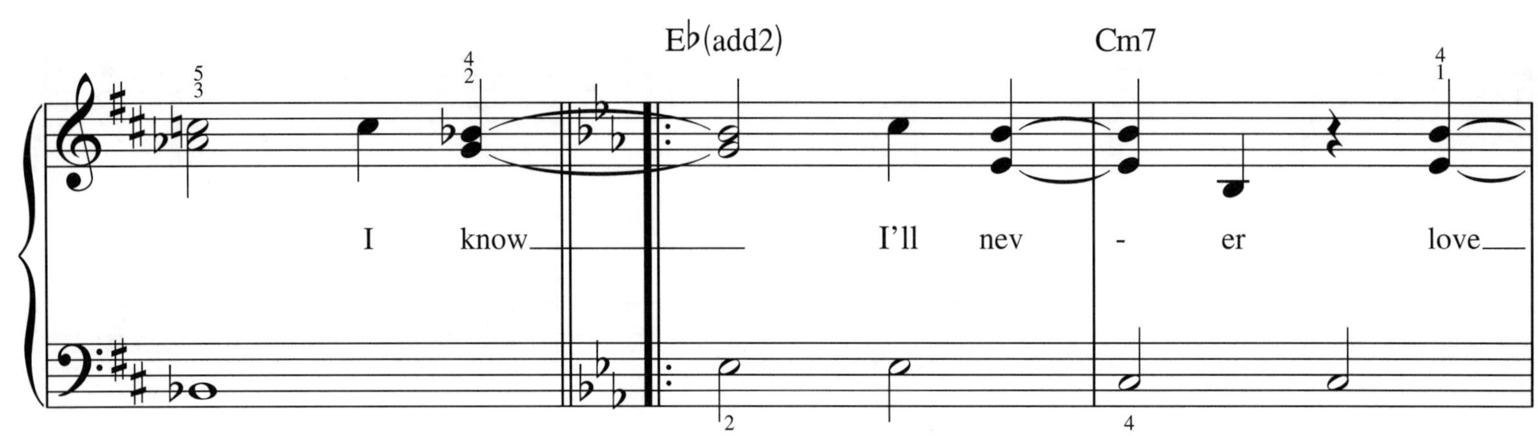
E♭(add2)
Cm7
I know
I'll nev - er love

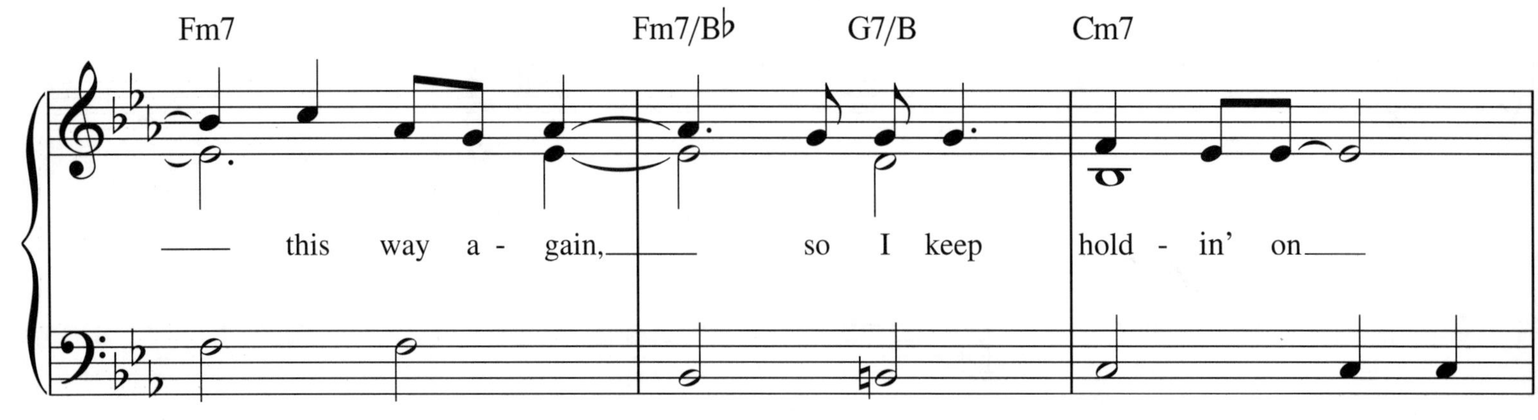
Fm7
Fm7/B♭
G7/B
Cm7
this way a - gain,
so I keep
hold - in' on

Cm7/F
F7
B♭7
be - fore the good is gone.
I know

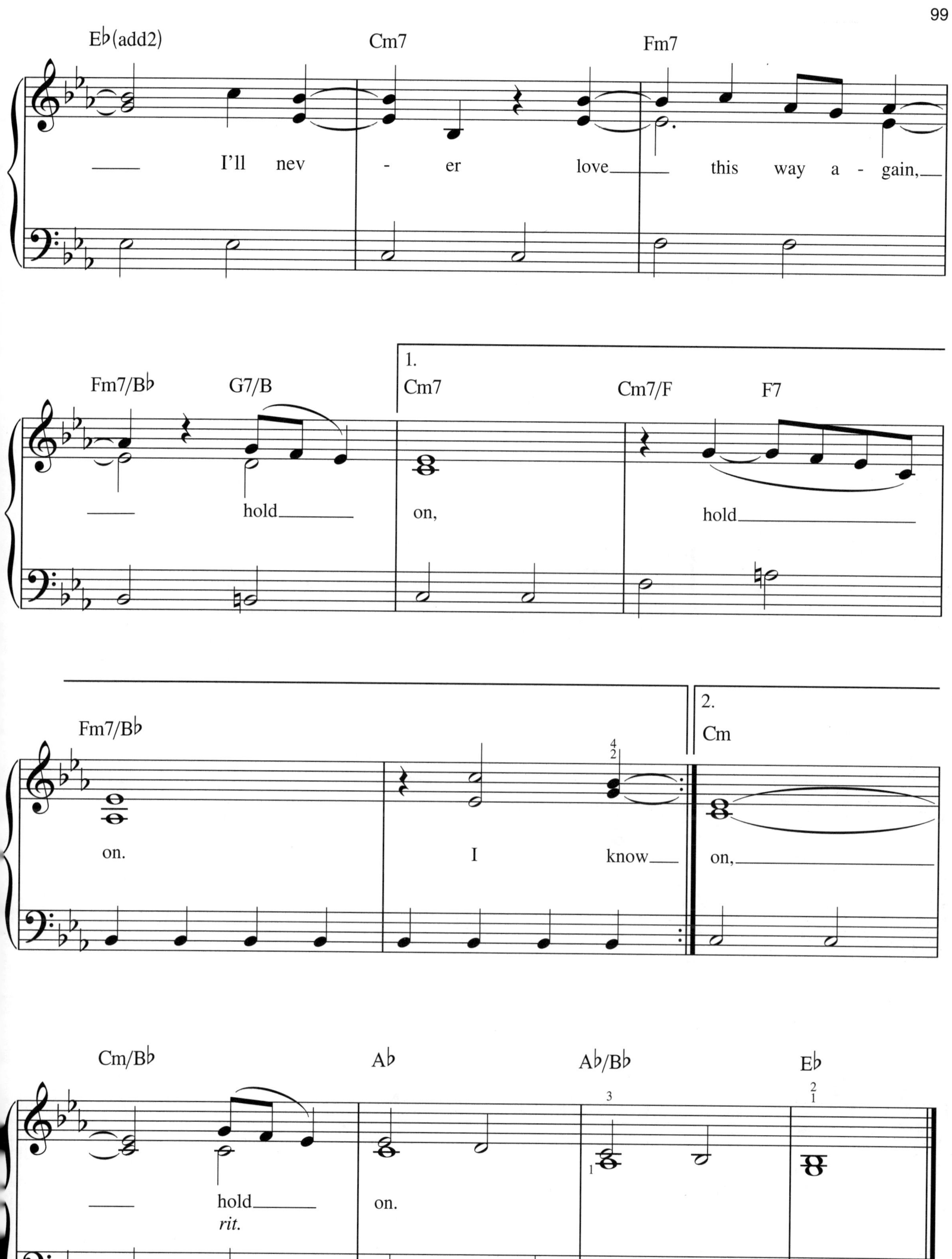

E♭(add2)
Cm7
Fm7
I'll nev - er love this way a - gain,
Fm7/B♭
G7/B
hold
1.
Cm7
on,
Cm7/F
F7
hold
Fm7/B♭
on.
I know
2.
Cm
on,
Cm/B♭
A♭
A♭/B♭
E♭
hold
rit.
on.

IF YOU LEAVE ME NOW

Words and Music by
PETER CETERA

Copyright © 1976 by BMG Songs, Inc. and Big Elk Music
International Copyright Secured All Rights Reserved

2.

C Am7 D7 G C G/C C

Ooh, girl, I just want you to stay.

F9sus Bbm/F F Am7

A love like ours is love that's hard to find. How could we let
We've come too far to leave it all be - hind. How could we end

F G

it slip a - way?
it all this way?

1.,3.

C Am7 E7

2.,3.
C
Em7
Am7
When to - mor - row comes, then we'll both re - gret the
Dm
Em
Fm
To Coda
things we said to - day.
Instrumental
Cmaj7
Am7
Em7
Am7
D
G
C

Am7
D7
G
C
G
C

D.S. al Coda
(with repeats)

CODA
Cmaj7
If you leave me now, you'll

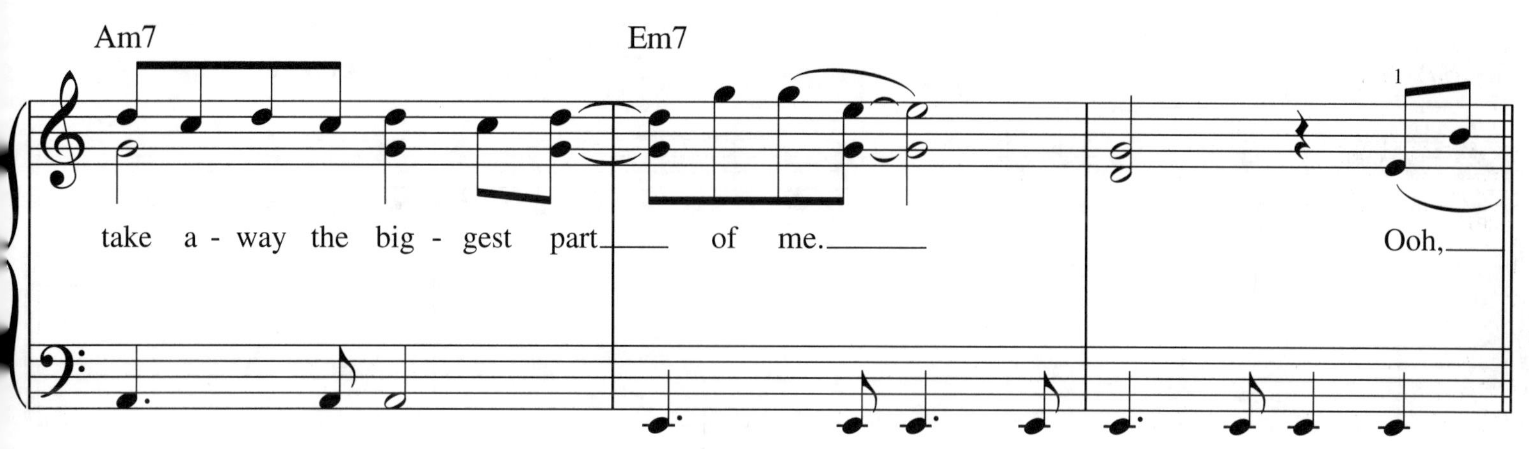
Am7
Em7
take a - way the big - gest part of me.
Ooh,

Am7
D7
G
C
no, ba - by, please don't go.

Am7
D7
G
C G C G C G C
Am7
D7
G
C
Ooh, girl, just got to have you by my side.
Ooh, ma - ma, I just got to have your lov - in'.
Am
D7
G
1.
C G C G C G C
Ooh,
2.
C G C G C G C
rit.

IT'S TOO LATE

Words by TONI STERN
Music by CAROLE KING

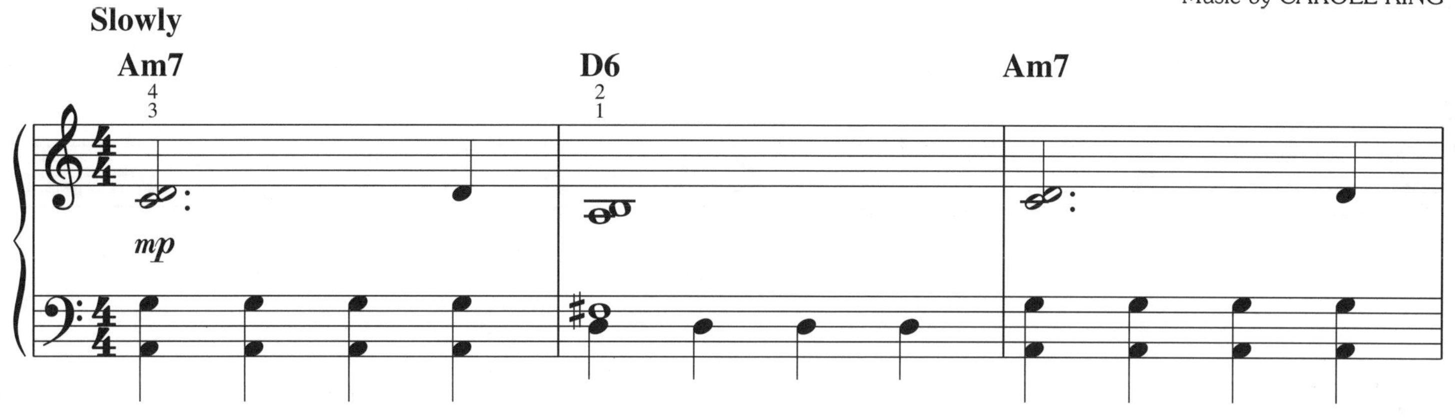

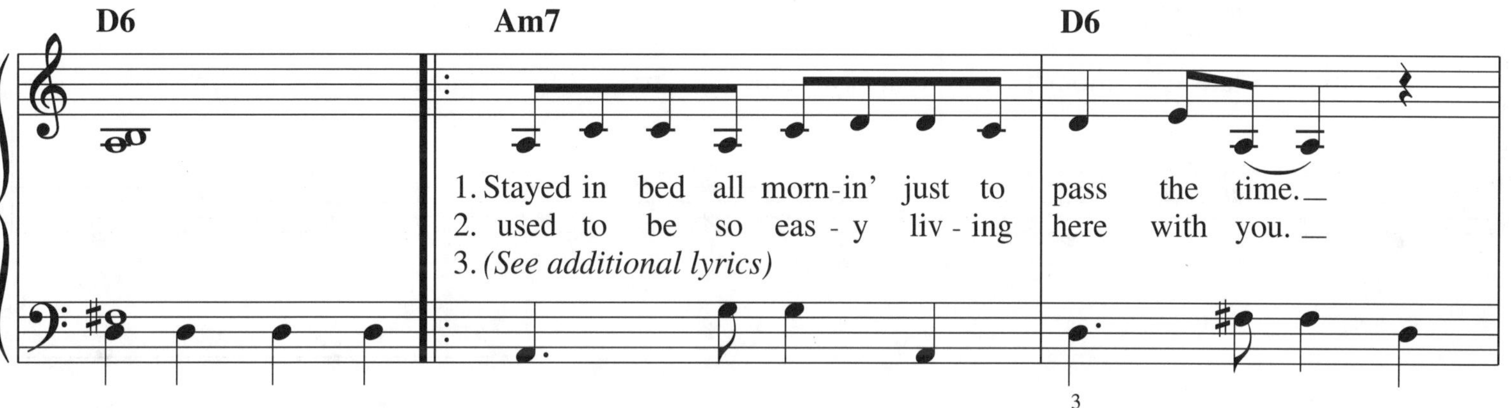

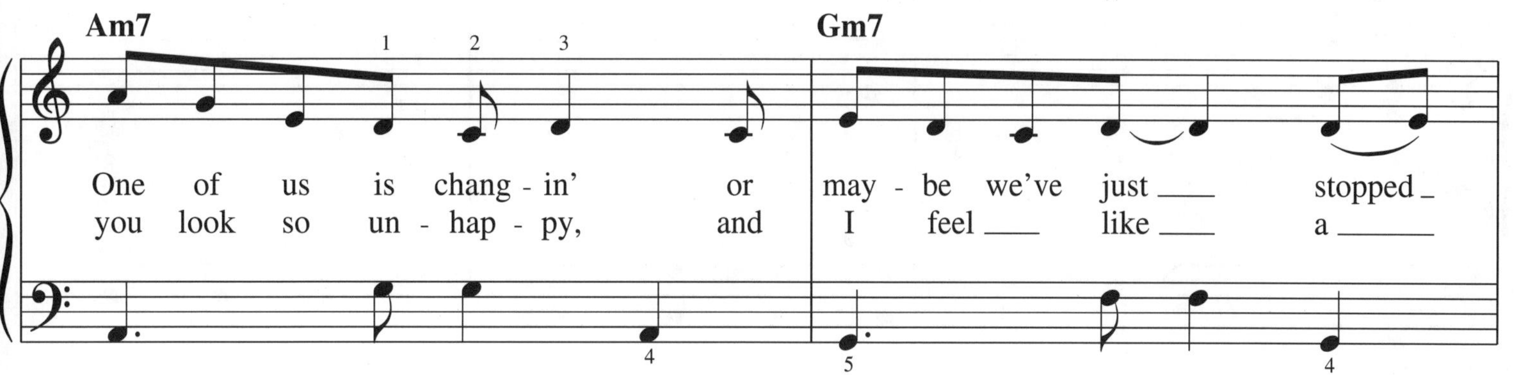

© 1971 (Renewed 1999) COLGEMS-EMI MUSIC INC.
All Rights Reserved International Copyright Secured Used by Permission

Fmaj7
Chorus
B♭maj7
try in'.
fool.
And it's
too late, ba - by, now

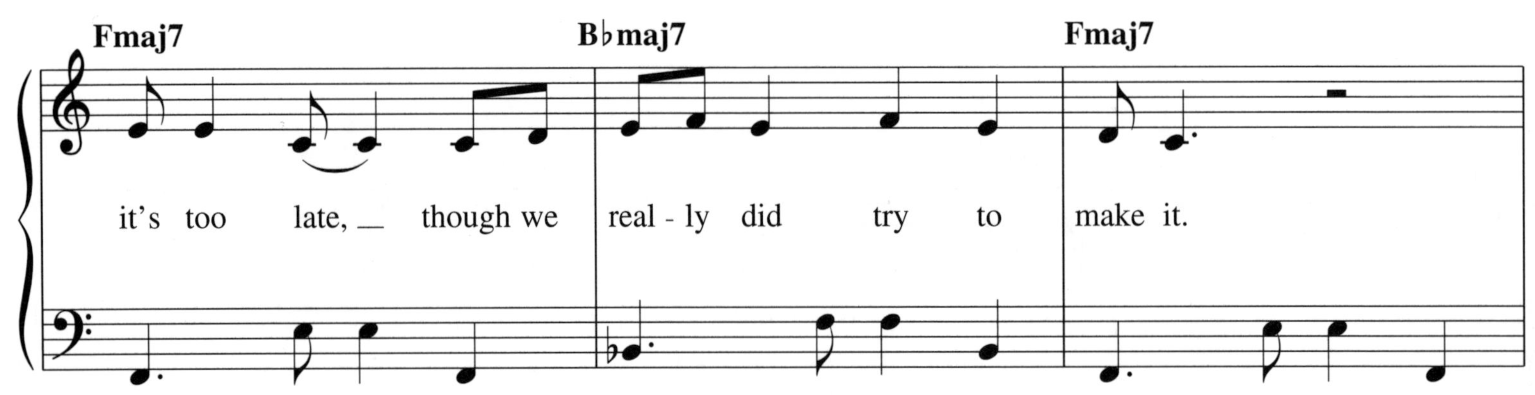
Fmaj7
B♭maj7
Fmaj7
it's too late, though we
real - ly did try to
make it.

B♭maj7
Fmaj7
1.,2.
Dm7
Fmaj7
Some-thin' in - side has
died, and I can't
hide and I just can't

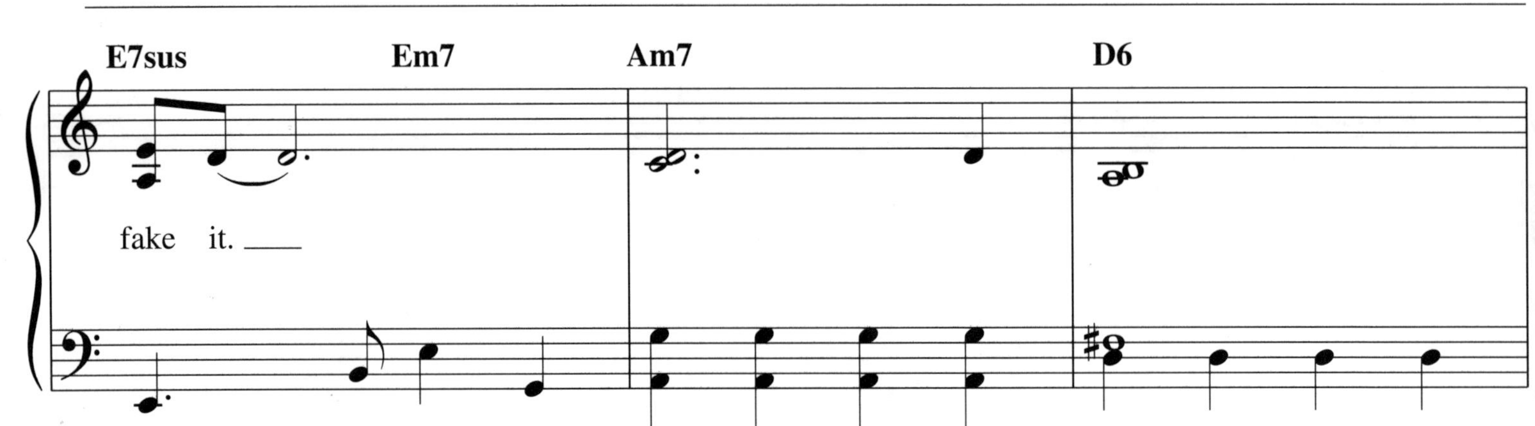
E7sus
Em7
Am7
D6
fake it.

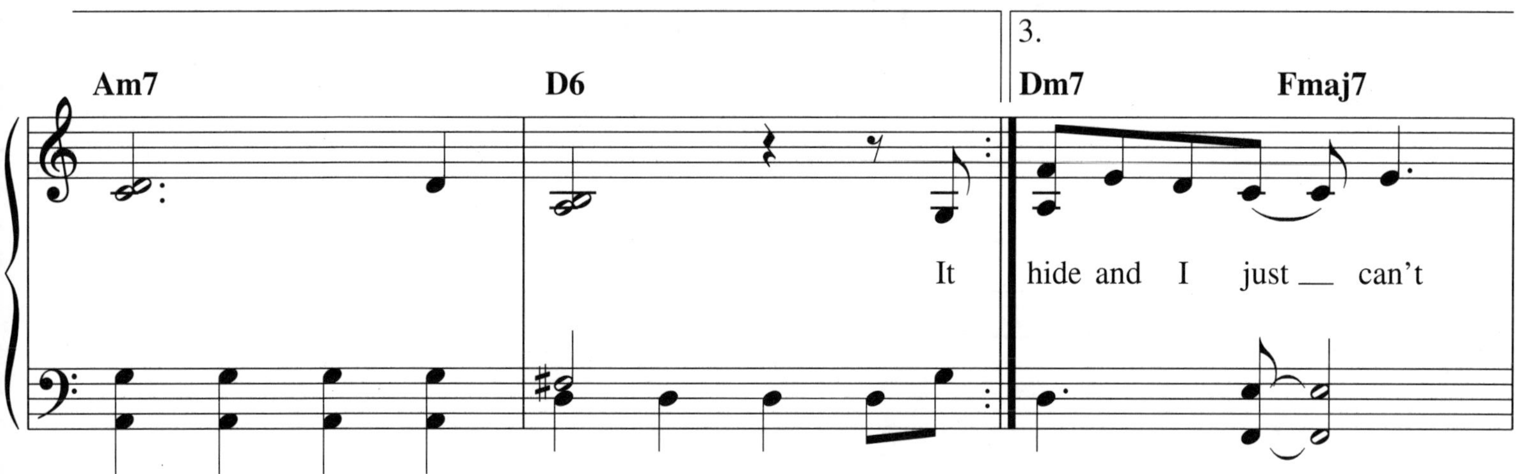

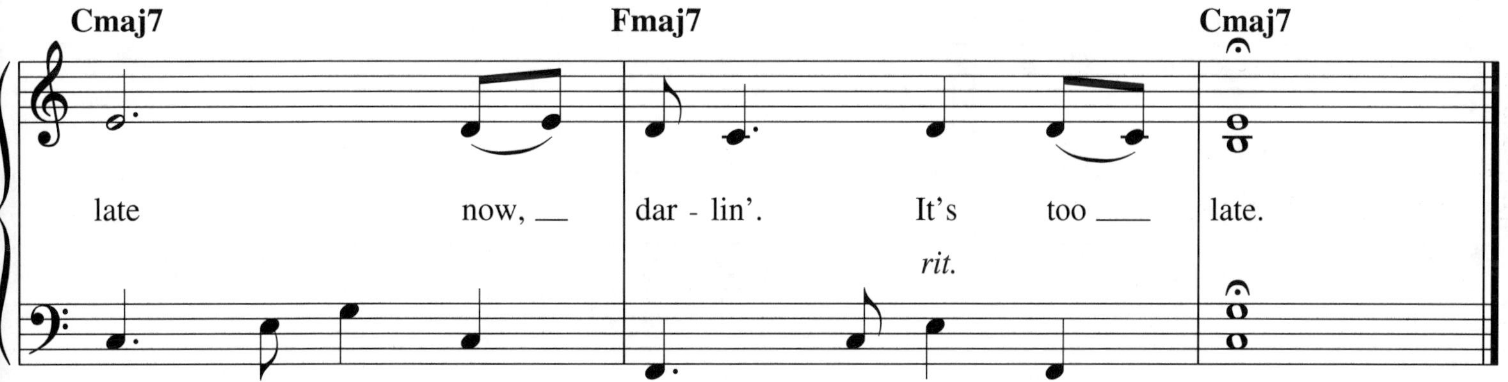

Additional Lyrics

3. There'll be good times again for me and you,
But we just can't stay together.
Don't you feel it, too?
Still I'm glad for what we had
And how I once loved you.
Chorus

IT'S IMPOSSIBLE
(Somos Novios)

English Lyric by SID WAYNE
Spanish Words and Music by
ARMANDO MANZANERO

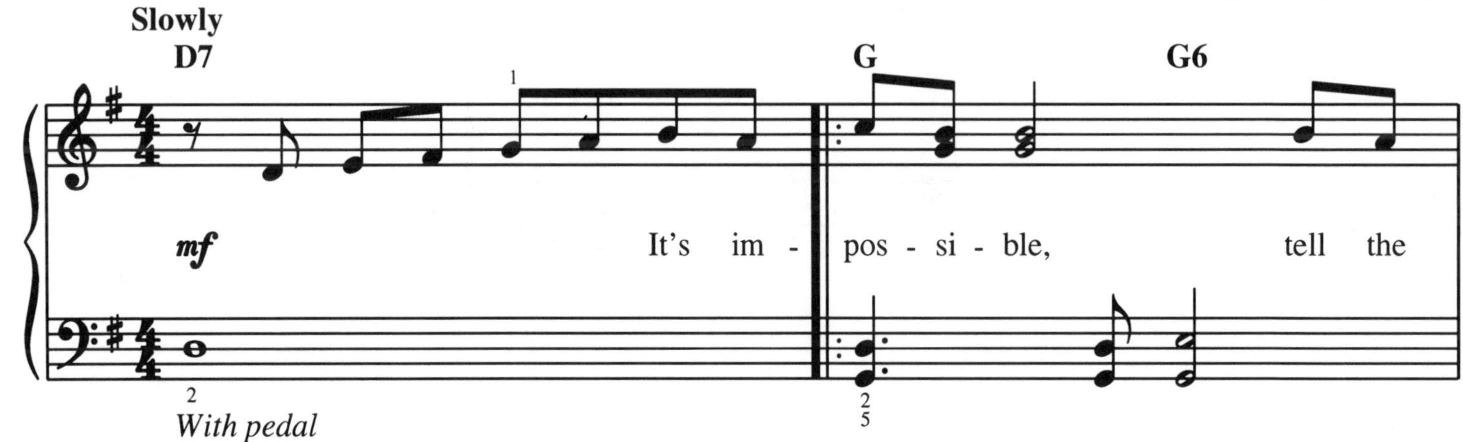

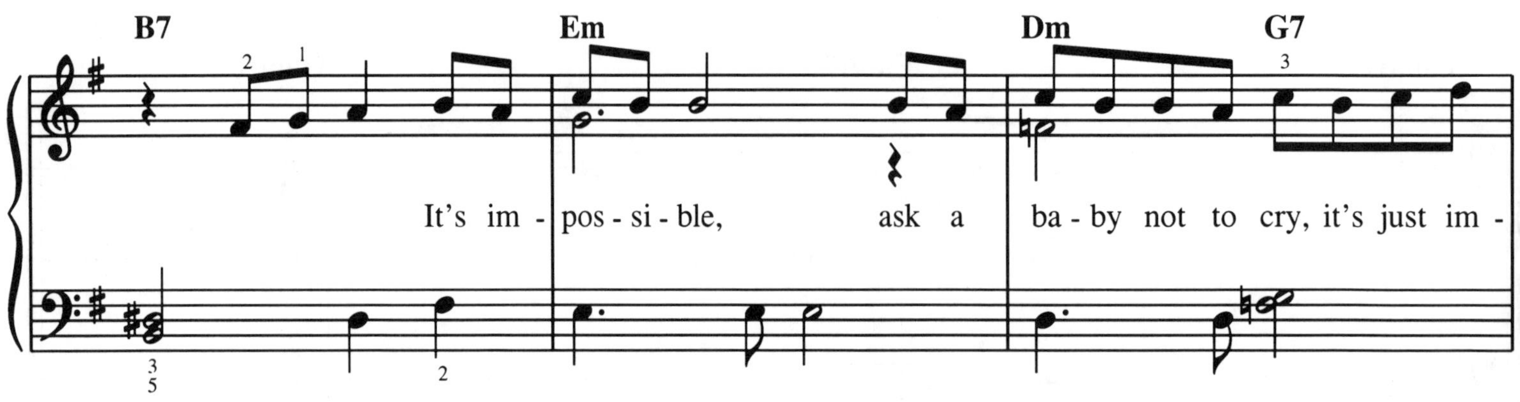

Copyright © 1968 by BMG Edim., S.A. de C.V.
Copyright Renewed
All Rights for the U.S. Administered by BMG Songs, Inc.
International Copyright Secured All Rights Reserved

Cm
G/D
E7♭9
to me, and not feel you go-ing through me? Split the
Am
A7
sec-ond that I nev-er think of you? Oh, how im-
D7
Am7
D7
G
G6
pos-si-ble. Can the o-cean keep from
Gmaj7
G6
F♯m7♭5
rush-ing to the shore? It's just im-pos-si-ble.

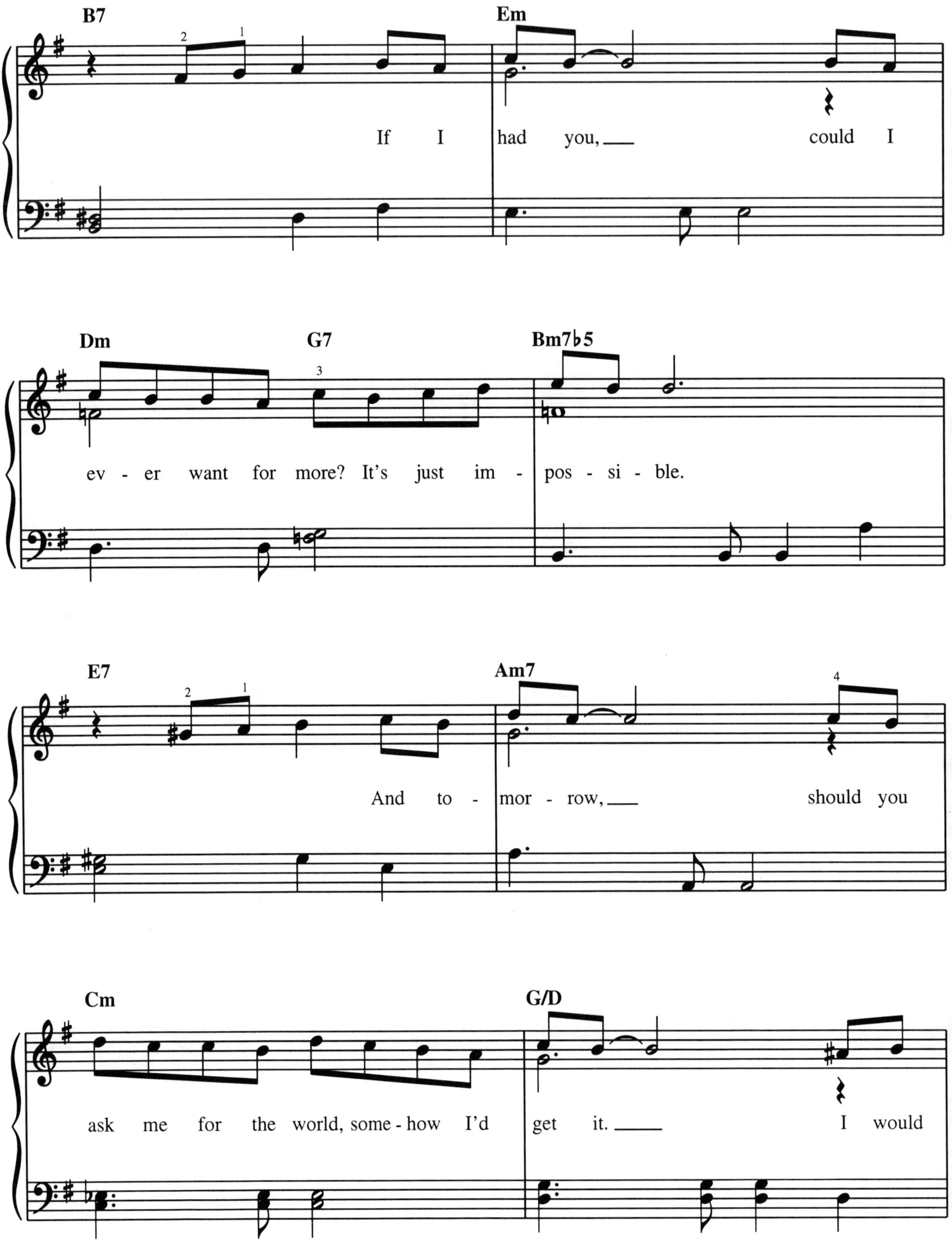

B7 Em

2 1

If I had you, ___ could I

Dm G7 Bm7♭5

3

ev - er want for more? It's just im - pos - si - ble.

E7♭9
Am
sell my ver - y soul and not re - gret it, ___ for to
4
D7
1.
G
live with - out your love is just im - pos - si - ble.
1
2
Am7
D7
4
2.
G
Em
It's im - pos - si - ble. Im - pos - si - ble.
Am7
D7
G
Cm
G
Mm, ___ im - pos - si - ble.
rit.

JOY TO THE WORLD

Words and Music by
HOYT AXTON

Copyright © 1970 Irving Music, Inc.
International Copyright Secured All Rights Reserved

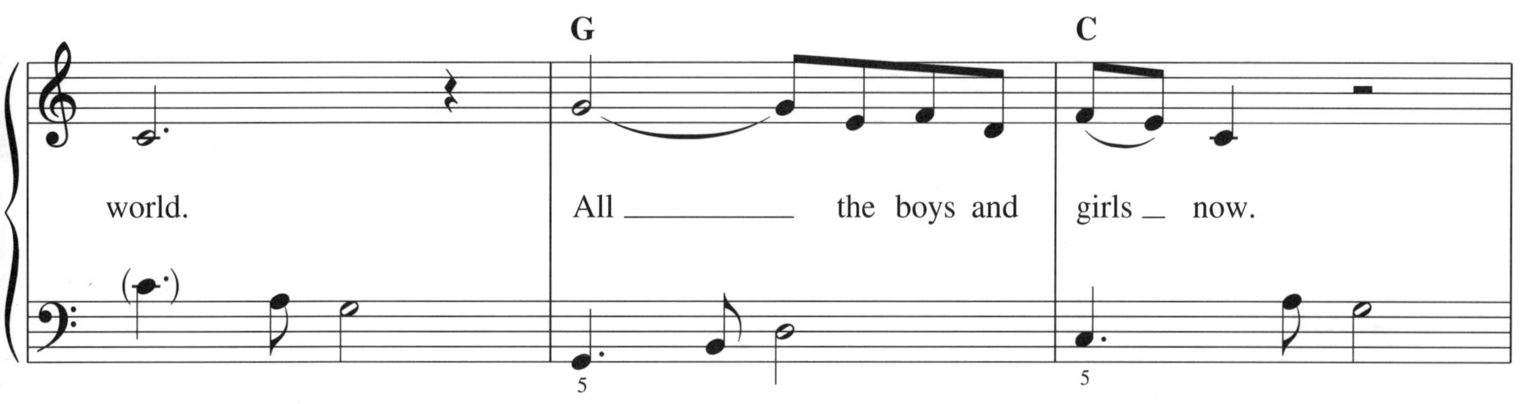
G
C
world.
All the boys and
girls now.
5
5

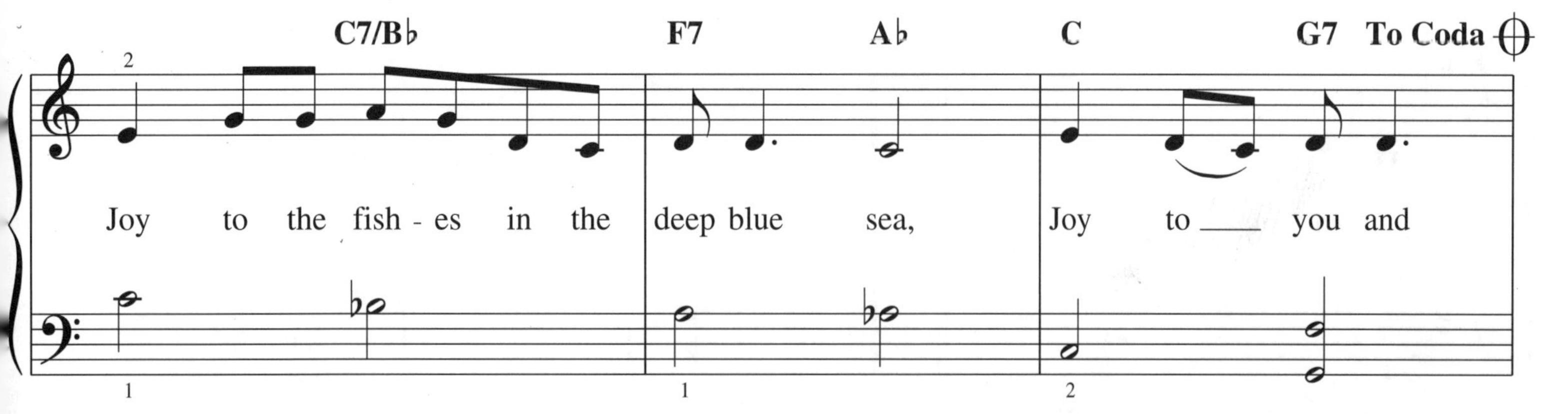
C7/B♭
F7
A♭
C
G7
To Coda
2
Joy to the fish - es in the
deep blue sea,
Joy to you and
1
1
2

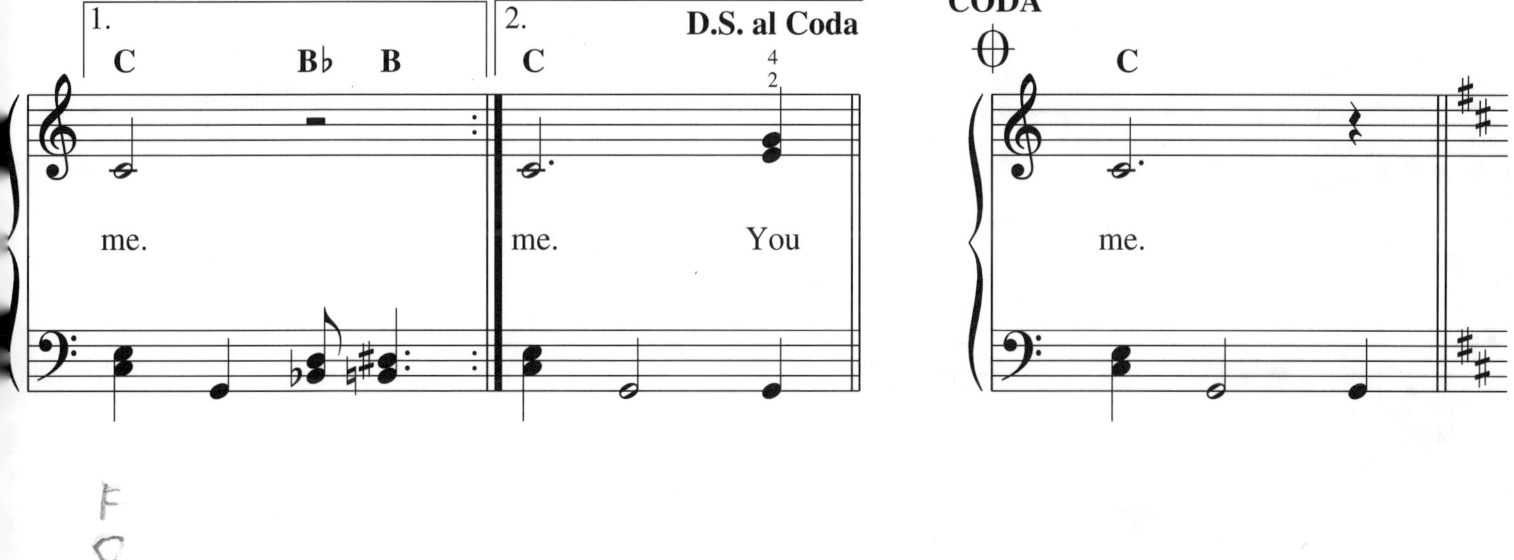
1.
2.
D.S. al Coda
CODA
C
B♭
B
C
C
4
2
me.
me.
You
me.

D
G
D
G
5
Joy
to the world.
All the
boys and girls.

D
G
D
Joy
to the world,
Joy
to

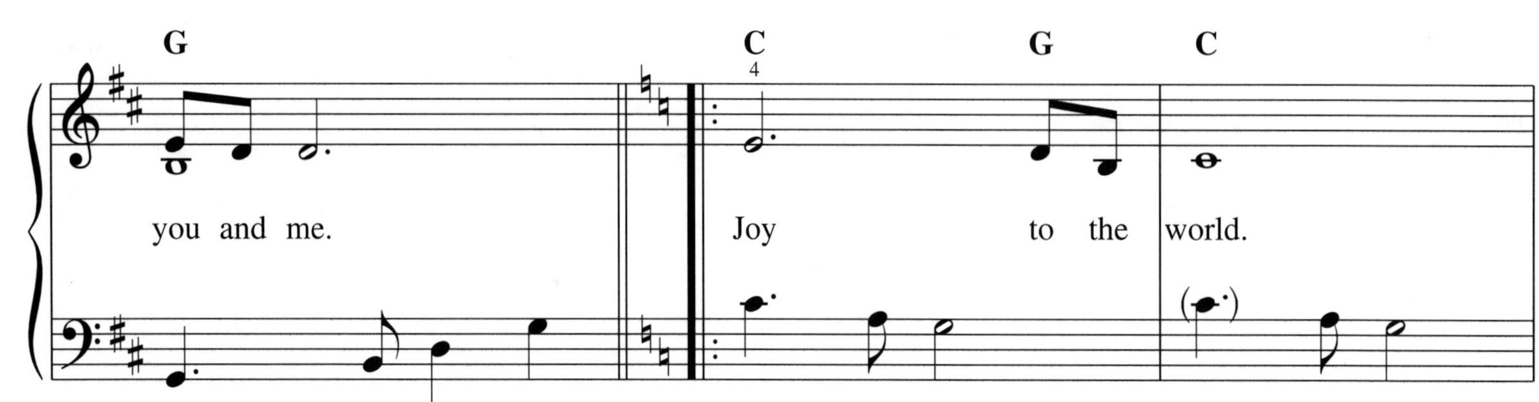
G
C
G
C
you and me.
Joy
to the
world.

G
C
C7/B♭
All ______ the boys and
girls.
Joy to the fish - es in the

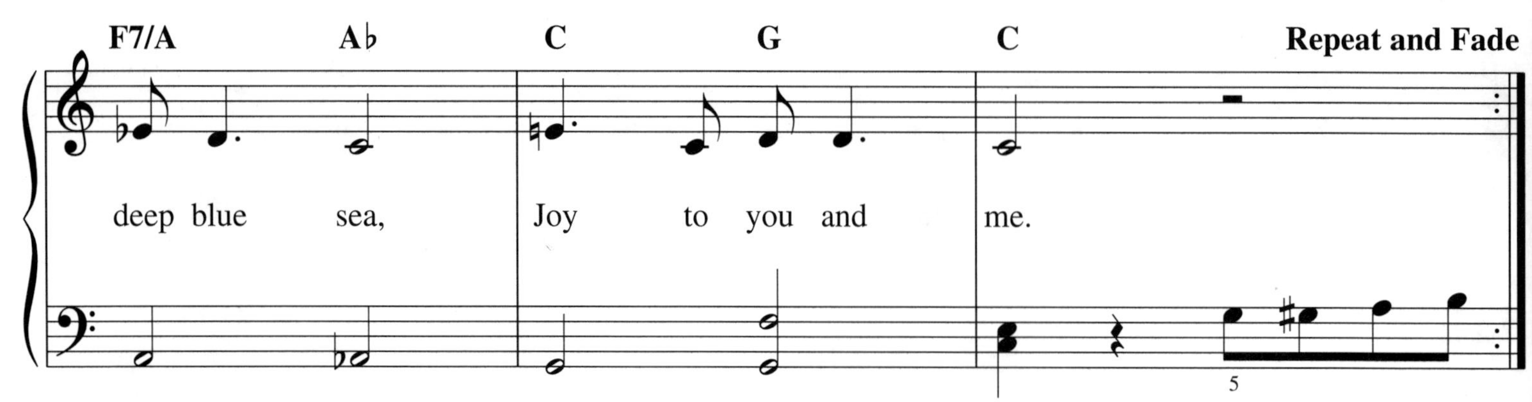
F7/A
A♭
C
G
C
Repeat and Fade
deep blue sea,
Joy to you and
me.

MAKE IT WITH YOU

Words and Music by
DAVID GATES

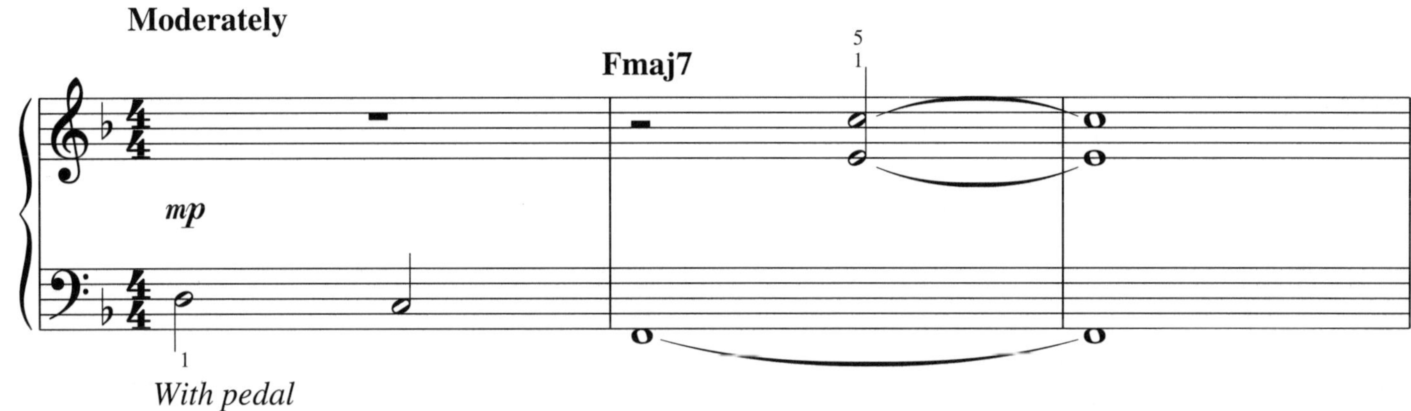

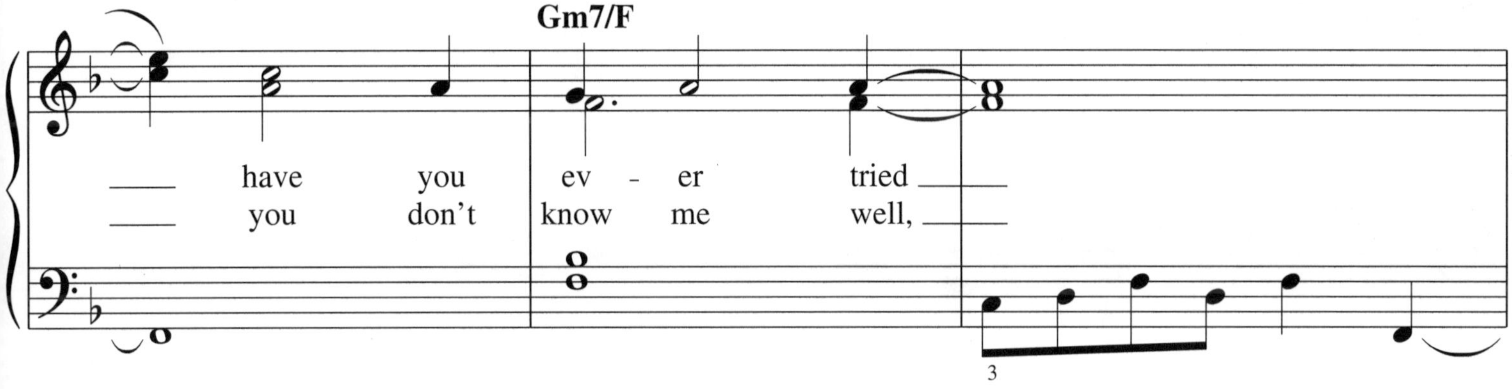

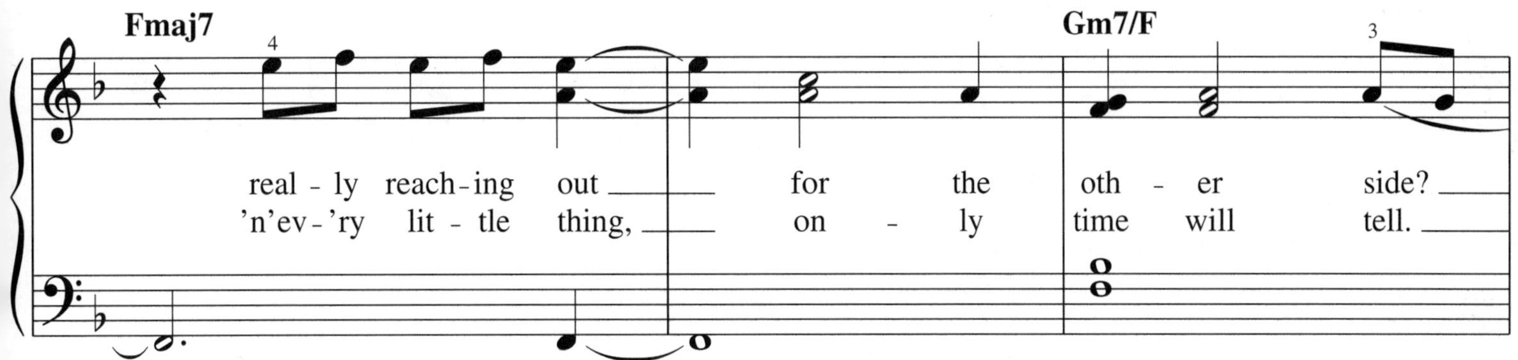

Copyright © 1970 Sony/ATV Tunes LLC
Copyright Renewed
All Rights Administered by Sony/ATV Music Publishing, 8 Music Square West, Nashville, TN 37203
International Copyright Secured All Rights Reserved

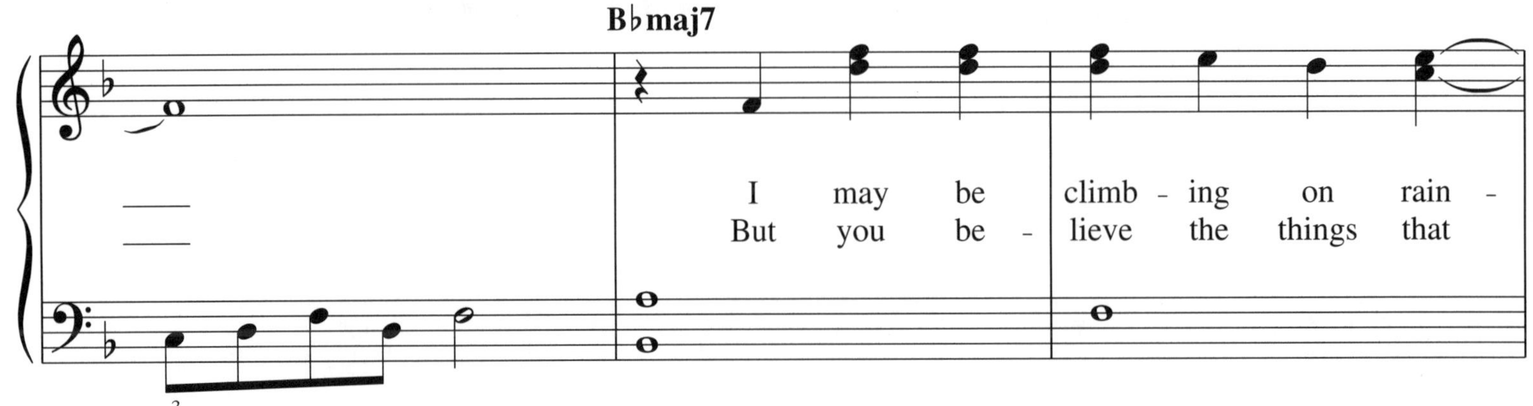
B♭maj7
I may be climb - ing on rain -
But you be - lieve the things that
3

Am7
Gm7
- bows but, ba - by, here goes.
I do, and we'll see it through.

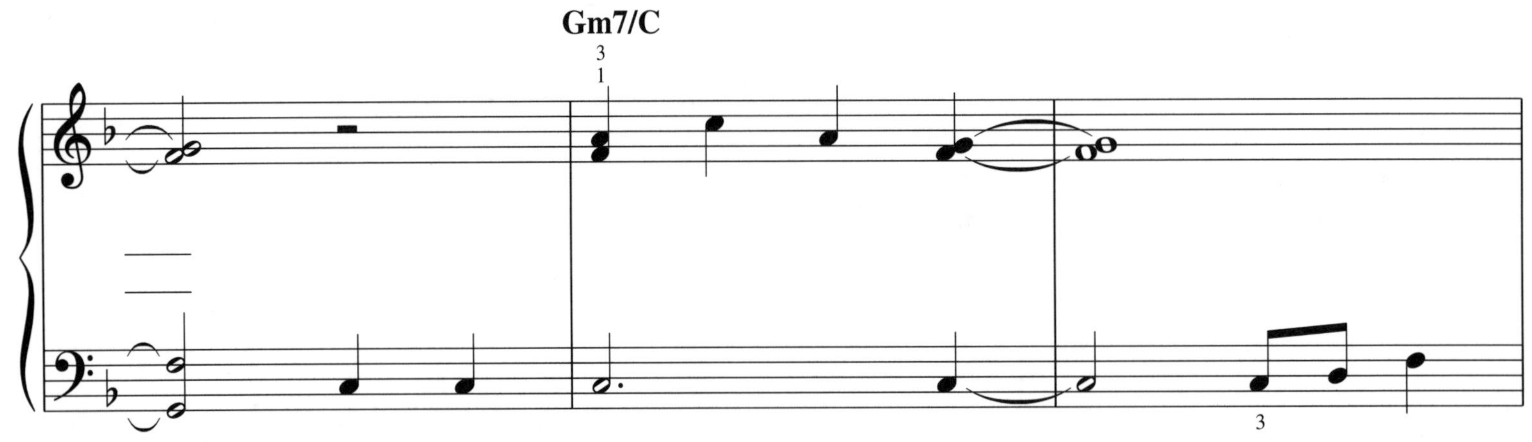
Gm7/C
3
1
3

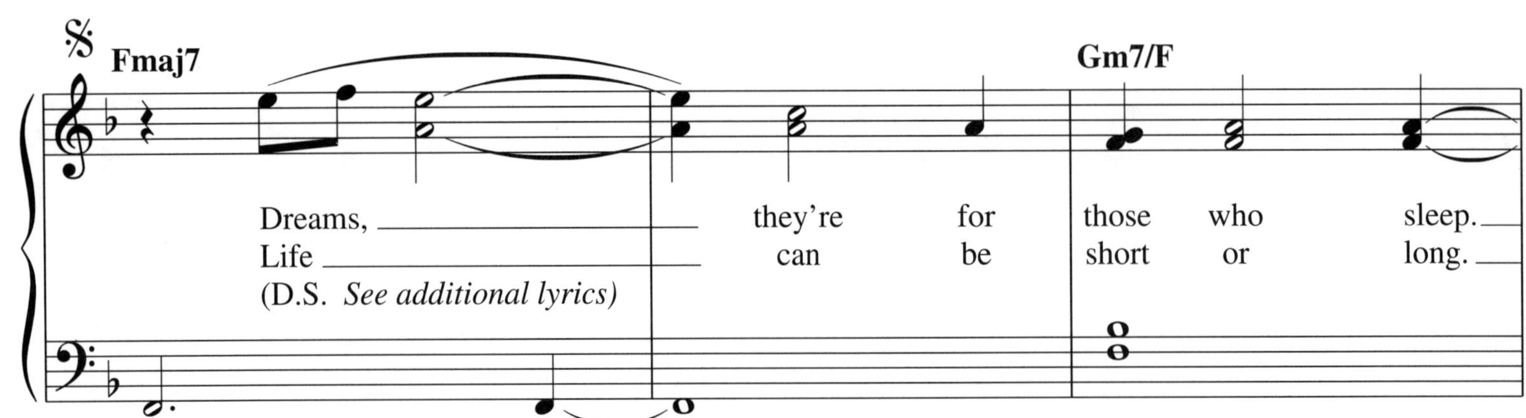
Fmaj7
Gm7/F
Dreams, they're for those who sleep.
Life can be short or long.
(D.S. See additional lyrics)

Fmaj7
Life, it's for
Love can be

Gm7/C
B♭maj7
us to keep. And if you're
right or wrong. And if I

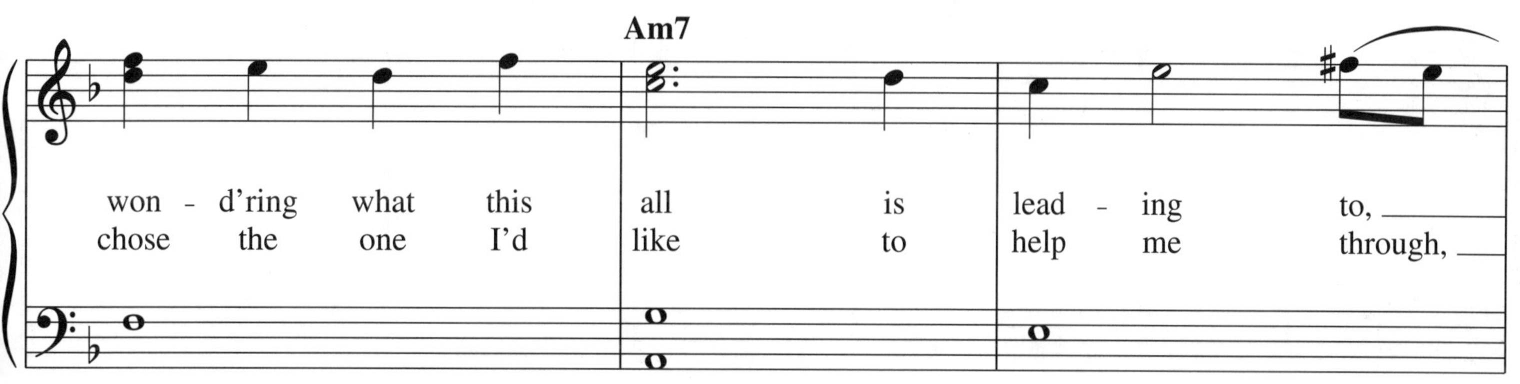
Am7
won - d'ring what this all is lead - ing to,
chose the one I'd like to help me through,

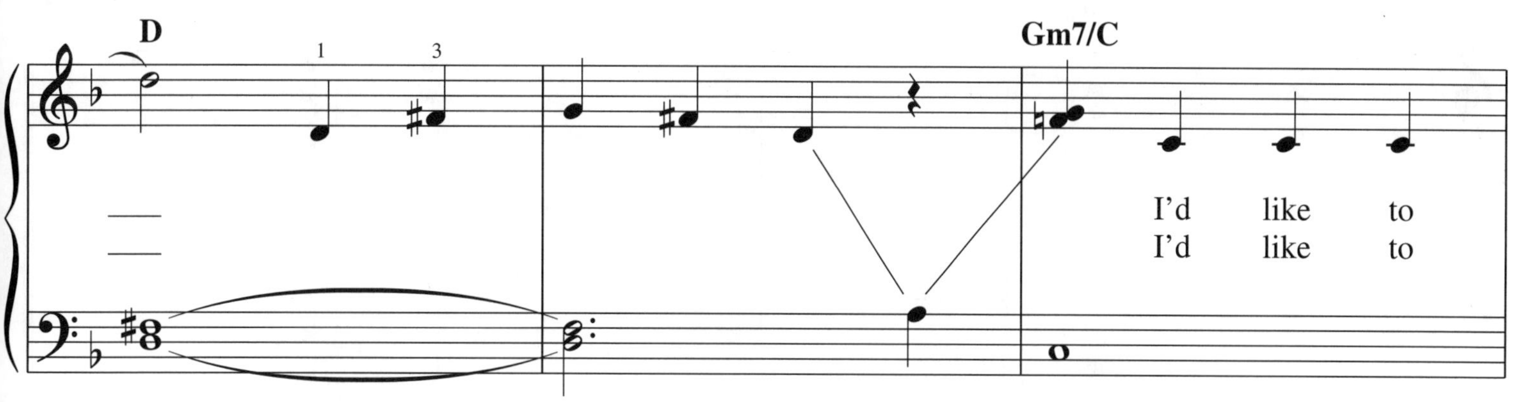
D
1
3
Gm7/C
I'd like to
I'd like to

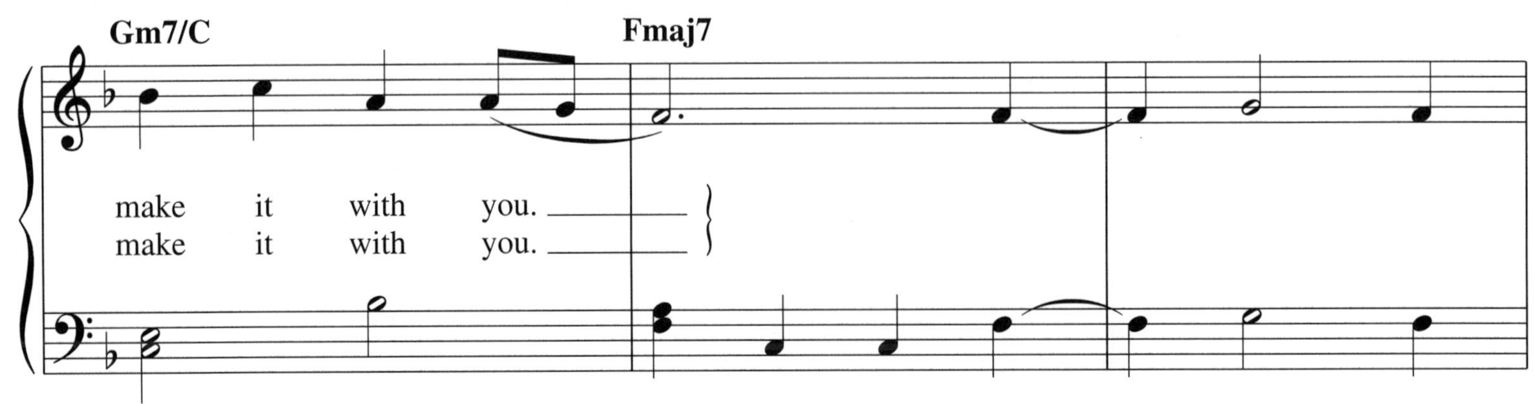
Gm7/C
Fmaj7
make it with you.
make it with you.

Gm7/C
Fmaj7
To Coda
I real - ly
think that we could
make it, girl.

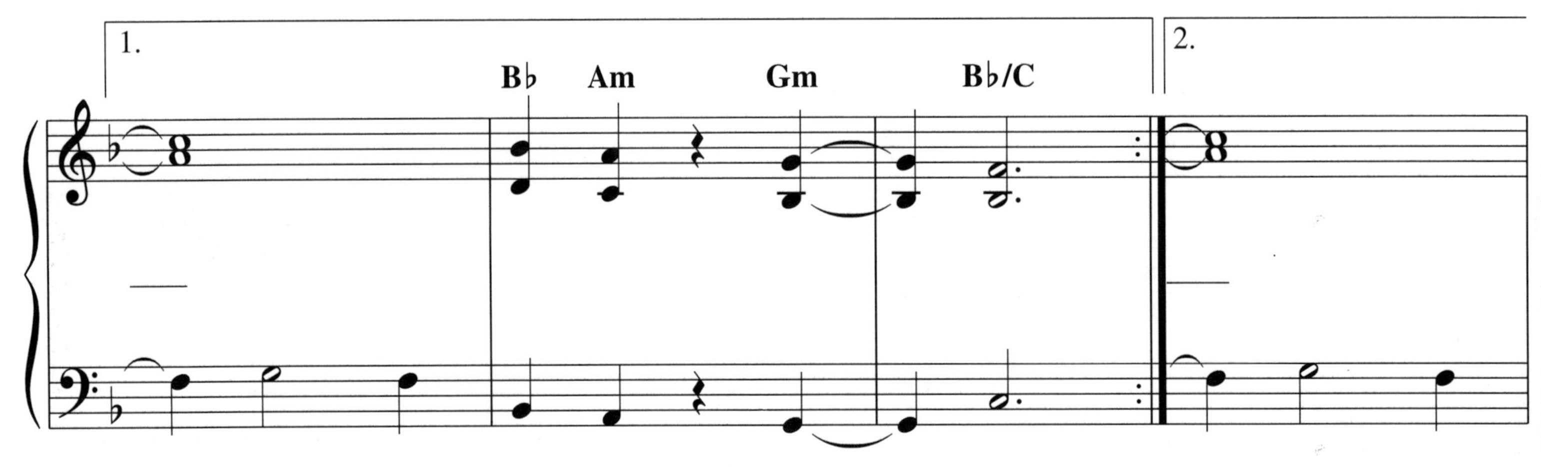
1.
B♭
Am
Gm
B♭/C
2.

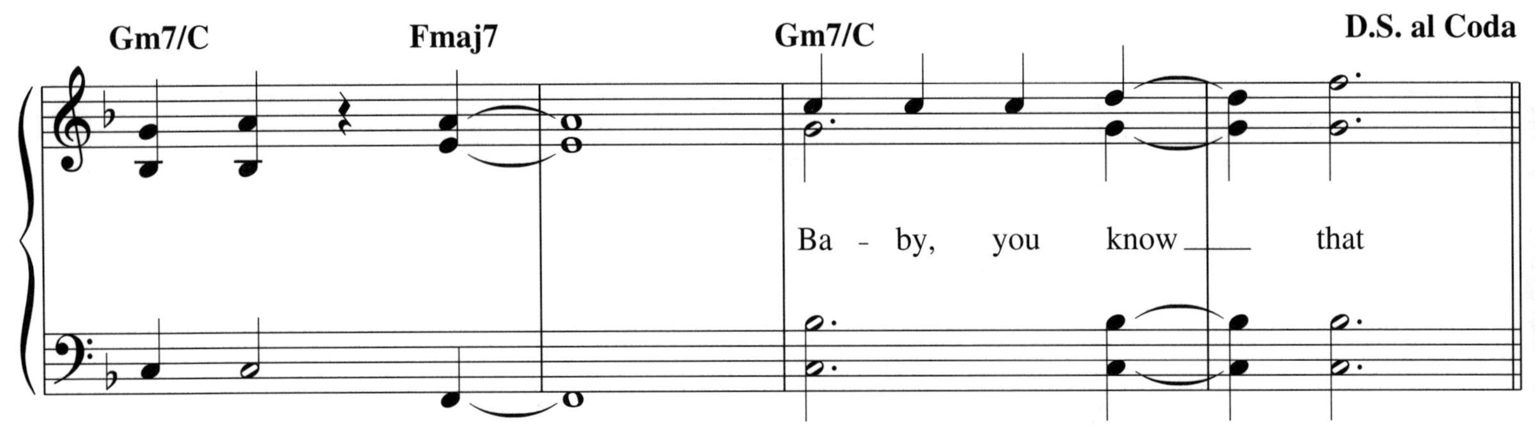
Gm7/C
Fmaj7
Gm7/C
D.S. al Coda
Ba - by, you know that

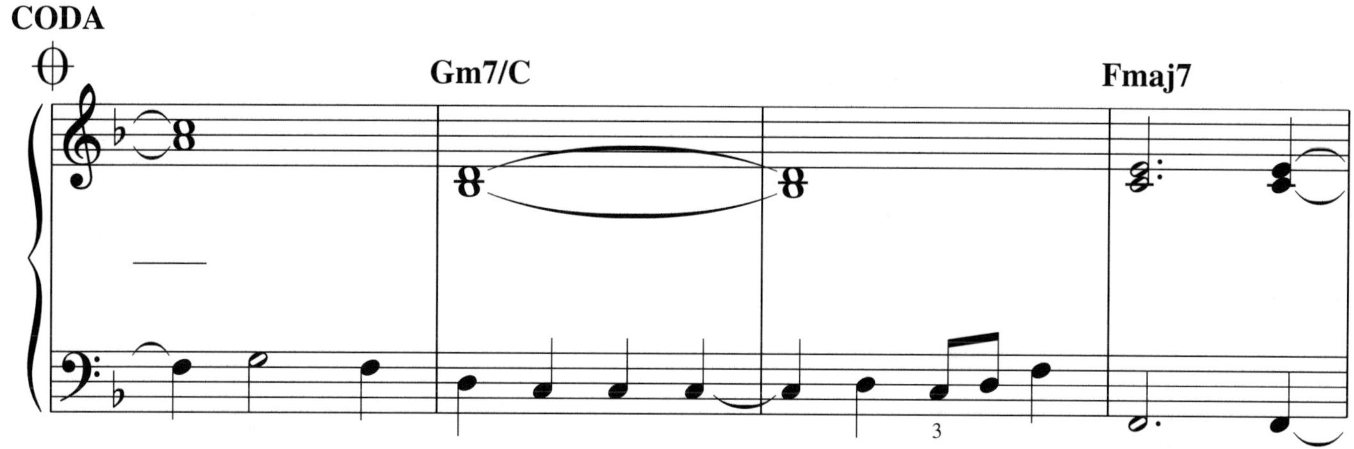

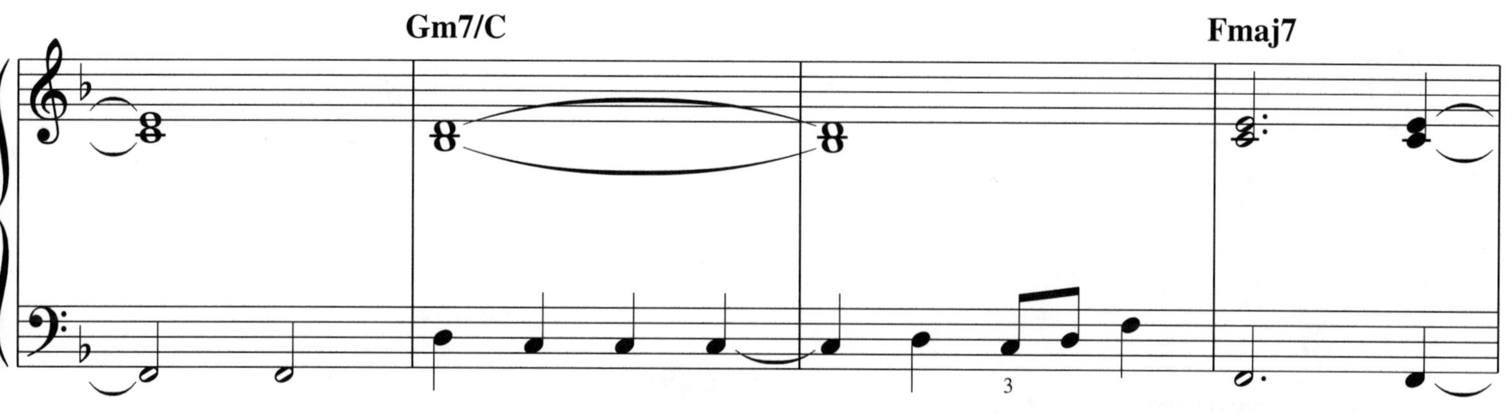

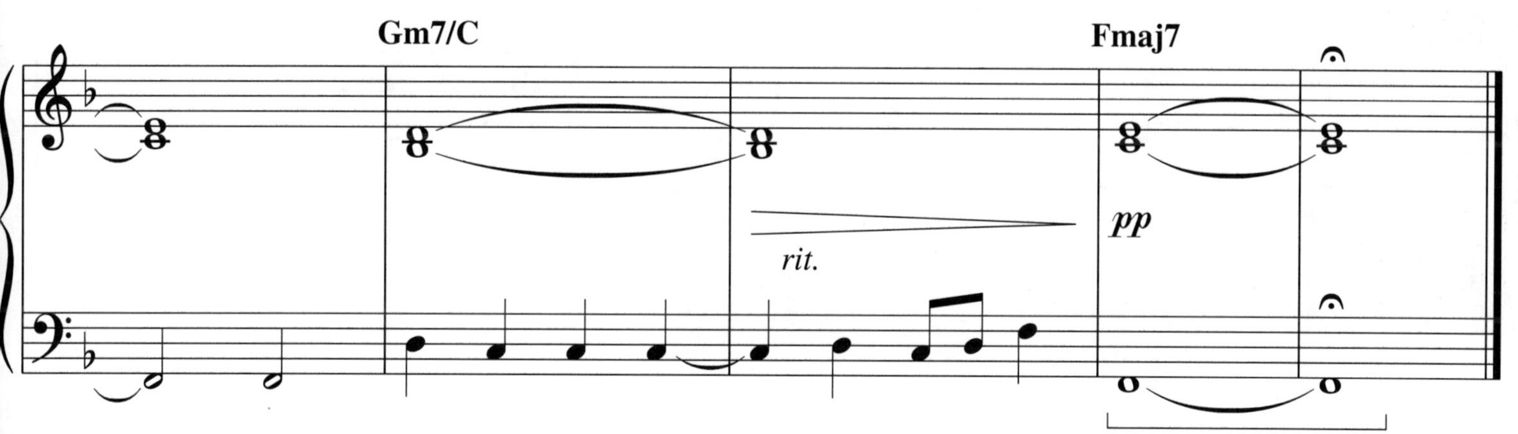

Additional Lyrics

D.S. (Baby, you know that)
Dreams, they're for those who sleep.
Life, it's for us to keep.
And if I chose the one I'd like to help me through,
I'd like to make it with you.
I really think that we could make it, girl.

LOOKS LIKE WE MADE IT

Words and Music by RICHARD KERR
and WILL JENNINGS

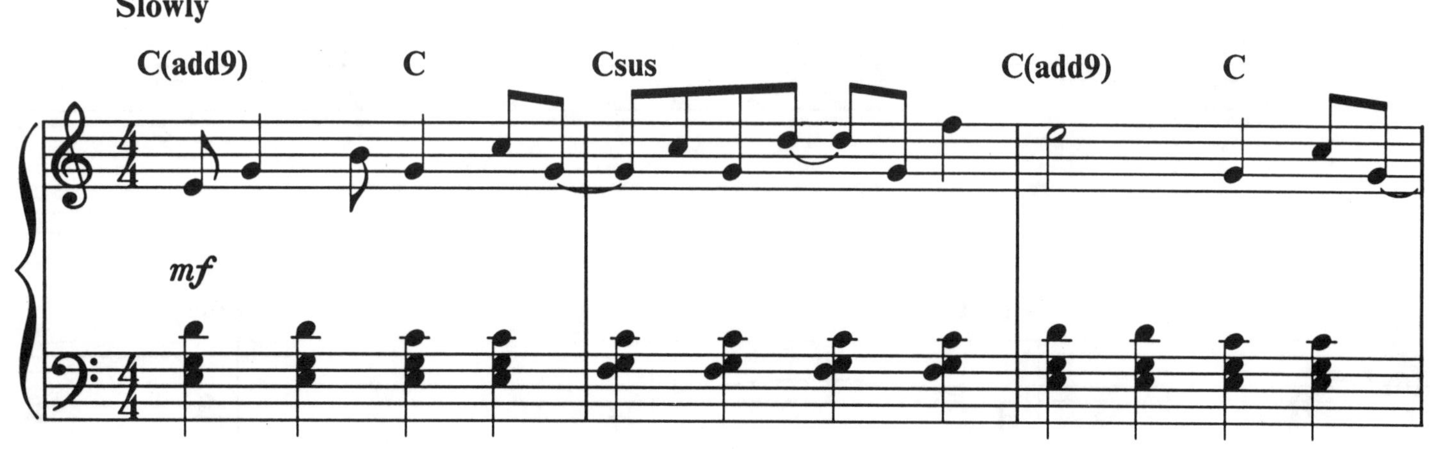

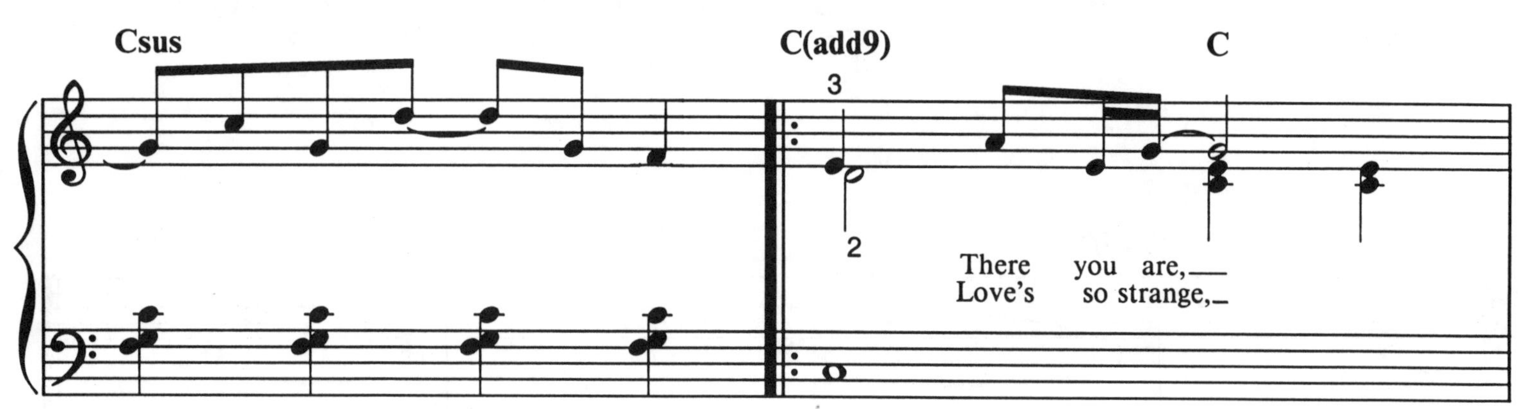

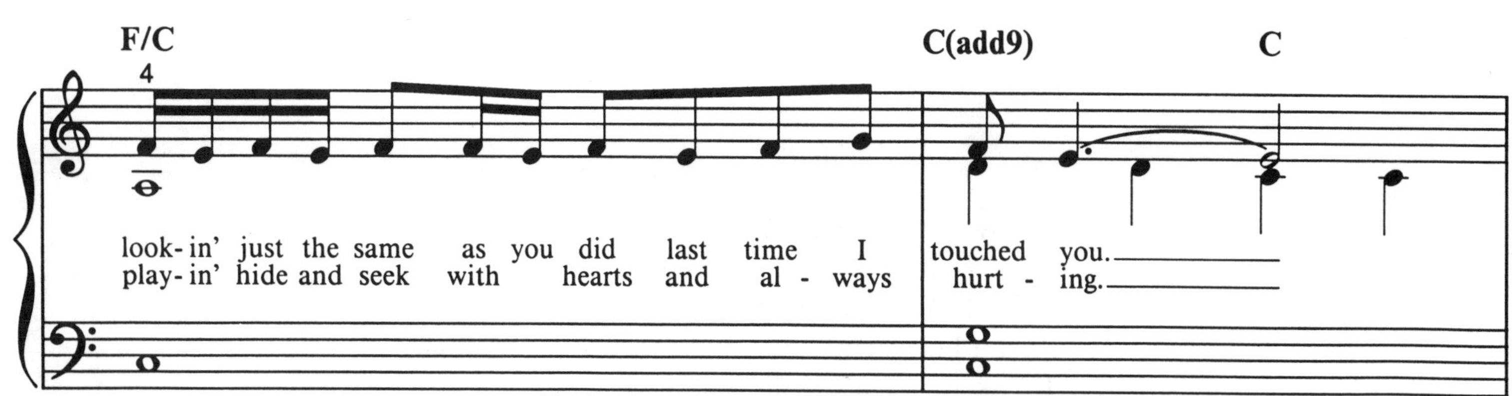

Copyright © 1976 RONDOR MUSIC (LONDON) LTD. and IRVING MUSIC, INC.
All Rights Reserved Used by Permission

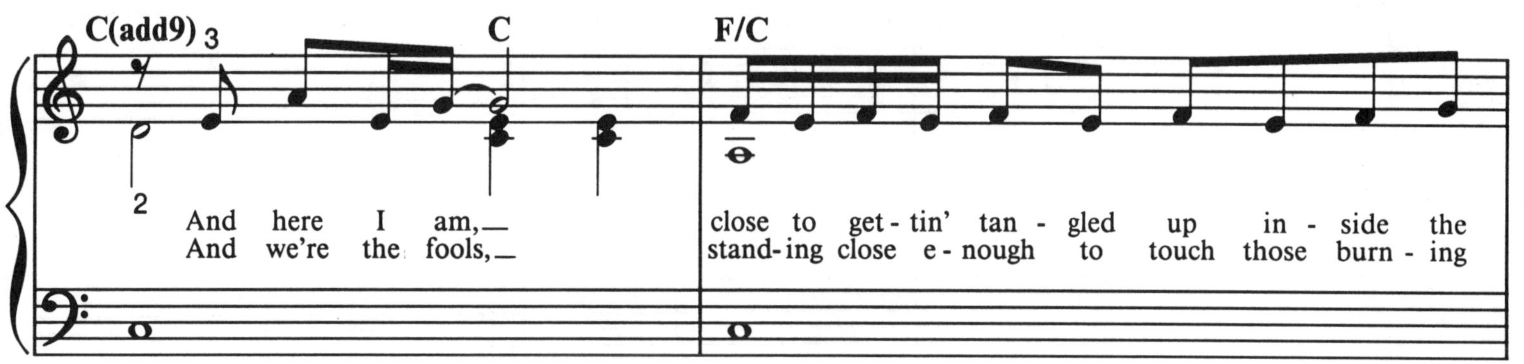
C(add9)
C
F/C
And here I am,
And we're the fools,
close to get-tin' tan-gled up in-side the
stand-ing close e-nough to touch those burn-ing

C(add9)
C
G/B
Am
D7sus
D7
thought of you.
mem-o-ries.
And
Do you
if I
love him as much as I love
hold you for the sake of all those

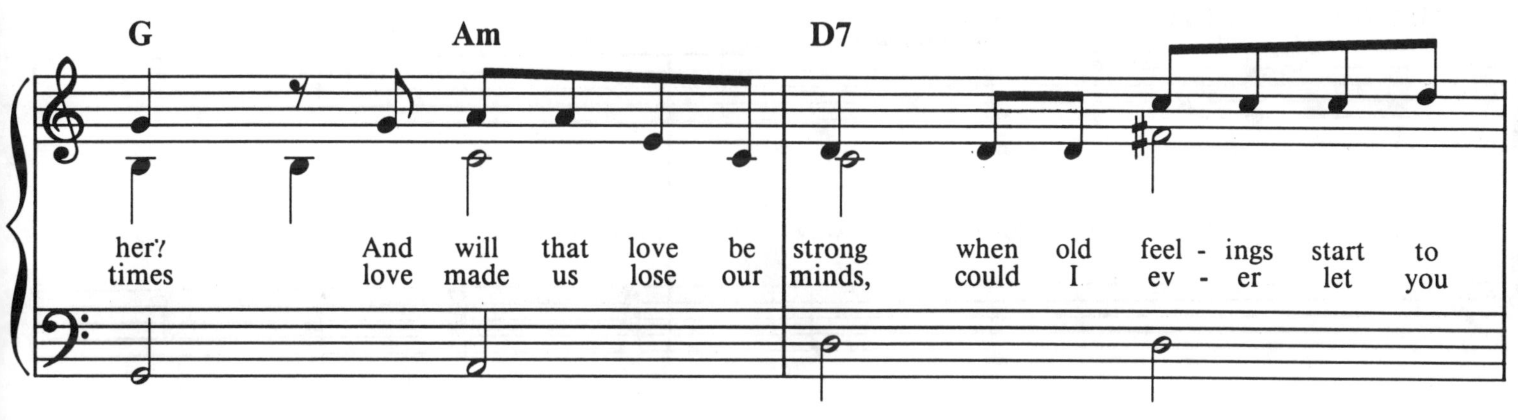
G
Am
D7
her?
times
And will that love be
love made us lose our
strong when old feel-ings start to
minds, could I ev-er let you

F/G
G
C
G/C
stir?
go?
Looks like we
Oh, no we've
made it,
made it,
Left each

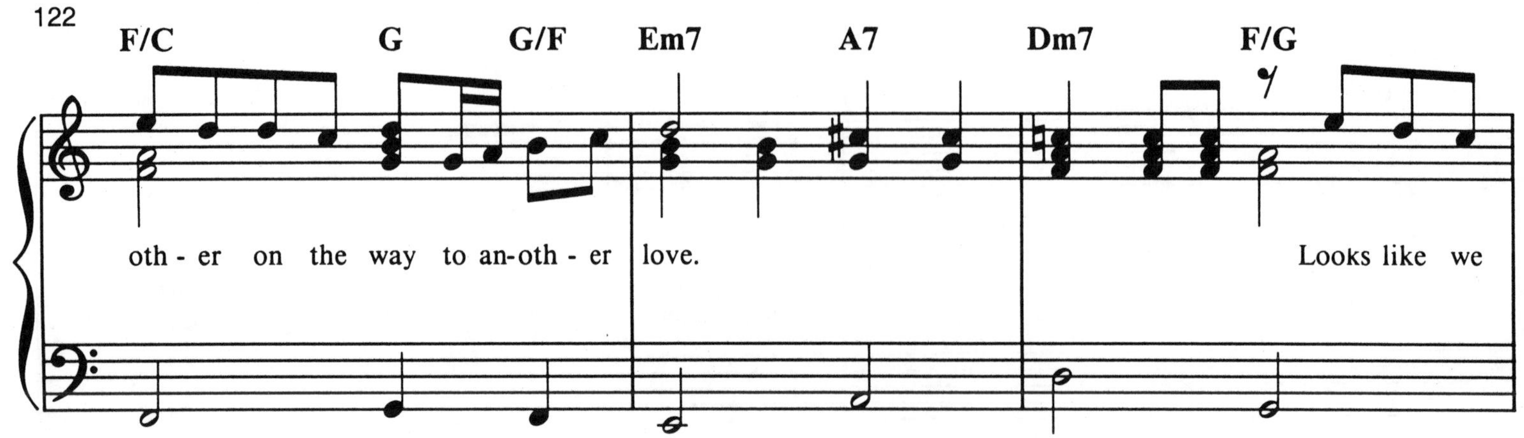
F/C G G/F Em7 A7 Dm7 F/G
oth - er on the way to an-oth - er love. Looks like we

C G/C F G G/F Em7 Am
3
3
made it, or I thought so till to- day un - til you were there, ev- 'ry- where, and

1.
Dm7 C/E F F/G C
all I could taste was love the way we made it.

G/C F/C
3
2.
Dm7 C/E F F/G
all I could taste was love the way we

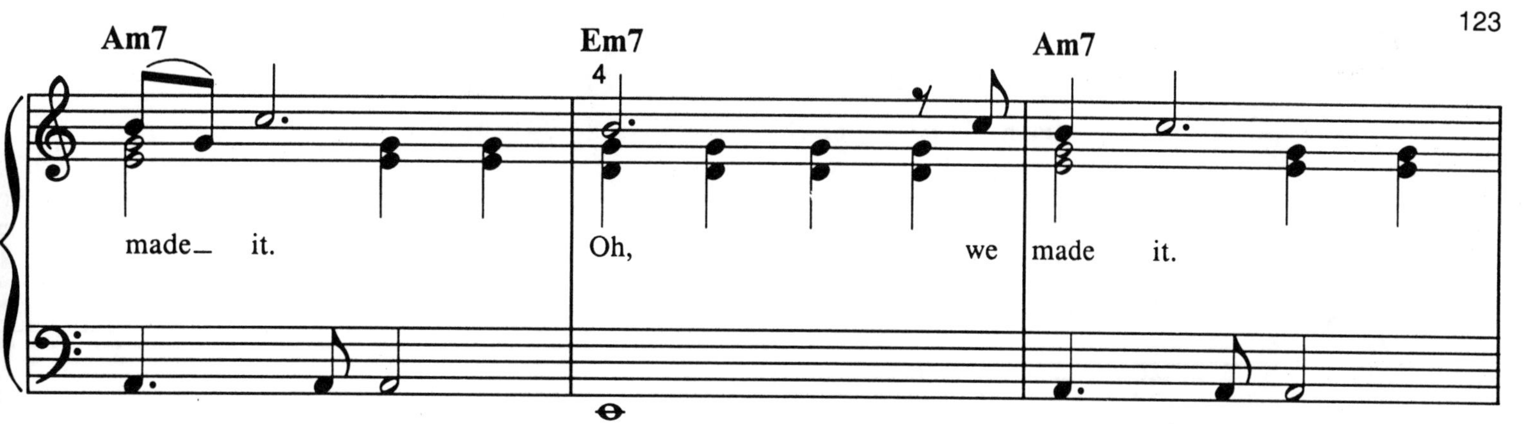
Am7
Em7
Am7
made it.
Oh, we made it.

F/G
C
G/C
Looks like we made it.

F/C
C
G/C
Looks like we made it.

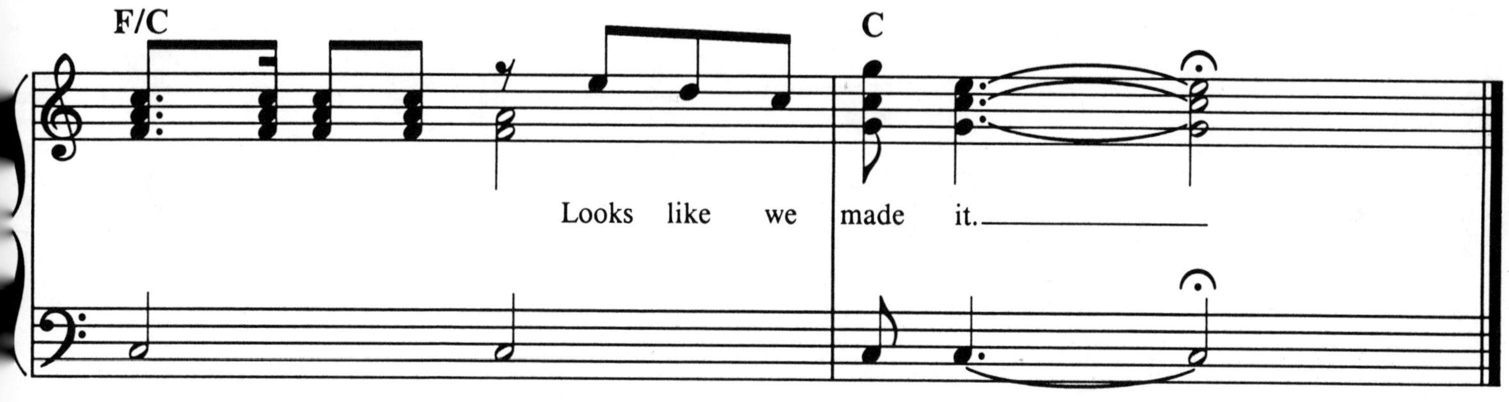
F/C
C
Looks like we made it.

NADIA'S THEME

from THE YOUNG AND THE RESTLESS

By BARRY DeVORZON
and PERRY BOTKIN, JR.

© 1971 (Renewed 1999) SCREEN GEMS-EMI MUSIC INC.
All Rights Reserved International Copyright Secured Used by Permission

loco
p
cresc.
rit.

mp
a tempo
p
rit.
decresc.
8va
pp

NIGHT FEVER

from SATURDAY NIGHT FEVER

Words and Music by BARRY GIBB, MAURICE GIBB and ROBIN GIBB

Copyright © 1977 by Gibb Brothers Music
All Rights Administered by Careers-BMG Music Publishing, Inc.
International Copyright Secured All Rights Reserved

Dm
F
B♭
danc - in' out there. __ If it's some - thin' we can share, we can
high - er in my walk - in'. And I'm glow - in' in the dark; I give you

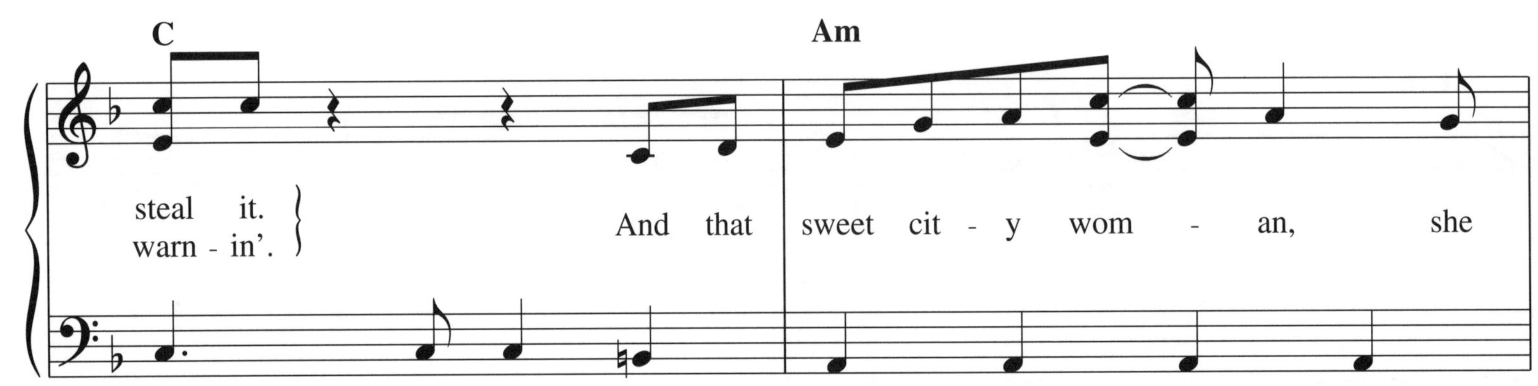
C
Am
steal it.
warn - in'.
And that sweet cit - y wom - an, she

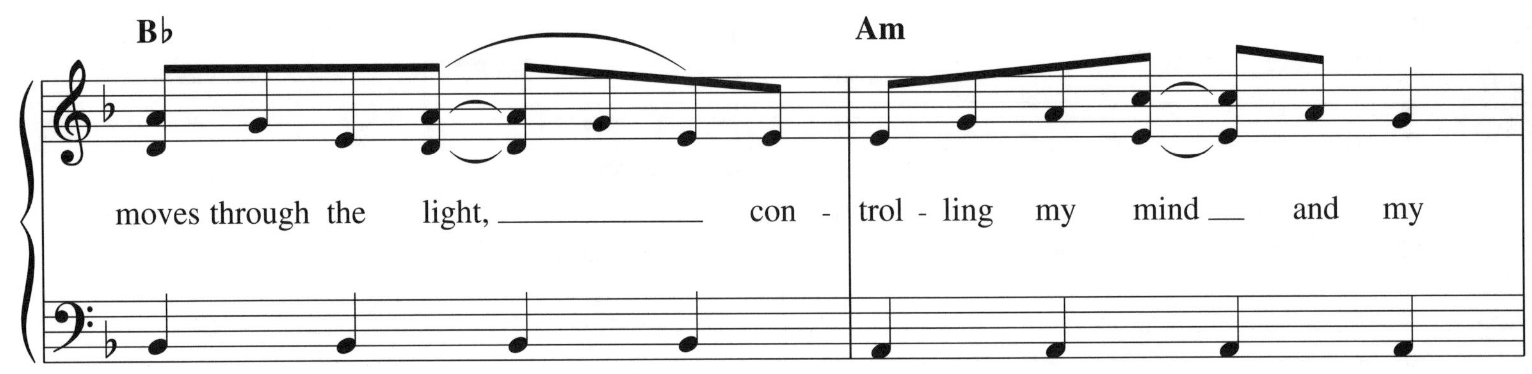
B♭
Am
moves through the light, ___ con - trol - ling my mind __ and my

Em
Am
soul. ___ When you reach out for me, __ yeah, and the

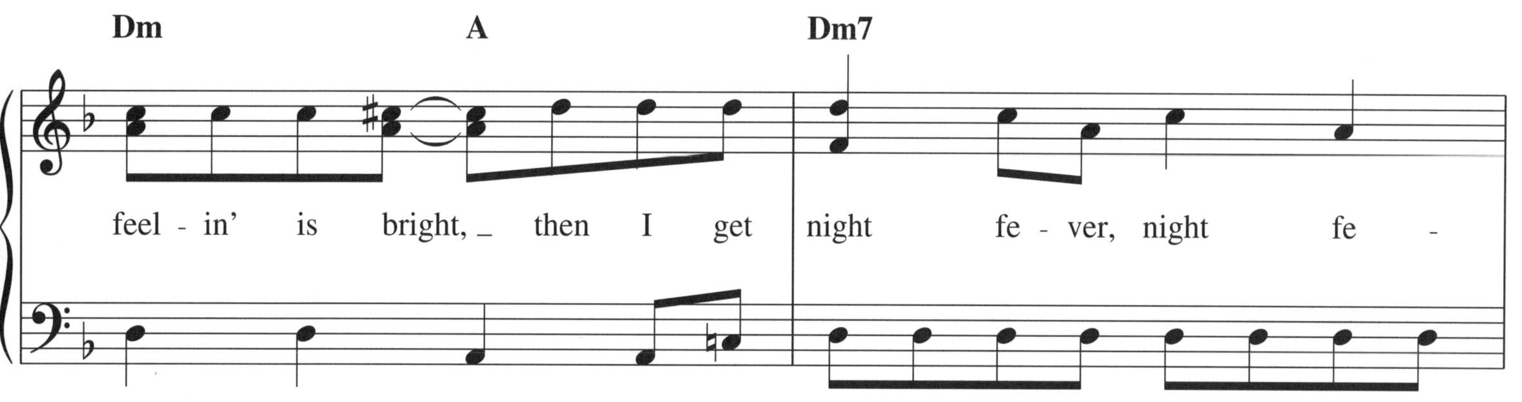
Dm
A
Dm7
feel - in' is bright, _ then I get night fe - ver, night fe -

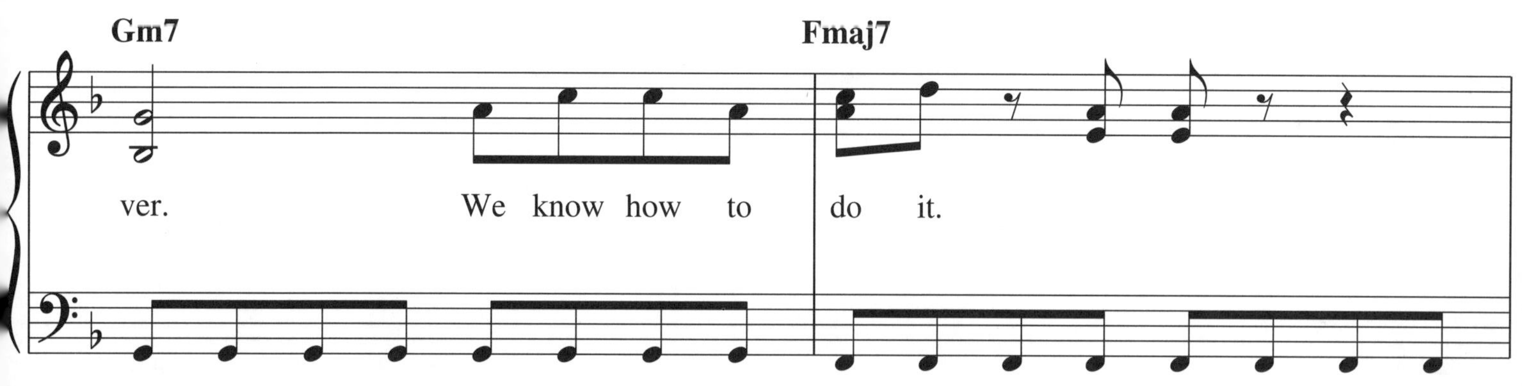
Gm7
Fmaj7
ver. We know how to do it.

Gm7
Dm7
Gim - me that night fe - ver, night fe -

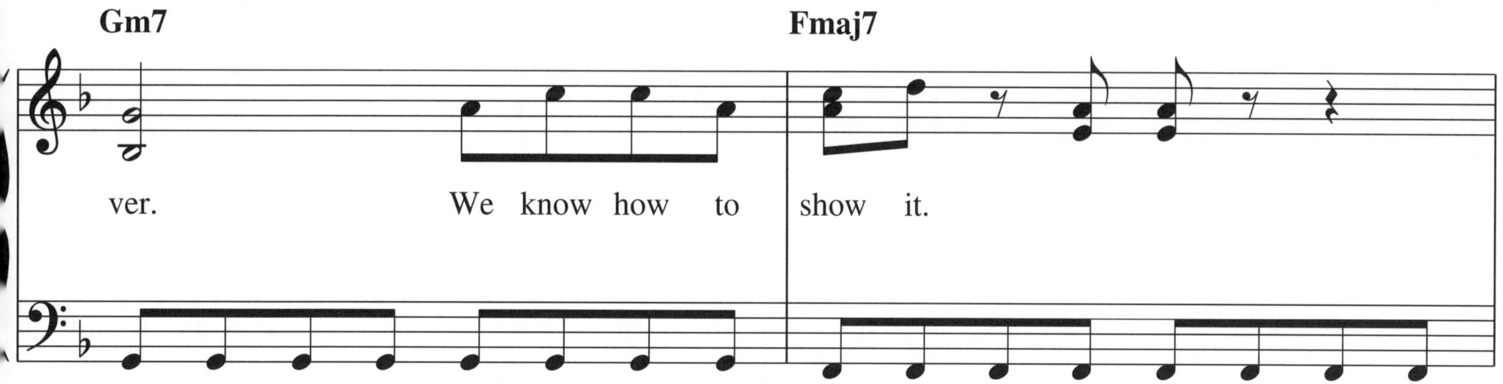
Gm7
Fmaj7
ver. We know how to show it.

Gm7
G
Here I am,

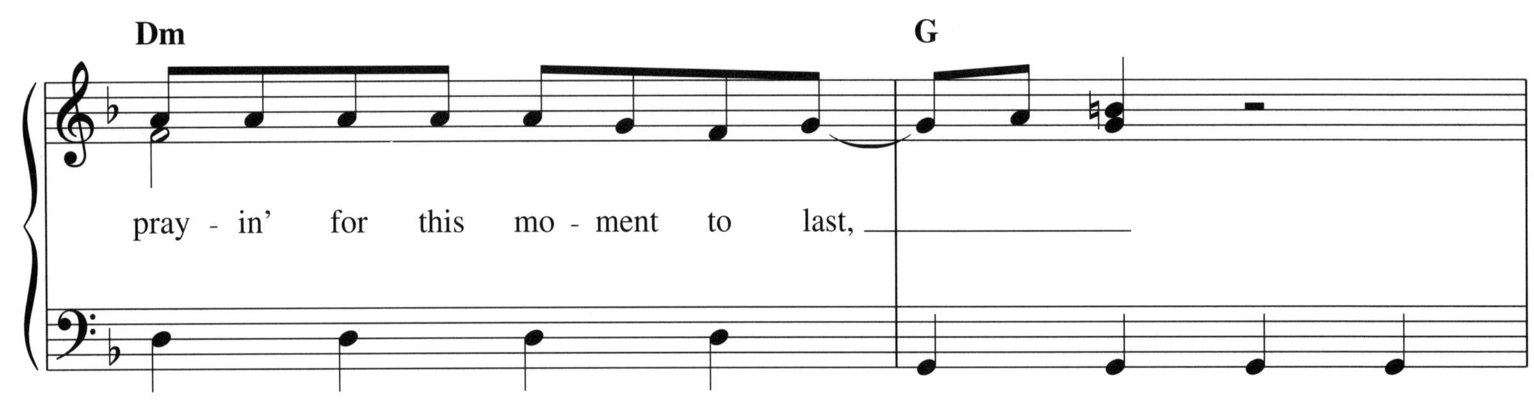
Dm
G
pray - in' for this mo - ment to last,

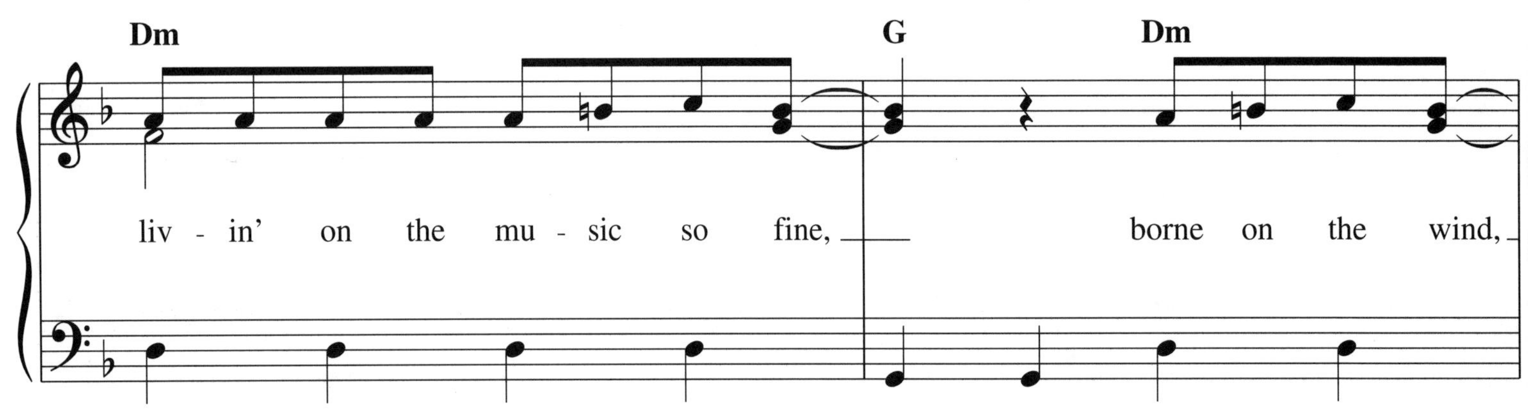
Dm
G
Dm
liv - in' on the mu - sic so fine,
borne on the wind,

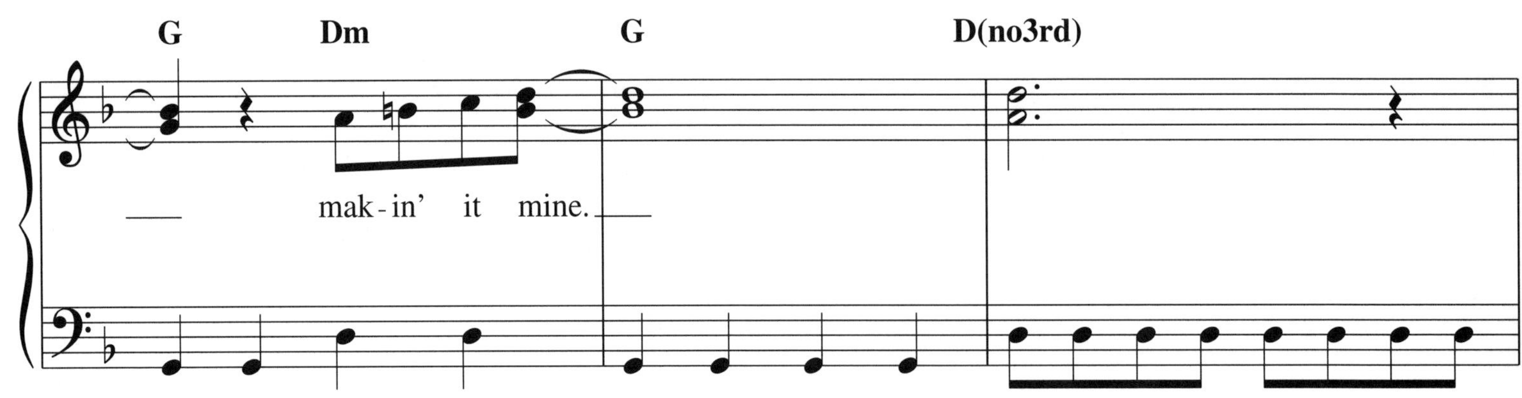
G
Dm
G
D(no3rd)
mak - in' it mine.

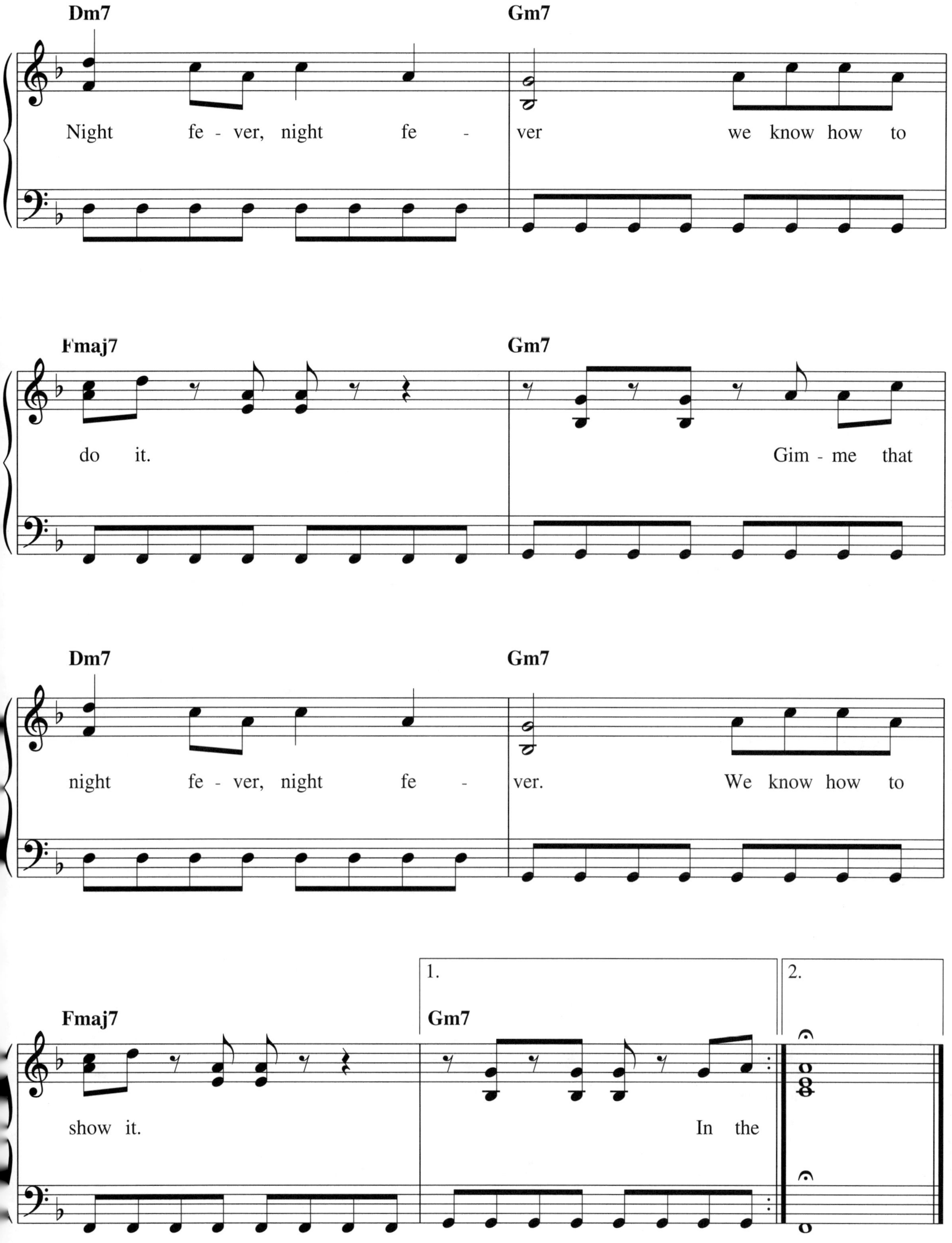
Dm7
Gm7
Night fe - ver, night fe - ver we know how to
Fmaj7
Gm7
do it. Gim - me that
Dm7
Gm7
night fe - ver, night fe - ver. We know how to
1.
2.
Fmaj7
Gm7
show it. In the

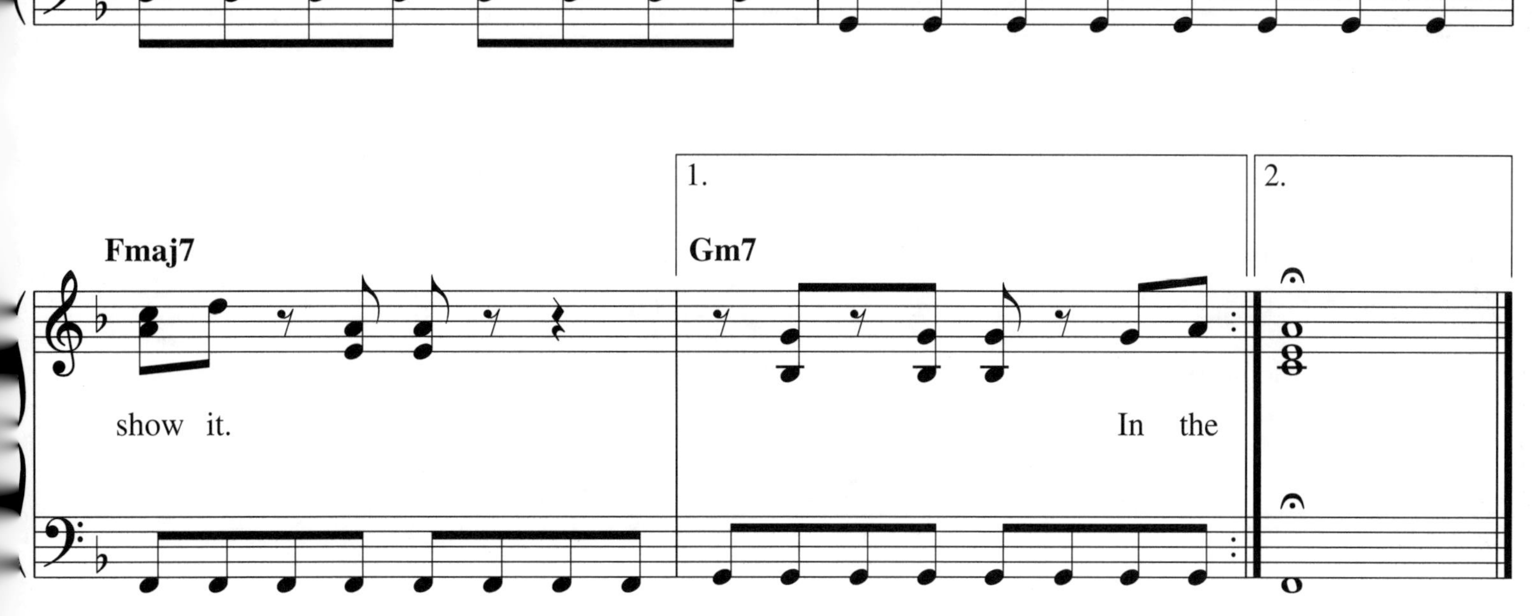

ONE LESS BELL TO ANSWER

Lyric by HAL DAVID
Music by BURT BACHARACH

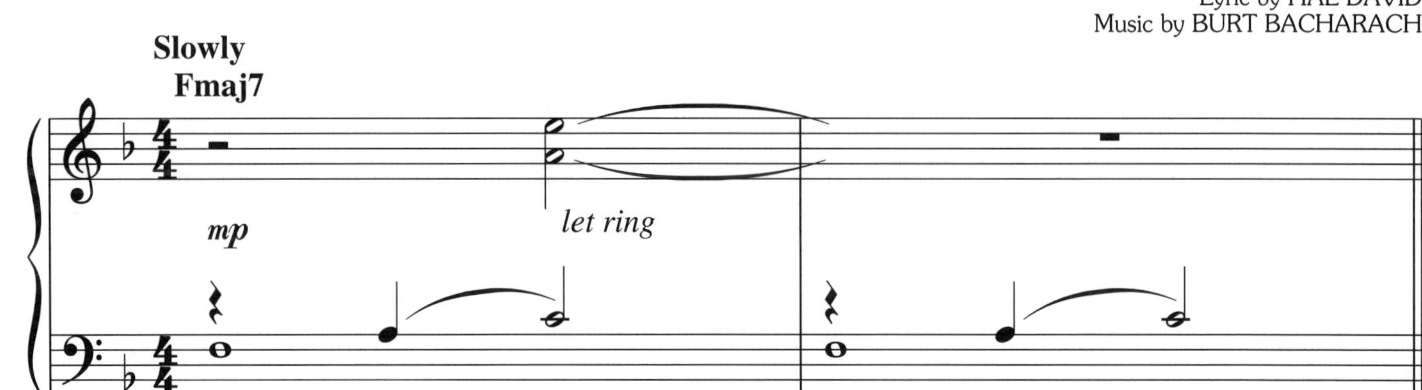

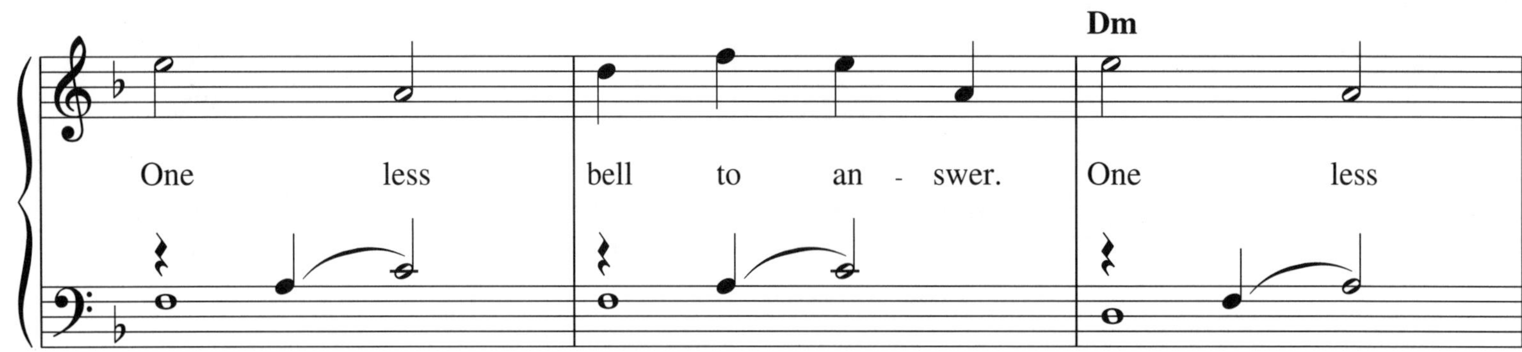

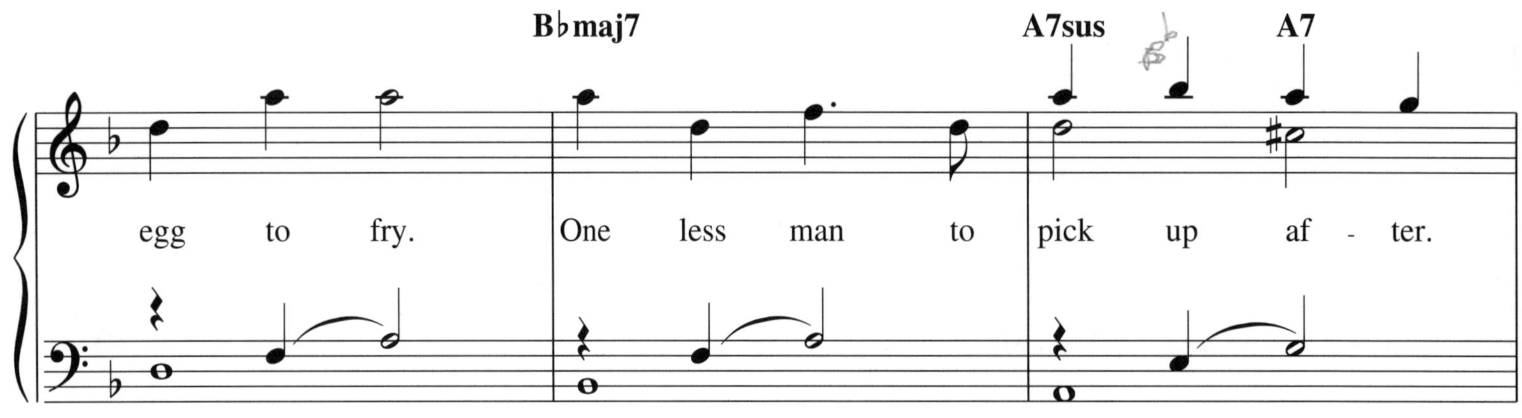

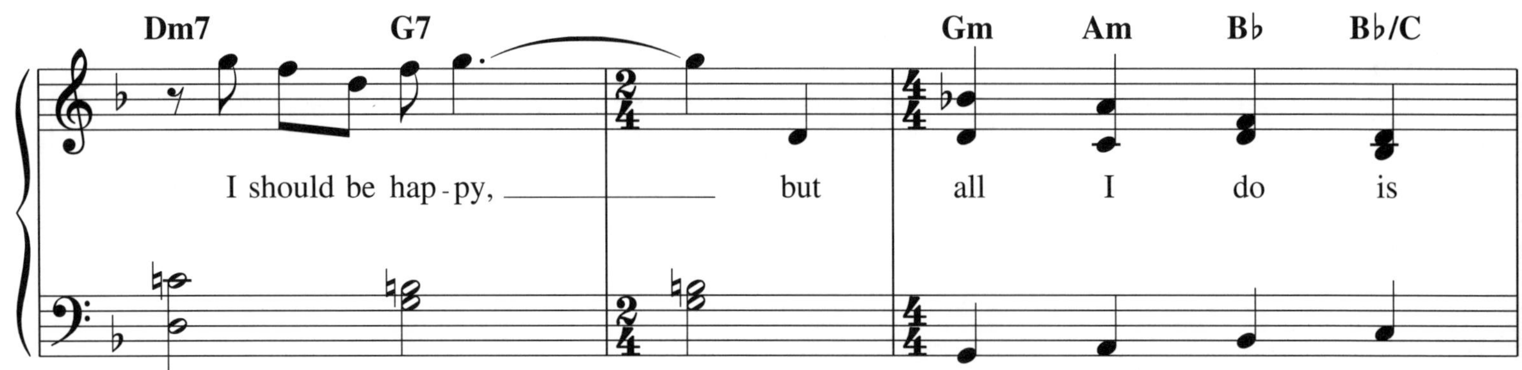

Copyright © 1967 (Renewed) Casa David and New Hidden Valley Music
International Copyright Secured All Rights Reserved

Fmaj7
Dm
cry, cry, no more laugh - ter. Oh, why

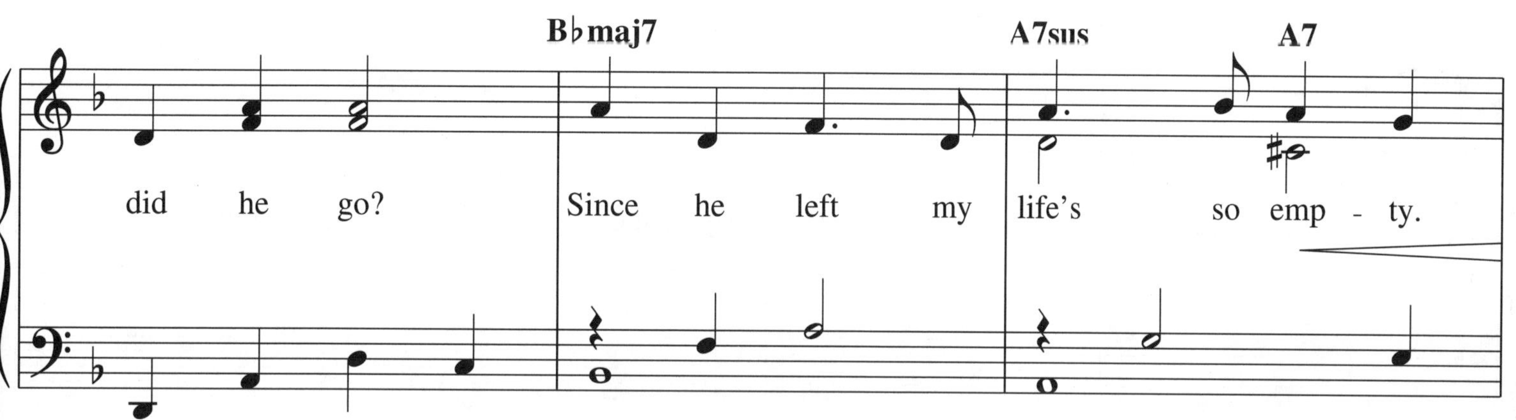
B♭maj7
A7sus
A7
did he go? Since he left my life's so emp - ty.

F♯
B♭m
Though I try to for - get, it just can't be done. Each time the
mf

B
A♭/B♭
B♭7
E♭maj7
Gm7
door - bell rings I still run. I don't know how in the world to stop

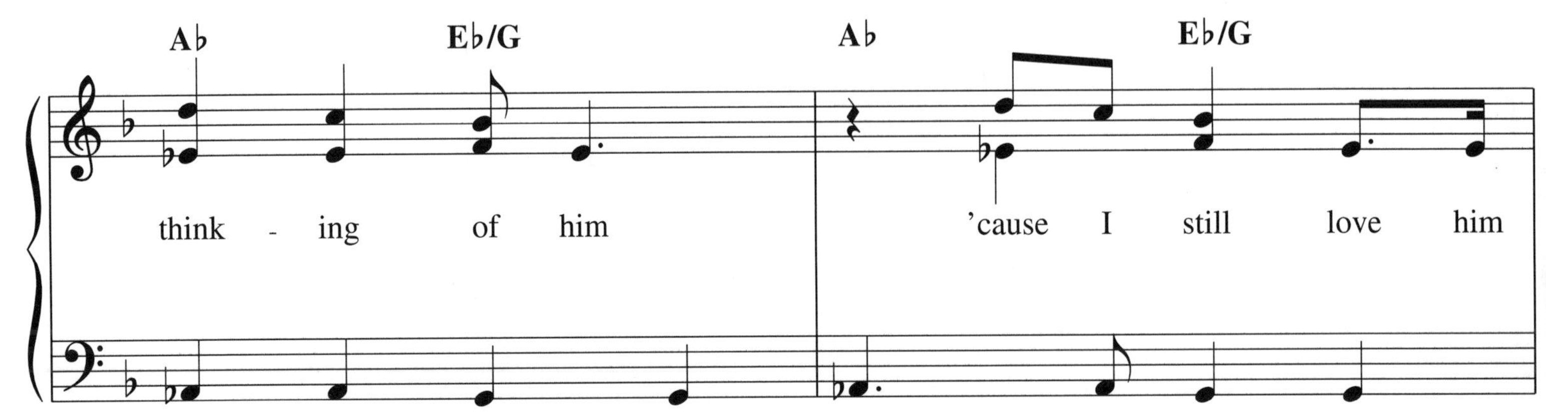
A♭
E♭/G
A♭
E♭/G
think - ing of him
'cause I still love him

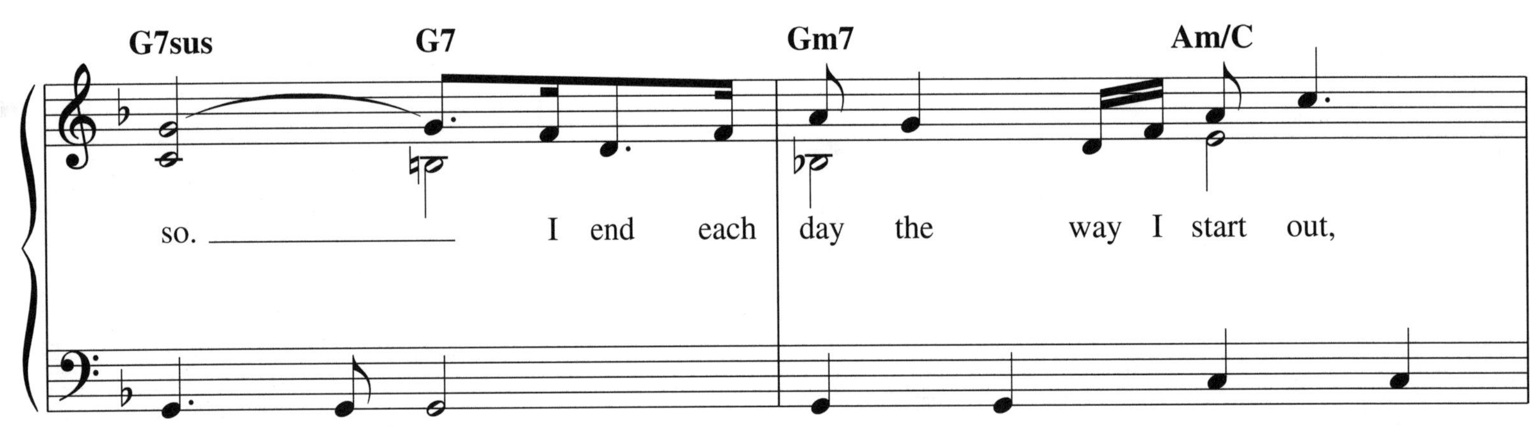
G7sus
G7
Gm7
Am/C
so. I end each
day the way I start out,

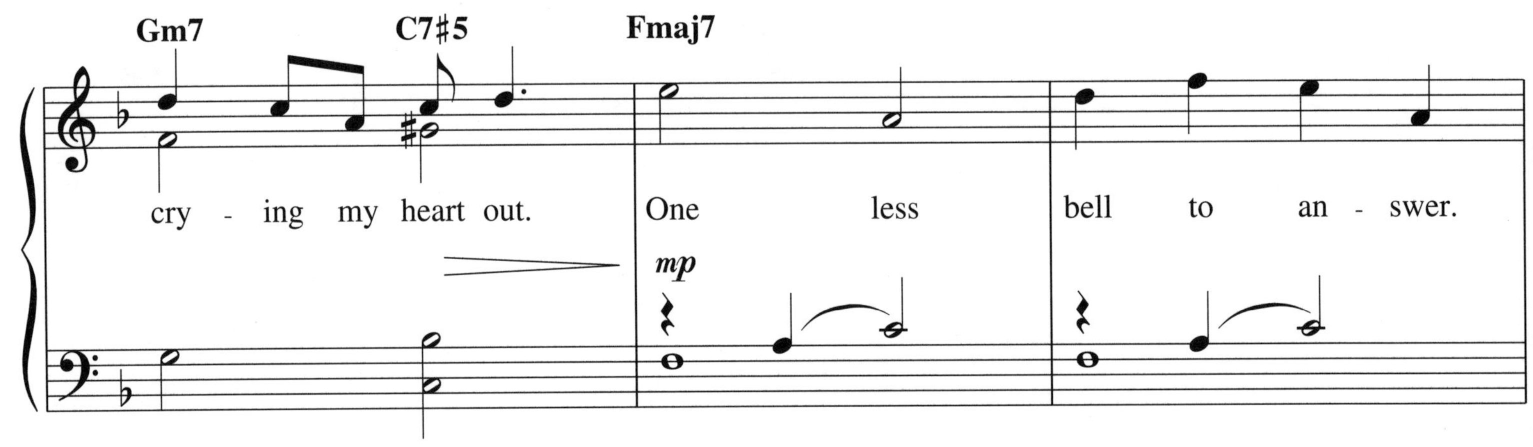
Gm7
C7♯5
Fmaj7
cry - ing my heart out.
One less
bell to an - swer.
mp

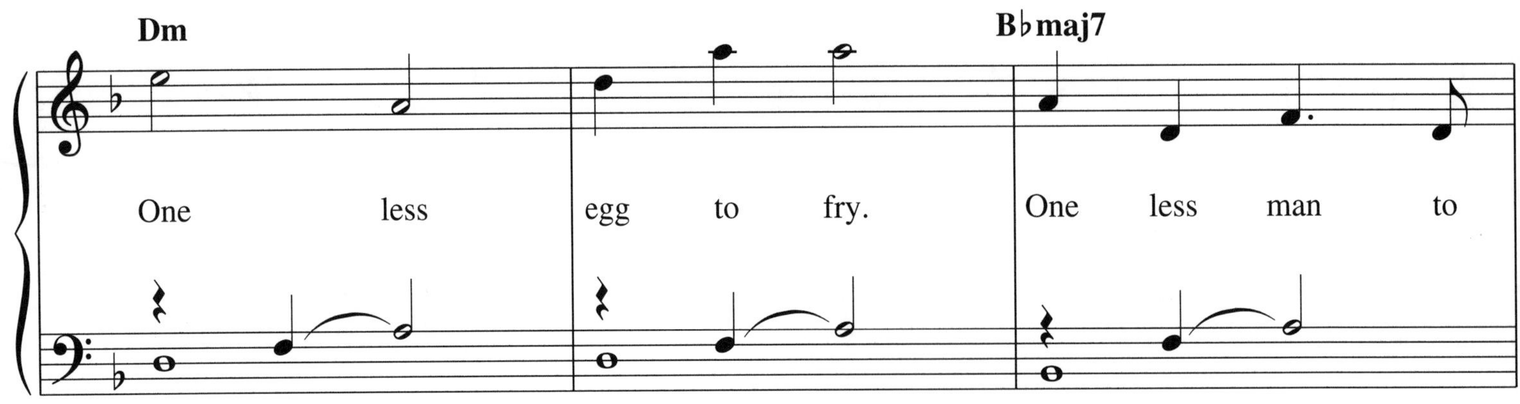
Dm
B♭maj7
One less
egg to fry.
One less man to

Am7
Dm7
Gm7
B♭/C
Am7♭5
D7♭9
pick up af - ter.
No more laugh - ter,
no more love
f
Gm7
Am7
B♭maj7
B♭/C
since he
went a - way.
Fmaj7
ff poco a poco dim.
Dm
B♭/C
Repeat ad lib.
Fmaj7
p

OUR HOUSE

Words and Music by
GRAHAM NASH

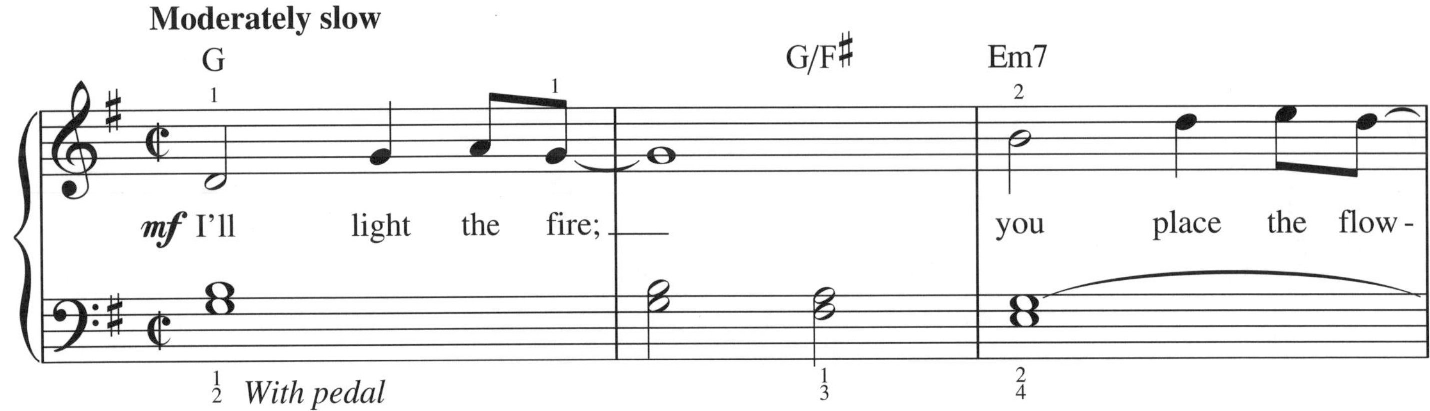

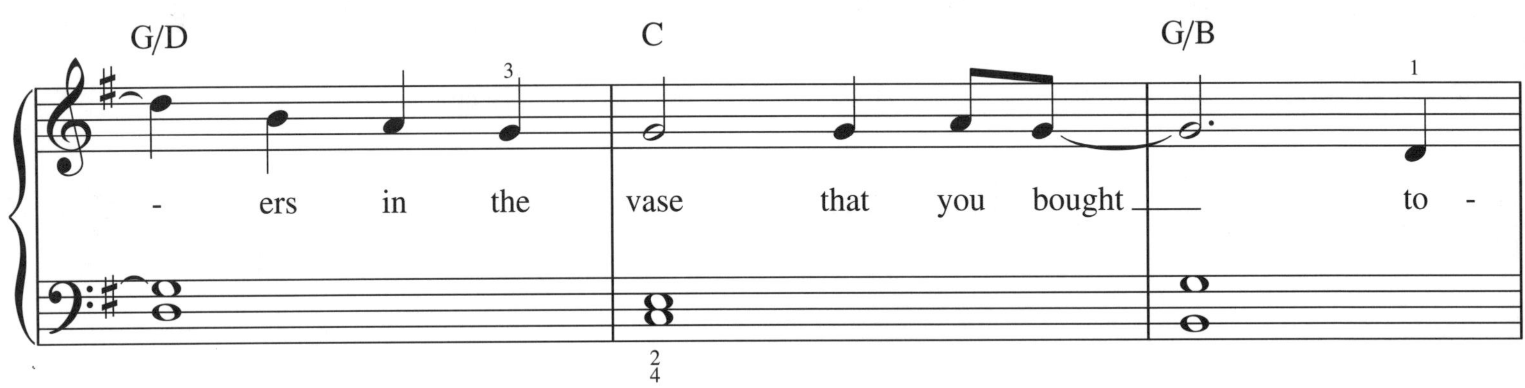

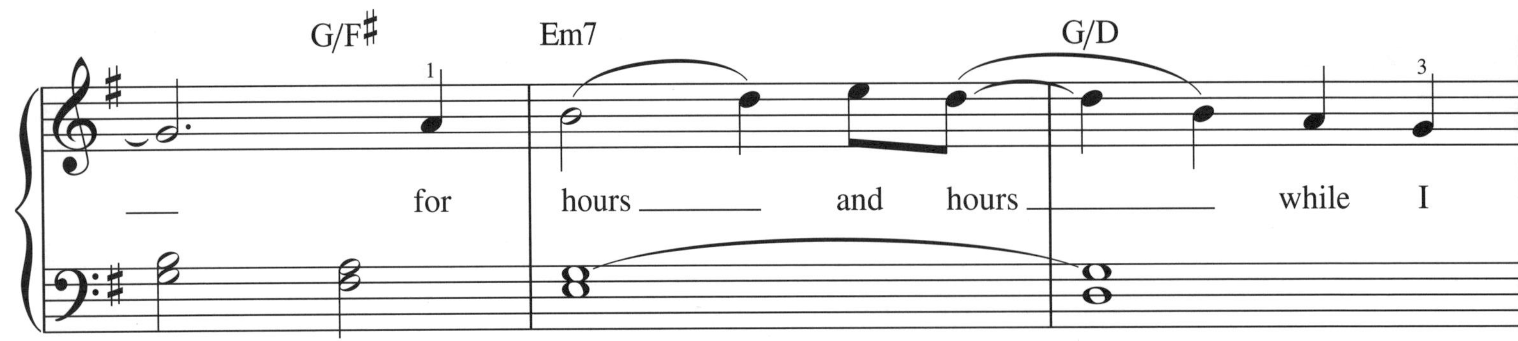

Copyright © 1970 Nash Notes
Copyright Renewed
All Rights Administered by Sony/ATV Music Publishing, 8 Music Square West, Nashville, TN 37203
International Copyright Secured All Rights Reserved

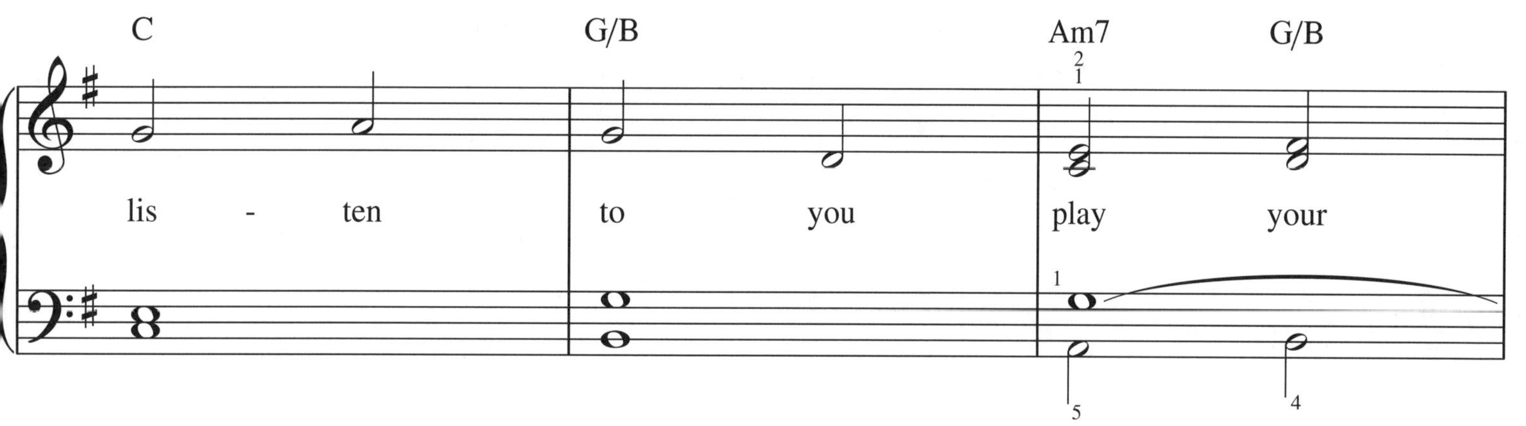
C
G/B
Am7
G/B
lis - ten
to you
play your

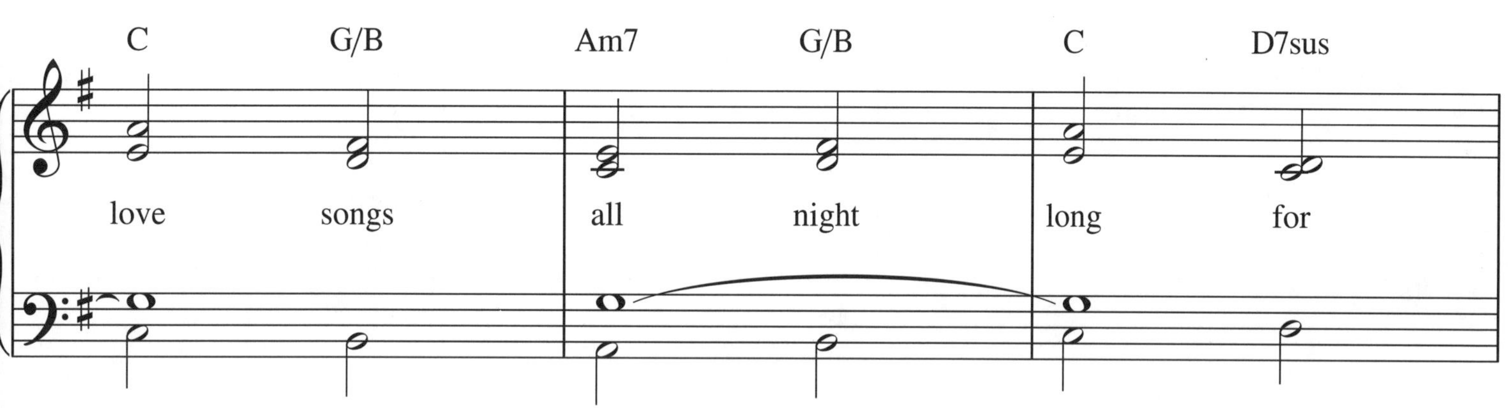
C
G/B
Am7
G/B
C
D7sus
love songs
all night
long for

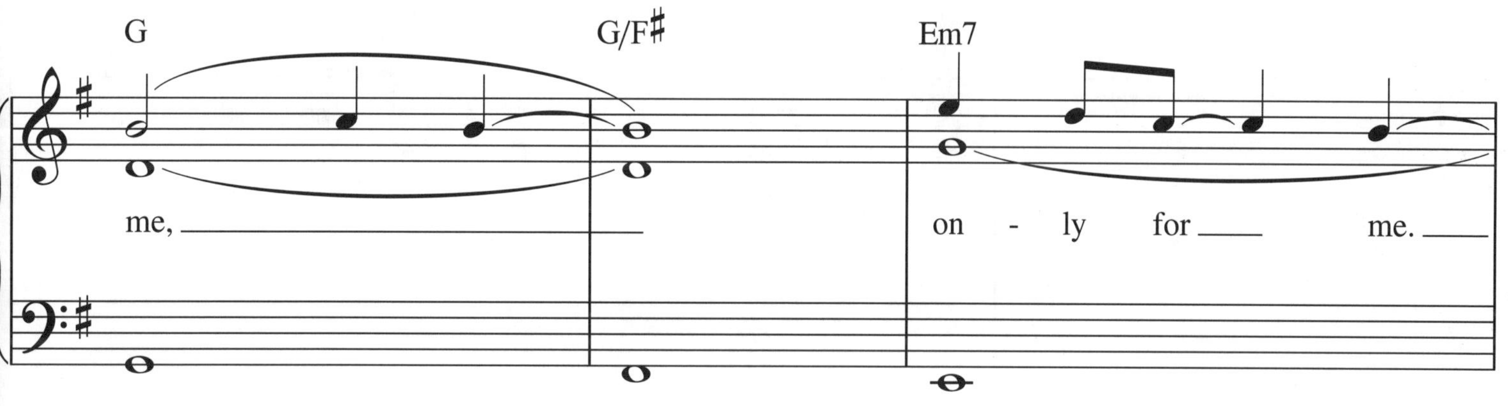
G
G/F♯
Em7
me,
on - ly for me.

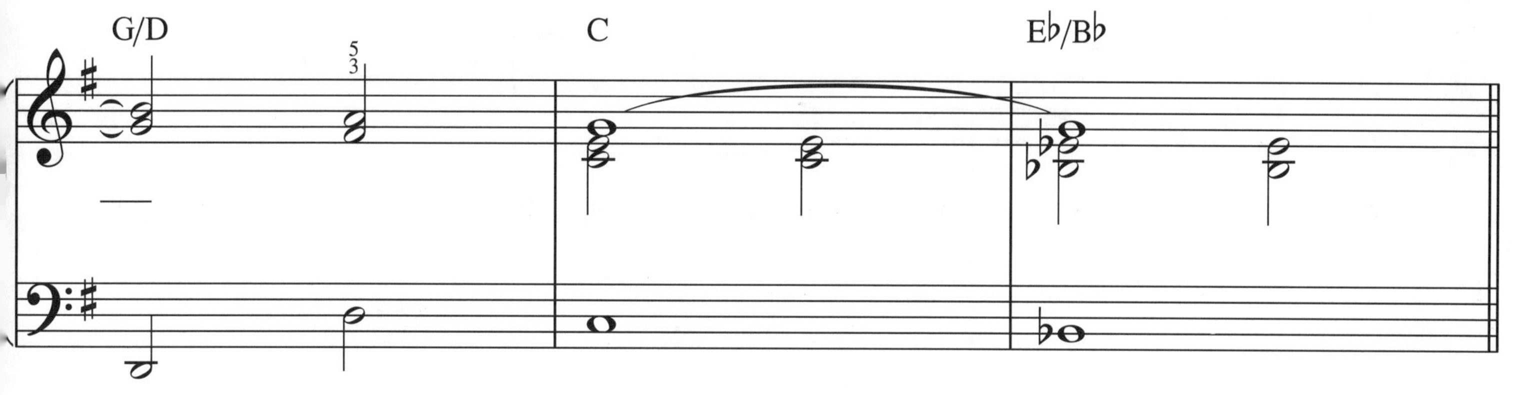
G/D
C
E♭/B♭

G
G/F♯
Em7
2
1
3
1
2
1
1
Come to me now and rest your head for just

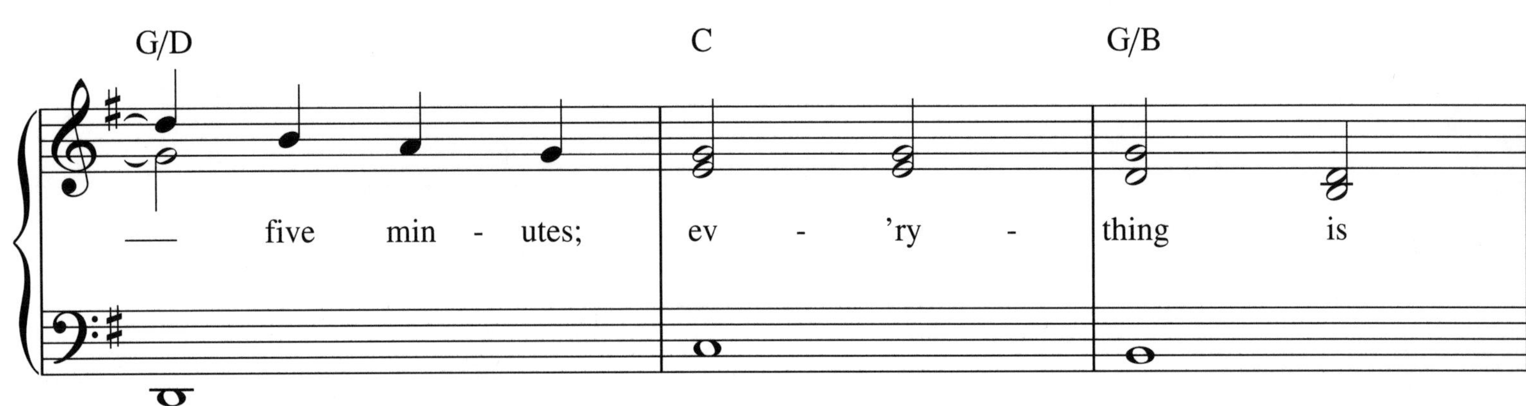
G/D
C
G/B
five min - utes; ev - 'ry - thing is

Am7
G
done.
Such a co - zy

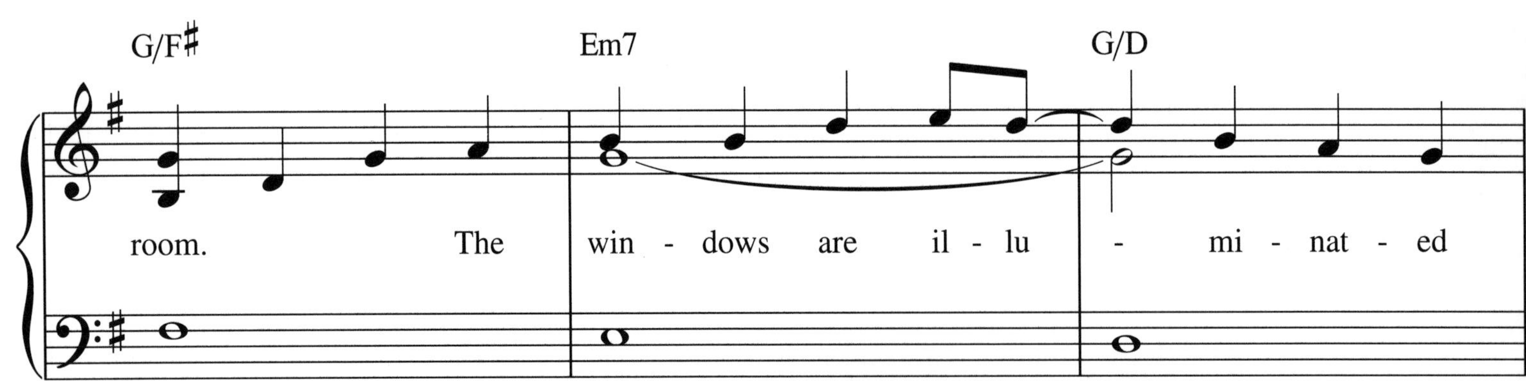
G/F♯
Em7
G/D
room. The win - dows are il - lu - mi - nat - ed

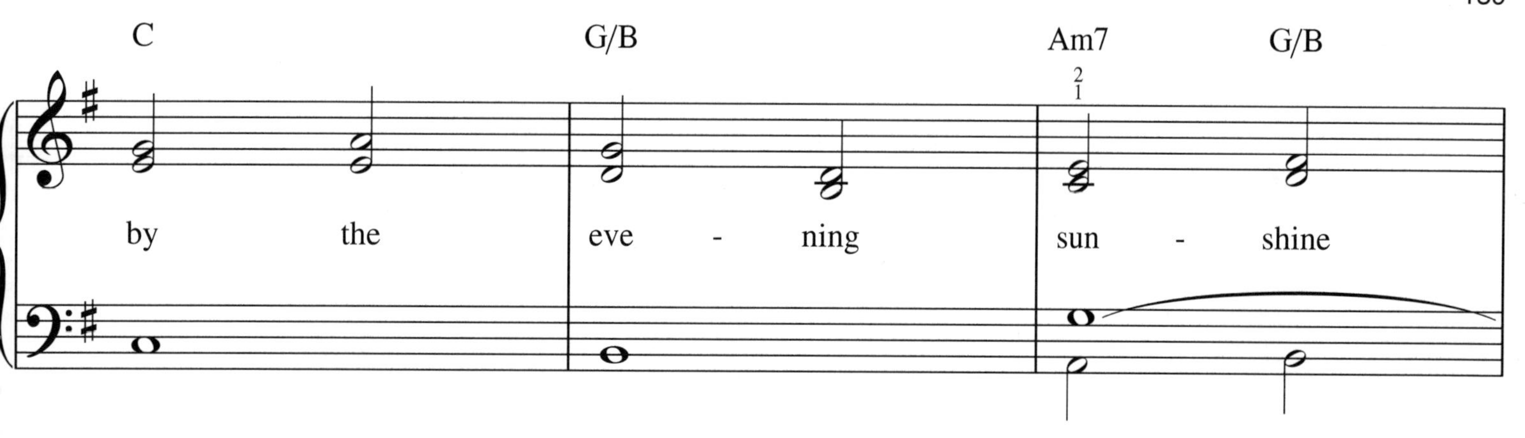
C
G/B
Am7
G/B
by the eve - ning sun - shine

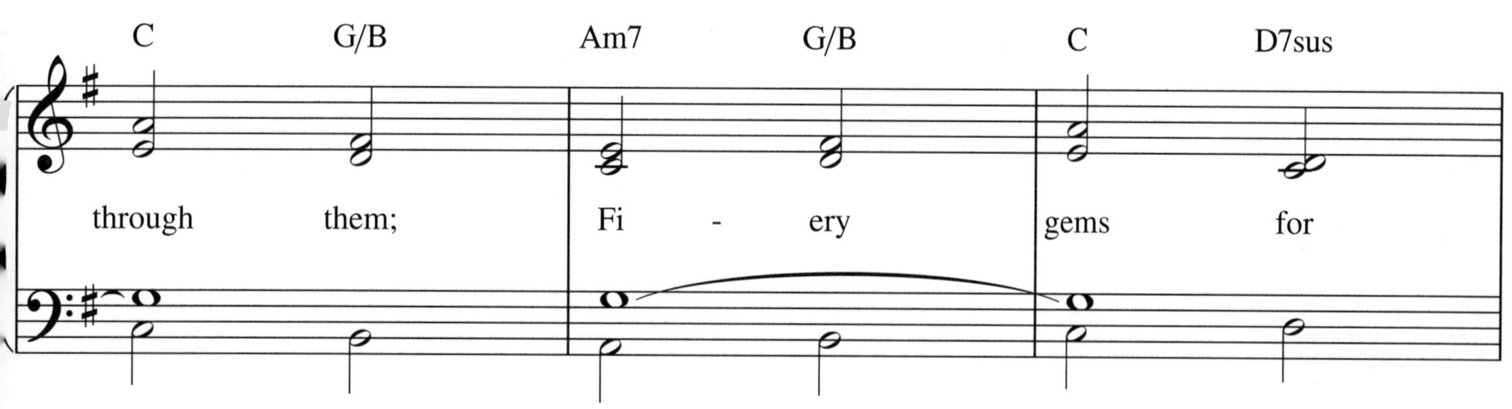
C
G/B
Am7
G/B
C
D7sus
through them; Fi - ery gems for

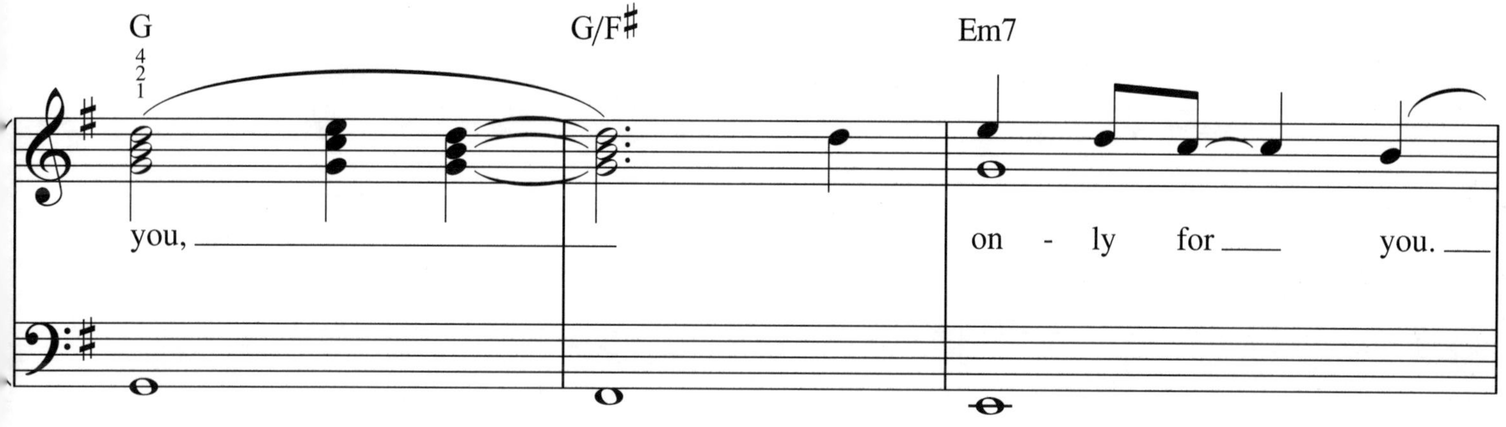
G
G/F♯
Em7
you, on - ly for you.

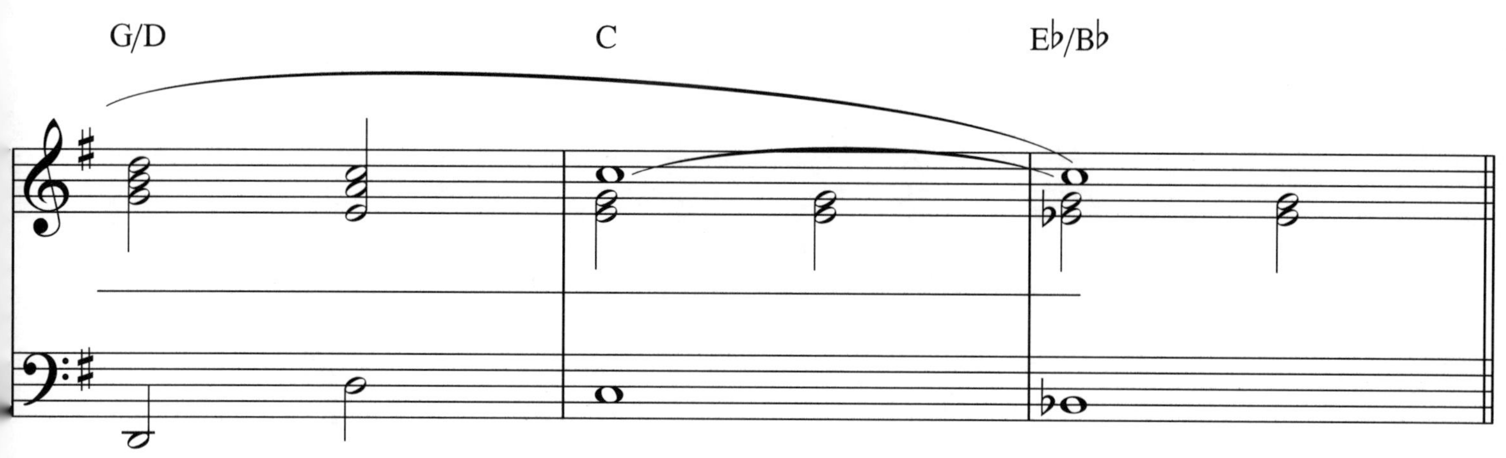
G/D
C
E♭/B♭

G
G/F♯
Em7
Our house is a ver - y, ver - y, ver - y fine

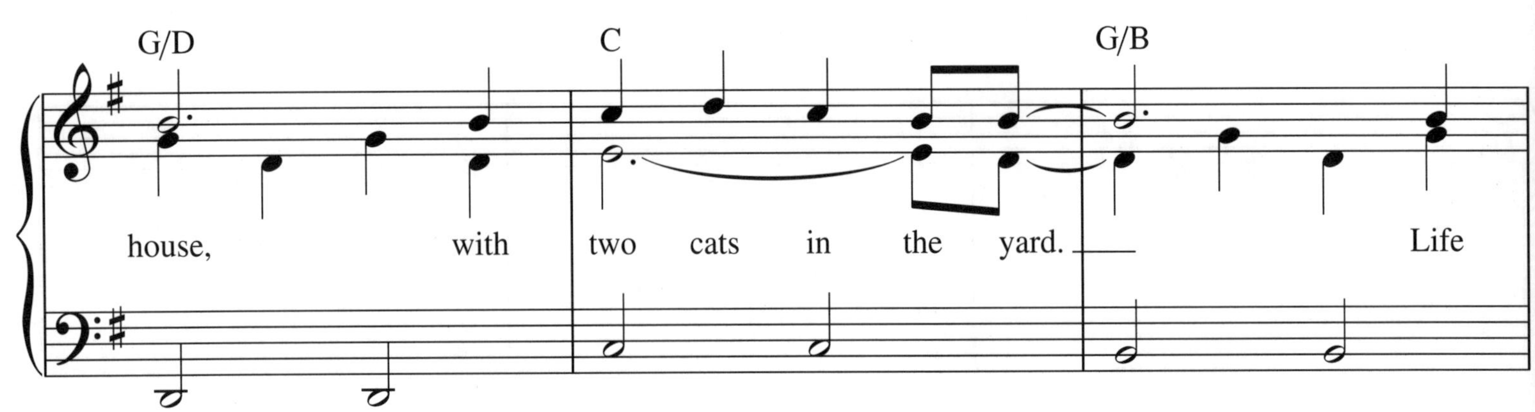
G/D
C
G/B
house, with two cats in the yard. Life

C
G/B
C
used to be so hard; now ev - 'ry - thing is eas -

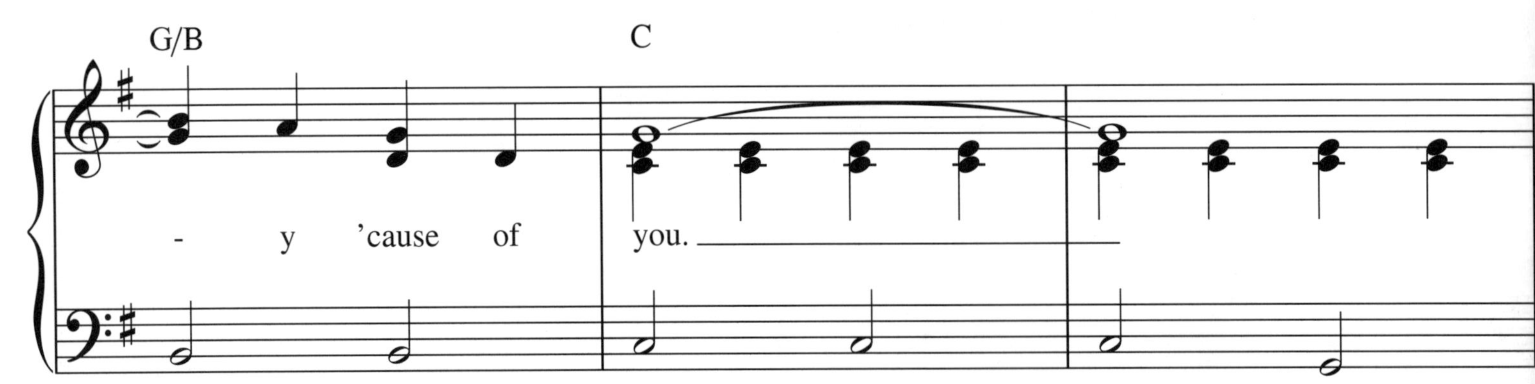
G/B
C
- y 'cause of you.

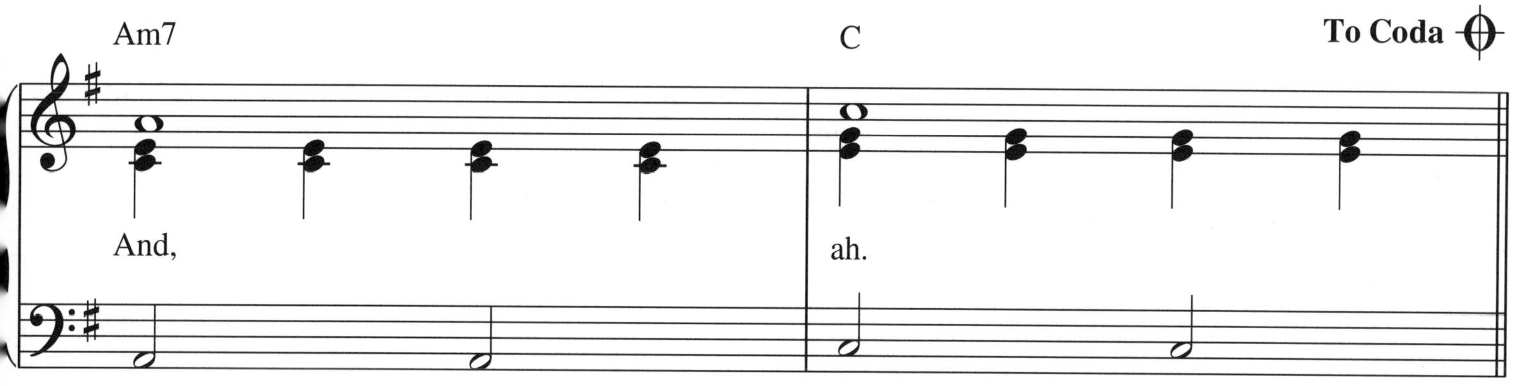
Am7
C
To Coda
And,
ah.

G
G/F♯
Em7
5
2
La la la la la la la la la la la

G/D
1.
C
G/B
la la la la la la la la la la la la la

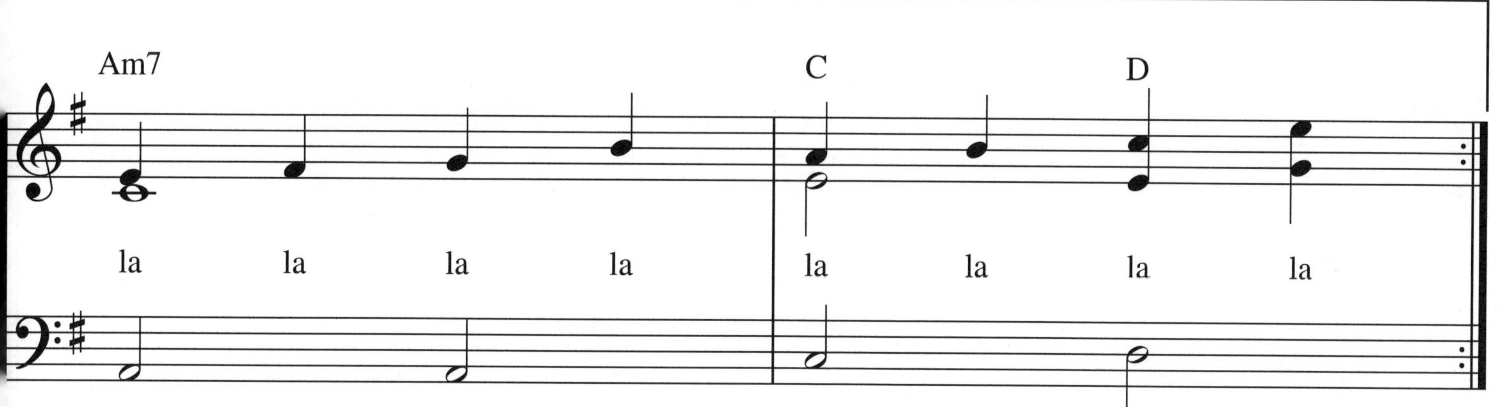
Am7
C
D
la la la la la la la la

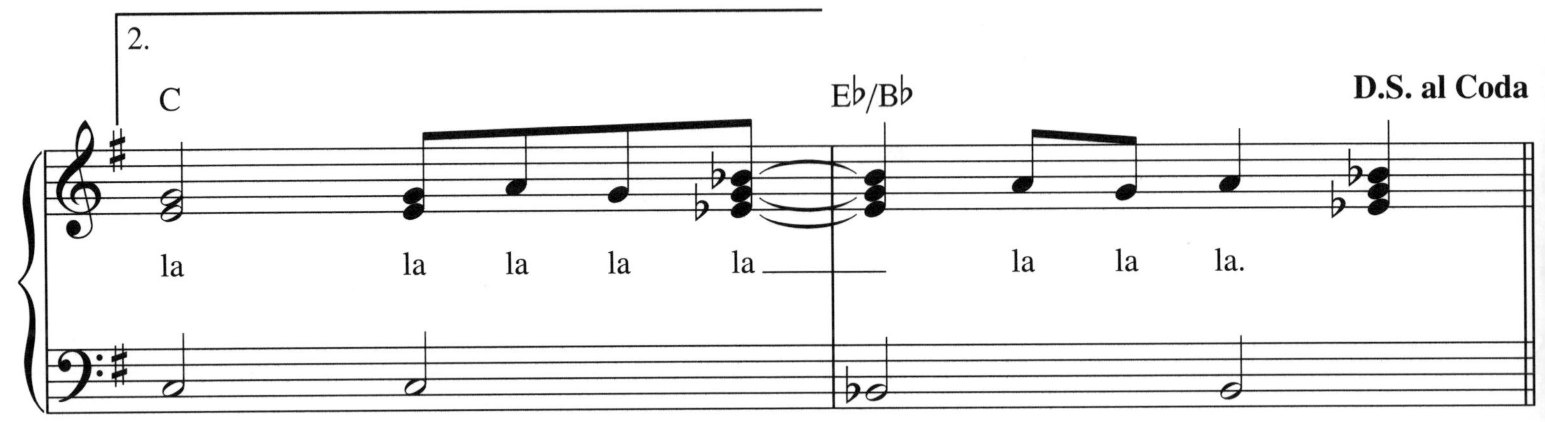
2.
C
E♭/B♭
D.S. al Coda
la la la la la
la la la.

CODA
Much slower, freely
G
G/F♯
I'll light the fire, while

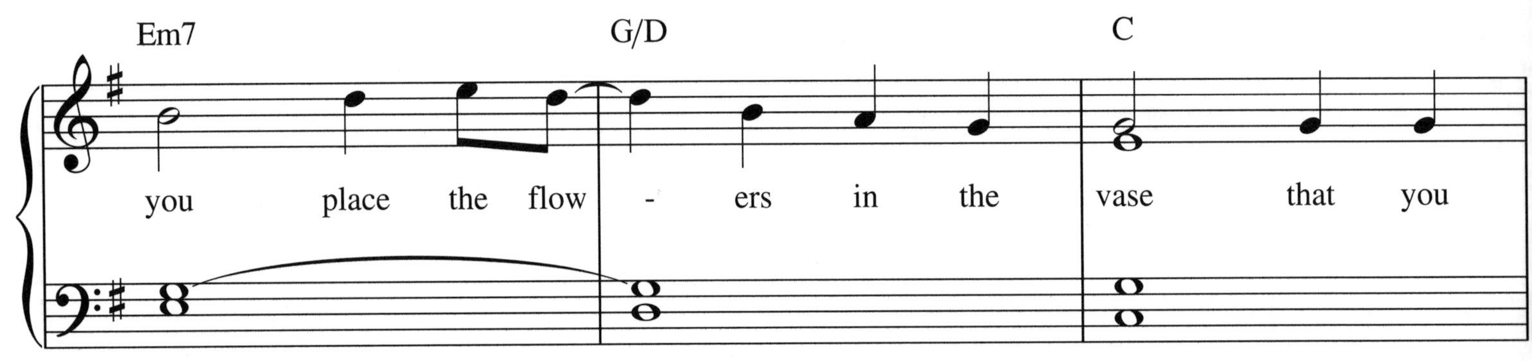
Em7
G/D
C
you place the flow - ers in the vase that you

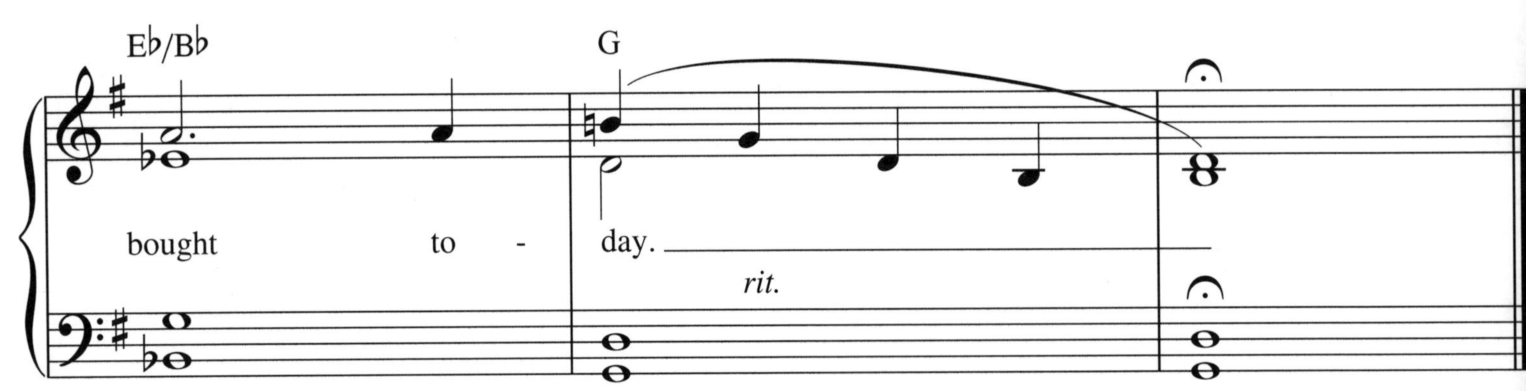
E♭/B♭
G
bought to - day.
rit.

OYE COMO VA

Words and Music by
TITO PUENTE

© 1963, 1970 (Renewed 1991, 1998) EMI FULL KEEL MUSIC
All Rights Reserved International Copyright Secured Used by Permission

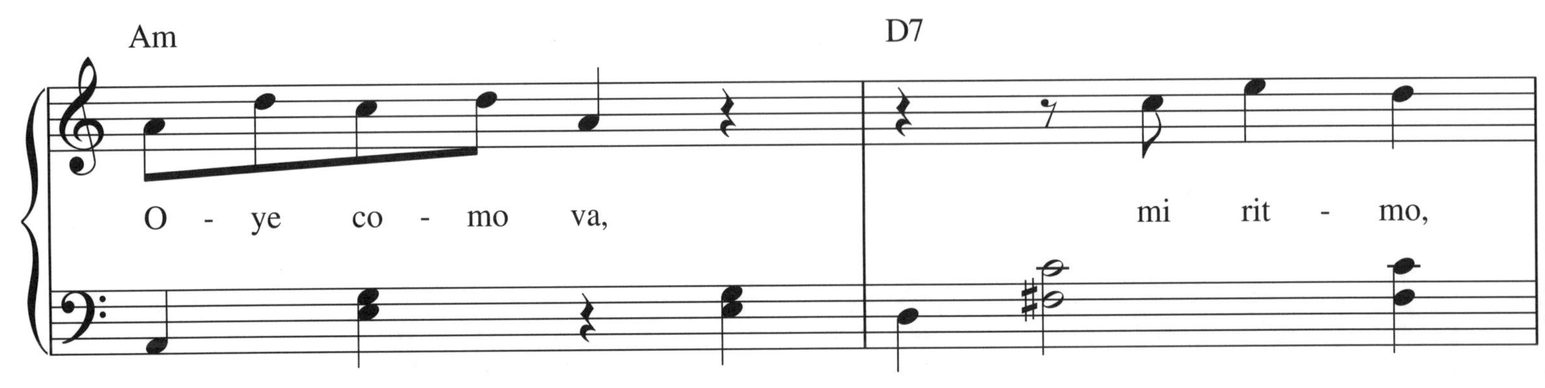
Am
D7
O - ye co - mo va,
mi rit - mo,

To Coda
Am
D7
bue - no pa go - zar,
mu - la - ta.

Am
D7
Am/E

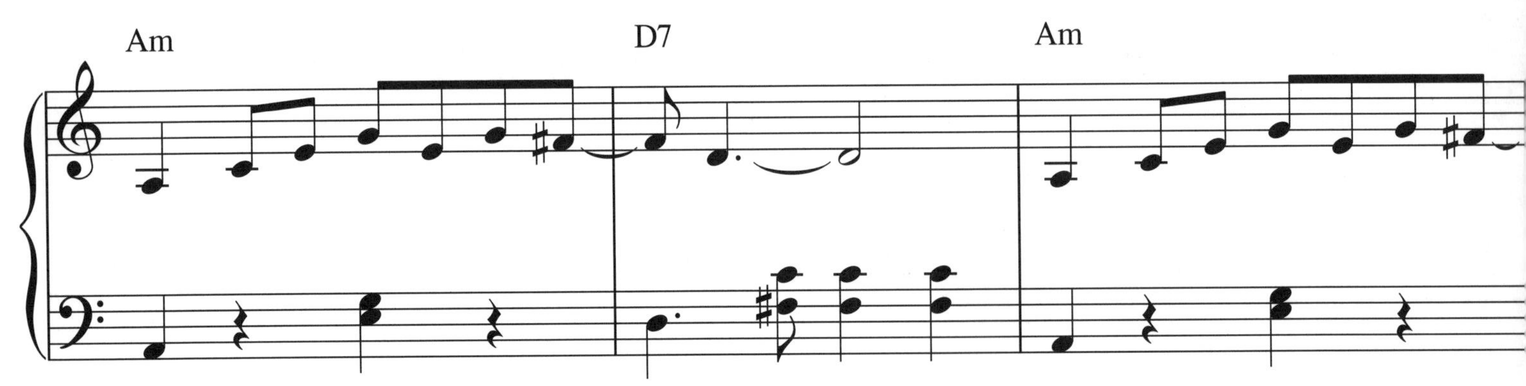
Am
D7
Am

D7
Am
D7

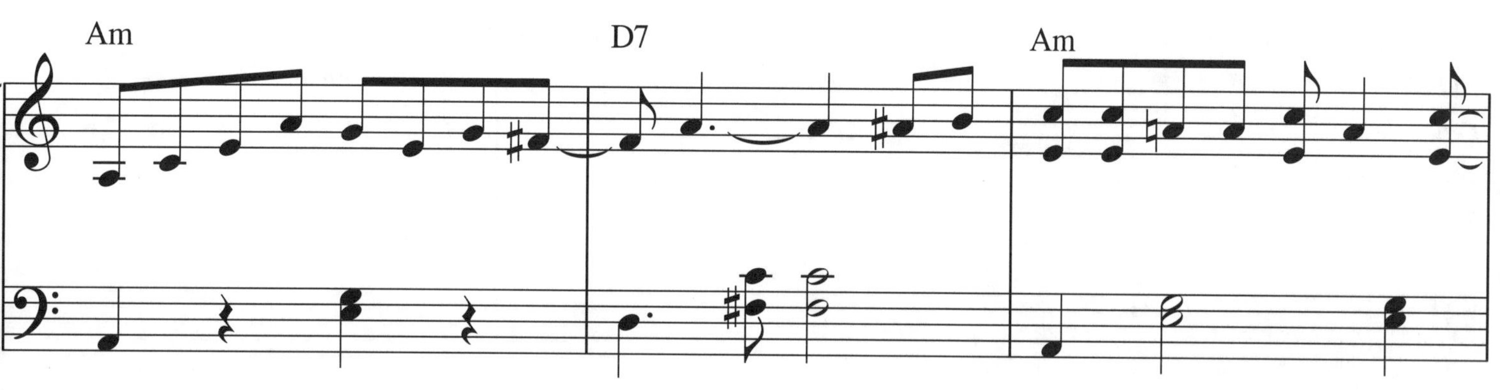
Am
D7
Am

D7
Am
D7

Am
D7
Am

D7
Am
D7
Am/E

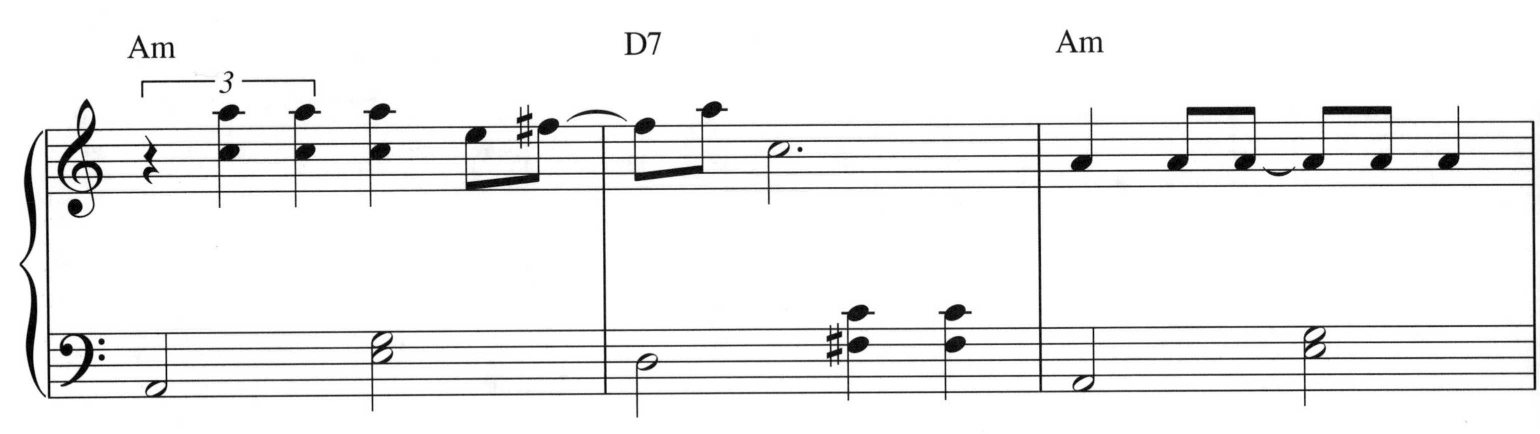
Am
3
D7
Am

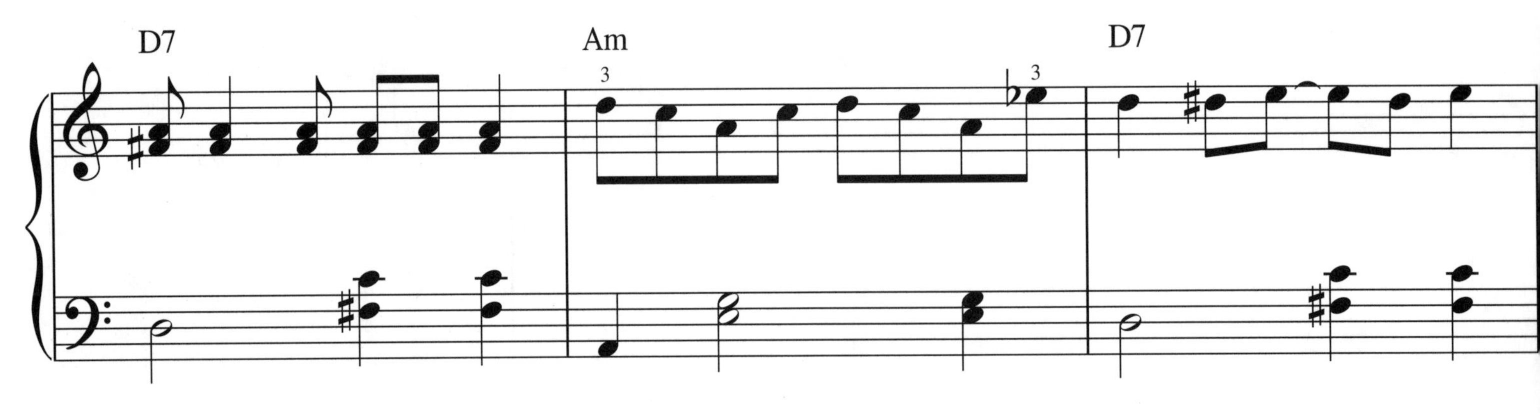
D7
Am
3
3
D7

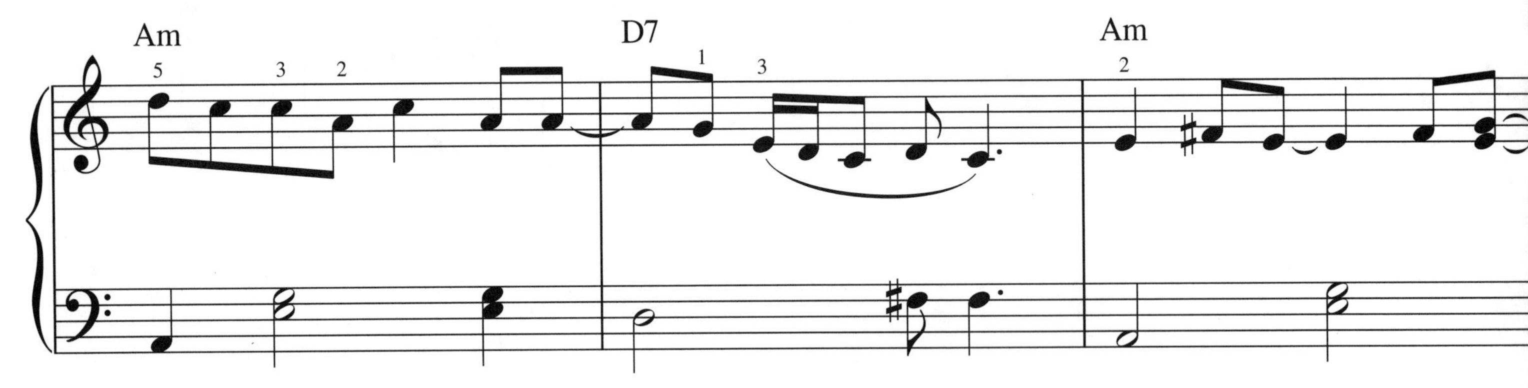
Am
5
3
2
D7
1
3
Am
2

D.S. al Coda

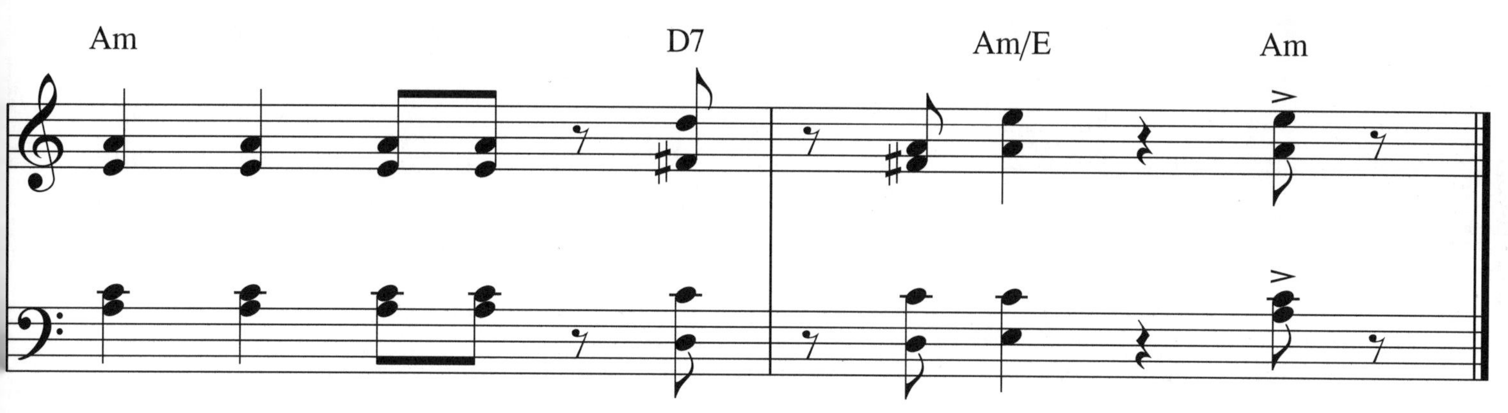

PRECIOUS AND FEW

Words and Music by
WALTER D. NIMS

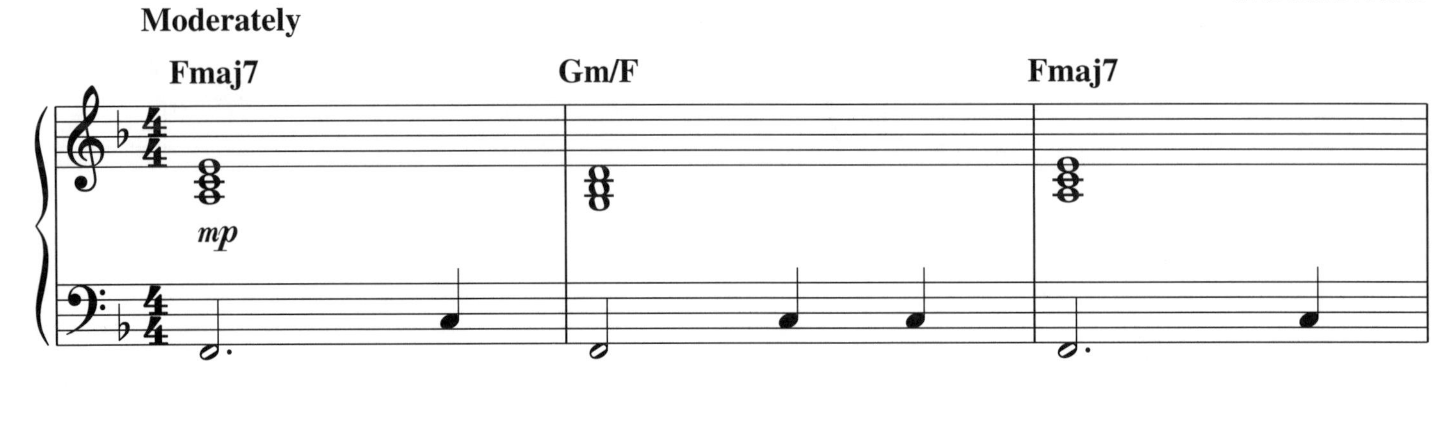

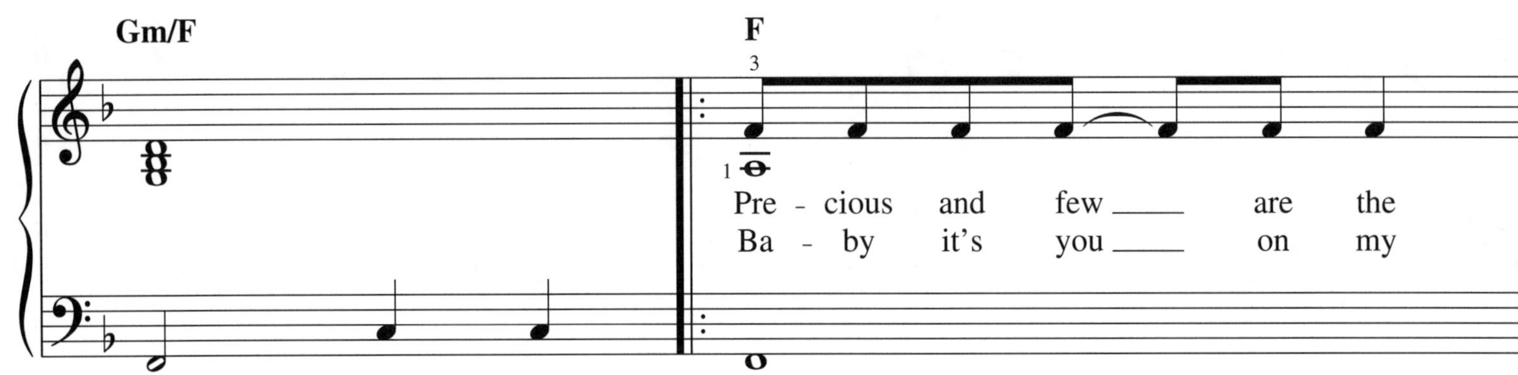

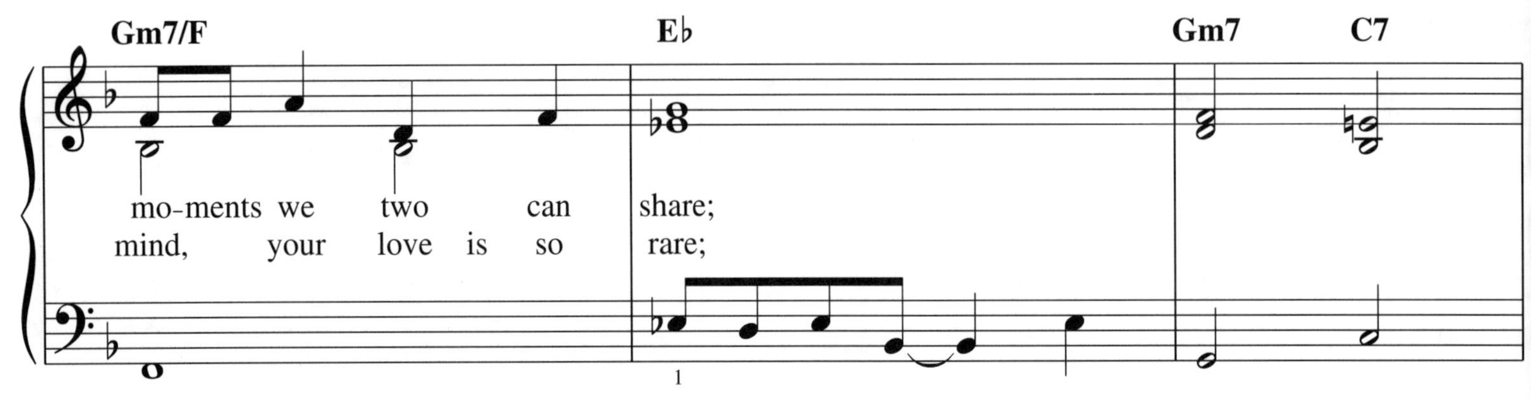

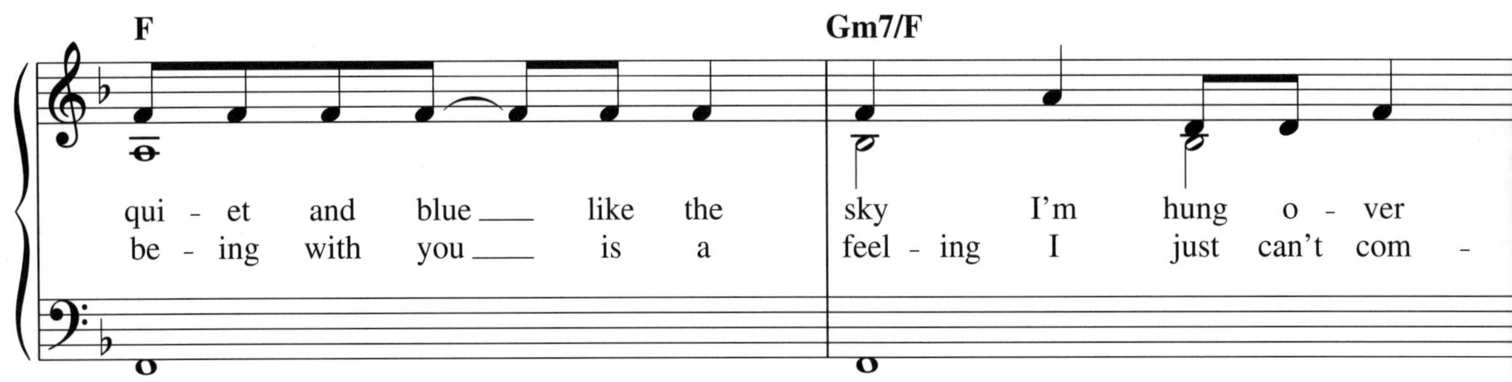

Copyright © 1970, 1972 (Renewed 1998, 2000) by Famous Music Corporation and Emerald City Music
All Rights for the World Controlled and Administered by Famous Music Corporation
International Copyright Secured All Rights Reserved

E♭/F
Gm7
C7
B♭maj7
you.
pare.
And if I
And if I
can't find my way _ back
can't find you in _ my

Em7
A7
Dm7
G7
Cmaj7
home
arms
it just would-n't be
it just would-n't be
fair, 'cause
fair, 'cause

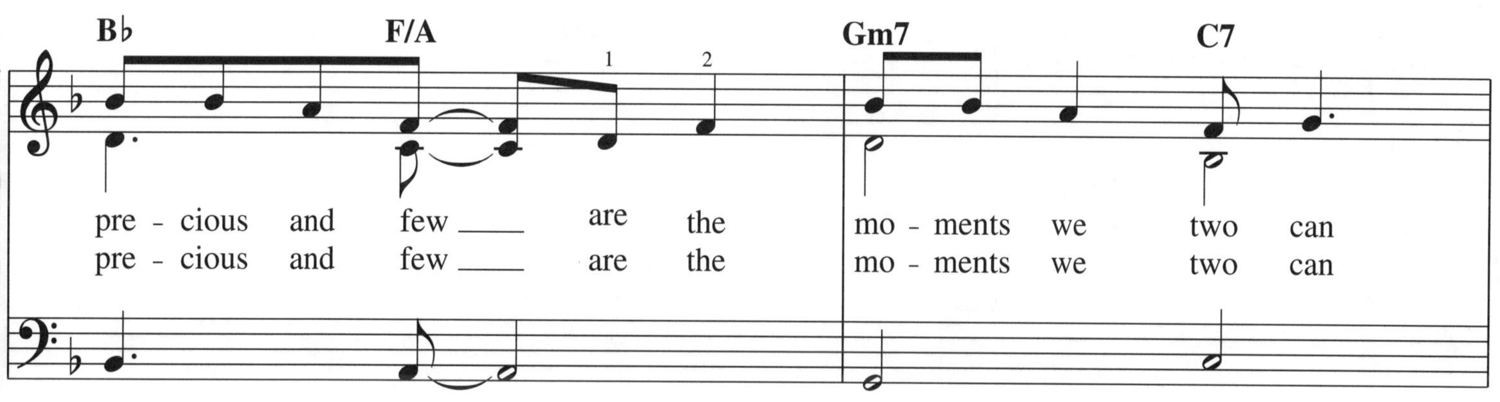
B♭
F/A
Gm7
C7
pre - cious and few _ are the
pre - cious and few _ are the
mo - ments we two can
mo - ments we two can

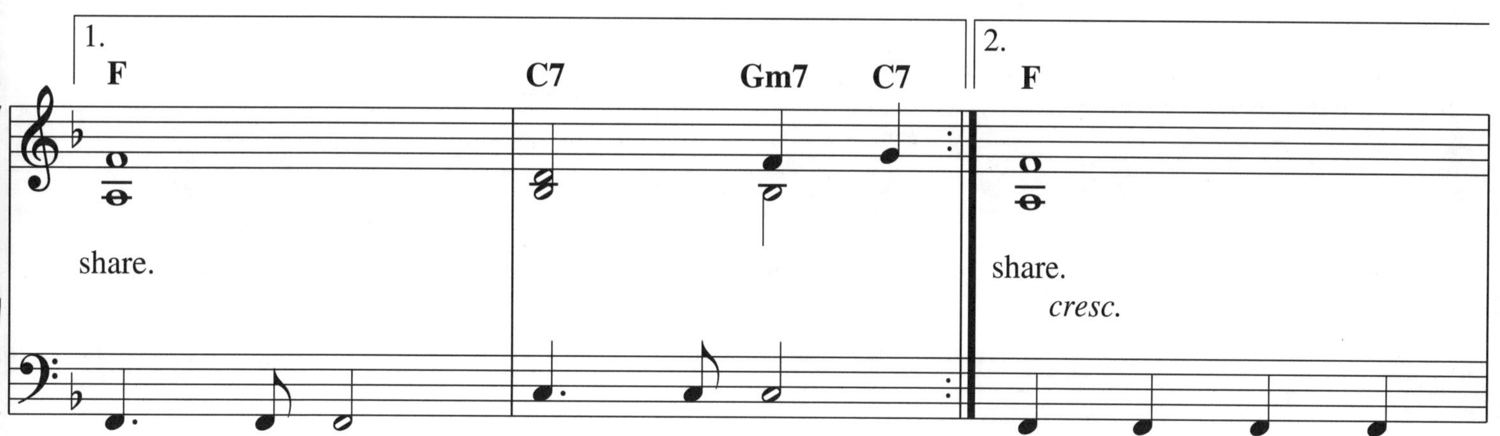
1.
F
C7
Gm7
C7
2.
F
share.
share.
cresc.

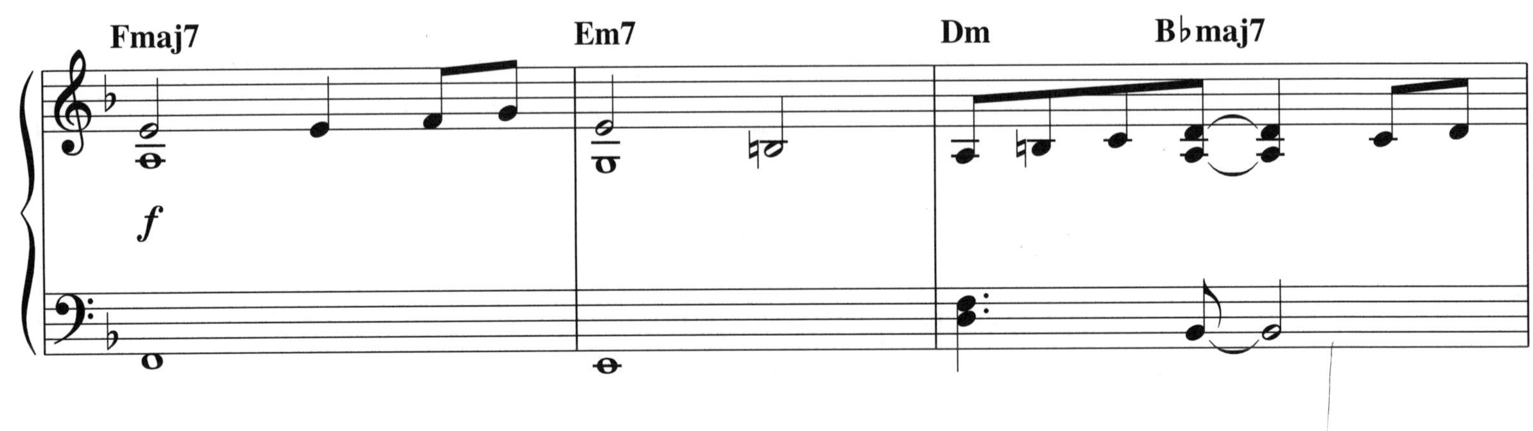
Fmaj7
Em7
Dm
B♭maj7
f

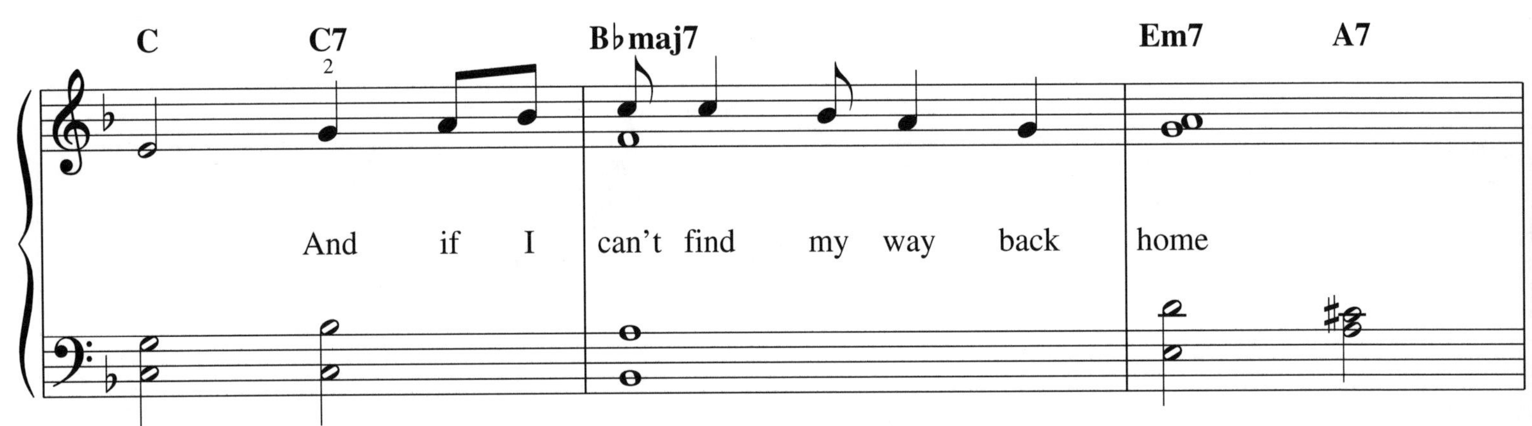
C
C7
B♭maj7
Em7
A7
And if I can't find my way back home

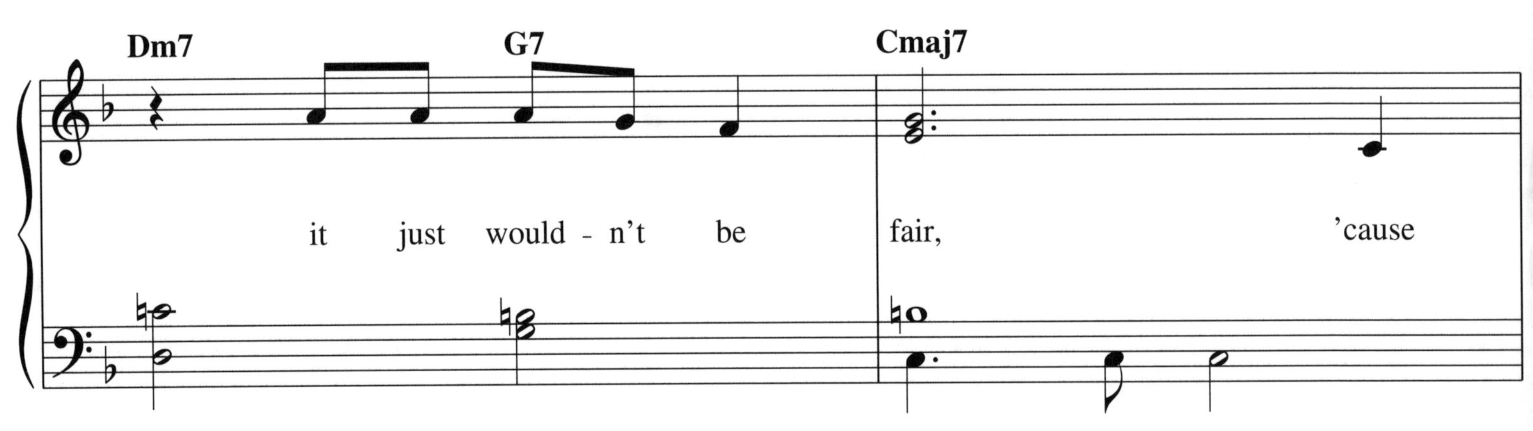
Dm7
G7
Cmaj7
it just would - n't be fair, 'cause

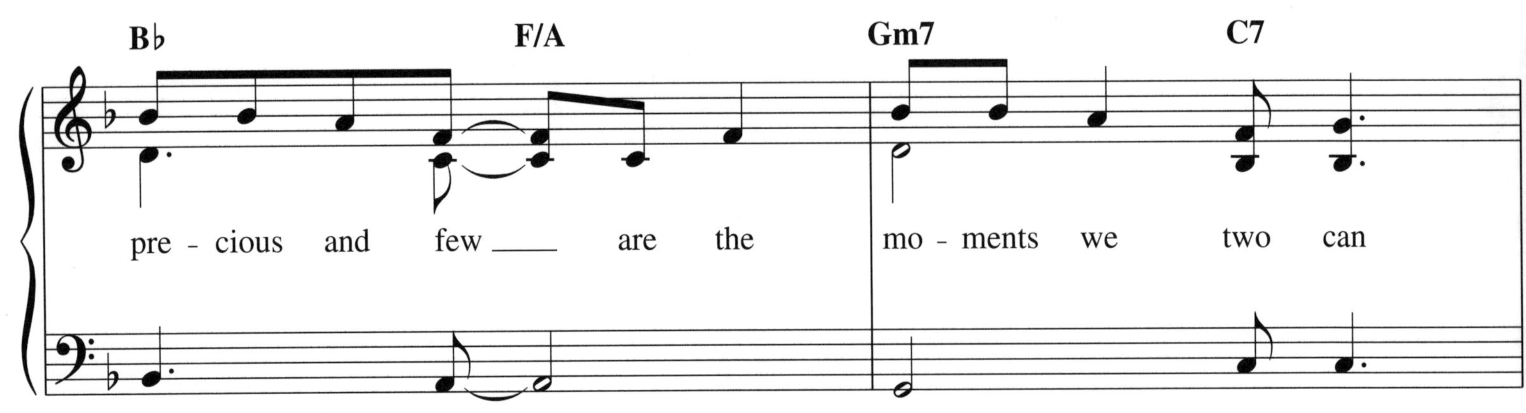
B♭
F/A
Gm7
C7
pre - cious and few ___ are the mo - ments we two can

F
D7
G
share.
Pre-cious and few __ are the
mf

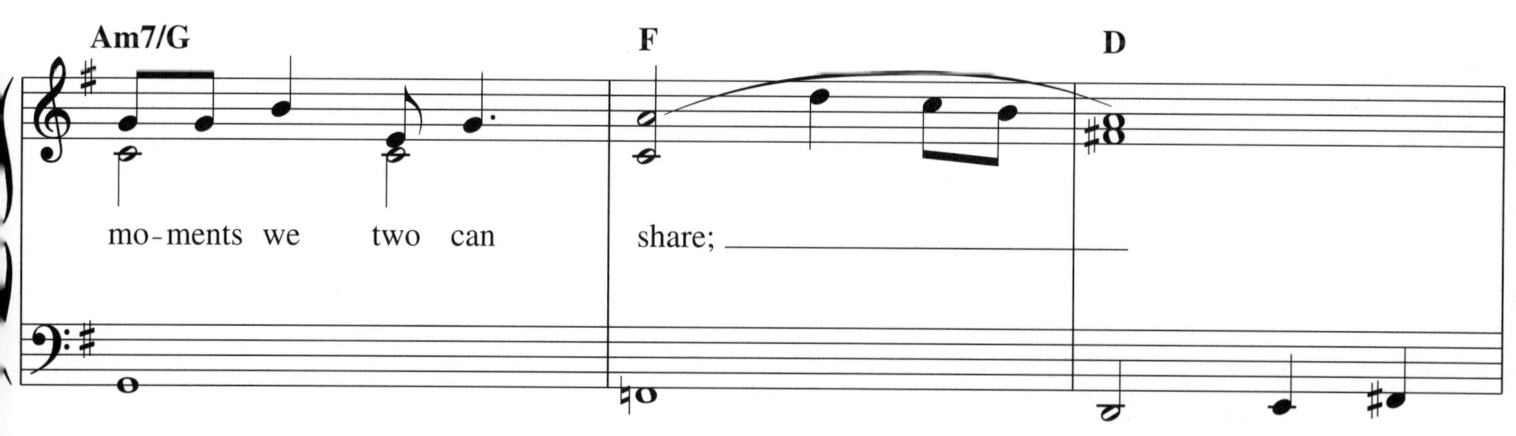
Am7/G
F
D
mo-ments we two can
share; ___

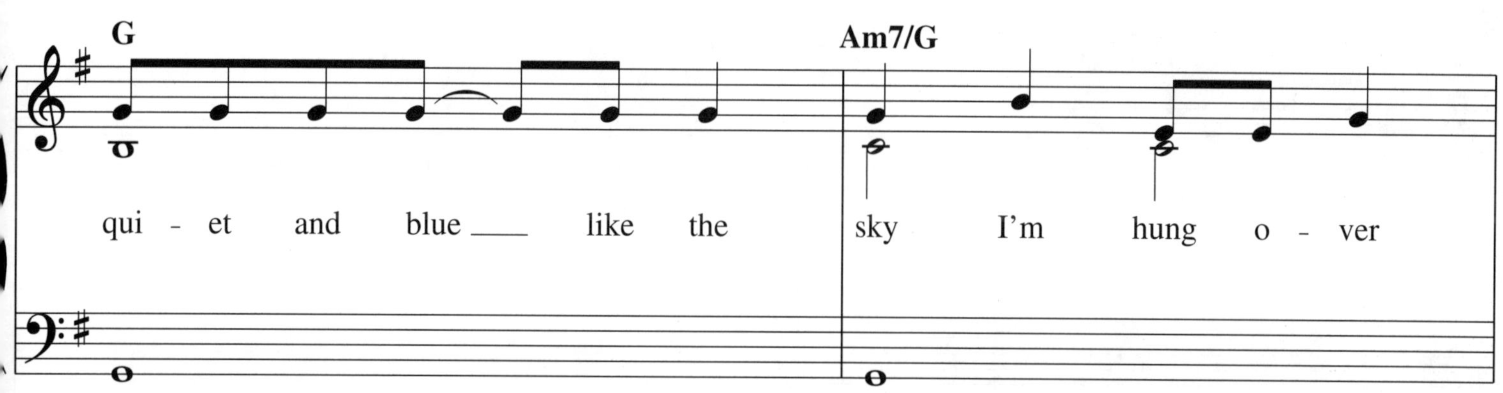
G
Am7/G
qui - et and blue __ like the
sky I'm hung o - ver

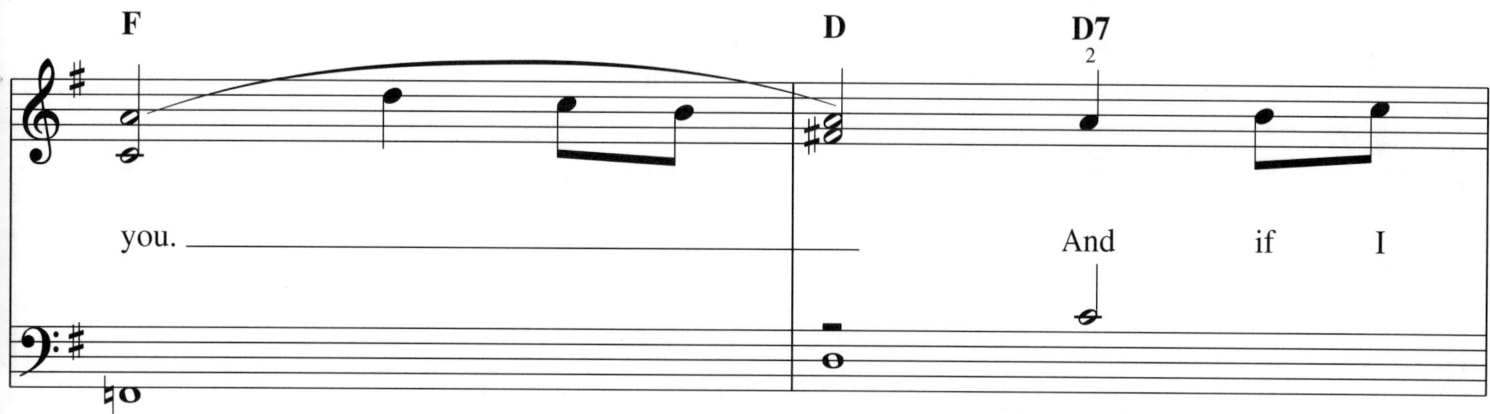
F
D
D7
2
you. ___
And if I

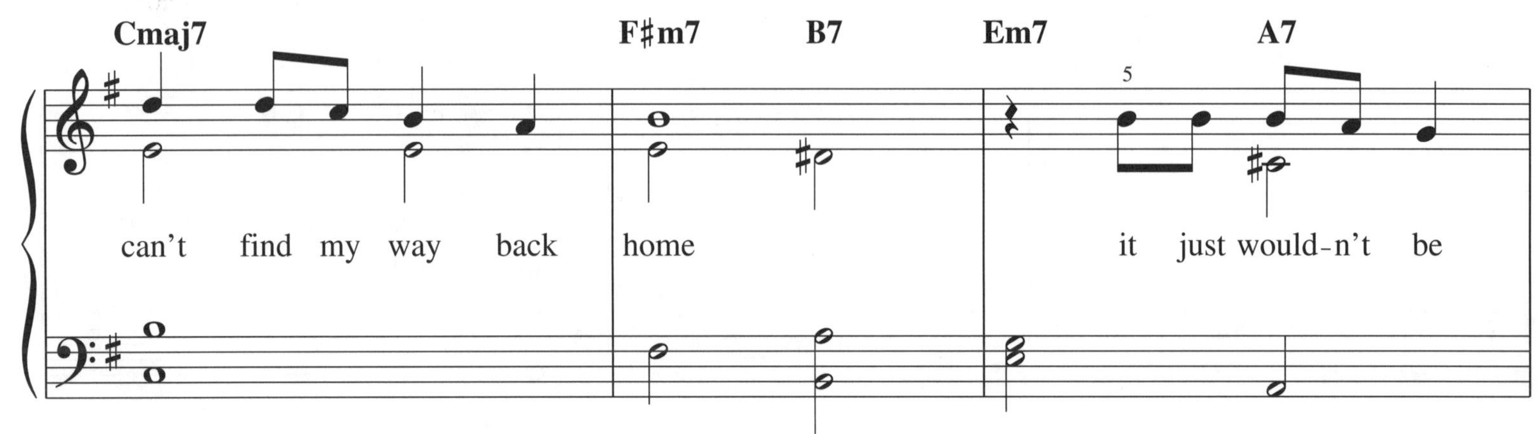
Cmaj7
F♯m7
B7
Em7
A7
5
can't find my way back home it just would-n't be

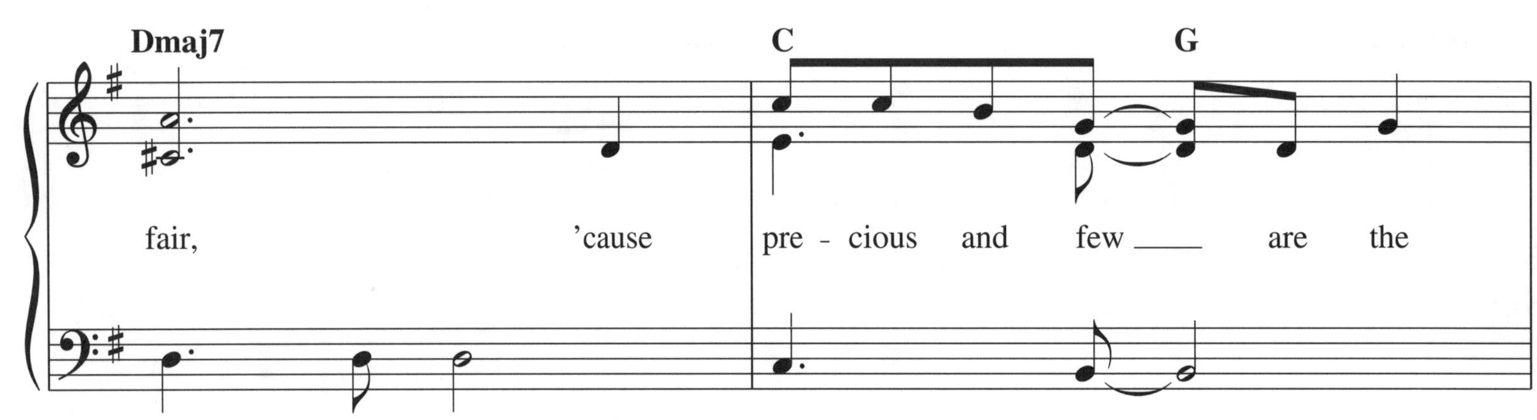
Dmaj7
C
G
fair, 'cause pre - cious and few are the

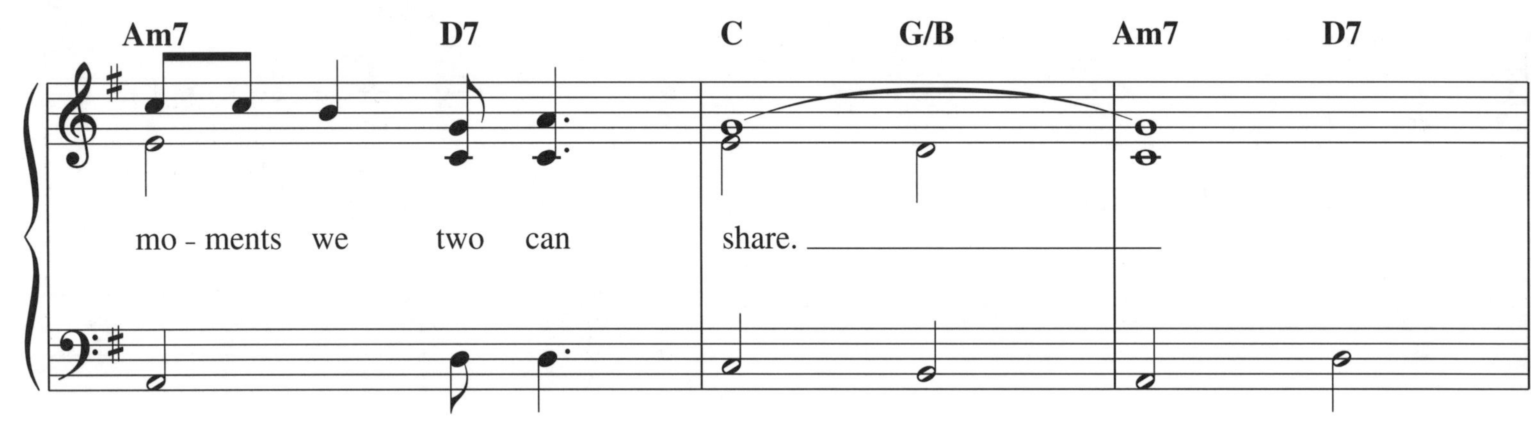
Am7
D7
C
G/B
Am7
D7
mo - ments we two can share.

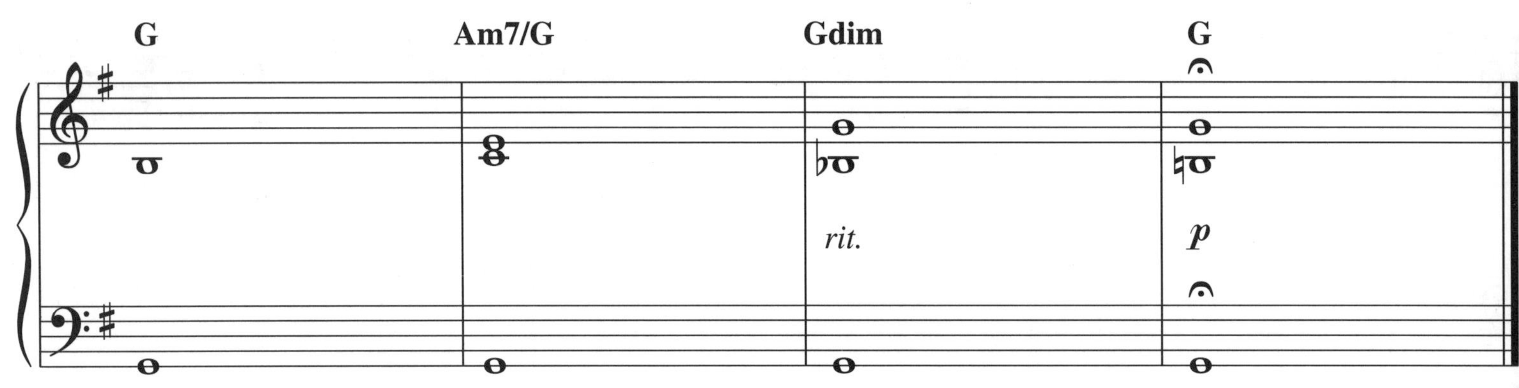
G
Am7/G
Gdim
G
rit.
p

READY TO TAKE A CHANCE AGAIN

(Love Theme)

from the Paramount Picture FOUL PLAY

Words by NORMAN GIMBEL
Music by CHARLES FOX

Moderately Slow

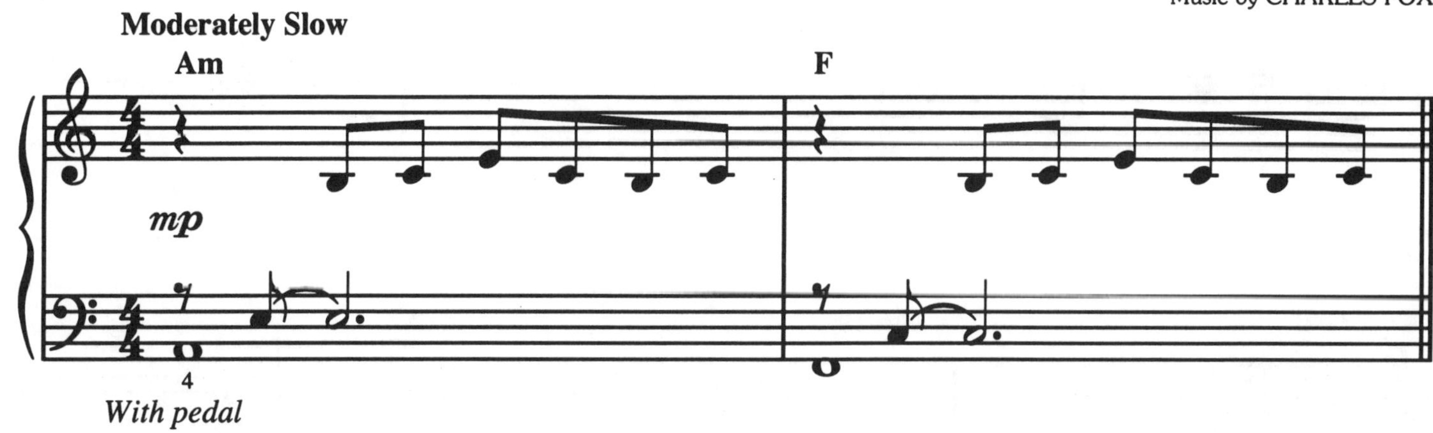

Copyright © 1977, 1978 by Ensign Music Corporation and Kamakazi Music Corporation
All Rights for the World Controlled and Administered by Ensign Music Corporation
International Copyright Secured All Rights Reserved

G7
G7sus
C
No jolts _ no sur -

G/B
Gm/B♭
A7
pris - es,
No cri - sis a - ris - es; My life _ goes a -

Dm
Dm/F
Dm/B
long as it should, _ it's all ver - y nice, _ but not ver - y good. _

E
Esus
E7
Am7
And I'm ready - y to take _ a
f

Dm7
G7
C/E
Am
E7
chance a - gain,
Read - y to put my
love on the line with
Am
Am/G
C7/G♭
Fmaj7
Em7
Dm7
you. Been
liv - ing with noth - ing to show
for it; You
G7sus
G7
To Coda
get what you get when you go
for it, And I'm
C/E
Fmaj7
E/G♯
read - y to take a
chance a - gain with
you.

N.C.
Am
E7/G♯
mp
When she left me in

A7/G
A7
Dm
all my de - spair,
I just held on, My hopes were all

Dm/C
Dm/B
E
Esus
E7
D.S. al Coda
gone, Then I found you there.
And I'm

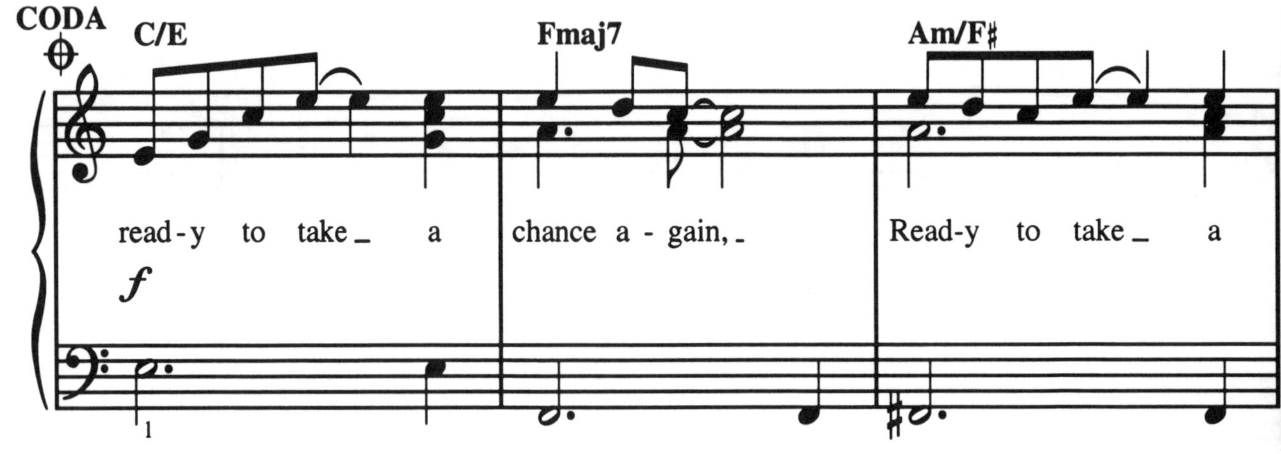
CODA
C/E
Fmaj7
Am/F♯
read-y to take a chance a - gain, Read-y to take a
f

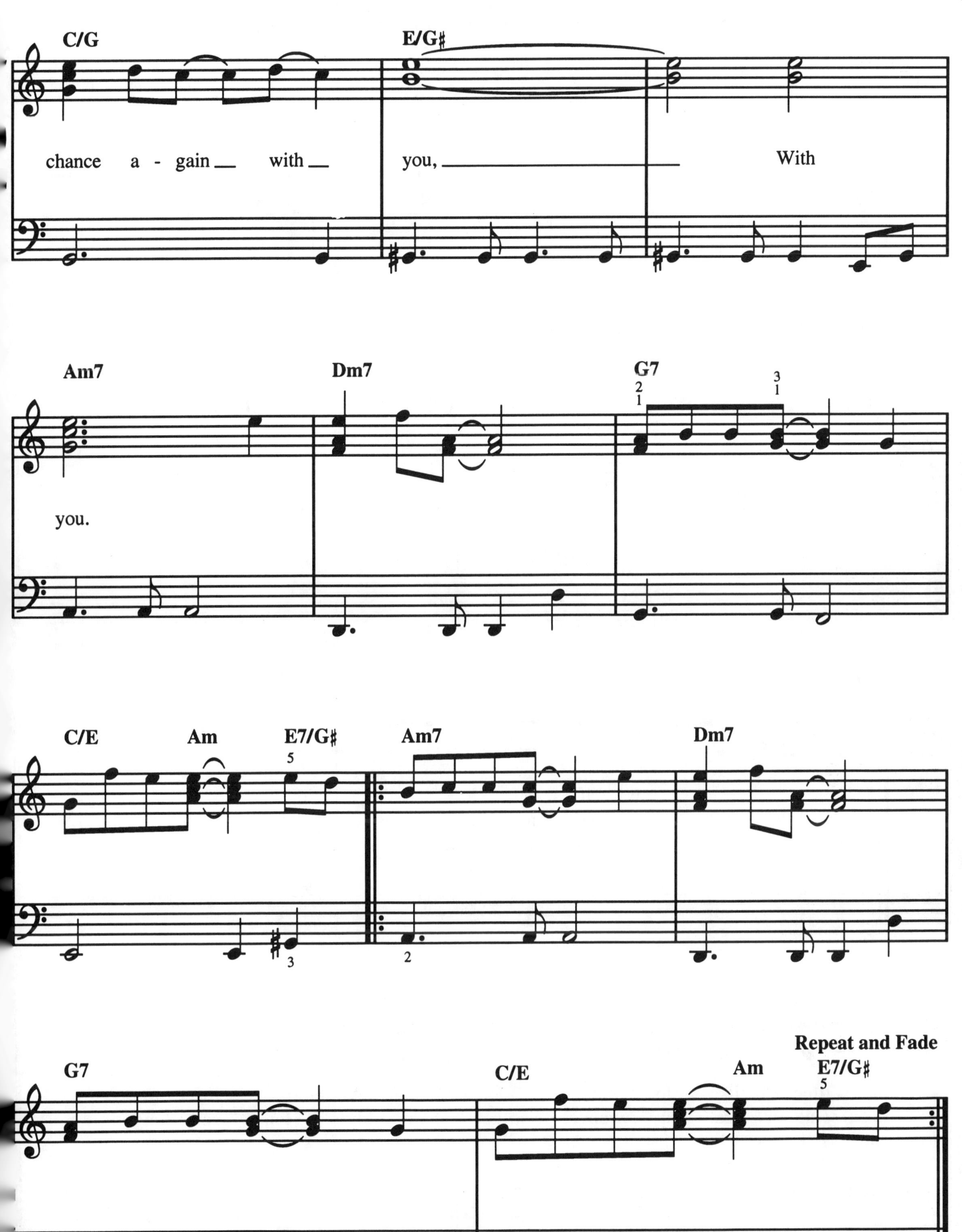
C/G
E/G♯
chance a - gain with
you,
With
Am7
Dm7
G7
you.
C/E
Am
E7/G♯
Am7
Dm7
G7
C/E
Repeat and Fade
Am
E7/G♯

RAINY DAYS AND MONDAYS

Lyrics by PAUL WILLIAMS
Music by ROGER NICHOLS

Copyright © 1970 ALMO MUSIC CORP.
Copyright Renewed
All Rights Reserved Used by Permission

Em7
Cmaj7
Am7
C/D
G
Hang - in' a - round
Walk - in' a - round
Hang - in' a - round
noth - ing to do but frown;
some kind of lone - ly clown;
noth - ing to do but frown;
Am7
C/D
G/D
D7sus
1.
G/D
D7sus
rain-y days and Mon-days al - ways get me down.
2.,3.
G/D
B/D♯
Em7
Cmaj7
Am7
D7
Gmaj7
Fun - ny but it seems I al - ways wind up here with you,
Bm7
Cmaj7
C/D
D
B7/D♯
nice to know some-bod - y loves me.

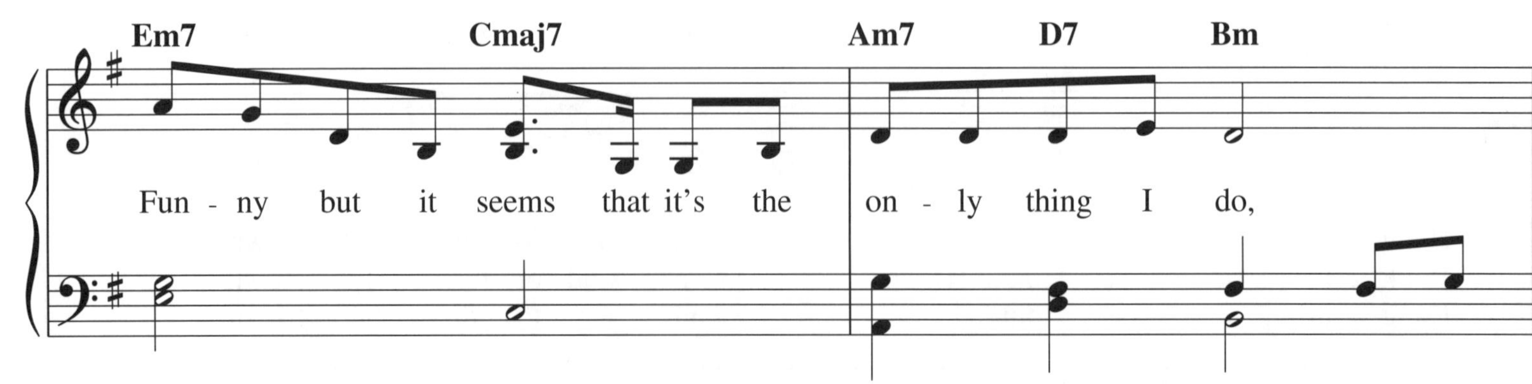
Em7
Cmaj7
Am7
D7
Bm
Fun - ny but it seems that it's the on - ly thing I do,

To Coda
D.S. al Coda
Bm7
Cmaj7
D7sus
D7
Am7
run and find the one who loves _ me.

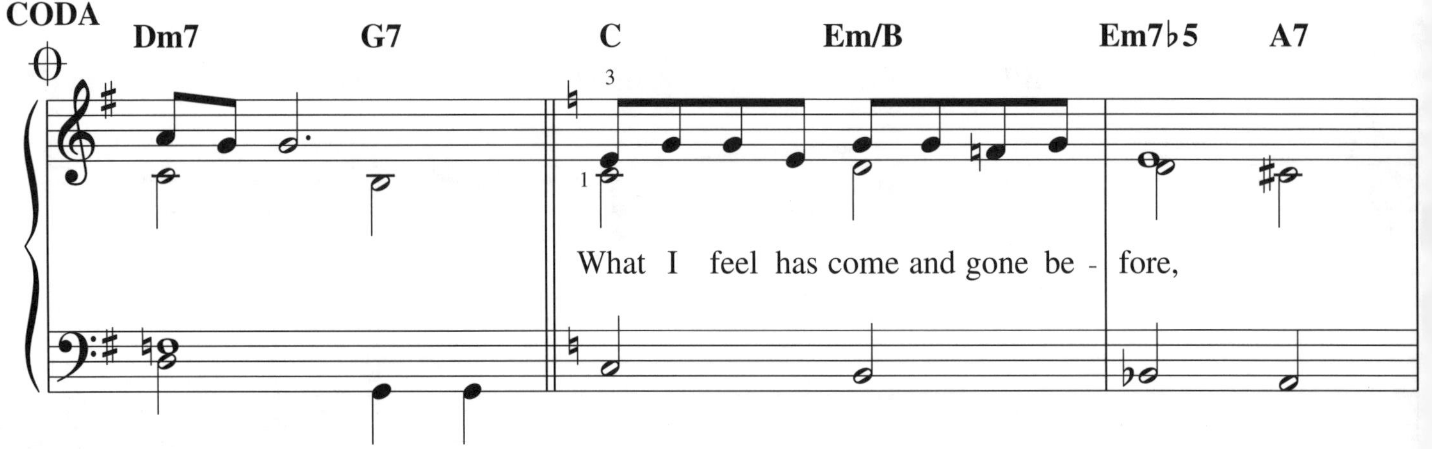
CODA
Dm7
G7
C
Em/B
Em7♭5
A7
What I feel has come and gone be - fore,

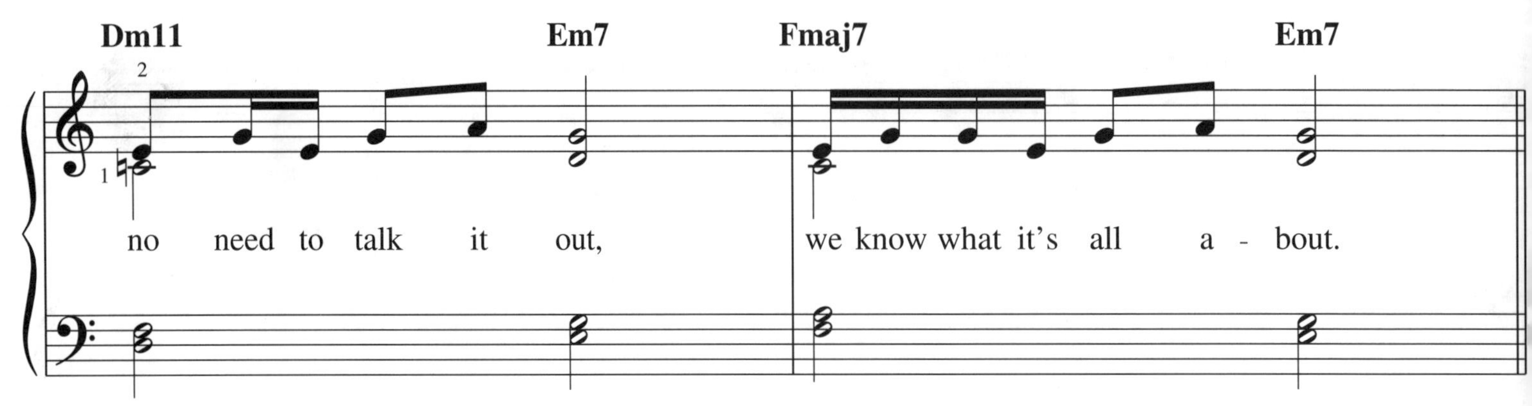
Dm11
Em7
Fmaj7
Em7
no need to talk it out, we know what it's all a - bout.

Am7
Fmaj7
Dm7
F/G
C
Hang - in' a - round noth - in' to do but frown;
1.
Dm7
F/G
C/G
E/G#
rain - y days and Mon - days al - ways get me down.
2.
Dm7
F/G
C/G
rain - y days and Mon - days al - ways get me down.
G7sus
C/G
G7sus
Cmaj7

SHE'S ALWAYS A WOMAN

Words and Music by
BILLY JOEL

© 1977, 1978 IMPULSIVE MUSIC
All Rights Reserved International Copyright Secured Used by Permission

1.
Am
Am/G
F
G7
C
Csus
hides like a child but she's al - ways a wom - an to me.
steals like a thief but she's al - ways a wom - an to
C
G
2.
C
Csus
C
Am
Am/G
She can lead you to me.
Oh,
Add pedal
D7/F#
D7
G
G/F#
Em
C
she takes care of her - self she can wait if she
F
F/E
Dm
G7
C
Csus
wants, she's a - head of her time.

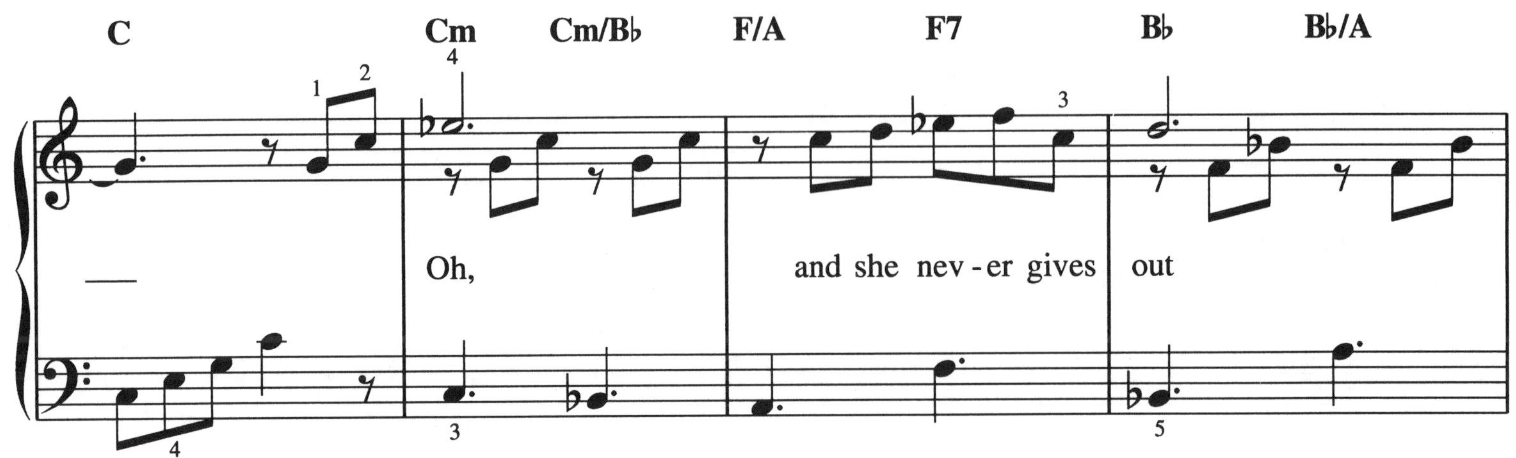
C
Cm
Cm/B♭
F/A
F7
B♭
B♭/A
Oh, and she nev - er gives out

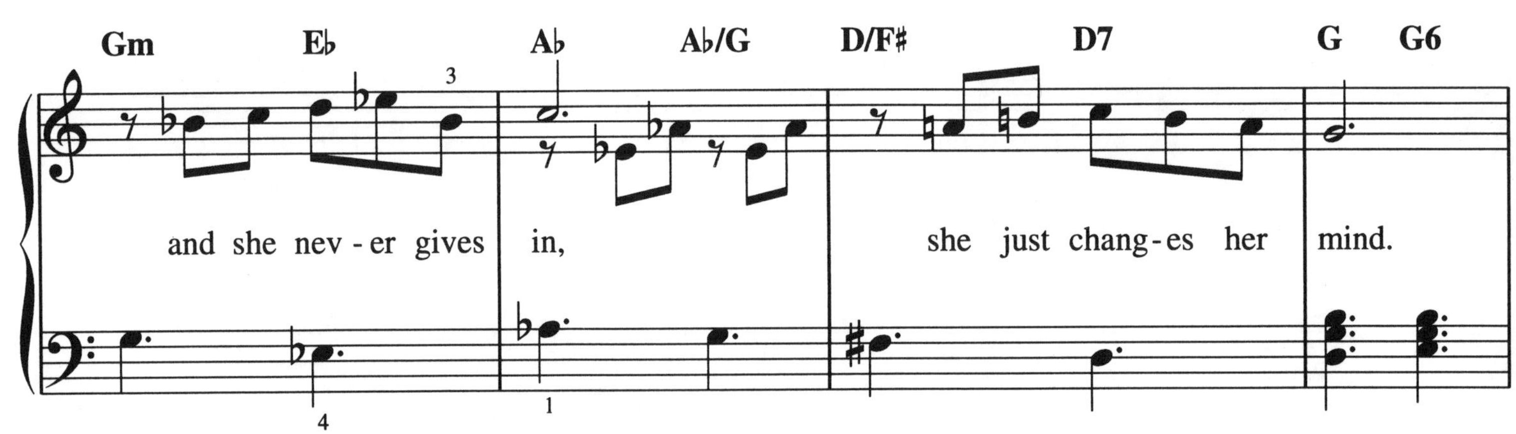
Gm
E♭
A♭
A♭/G
D/F♯
D7
G
G6
and she nev - er gives in, she just chang - es her mind.

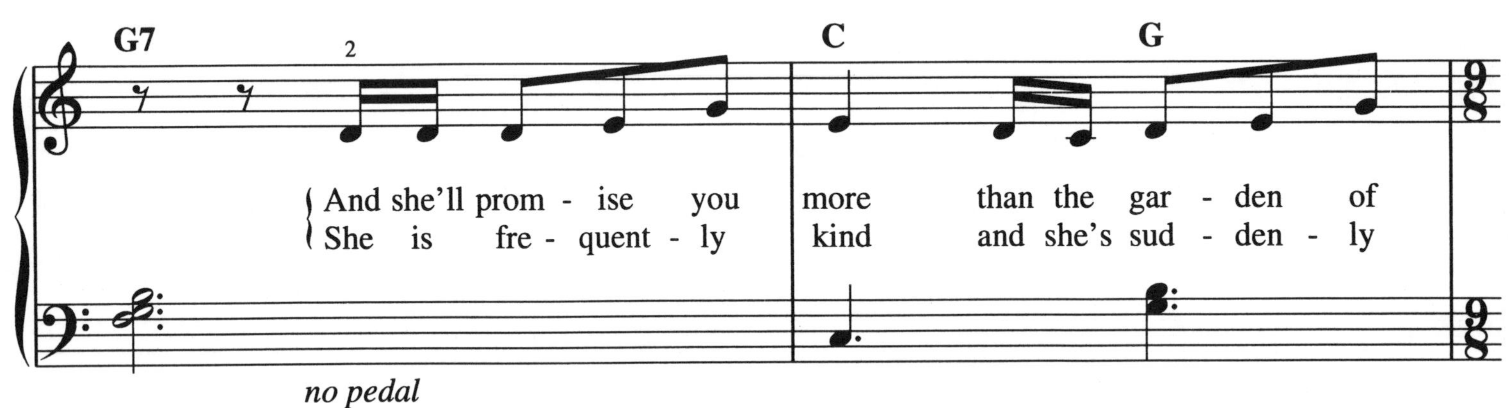
G7
C
G
And she'll prom - ise you more than the gar - den of
She is fre - quent - ly kind and she's sud - den - ly
no pedal

C
C7
F
F/E
E - den. Then she'll care - less - ly cut you and laugh while you're
cru - el. She can do as she pleas - es she's no - bo - dy's

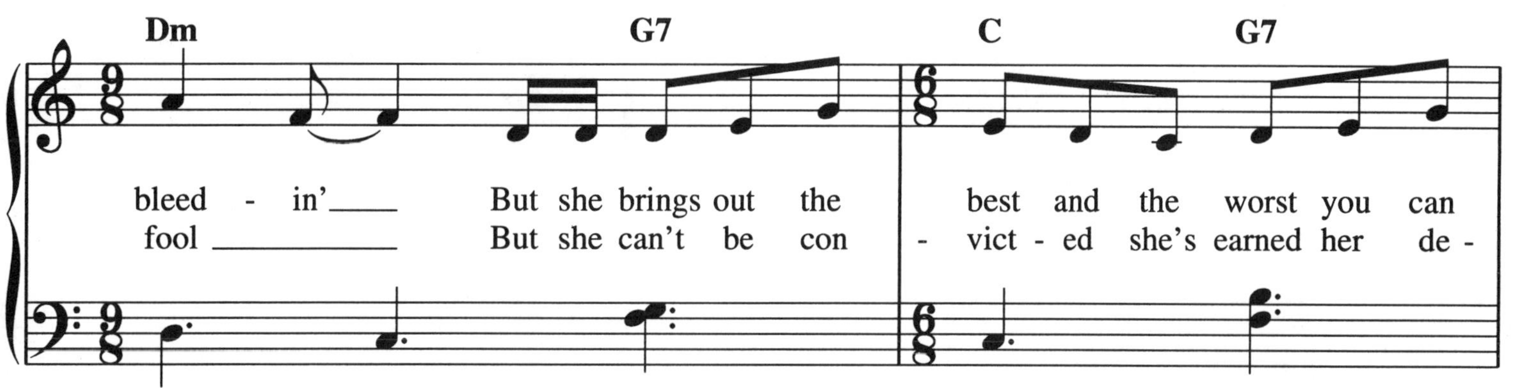
Dm
G7
C
G7
bleed - in' But she brings out the best and the worst you can
fool But she can't be con - vict - ed she's earned her de -

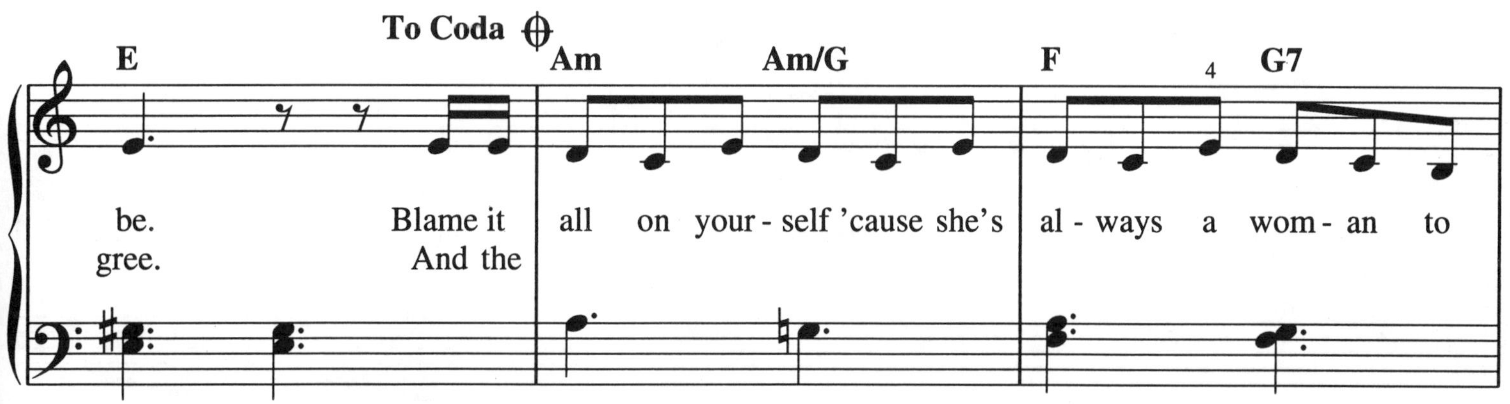
To Coda
E
Am
Am/G
F
G7
be. Blame it all on your - self 'cause she's al - ways a wom - an to
gree. And the

C
Csus
C
G
C
G
E
me.
(Hum)

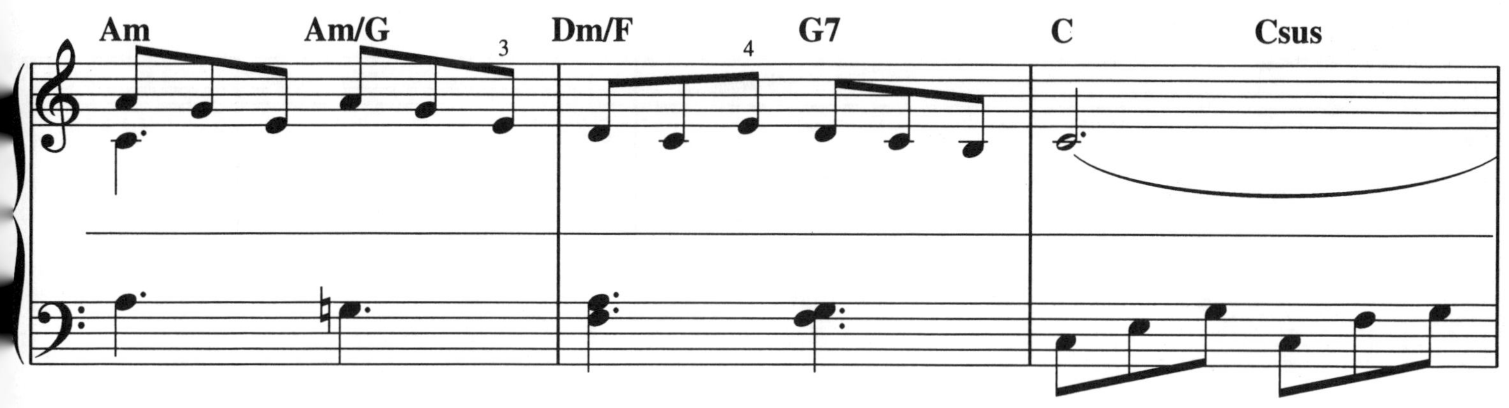
Am
Am/G
Dm/F
G7
C
Csus

C
D.S. al Coda

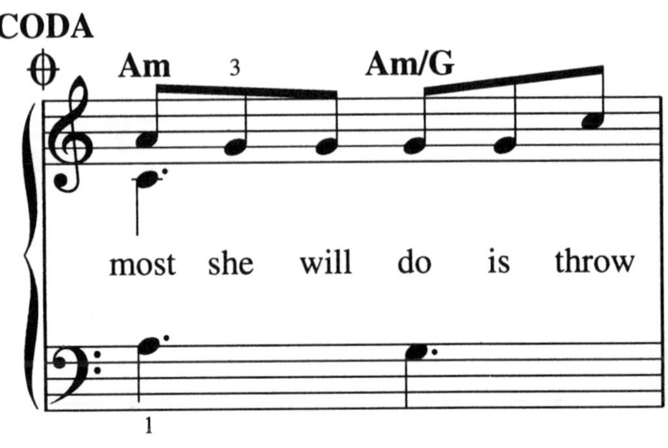
CODA
Am
Am/G
most she will do is throw

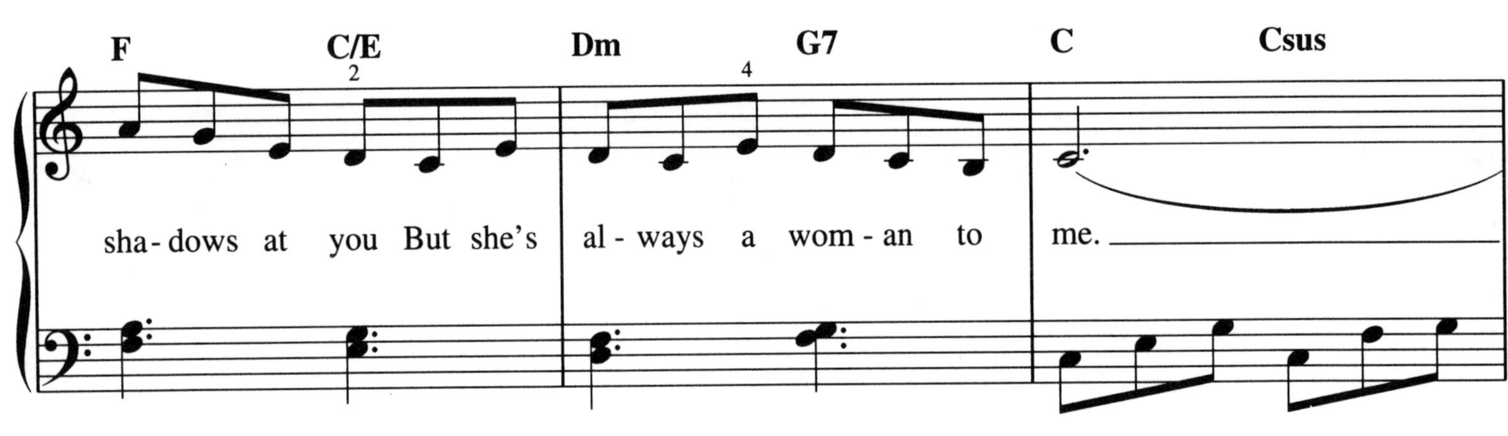
F
C/E
Dm
G7
C
Csus
sha-dows at you But she's al-ways a wom-an to me.

C
G
C
G7
E
(Hum)

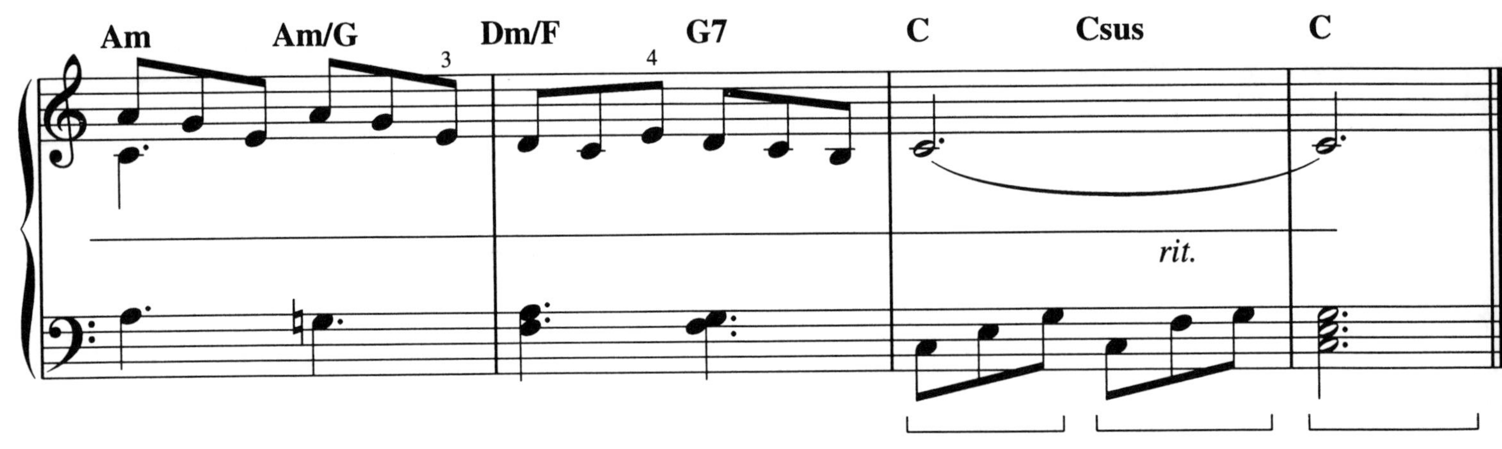
Am
Am/G
Dm/F
G7
C
Csus
C
rit.

SUMMER NIGHTS

from GREASE

Lyric and Music by WARREN CASEY and JIM JACOBS

© 1972 WARREN CASEY and JIM JACOBS
© Renewed 2000 JIM JACOBS and THE ESTATE OF WARREN CASEY
All Rights Administered by EDWIN H. MORRIS & COMPANY, A Division of MPL Communications, Inc.
All Rights Reserved

To Coda
D
G
A
B
Em
A7
Both: Sum-mer days drift - ing a - way, to uh, oh, those sum - mer nights.
Both: Sum-mer sun some-thing's be-gun, then uh, oh, those sum - mer nights.
Both: Sum-mer fling don't mean a thing, but
D
G
E
A
Chorus: Well-a, well-a, well-a, uh. Boys: Tell me more, tell me more, did you get ver - y
Chorus: Well-a, well-a, well-a, uh. Girls: Tell me more, tell me more, was it love at first
D
G
E
A
1.
D
G
A
G
far? Girls: Tell me more, tell me more, like, does he have a car?
sight? Boys: Tell me more, tell me more, did she put up a
2.
D
G
A
G
D.S. al Coda
fight?
CODA
Em
A
uh, oh, the sum - mer

B♭
E♭
A♭
F
B♭
nights.
Boys: Tell me more, tell me more, like you don't have to
E♭
A♭
F
B♭7
E♭
A♭
B♭
A♭
brag. Girls: Tell me more, tell me more, 'cause he sounds like a drag.
E♭
A♭
B♭
A♭
E♭
A♭
Girl: He got friend-ly hold-ing my hand.
Boy: She got friend-ly
B♭
A♭
E♭
A♭
B♭
C
down on the sand.
Girl: He was sweet, just turned eight-een.

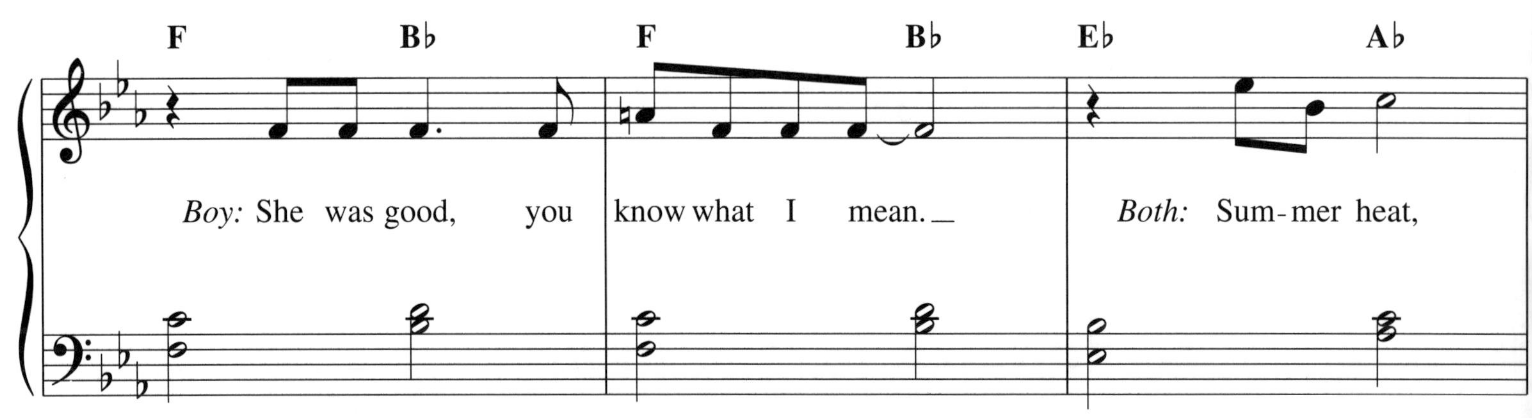
F
B♭
F
B♭
E♭
A♭
Boy: She was good, you know what I mean.
Both: Sum-mer heat,

B♭
C
Fm
B♭7
E♭
C7
boy and girl meet, then, uh, oh, those sum - mer nights.

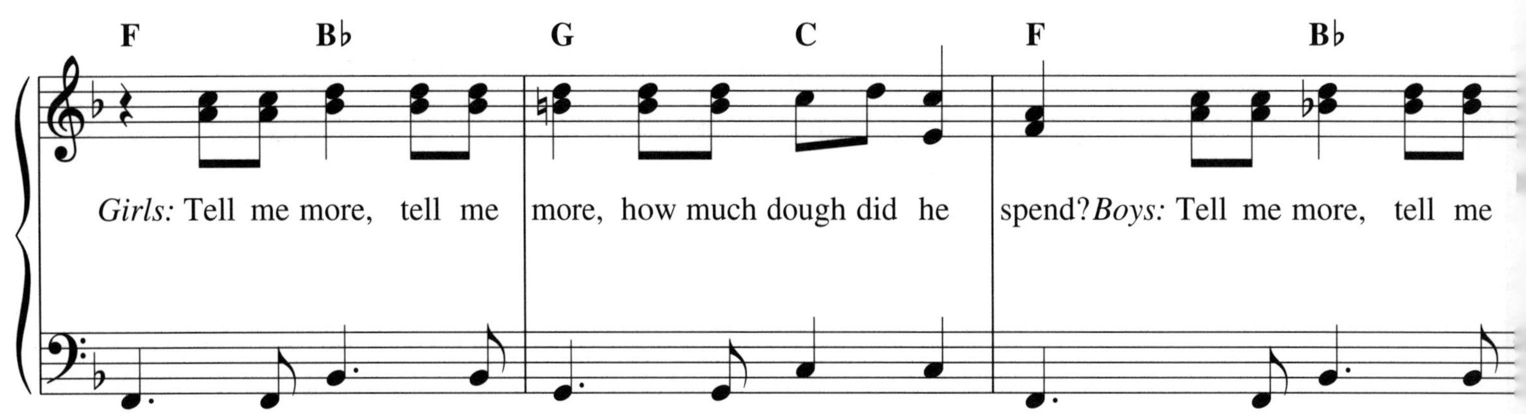
F
B♭
G
C
F
B♭
Girls: Tell me more, tell me more, how much dough did he spend?
Boys: Tell me more, tell me

G
C7
F
B♭
E♭
A♭
more, could she get me a friend?
Girl: It turned cold-er,

B♭
A♭
E♭
A♭
B♭
A♭
that's where it ends.
Boy: So I told her
we'd still be friends.
E♭
A♭
B♭
C
E
A
Girl: Then we made
our true love vow.
Boy: Won-der what
Lightly
E
A
D
G
A
B
she's do-in' now.
Both: Sum-mer dreams
ripped at the seams, but
Em
A
D♭
D
G
D
oh, those sum-mer
nights.
Chorus: Tell me more, tell me
more.

SO FAR AWAY

Words and Music by
CAROLE KING

© 1971 (Renewed 1999) COLGEMS-EMI MUSIC INC.
All Rights Reserved International Copyright Secured Used by Permission

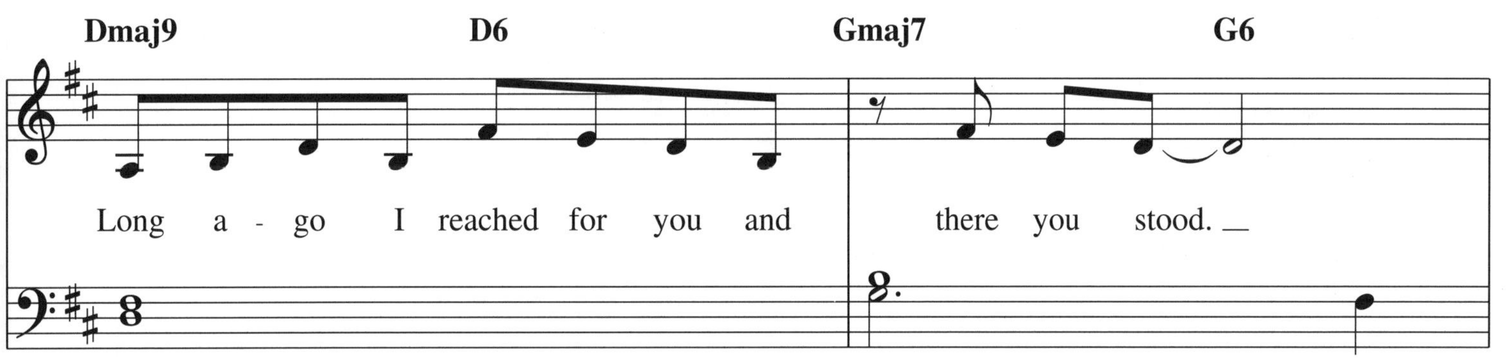
Dmaj9
D6
Gmaj7
G6
Long a - go I reached for you and
there you stood.

Em7
G/A
Dmaj7
G/D Dmaj7
Hold - ing you a - gain could on - ly
do me good.

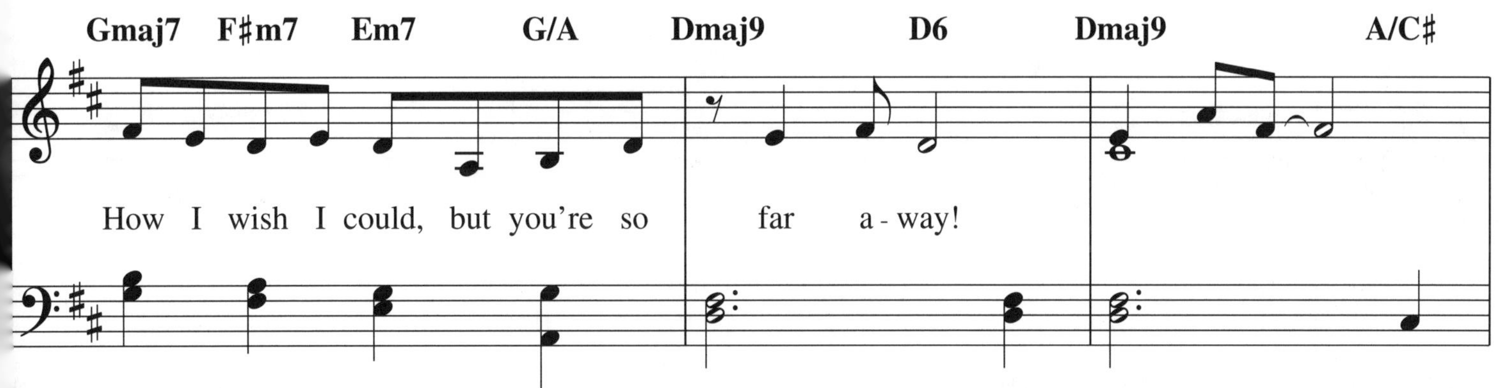
Gmaj7
F♯m7
Em7
G/A
Dmaj9
D6
Dmaj9
A/C♯
How I wish I could, but you're so
far a - way!

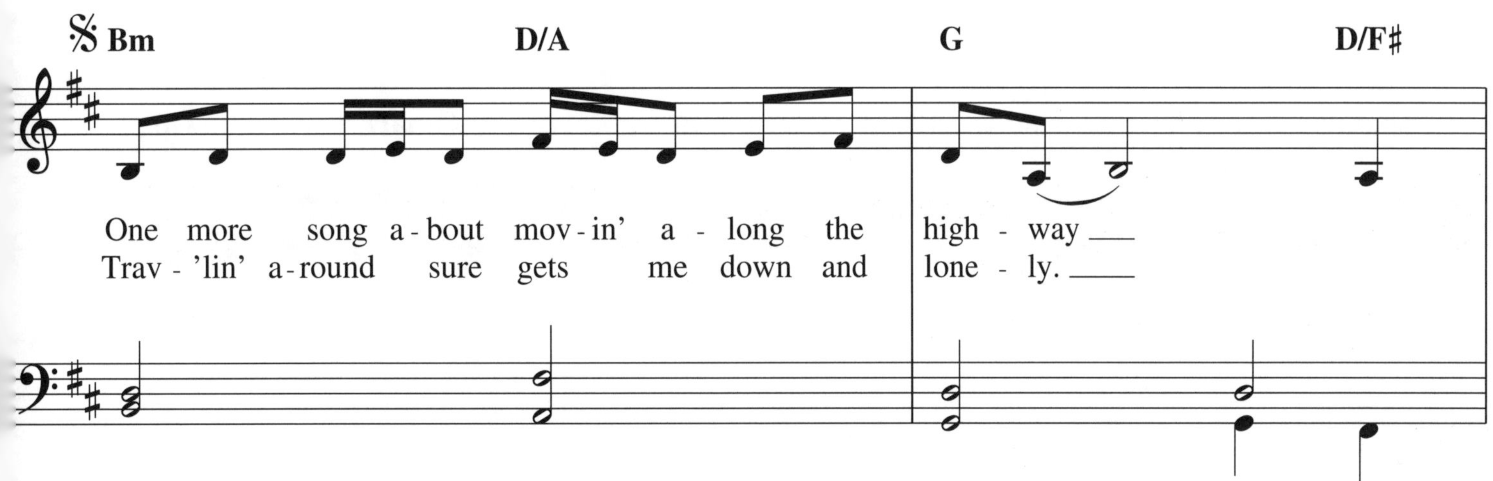
Bm
D/A
G
D/F♯
One more song a - bout mov - in' a - long the
Trav - 'lin' a - round sure gets me down and
high - way
lone - ly.

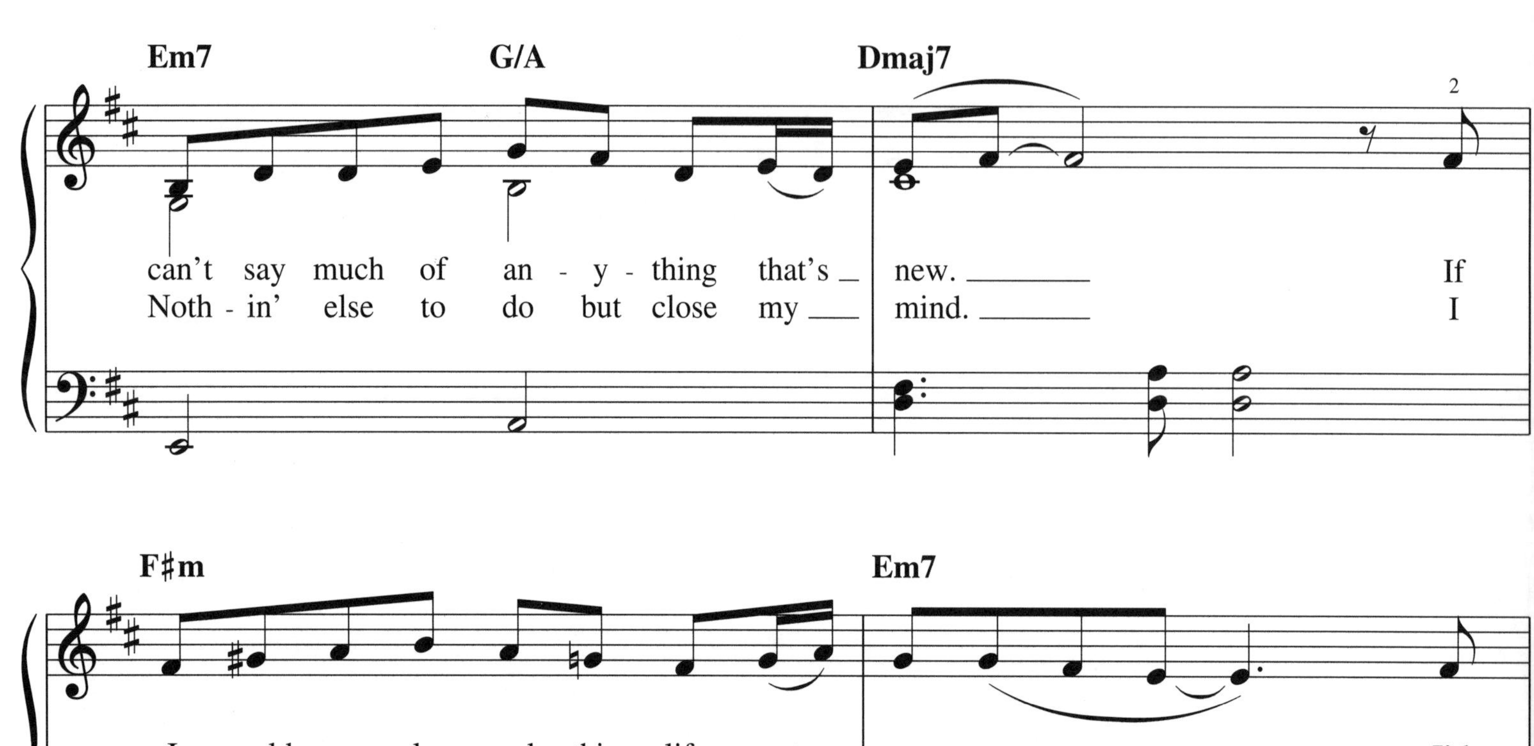
Em7
G/A
Dmaj7
2
can't say much of an - y - thing that's new. If
Noth - in' else to do but close my mind. I

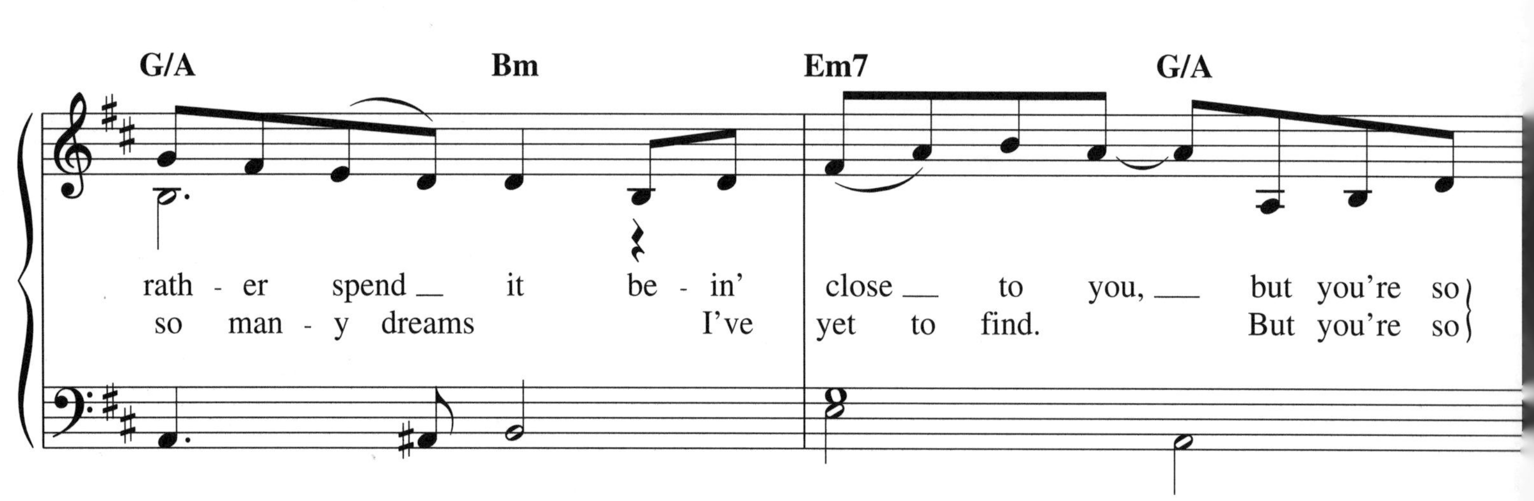
F♯m
Em7
G/A
Bm
Em7
G/A
I could on - ly work this life out my way, I'd
sure hope the road don't come to own me. There's
rath - er spend it be - in' close to you, but you're so
so man - y dreams I've yet to find. But you're so

Dmaj9
D6
Dmaj9
D6
Gmaj7
G6
far a - way! Does - n't an - y - bod - y stay in one place an - y - more?

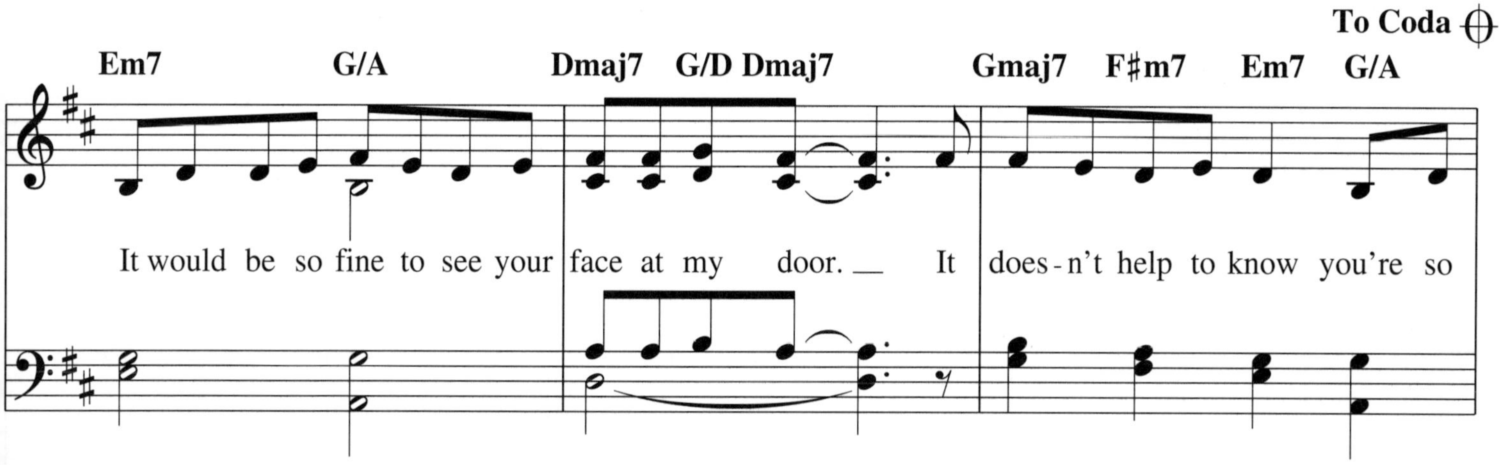
To Coda
Em7
G/A
Dmaj7
G/D Dmaj7
Gmaj7
F♯m7
Em7
G/A
It would be so fine to see your face at my door. It does-n't help to know you're so

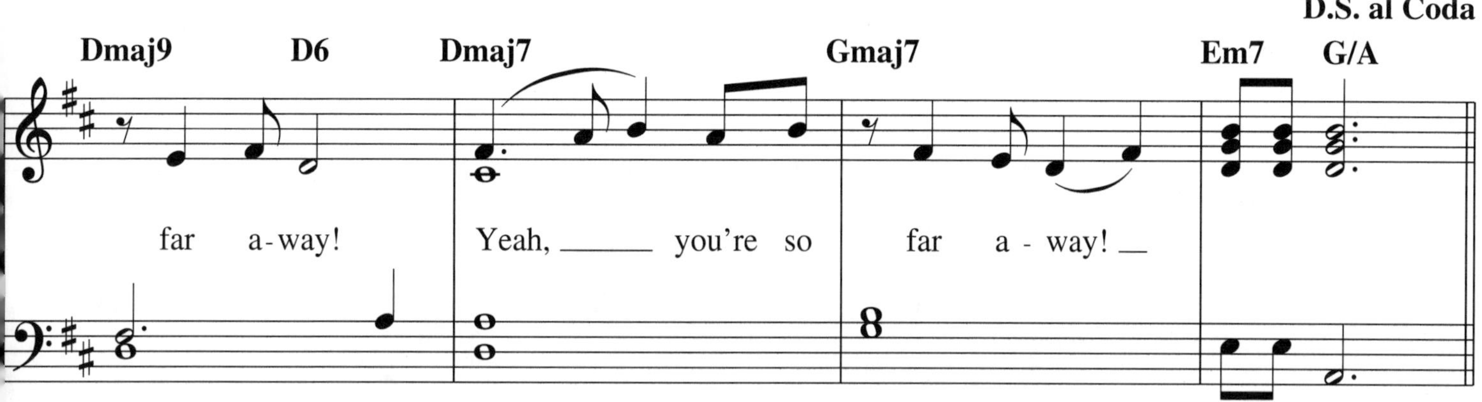
D.S. al Coda
Dmaj9
D6
Dmaj7
Gmaj7
Em7
G/A
far a-way! Yeah, you're so far a - way!

CODA
Dmaj9
D6
Dmaj7
D6
far a - way! Yeah, you're so

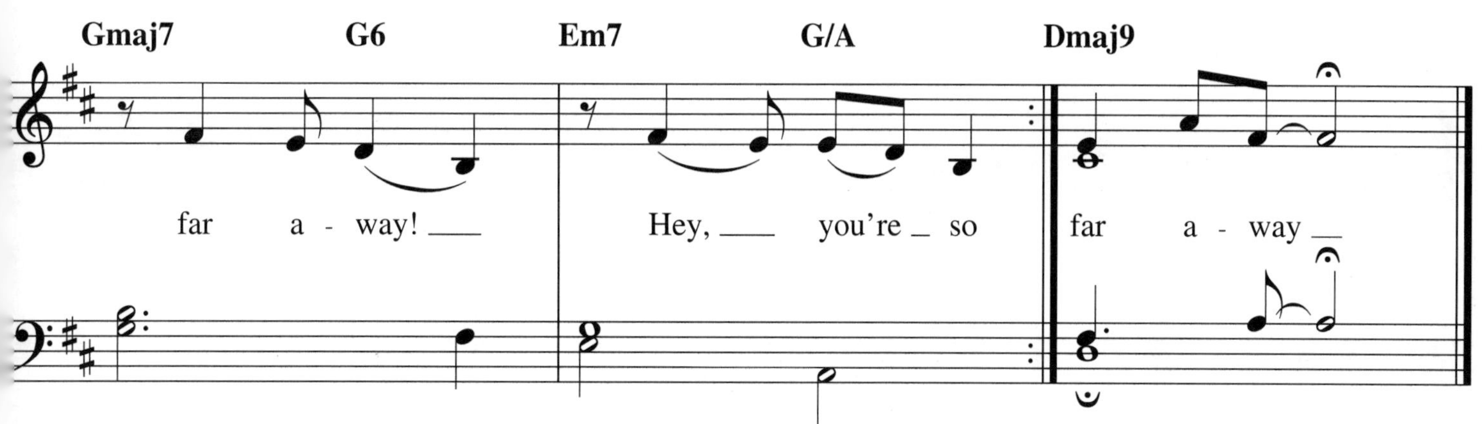
Gmaj7
G6
Em7
G/A
Dmaj9
far a - way! Hey, you're so far a - way

SPEAK SOFTLY, LOVE

(Love Theme)

from the Paramount Picture THE GODFATHER

Words by LARRY KUSIK
Music by NINO ROTA

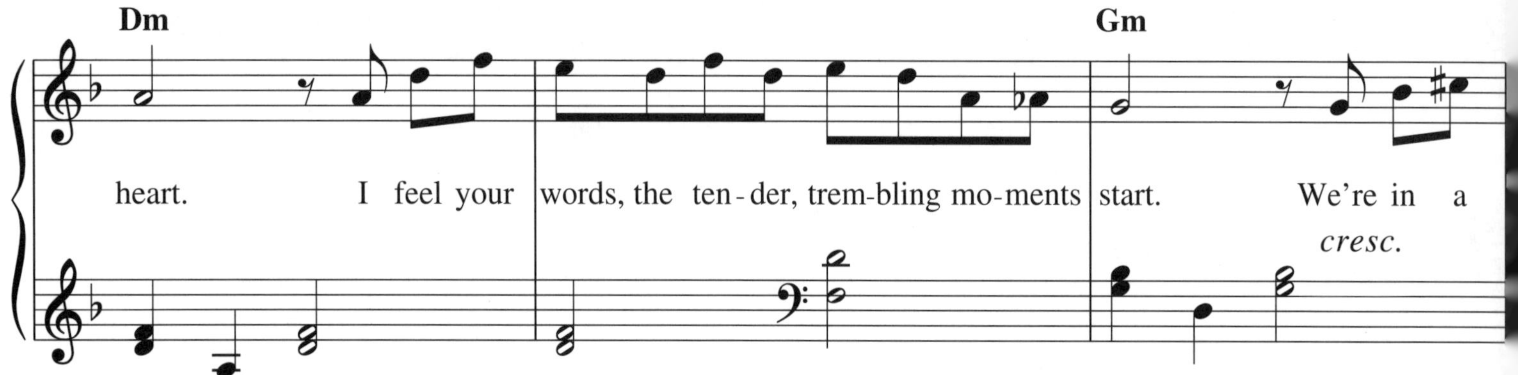

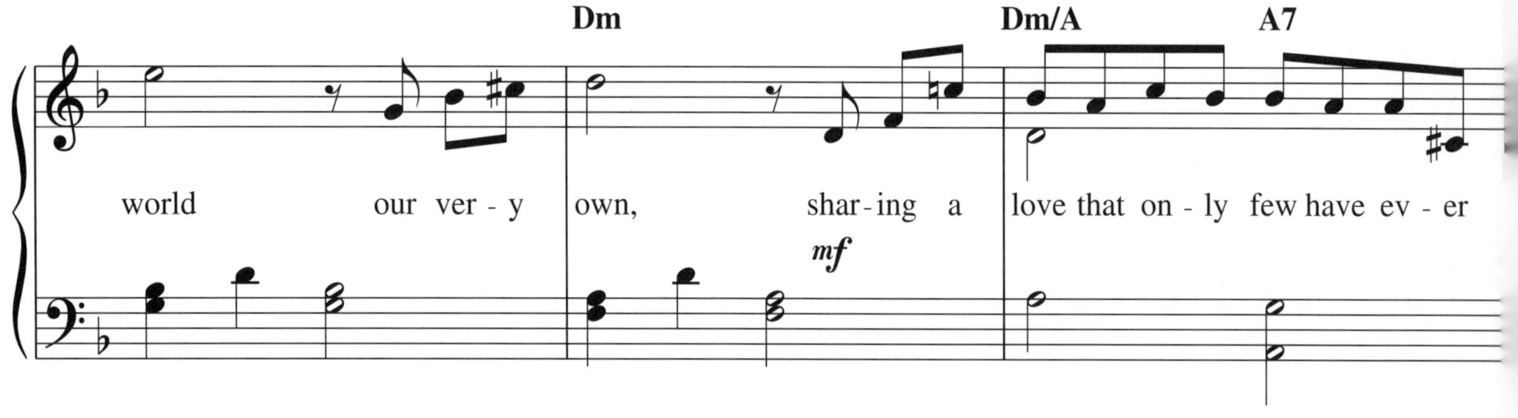

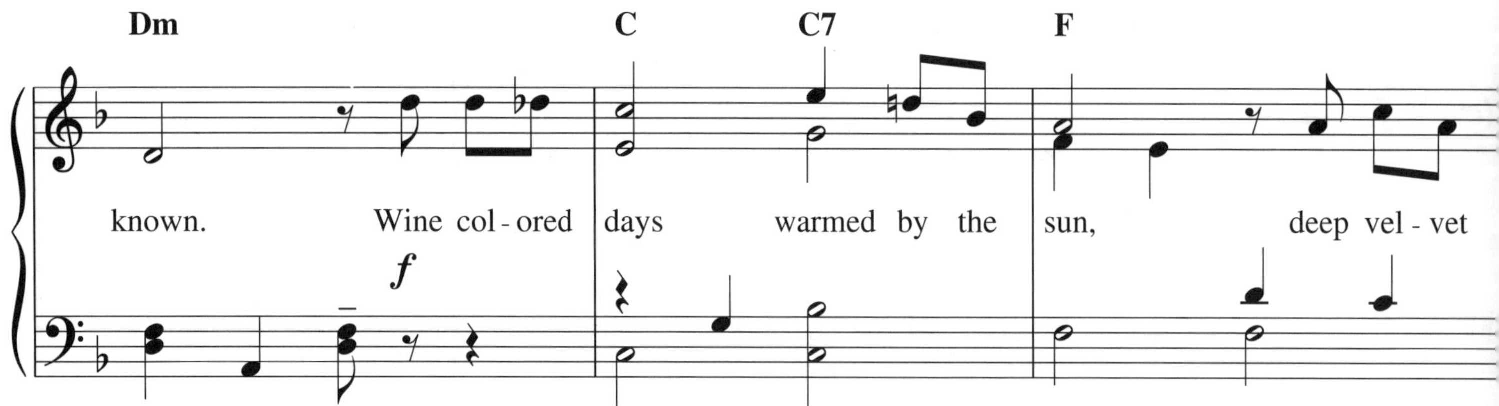

Copyright © 1972 (Renewed 2000) by Famous Music Corporation
International Copyright Secured All Rights Reserved

E♭/G
Gm/B♭
A
N.C.
Dm
Gm/D
nights when we are one. Speak soft - ly, love, so no one hears us but the
dim.
mp
Dm
sky. The vows of love we make will live un - til we
Gm
Dm
die. My life is yours and all be - cause you came in -
cresc.
mf
Dm/A
A7
1.
Dm
2.
Dm
to my world with love so soft - ly, love. Speak soft - ly, love.
p
rit.

TEACH YOUR CHILDREN

Words and Music by
GRAHAM NASH

Copyright © 1970 Nash Notes
Copyright Renewed
All Rights Administered by Sony/ATV Music Publishing, 8 Music Square West, Nashville, TN 37203
International Copyright Secured All Rights Reserved

G7
5
1
be - come your - self, be - cause the past

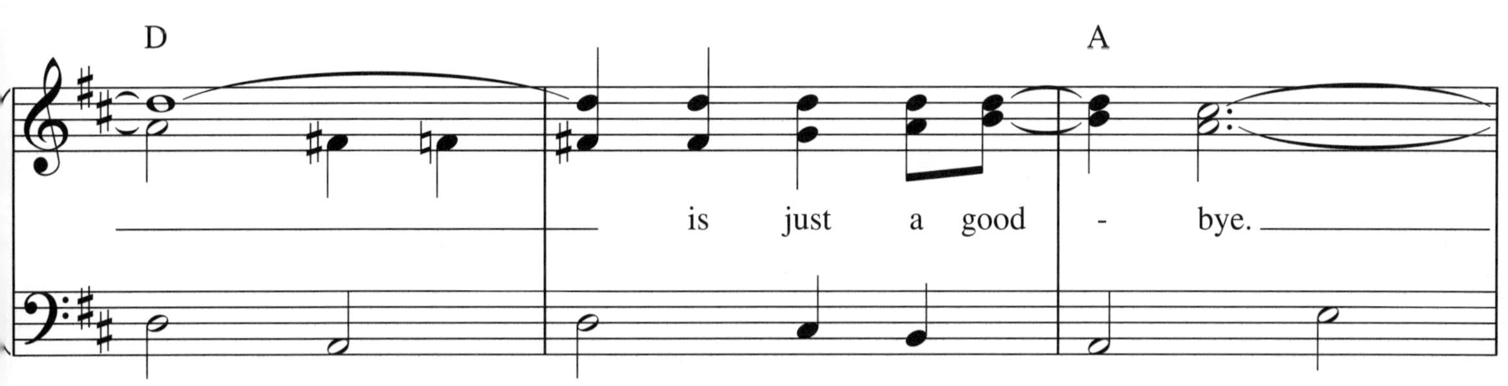
D
A
is just a good - bye.

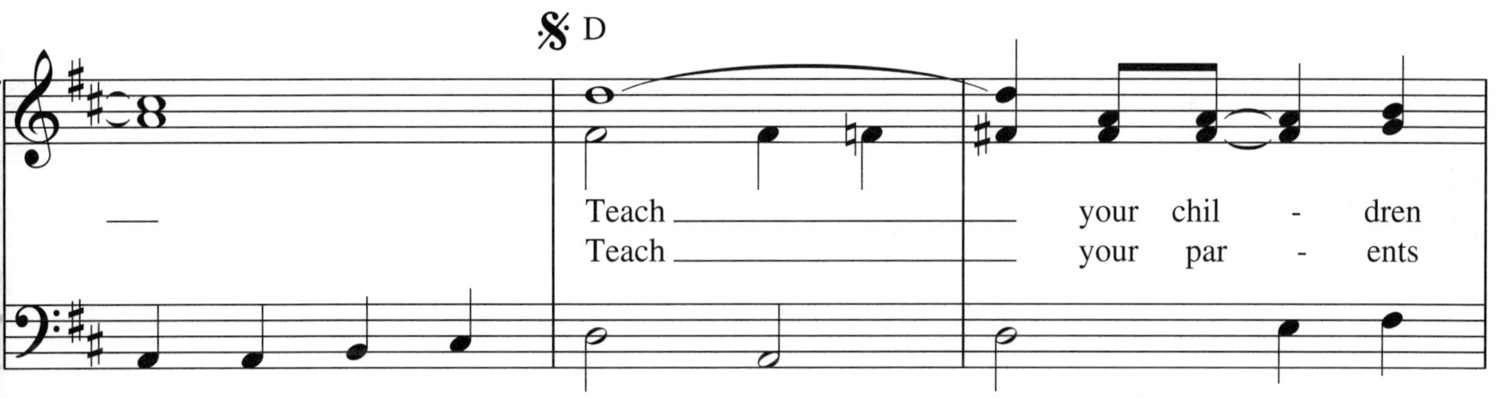
D
Teach your chil - dren
Teach your par - ents

G7
D
well; their fa - ther's hell
well; their chil - dren's hell

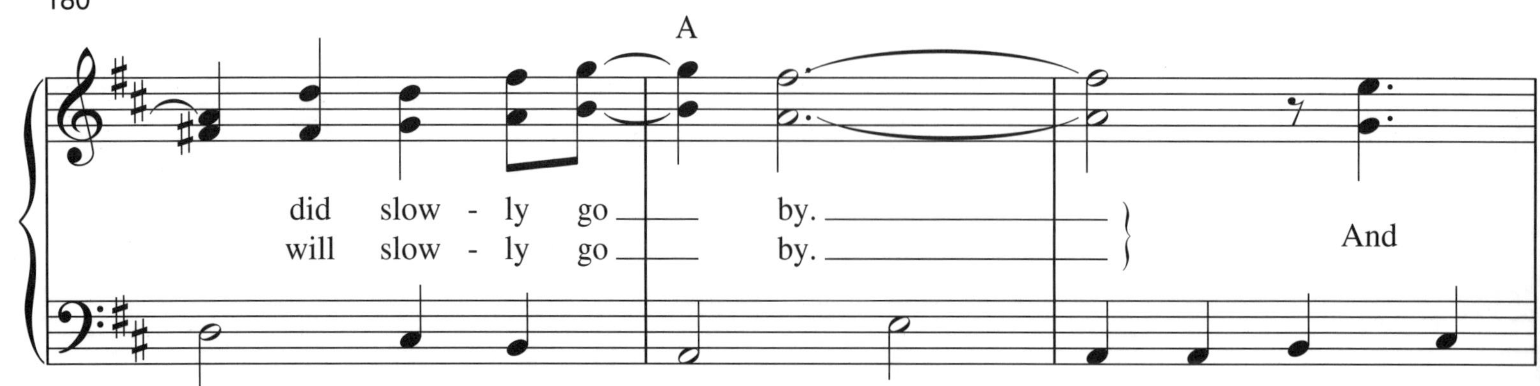
A
did slow - ly go by.
will slow - ly go by.
And

D
G7
feed them on your dreams,

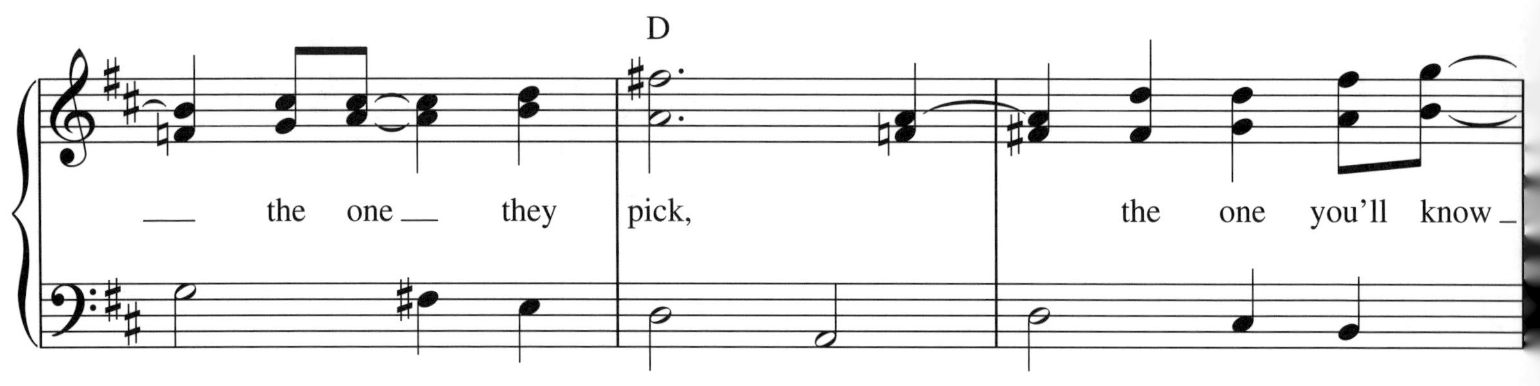
D
the one they pick,
the one you'll know

A
D
by.
Don't you ev -

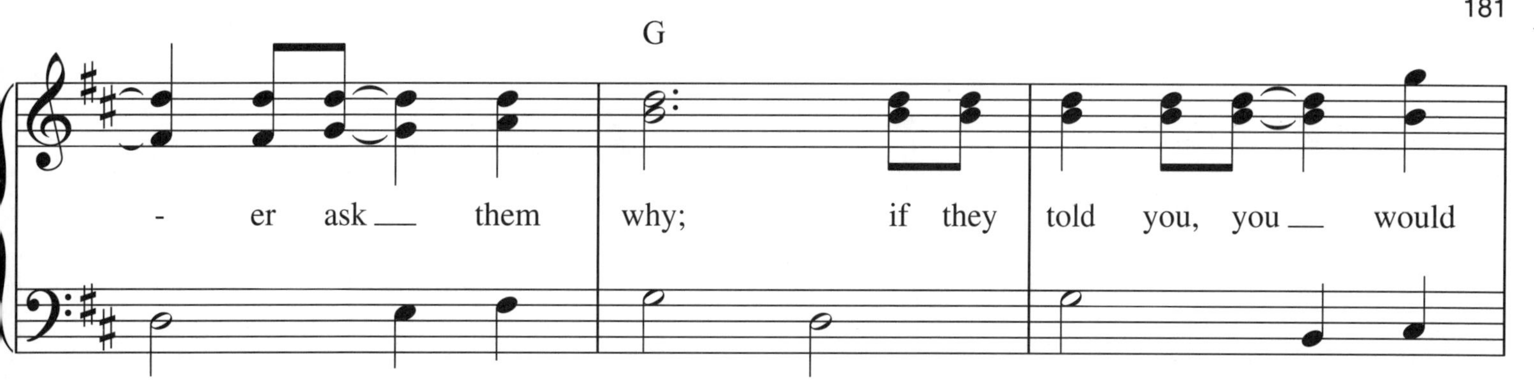
G
- er ask them why; if they told you, you would

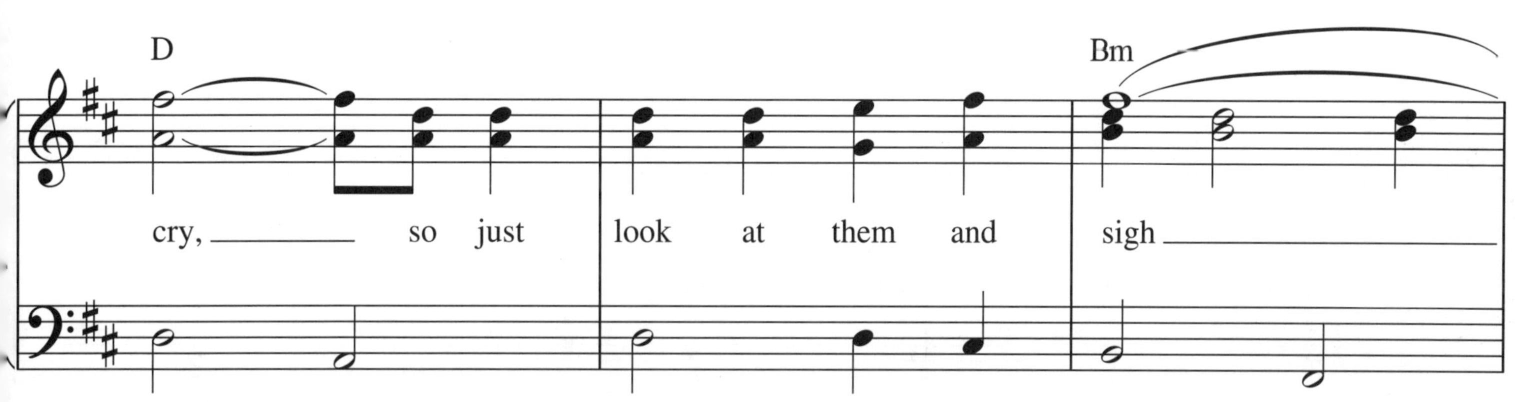
D
Bm
cry, so just look at them and sigh

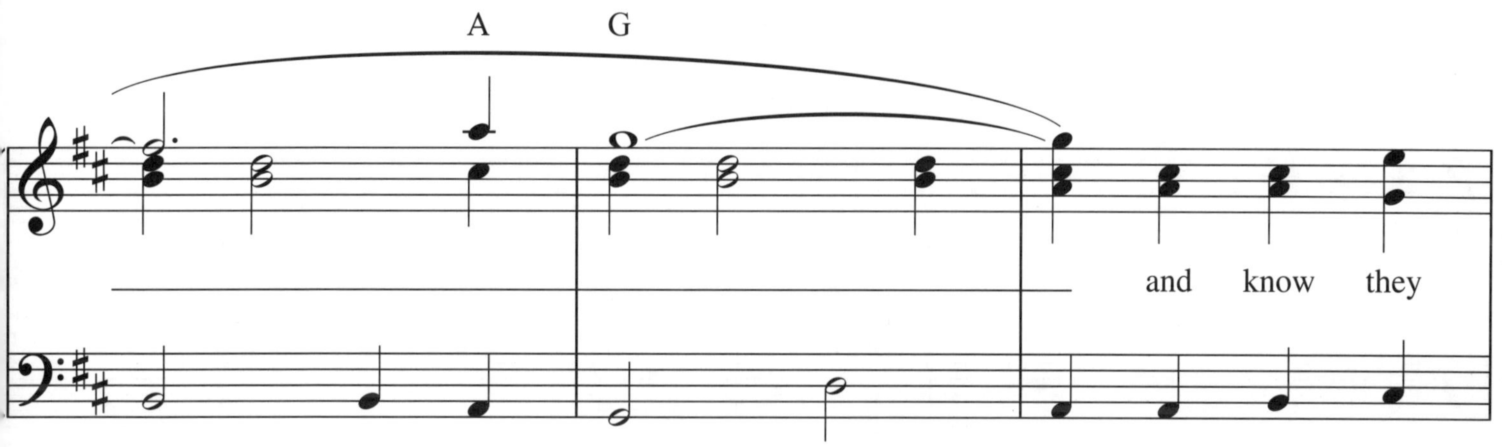
A
G
and know they

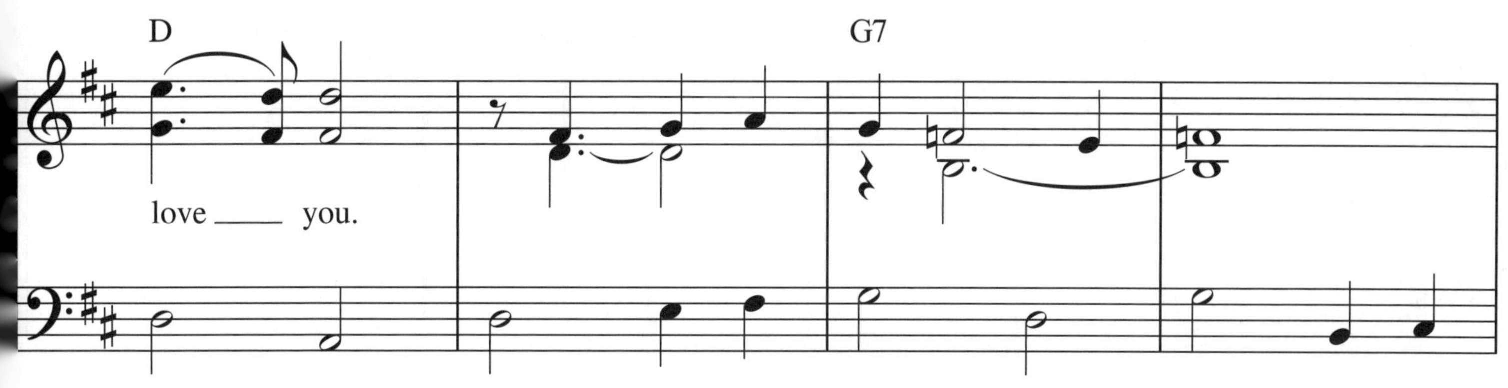
D
G7
love you.

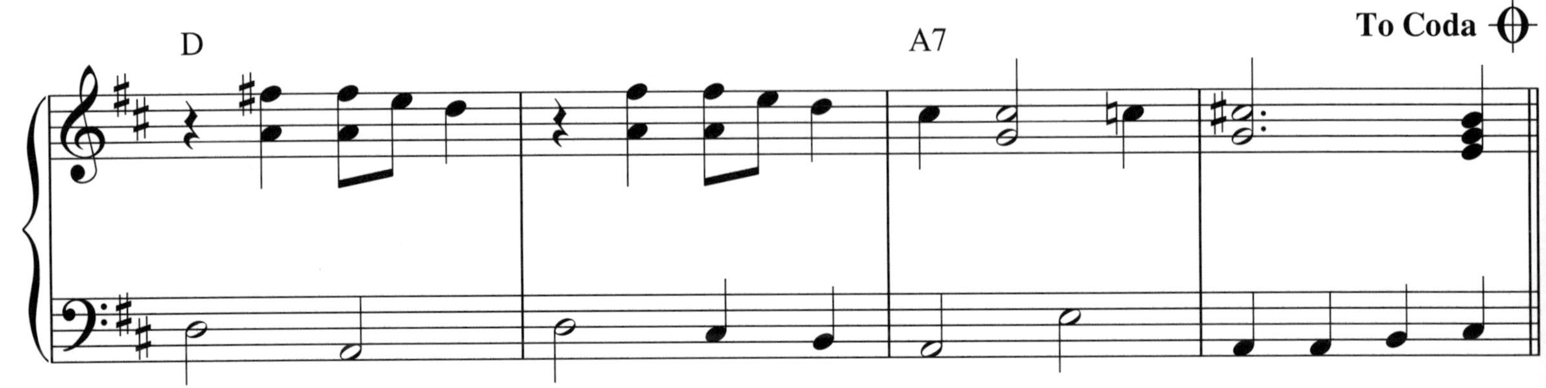
D
A7
To Coda

D
G
Can you hear and do you
teach your chil - dren? You'll be -

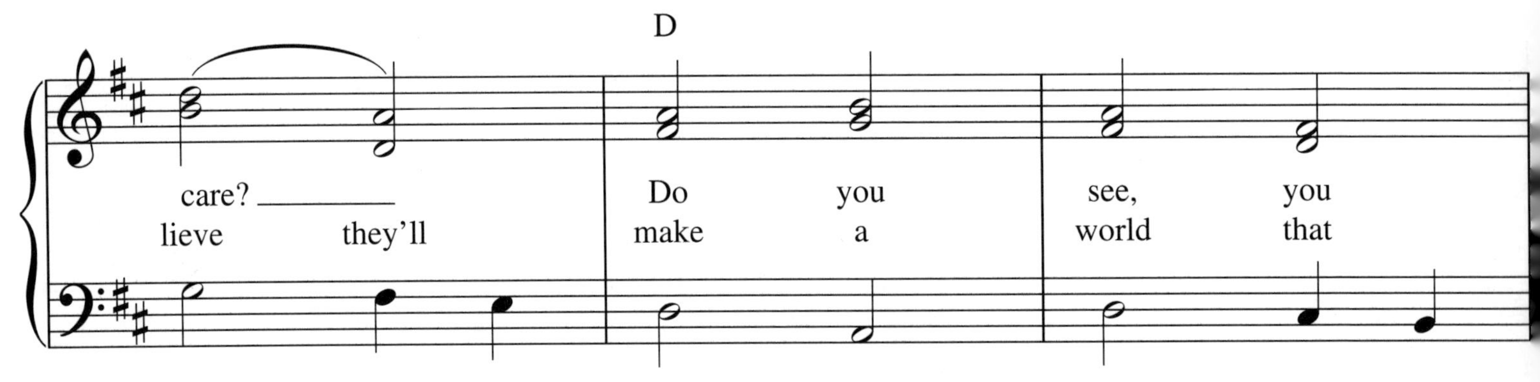
D
care? ___ Do you see, you
lieve they'll make a world that

A
D.S. al Coda
must be free to
we can live in.

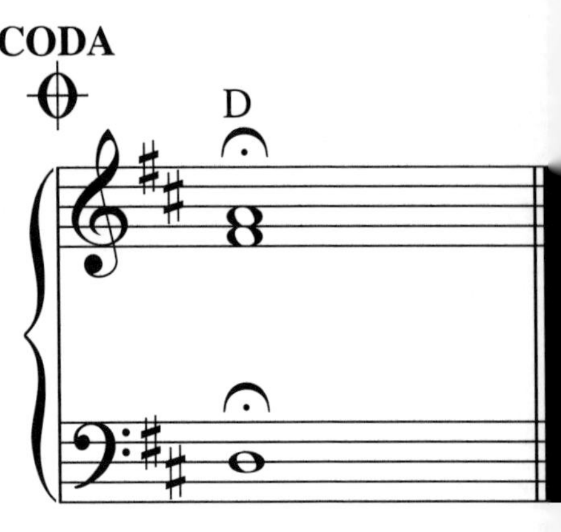
CODA
D

THREE TIMES A LADY

Words and Music by
LIONEL RICHIE

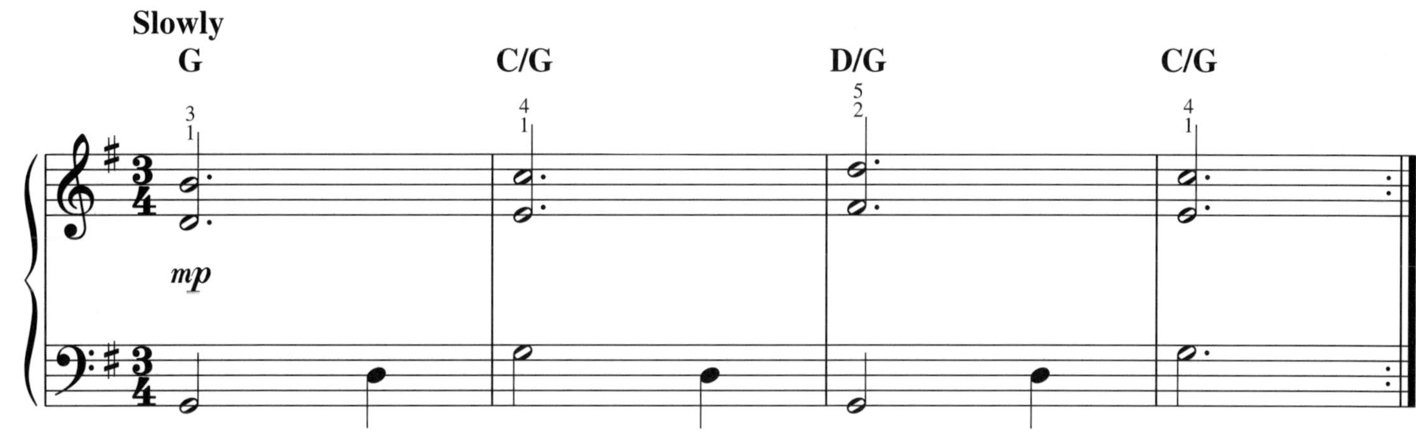

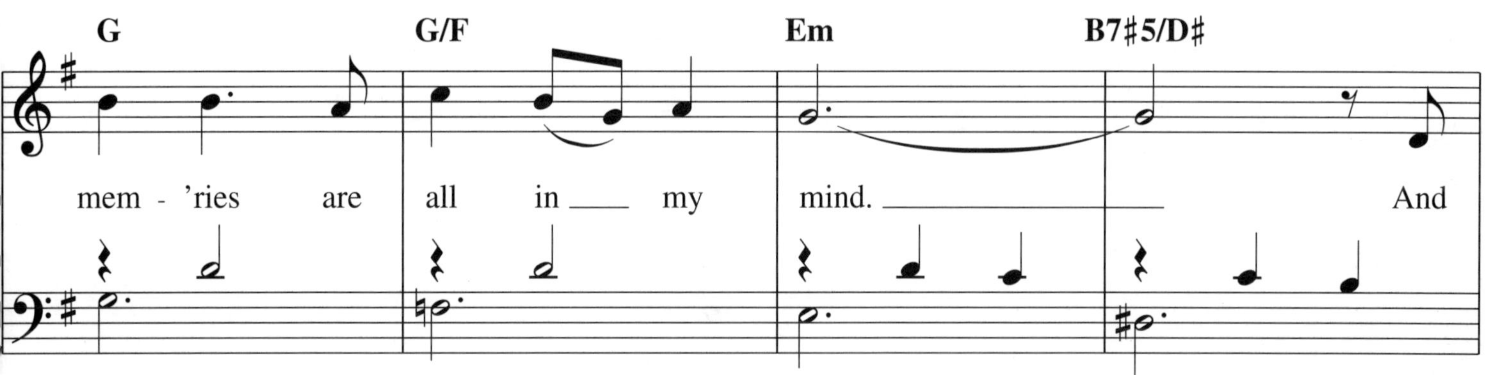

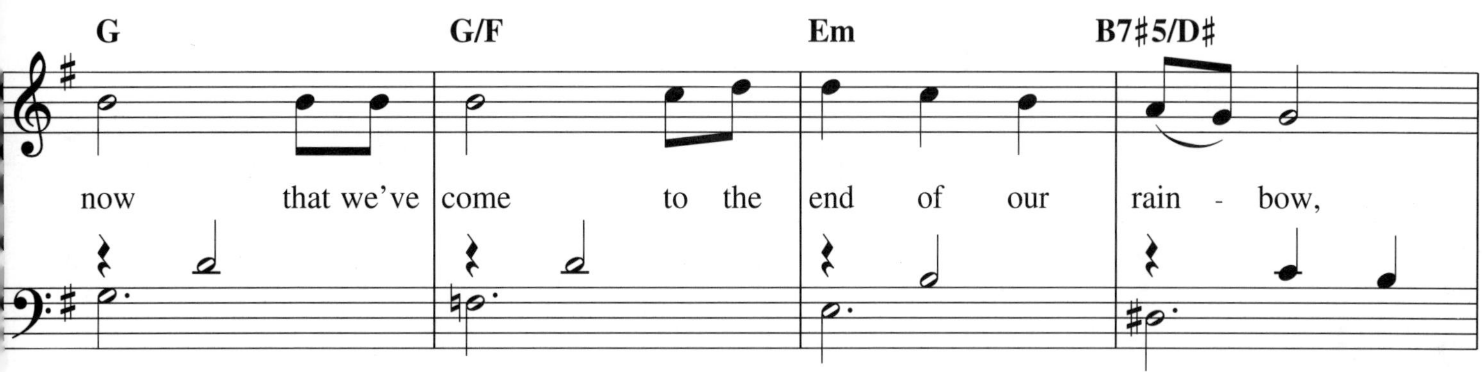

© 1978 JOBETE MUSIC CO., INC. and LIBREN MUSIC
All Rights Controlled and Administered by EMI APRIL MUSIC INC.
All Rights Reserved International Copyright Secured Used by Permission

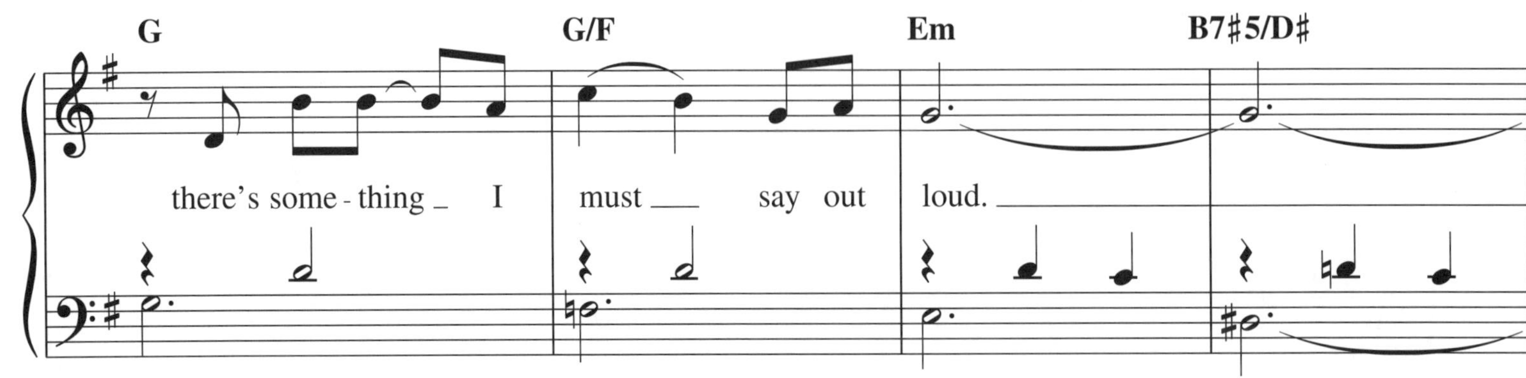
G
G/F
Em
B7♯5/D♯
there's some - thing _ I
must ___ say out
loud. ___

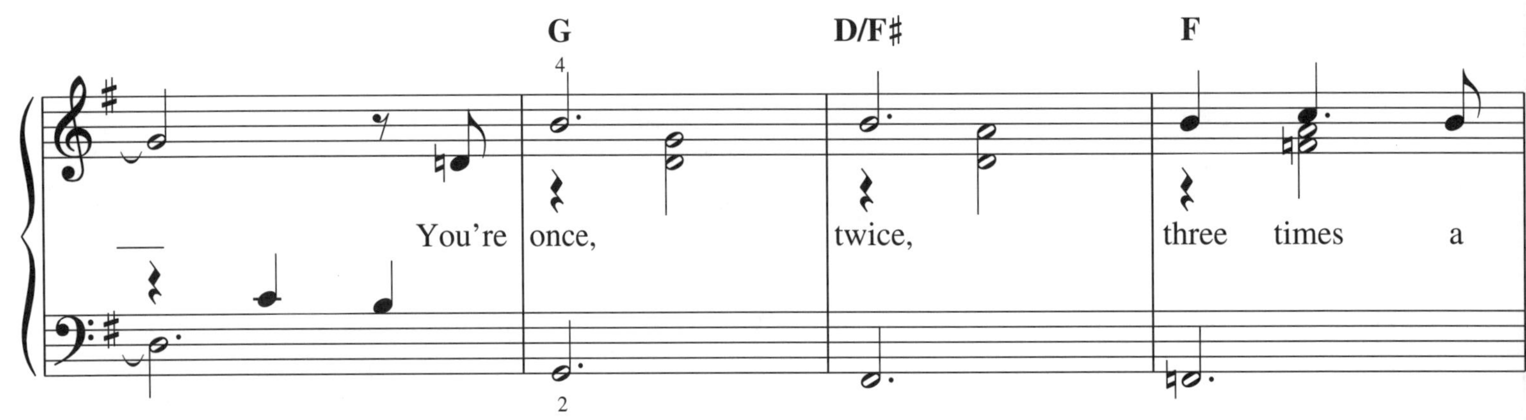
G
D/F♯
F
You're
once,
twice,
three times a

C/E
Am7
G
D
la - dy,
and I
love ___
you. ___

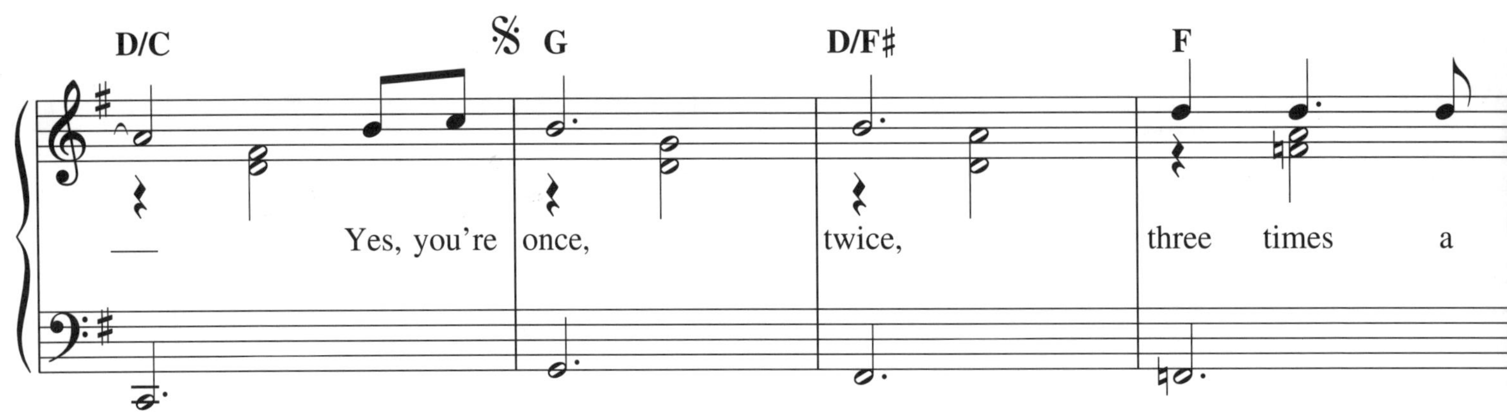
D/C
G
D/F♯
F
Yes, you're
once,
twice,
three times a

C/E
Am7
G
D
la - dy, and I love you,

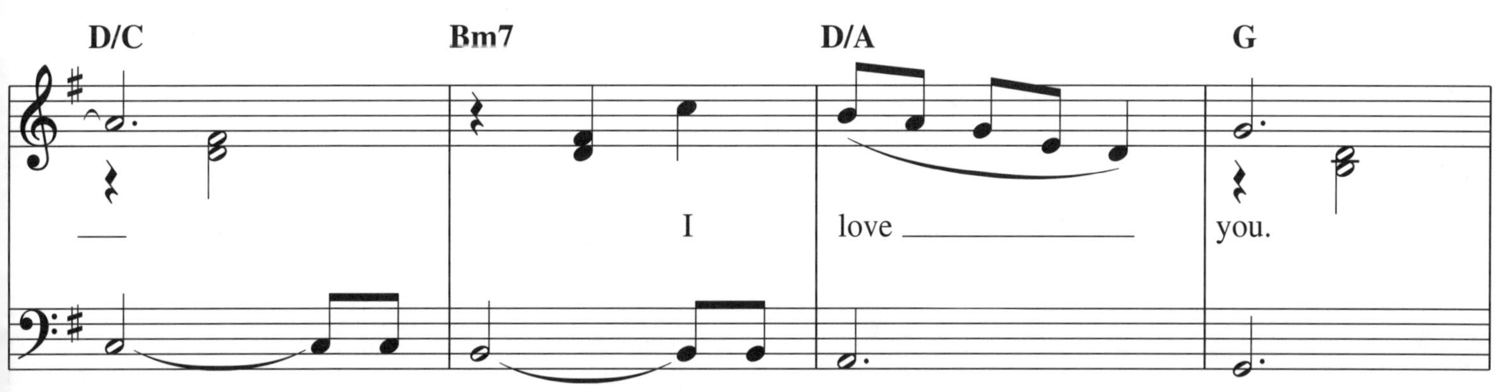
D/C
Bm7
D/A
G
I love you.

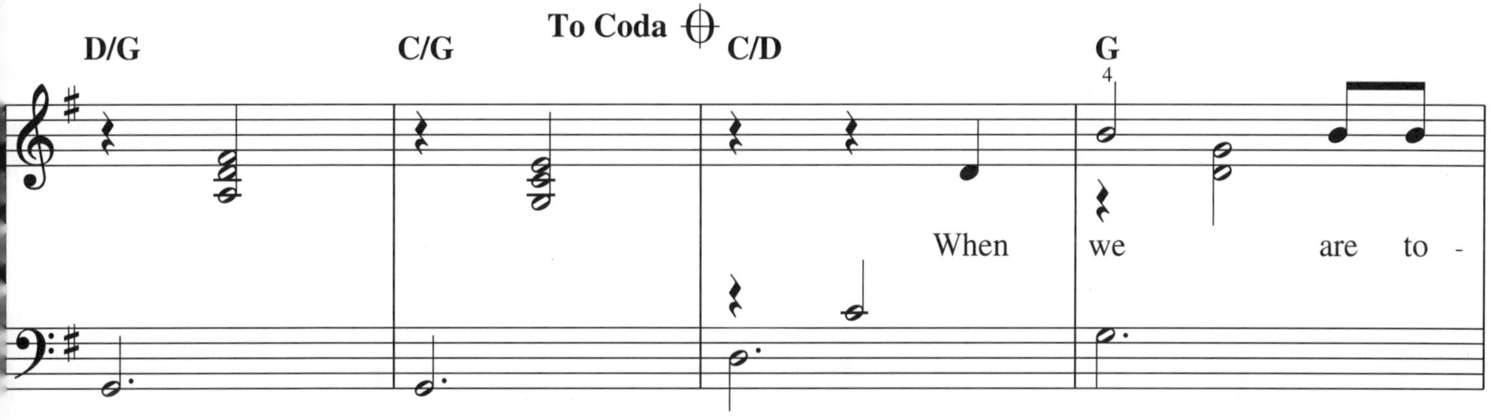
To Coda
D/G
C/G
C/D
G
When we are to -

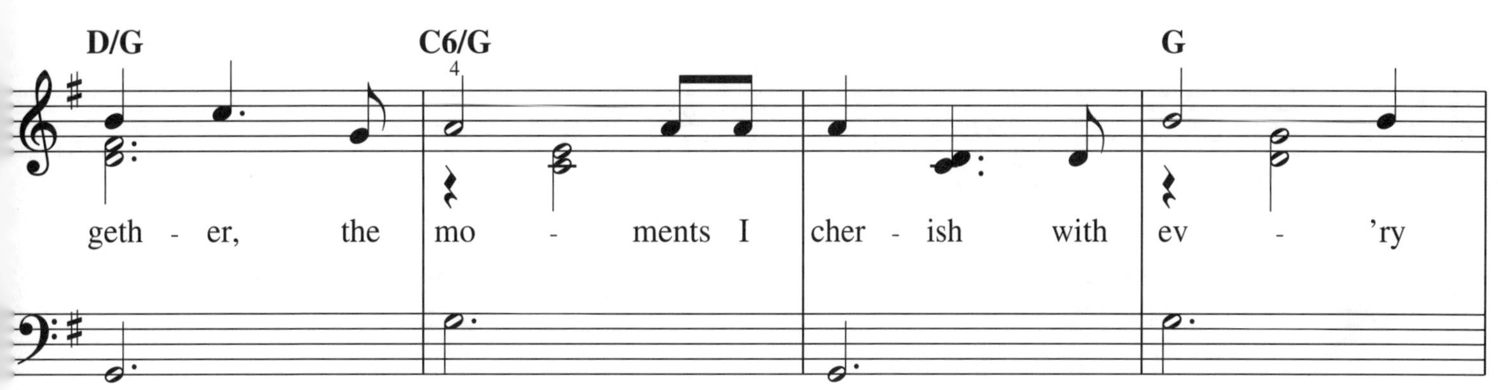
D/G
C6/G
G
geth - er, the mo - ments I cher - ish with ev - 'ry

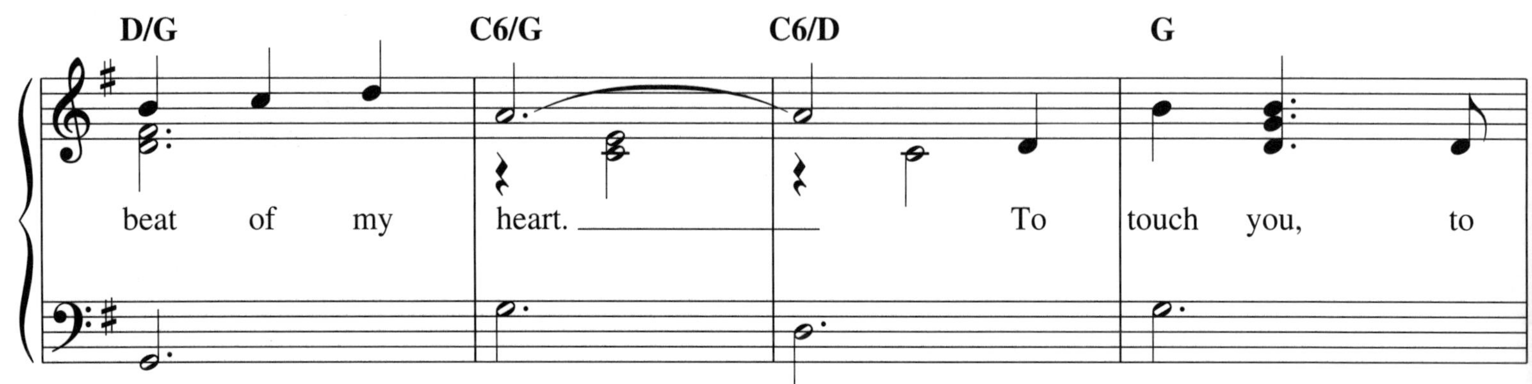
D/G
C6/G
C6/D
G
beat of my heart. To touch you, to

D/G
C6/G
G
hold you, to feel you, to need you; there's noth - ing to

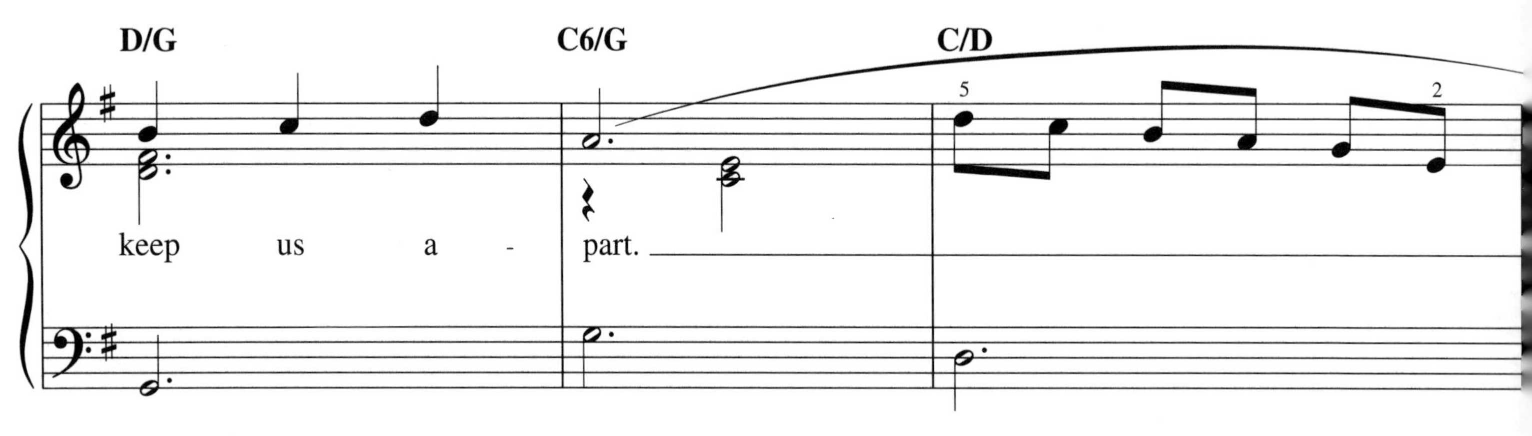
D/G
C6/G
C/D
keep us a - part.

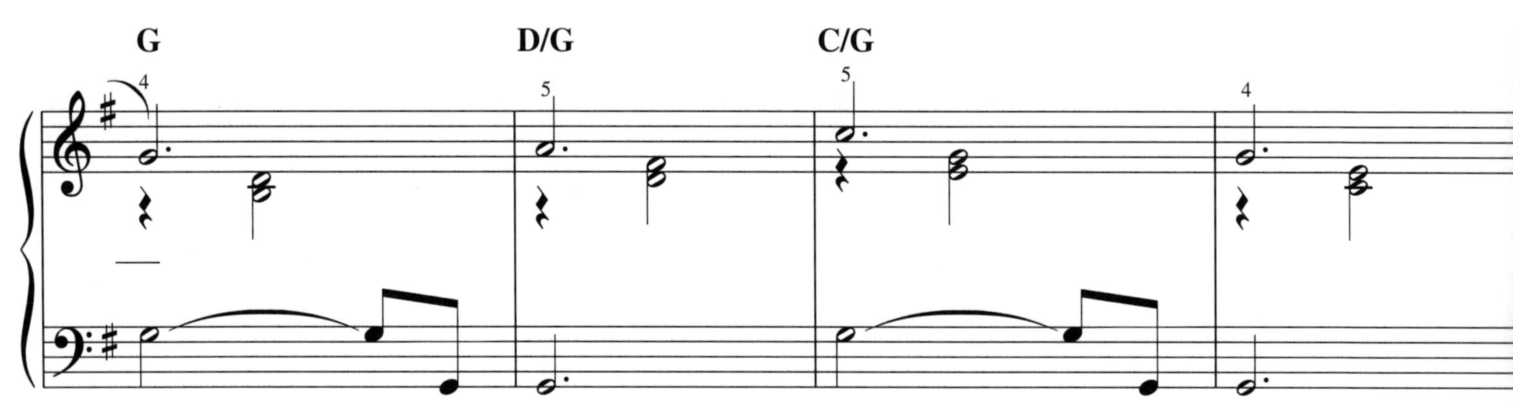
G
D/G
C/G

G
5
D/G
C/G

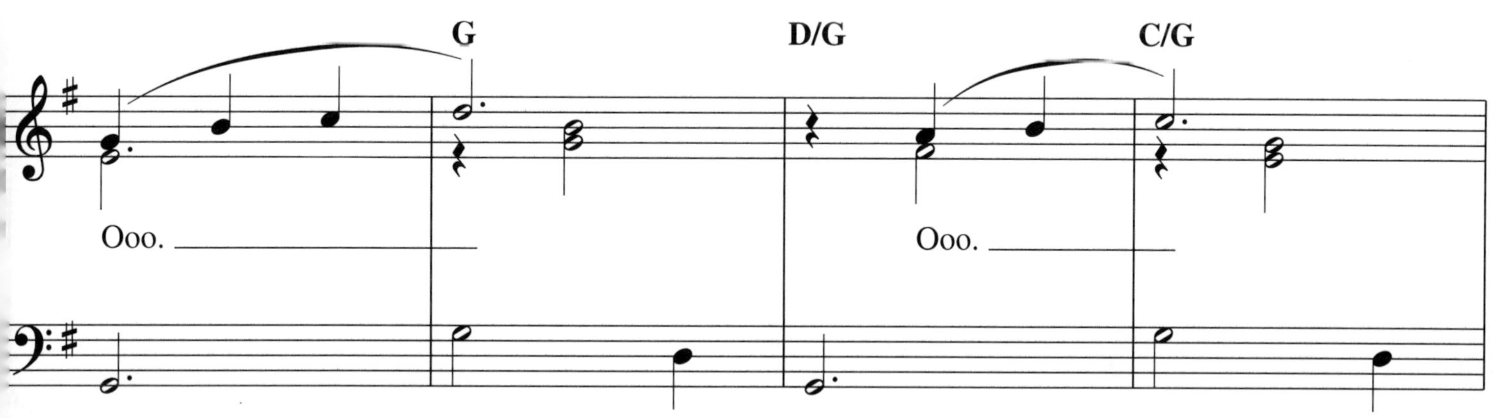
G
D/G
C/G
Ooo.
Ooo.

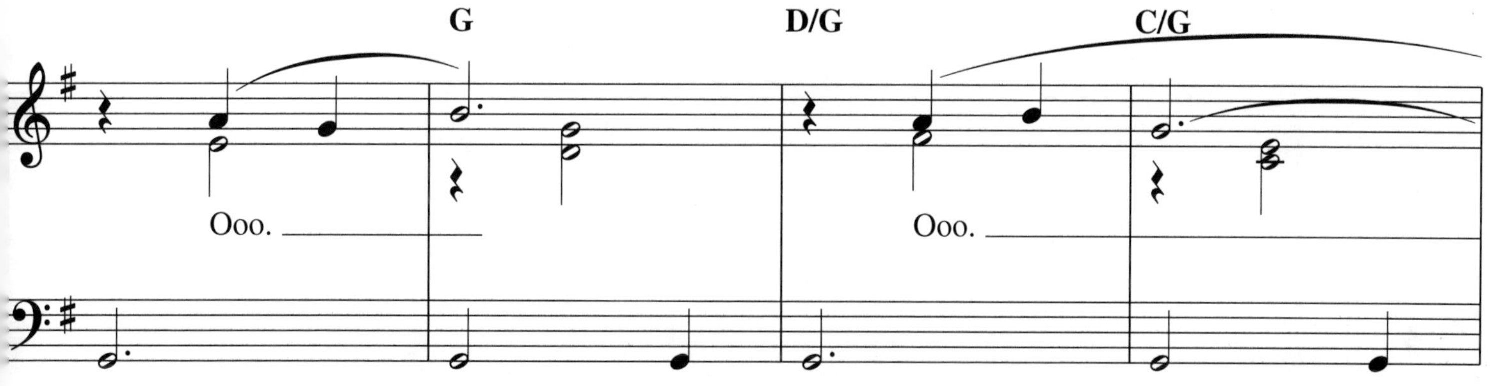
G
D/G
C/G
Ooo.
Ooo.

D.S. al Coda
You're

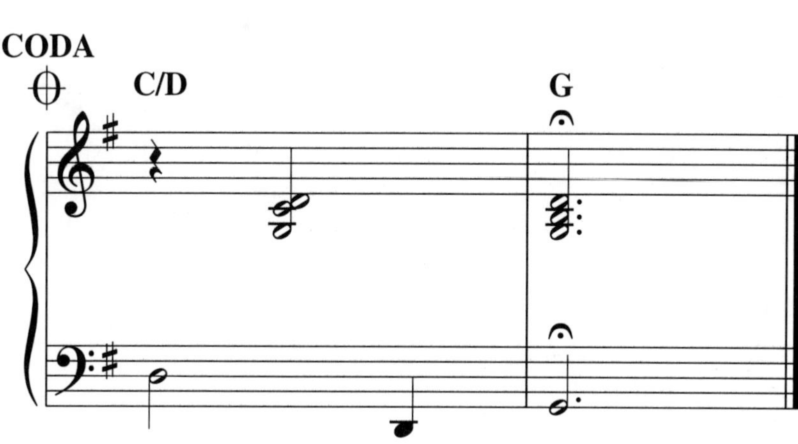
CODA
C/D
G

TOP OF THE WORLD

Words and Music by JOHN BETTIS
and RICHARD CARPENTER

Copyright © 1972 ALMO MUSIC CORP. and HAMMER AND NAILS MUSIC
Copyright Renewed
All Rights Administered by ALMO MUSIC CORP.
All Rights Reserved Used by Permission

D
G
see, ___
same, ___
not a
in the
cloud in the
leaves on the

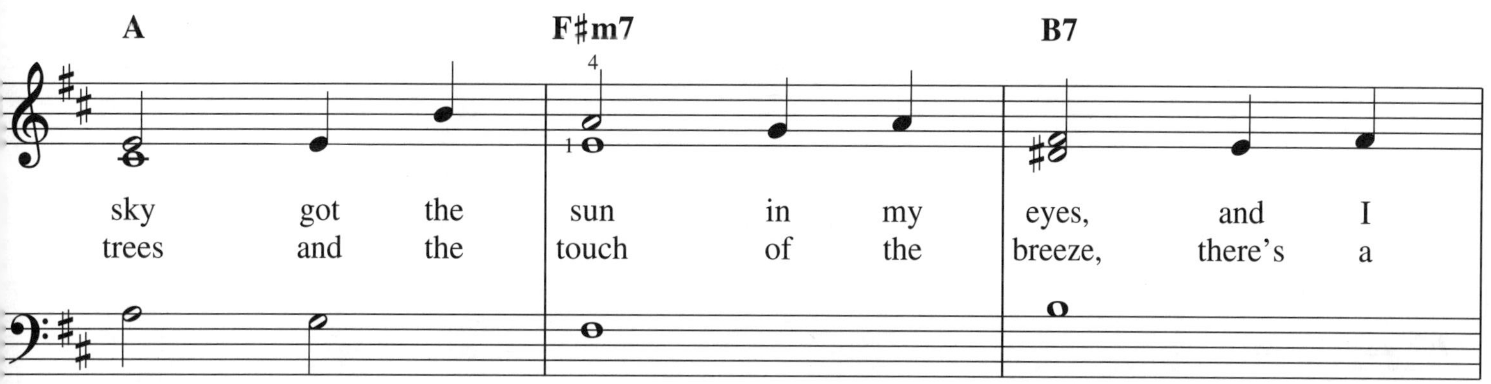
A
F♯m7
B7
sky got the
trees and the
sun in my
touch of the
eyes, and I
breeze, there's a

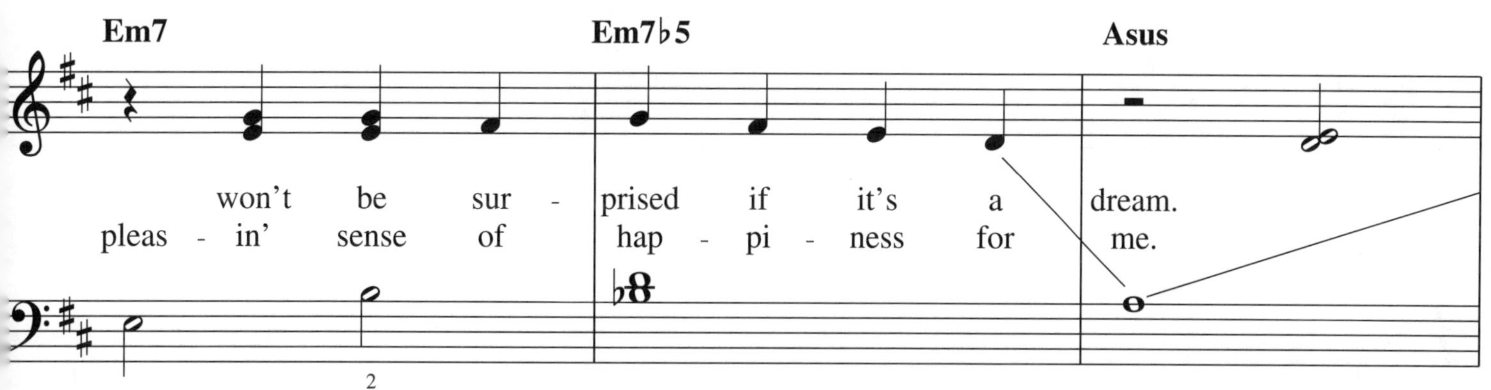
Em7
Em7♭5
Asus
won't be sur - prised if it's a dream.
pleas - in' sense of hap - pi - ness for me.

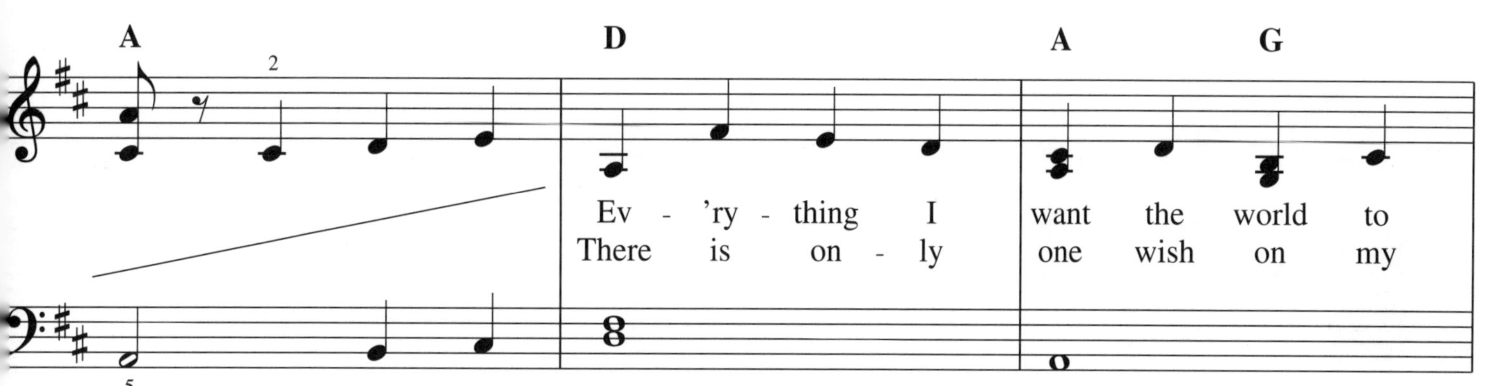
A
D
A
G
Ev - 'ry - thing I want the world to
There is on - ly one wish on my

D
F♯m
be, is now com - ing true es -
mind, when this day is through I

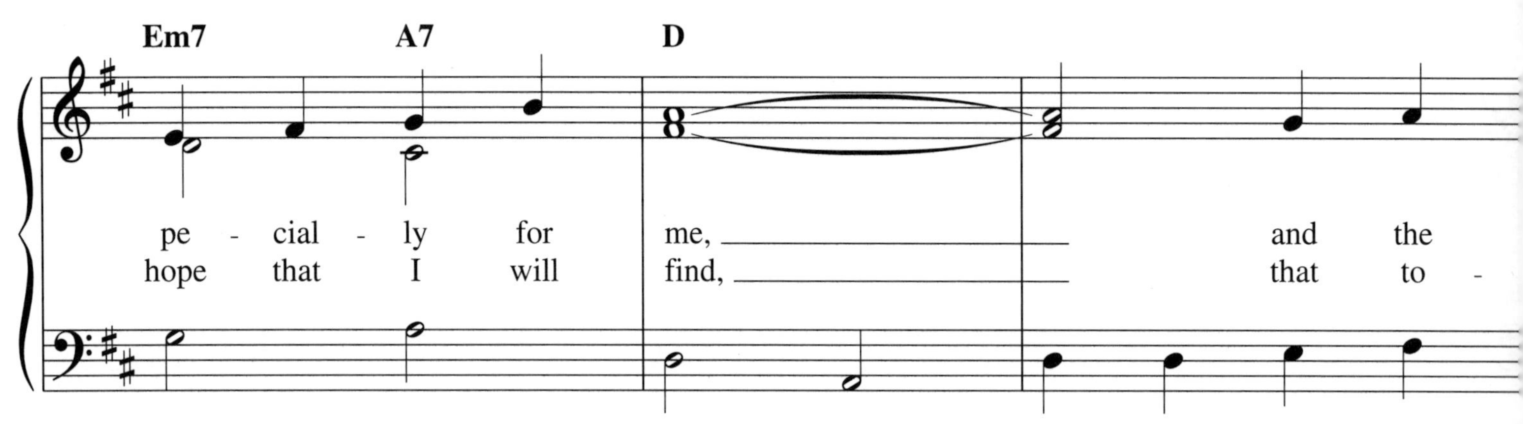
Em7
A7
D
pe - cial - ly for me, and the
hope that I will find, that to -

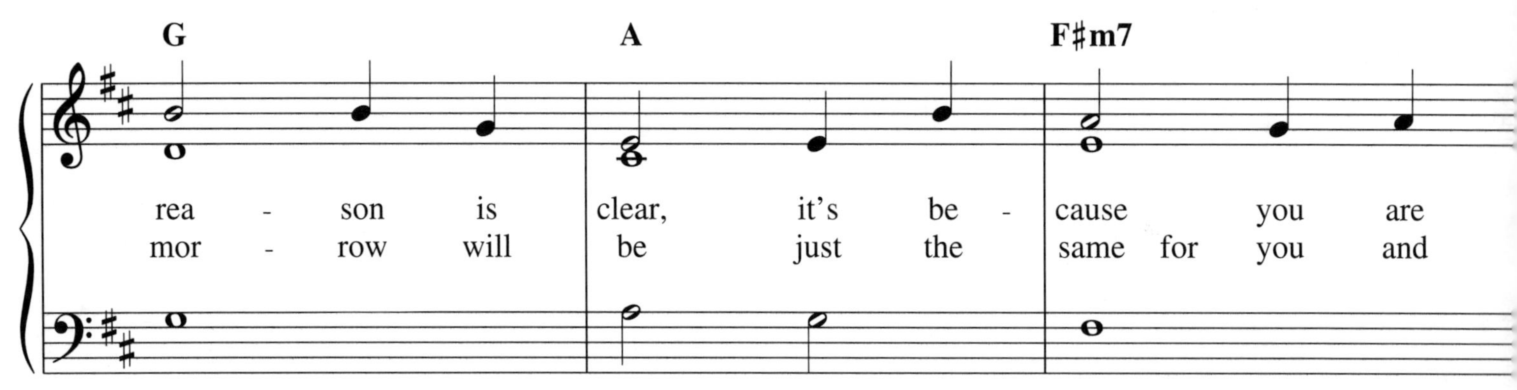
G
A
F♯m7
rea - son is clear, it's be - cause you are
mor - row will be just the same for you and

B7
Em7
Em7♭5
here, you're the near - est thing to heav - en that I've
me, all I need will be mine if you are

Asus
A
D
seen.
here.
I'm on the
top of the world

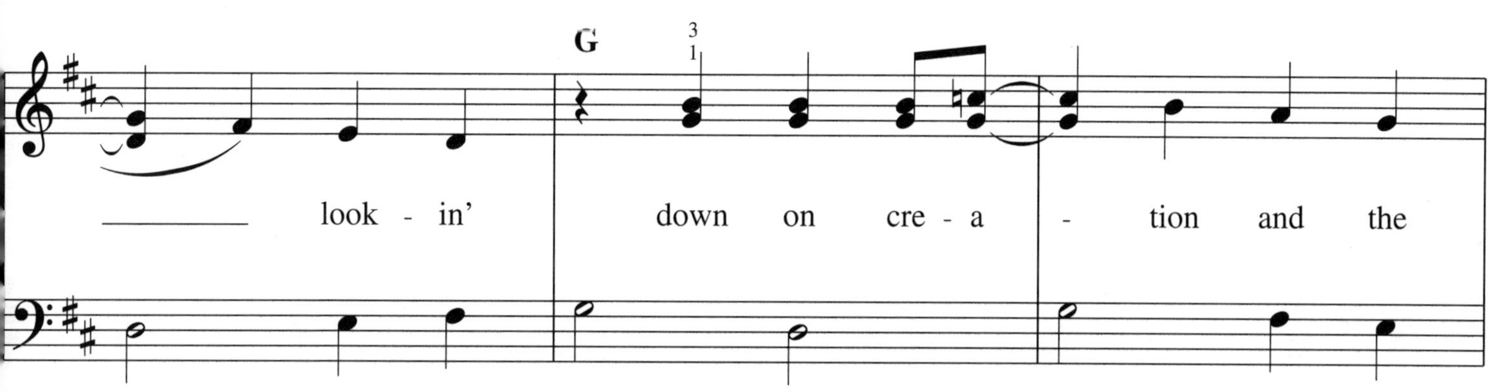
G
look - in'
down on cre - a
- tion and the

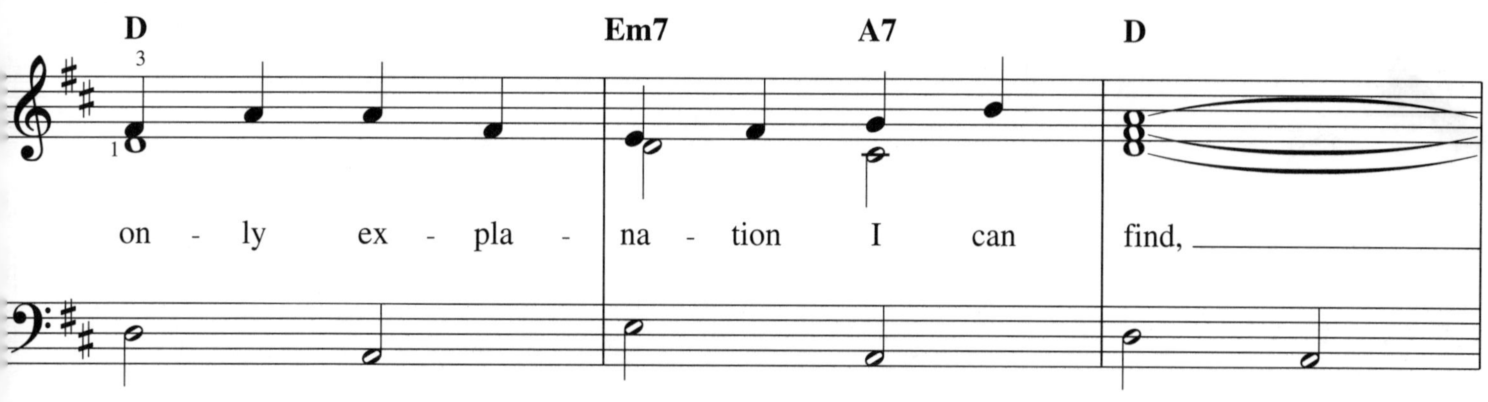
D
Em7
A7
D
on - ly ex - pla -
na - tion I can
find,

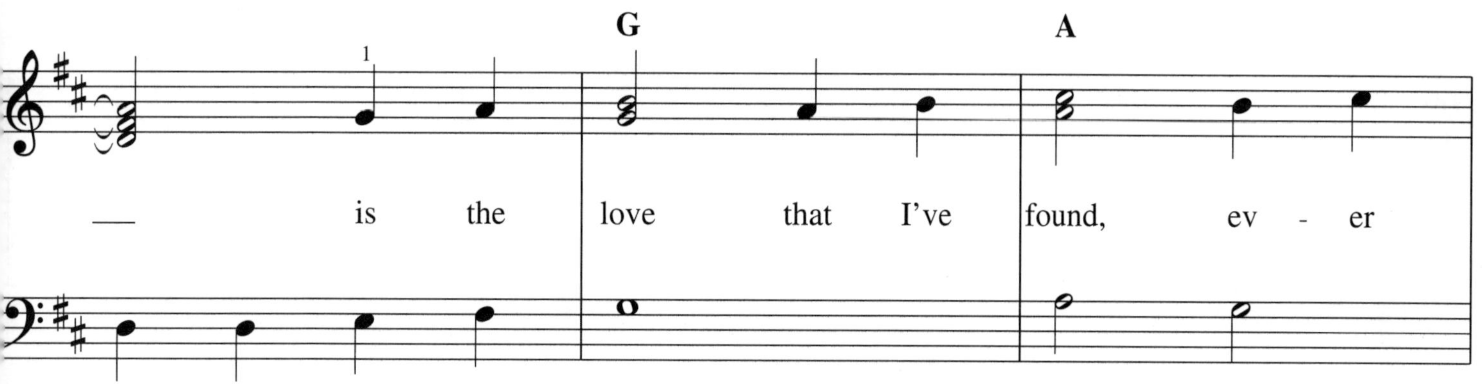
G
A
is the
love that I've
found, ev - er

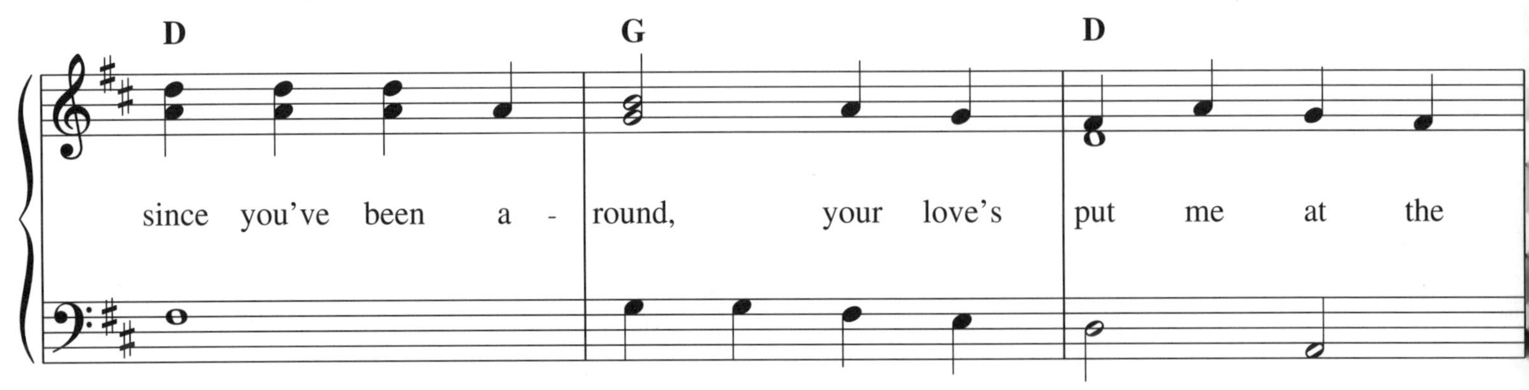
D
G
D
since you've been a - round, your love's put me at the

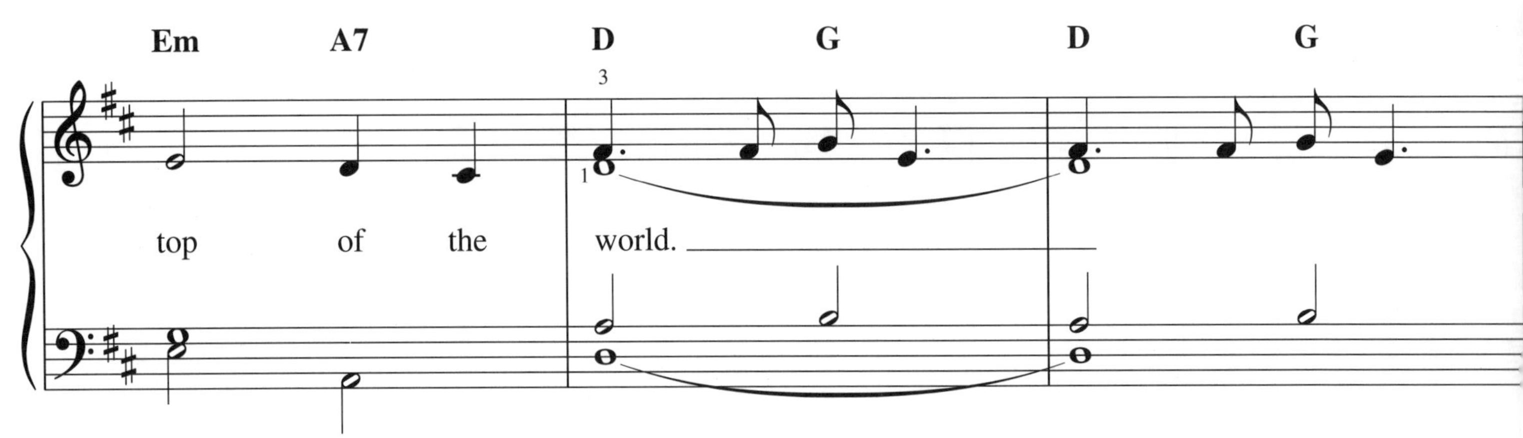
Em
A7
D
G
D
G
top of the world.

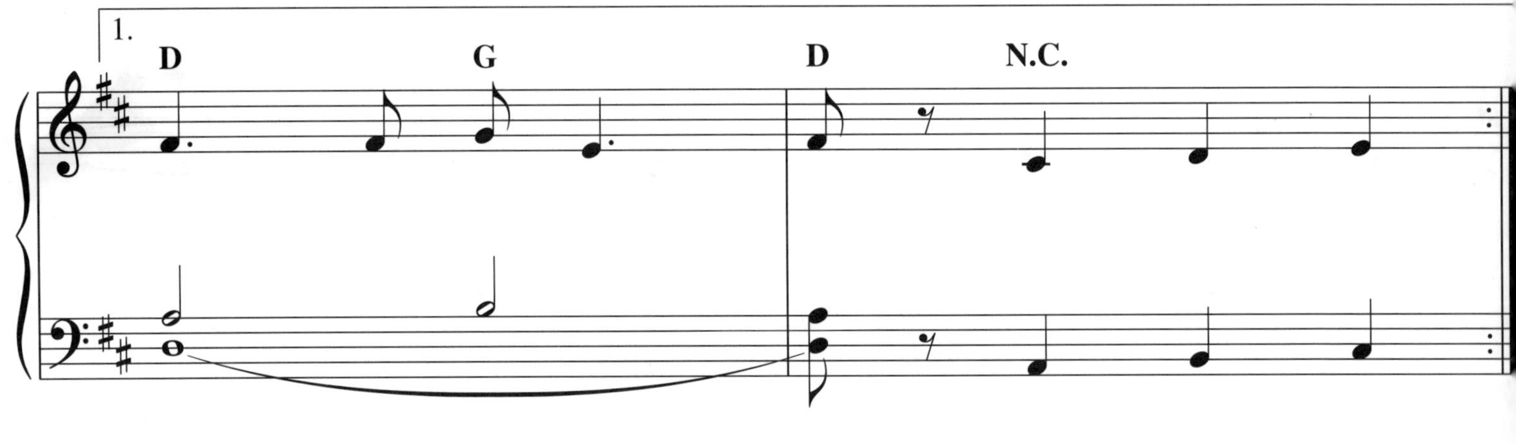
1.
D
G
D
N.C.

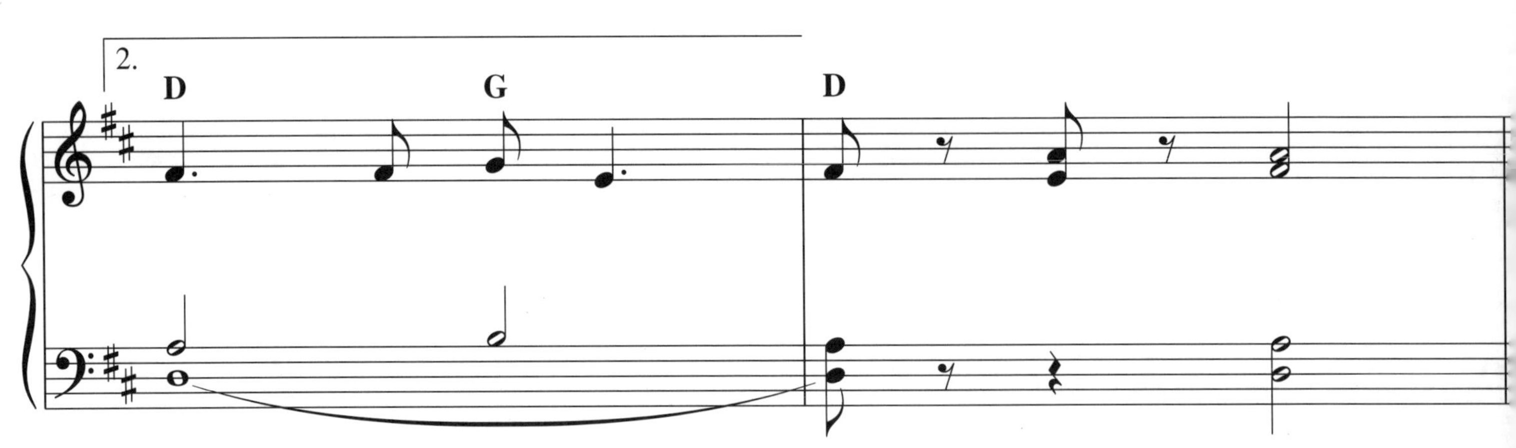
2.
D
G
D

YESTERDAY ONCE MORE

Words and Music by JOHN BETTIS
and RICHARD CARPENTER

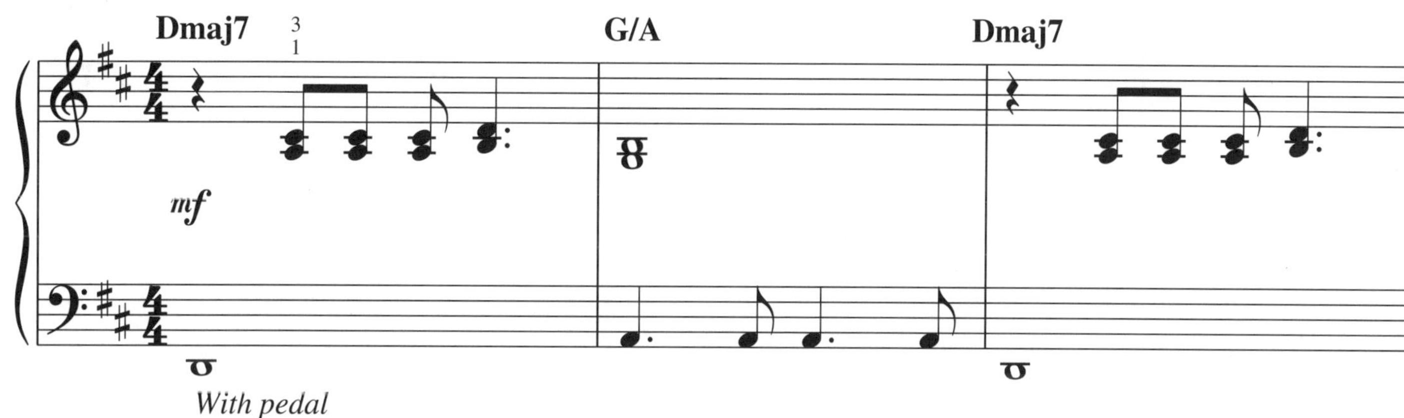

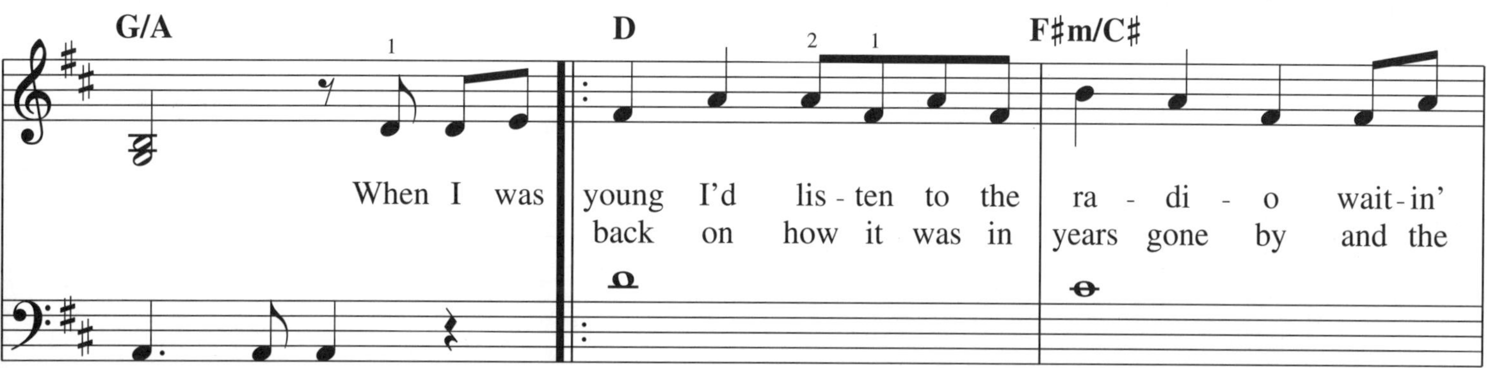

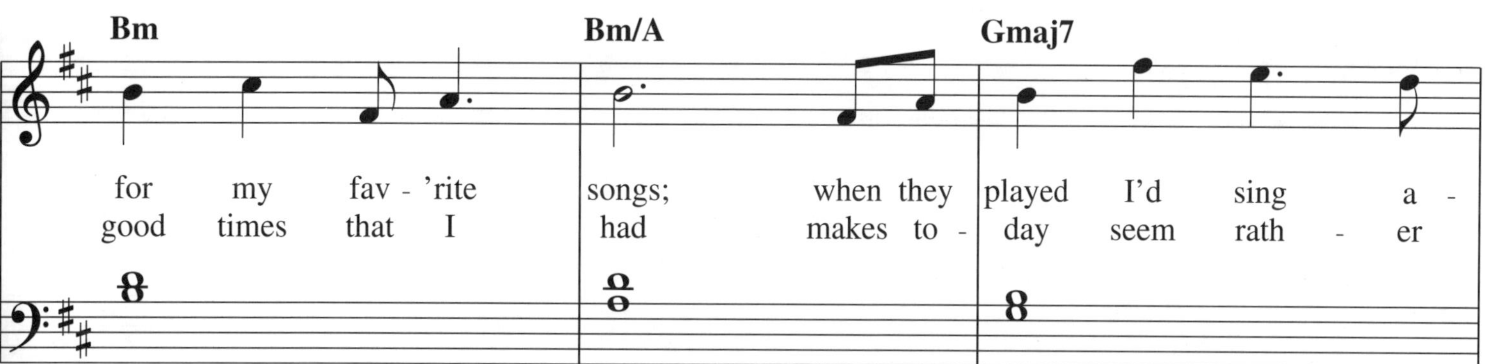

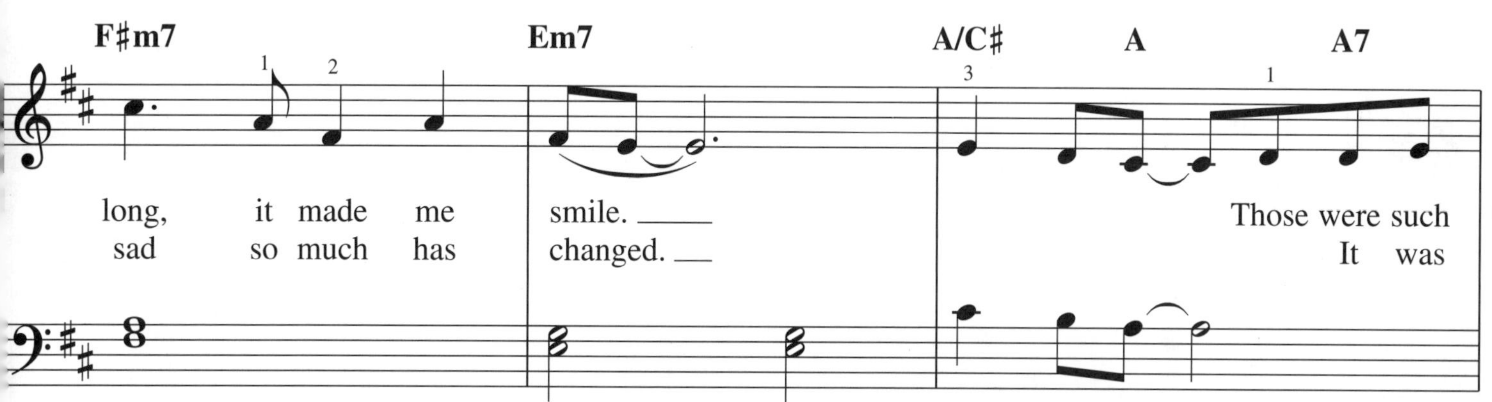

Copyright © 1973 ALMO MUSIC CORP. and HAMMER AND NAILS MUSIC
Copyright Renewed
All Rights Administered by ALMO MUSIC CORP.
All Rights Reserved Used by Permission

D
F♯m/C♯
hap - py times and not so long a - go how I
songs of love that I would sing to then and I'd

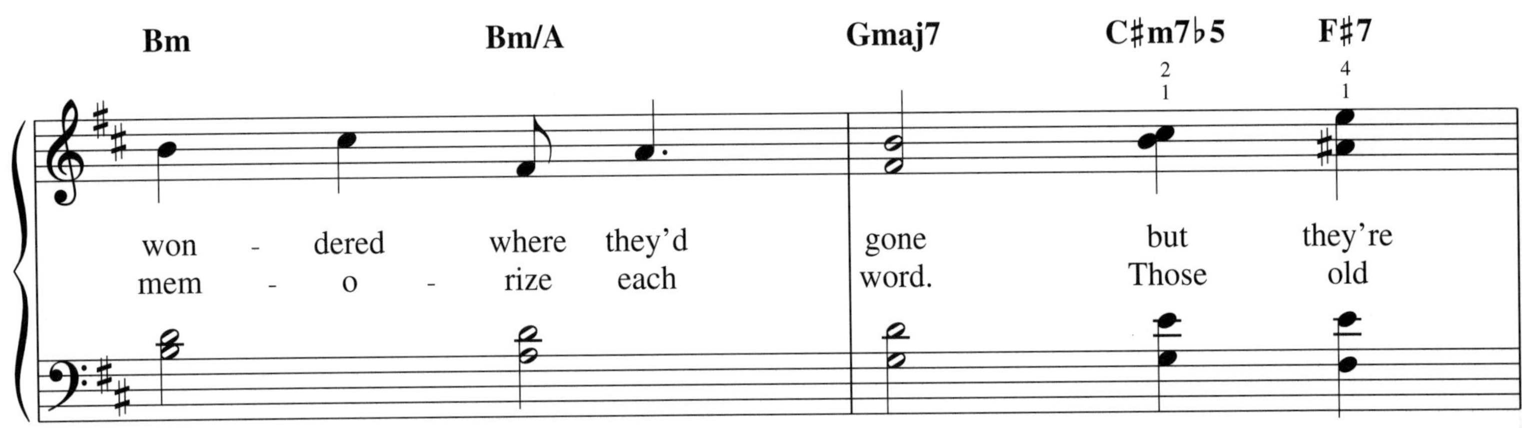
Bm
Bm/A
Gmaj7
C♯m7♭5
F♯7
won - dered where they'd gone but they're
mem - o - rize each word. Those old

Bm
Bm/A
back a - gain just like a long lost friend all the
mel - o - dies still sound so good to me as they

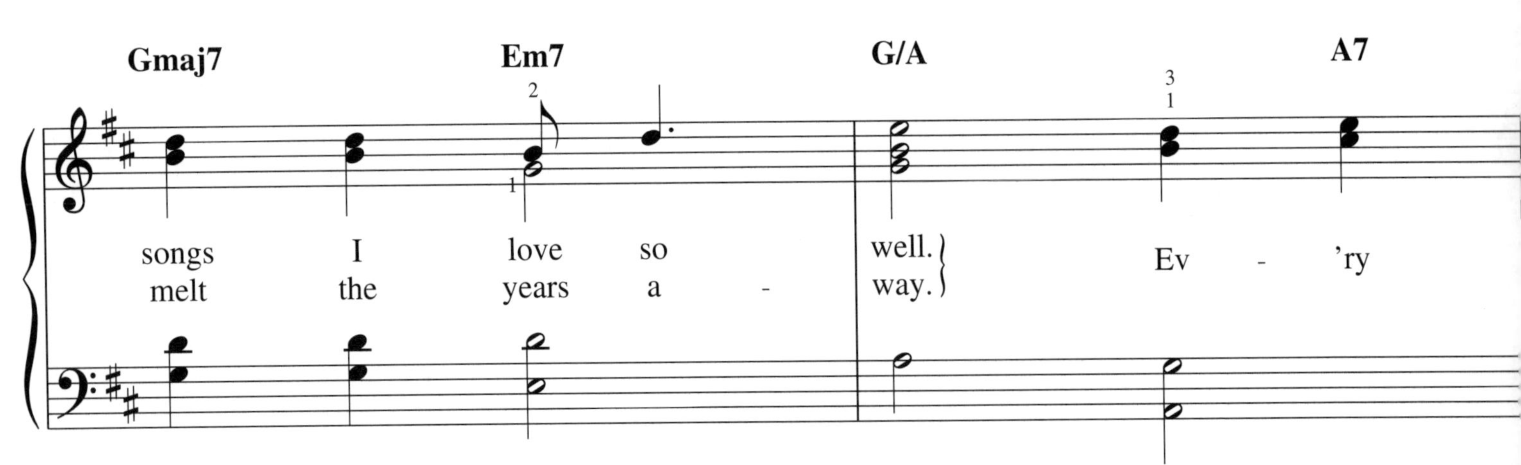
Gmaj7
Em7
G/A
A7
songs I love so well.
melt the years a - way.
Ev - 'ry

D
Bm
sha - la - la - la ev - 'ry
wo wo still
D
Bm7
shines.
Ev - 'ry
D
Bm
shing - a - ling - a - ling that they're
start - in' to sing so
Em7
A7
fine.
When they
All my

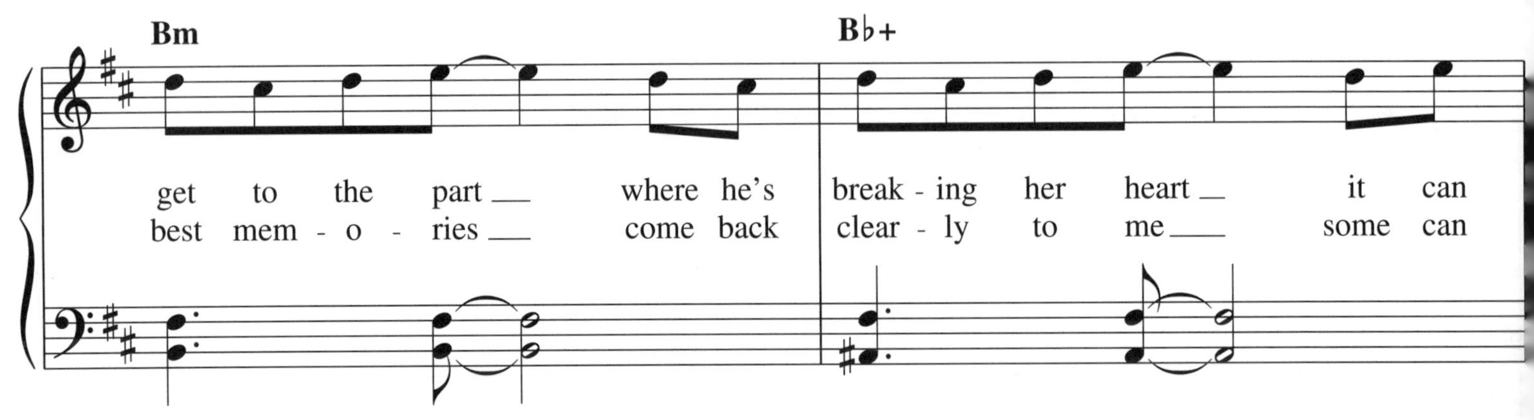
Bm
B♭+
get to the part where he's breaking her heart it can
best mem-o-ries come back clear-ly to me some can

D/A
G♯m7♭5
D/A
real-ly make me cry just like be-fore.
e-ven make me cry just like be-fore.

G/A
Dmaj7
1.
G/A
It's yes-ter-day once more.

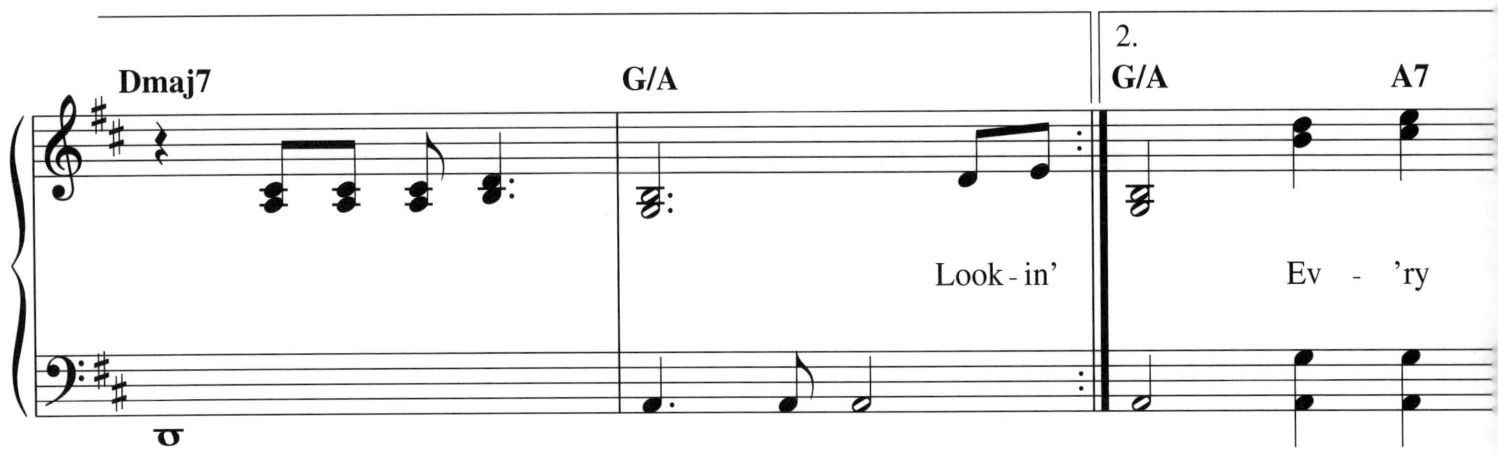
Dmaj7
G/A
2.
G/A
A7
Look-in'
Ev-'ry

D
Bm
D
sha - la - la - la ev - 'ry wo wo still shines.
Bm7
D
Ev - 'ry shing - a - ling - a - ling that they're
Bm7
Em7
1.
A7
G/A
A7
start - in' to sing so fine. Ev - 'ry
2.
A7
G/A
Dmaj7

THE WAY WE WERE

from the Motion Picture THE WAY WE WERE

Words by ALAN and MARILYN BERGMAN
Music by MARVIN HAMLISCH

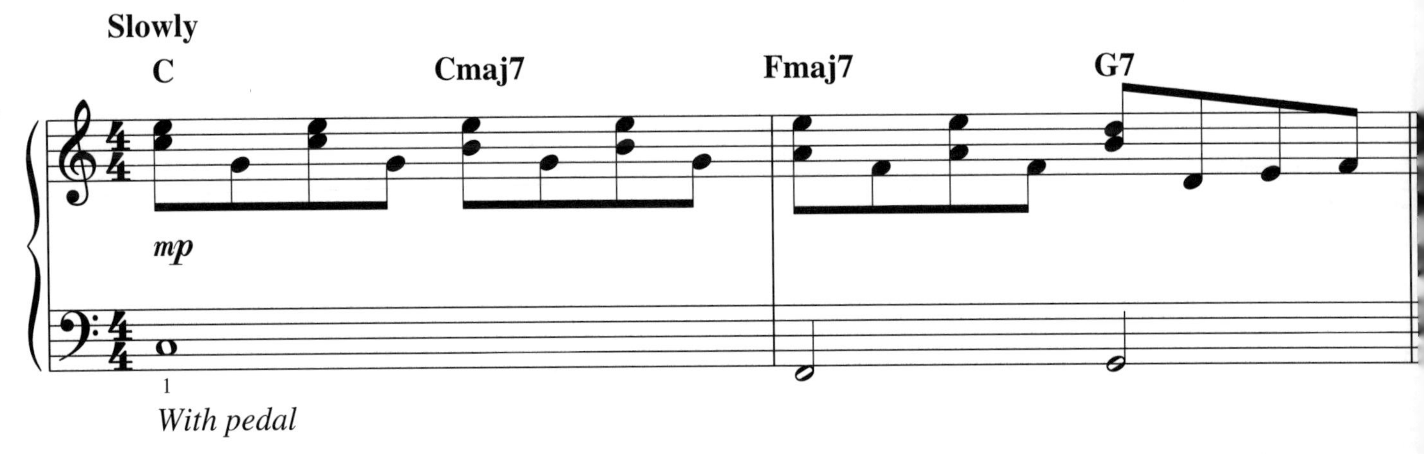

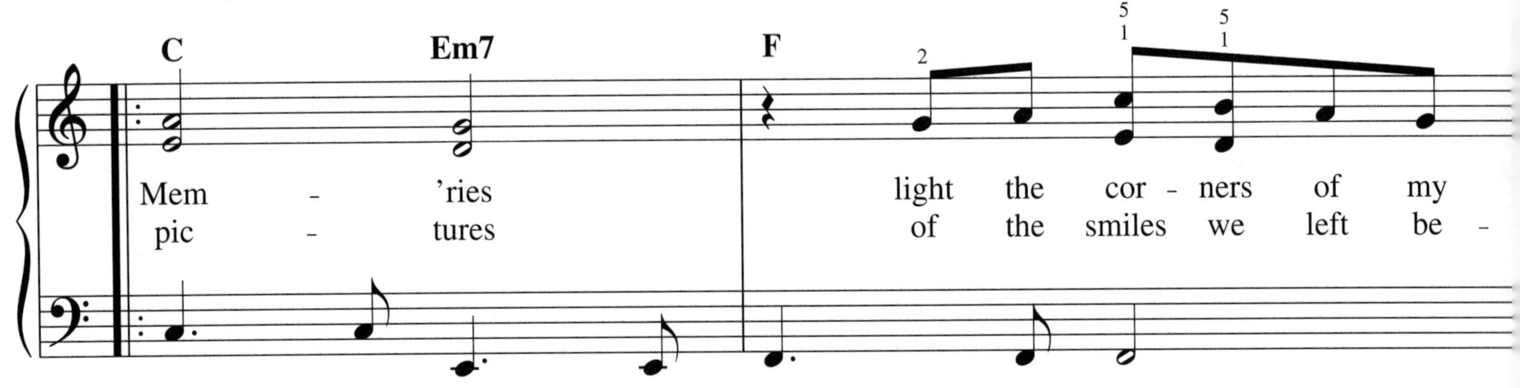

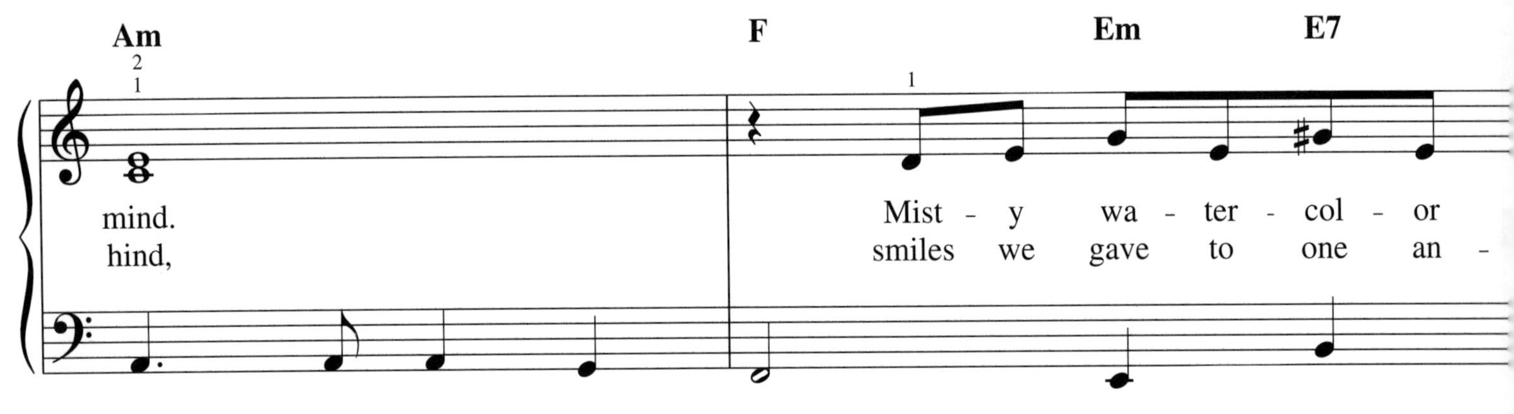

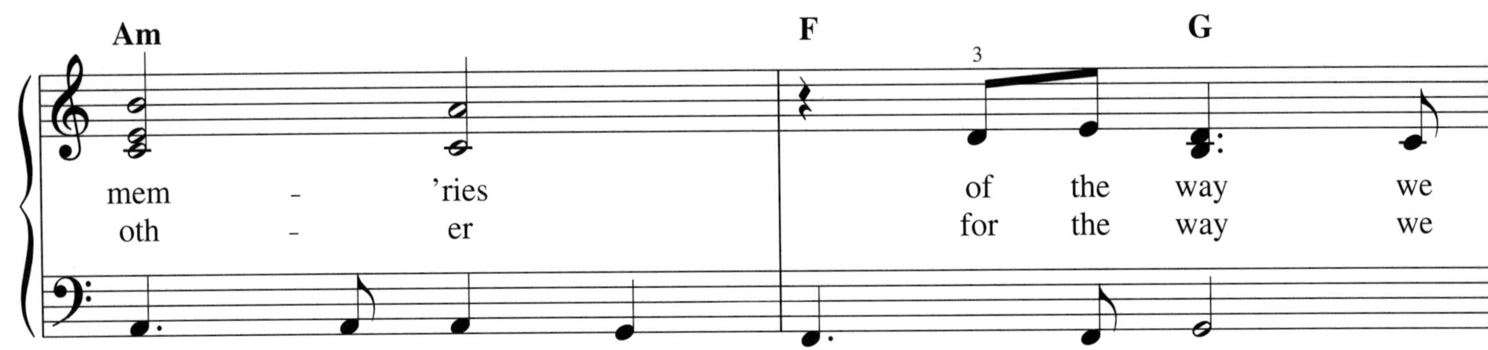

© 1973 (Renewed 2001) COLGEMS-EMI MUSIC INC.
All Rights Reserved International Copyright Secured Used by Permission

1.
Cmaj7
Am
Dm7
Gsus
were.
Scat - tered
2.
Cmaj7
Gm7
C7sus
F
were.
Can it be that it was all so
Dm
Em
Em(maj7)
sim - ple then,
or has time re - writ - ten ev - 'ry
Em7/D
A7
Dm
Dm(maj7)
line?
If we had the chance to do it

Dm7
G7
Cmaj7
Dm7
G7
all a-gain, tell me would we?
Could we?

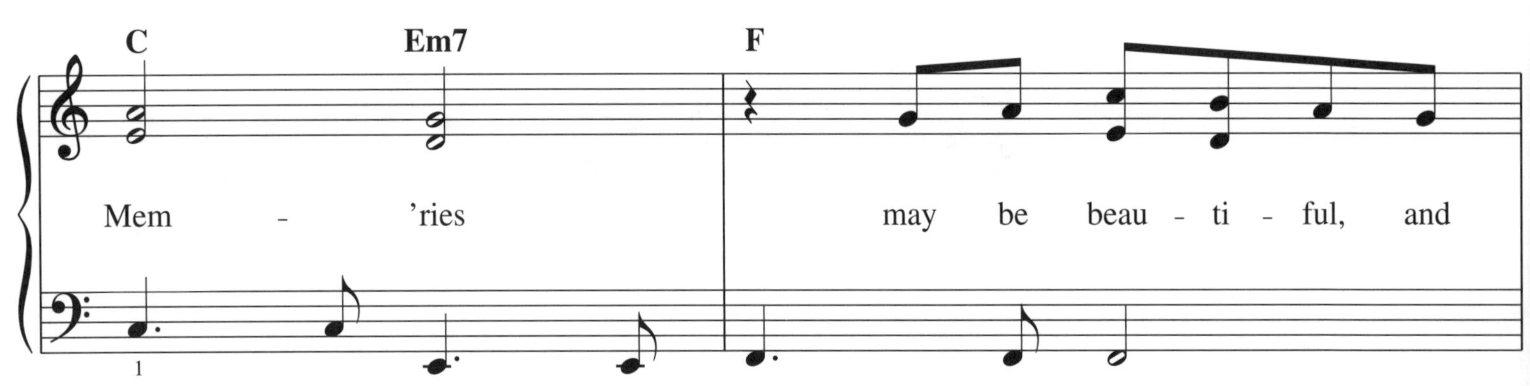
C
Em7
F
Mem - 'ries may be beau - ti - ful, and

Am
F
Em
E7
yet, what's too pain - ful to re -

Am
F
E7
Am
mem - ber we sim-ply choose to for - get.

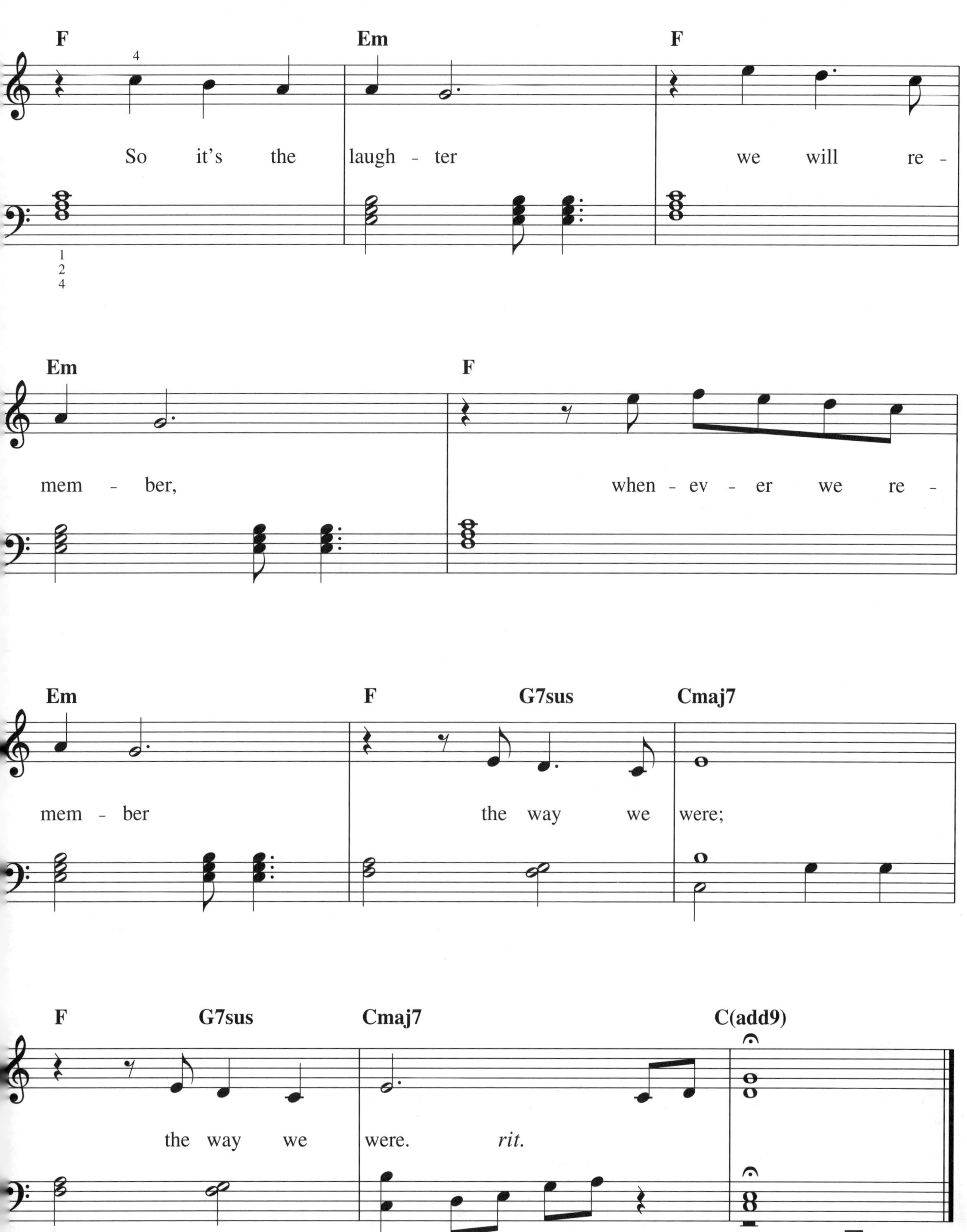
F
Em
F
So it's the laugh - ter we will re -
Em
F
mem - ber, when - ev - er we re -
Em
F
G7sus
Cmaj7
mem - ber the way we were;
F
G7sus
Cmaj7
C(add9)
the way we were. rit.

WE'VE ONLY JUST BEGUN

Words and Music by ROGER NICHOLS
and PAUL WILLIAMS

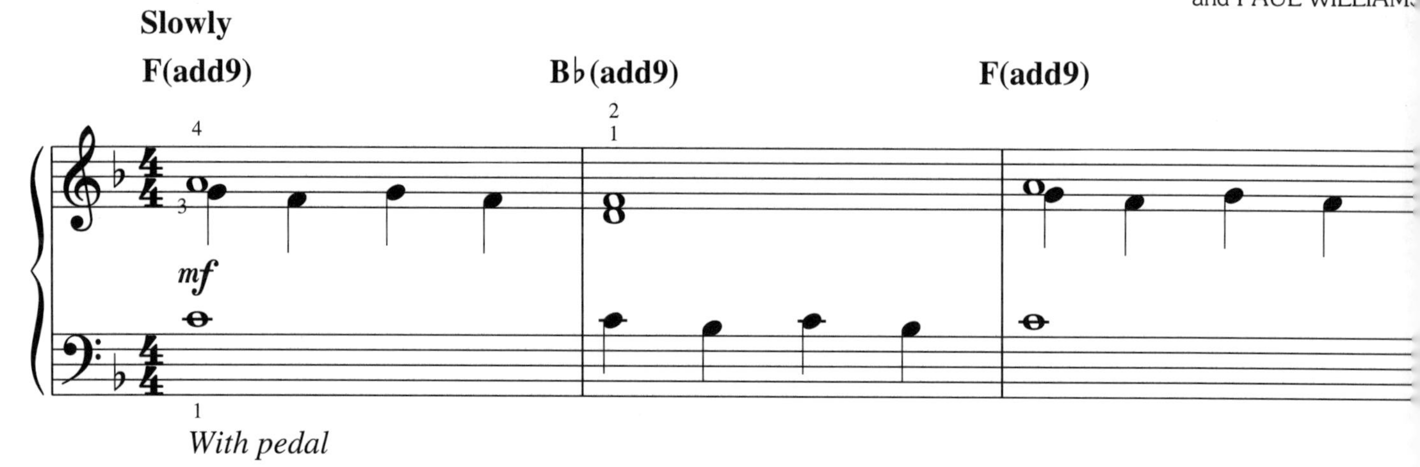

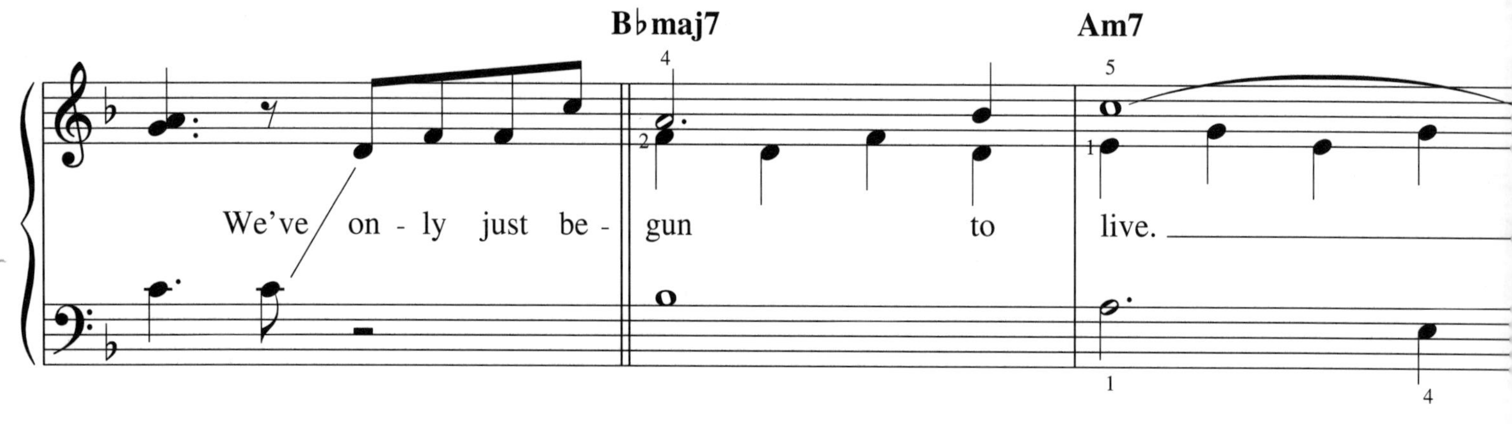

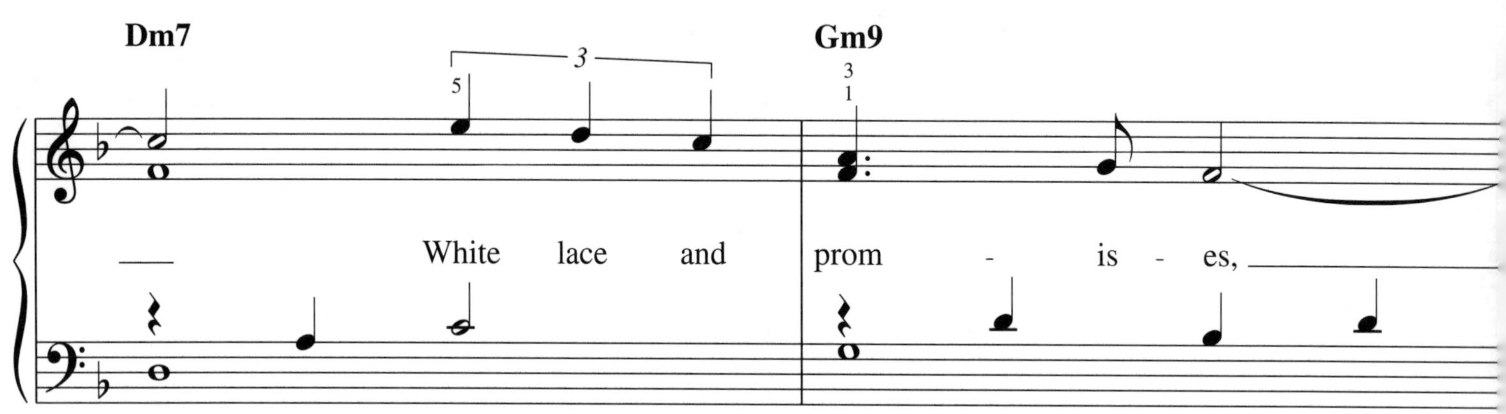

Copyright © 1970 IRVING MUSIC, INC.
Copyright Renewed
All Rights Reserved Used by Permission

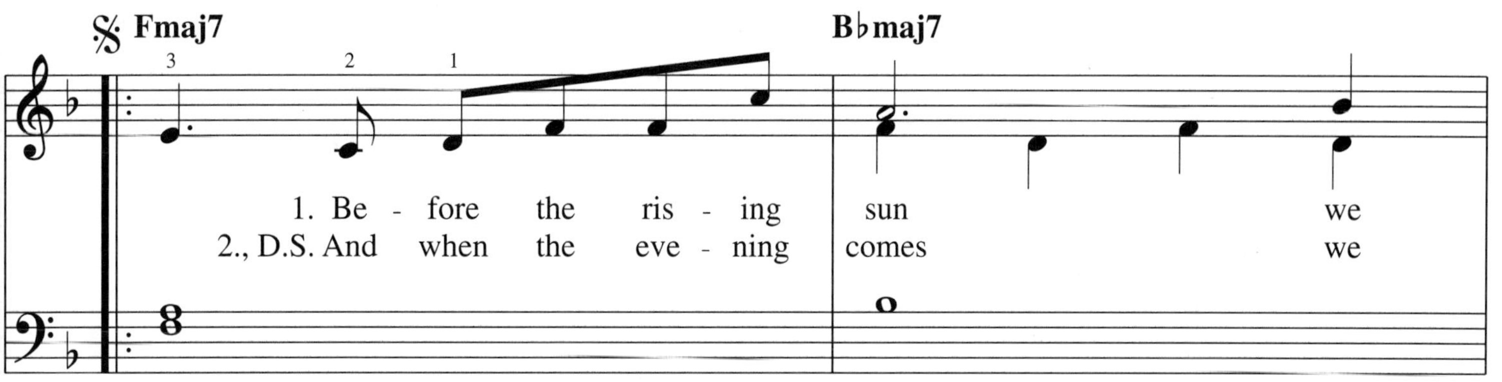
Fmaj7
B♭maj7
1. Be - fore the ris - ing sun we
2., D.S. And when the eve - ning comes we

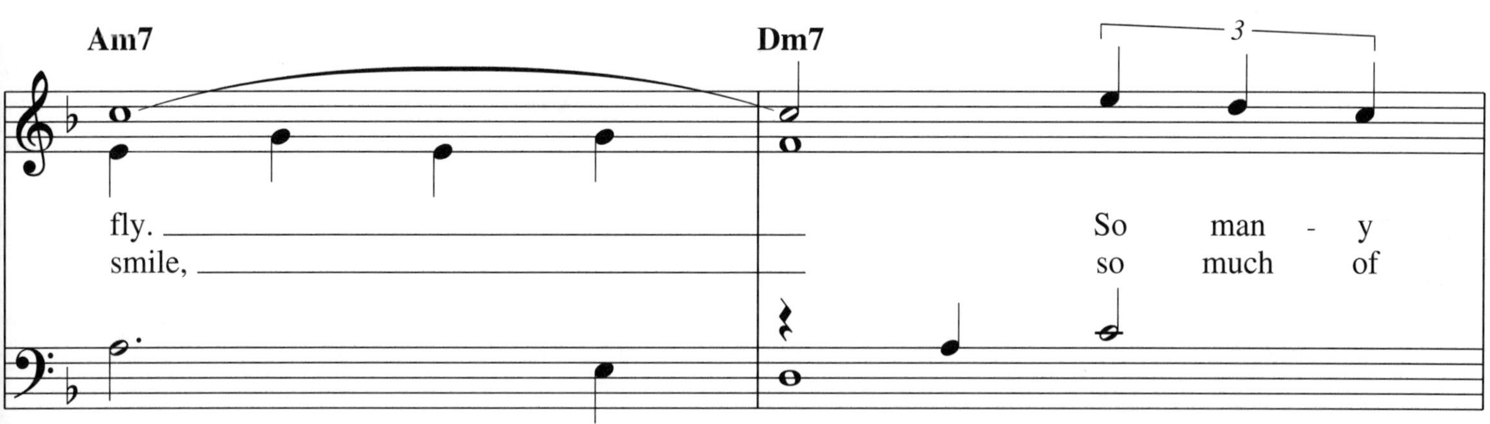
Am7
Dm7
fly. So man - y
smile, so much of

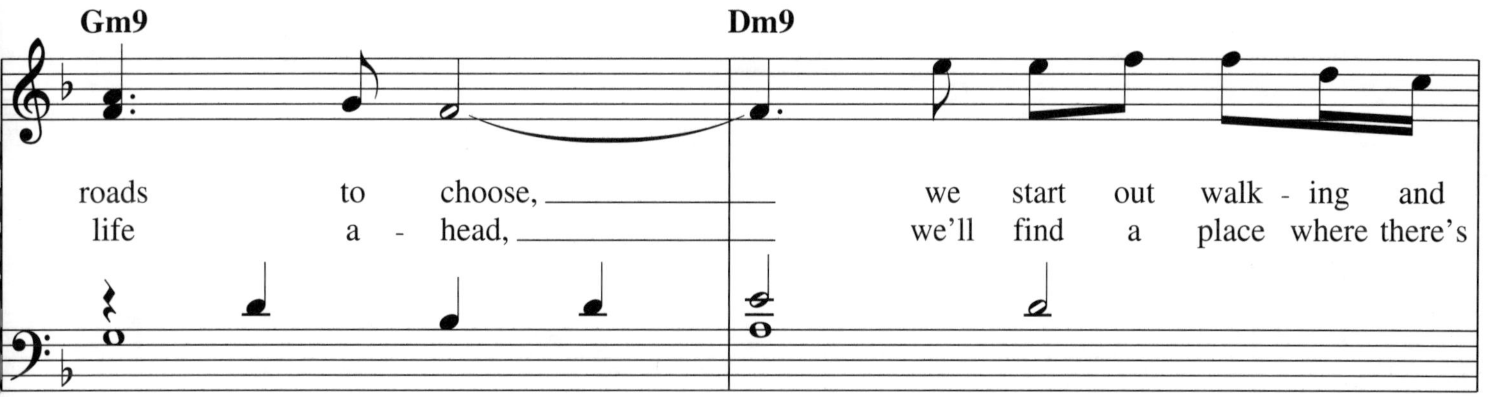
Gm9
Dm9
roads to choose, we start out walk - ing and
life a - head, we'll find a place where there's

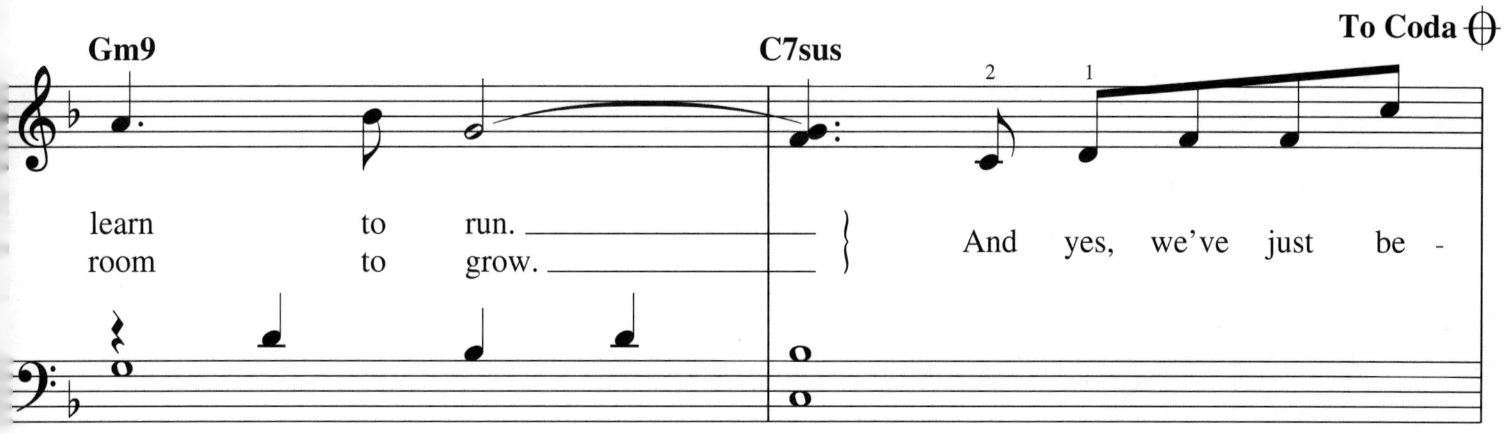
Gm9
C7sus
To Coda
learn to run.
room to grow.
And yes, we've just be -

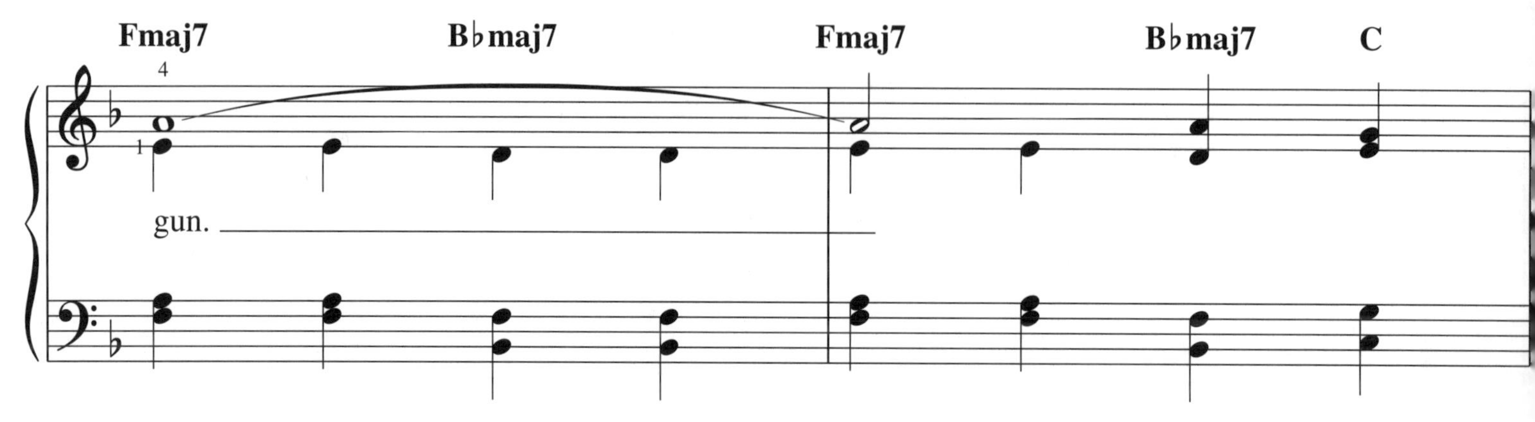
Fmaj7
B♭maj7
Fmaj7
B♭maj7
C
gun.

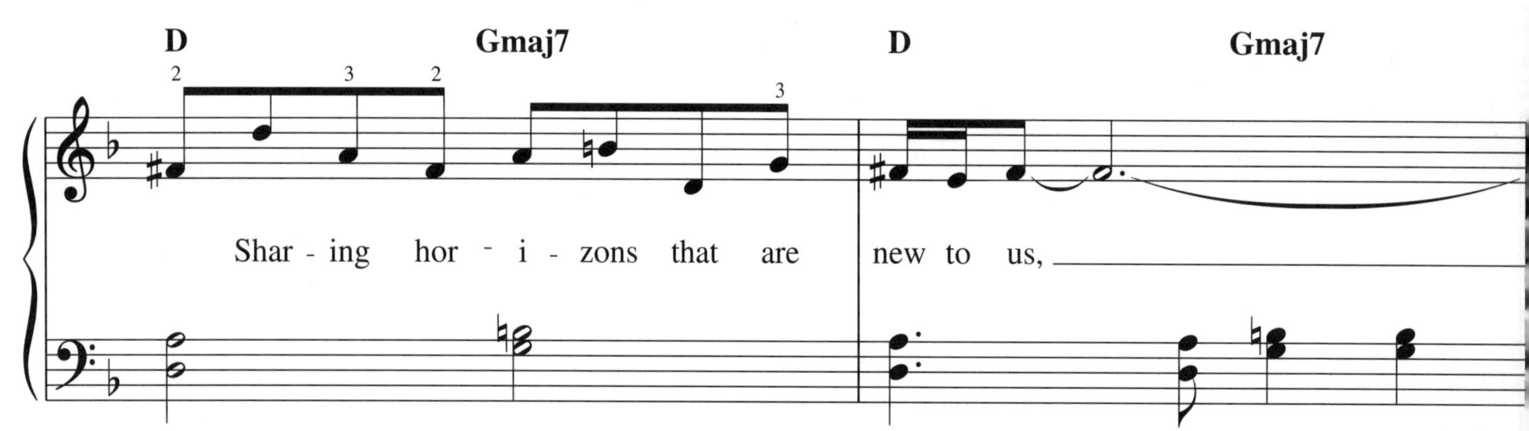
D
Gmaj7
D
Gmaj7
Shar - ing hor - i - zons that are
new to us,

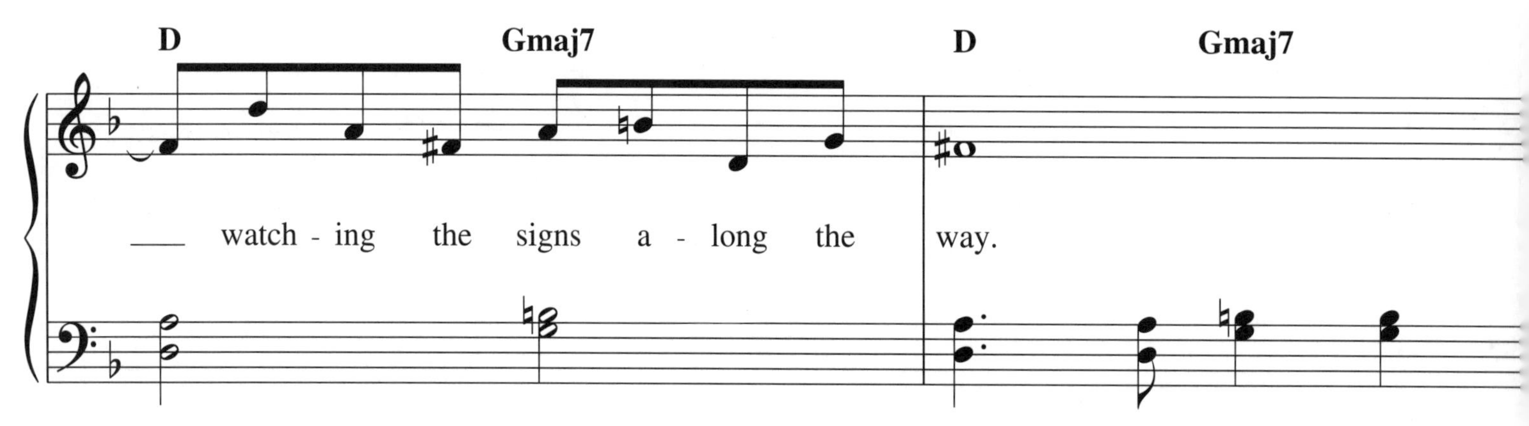
D
Gmaj7
D
Gmaj7
watch - ing the signs a - long the
way.

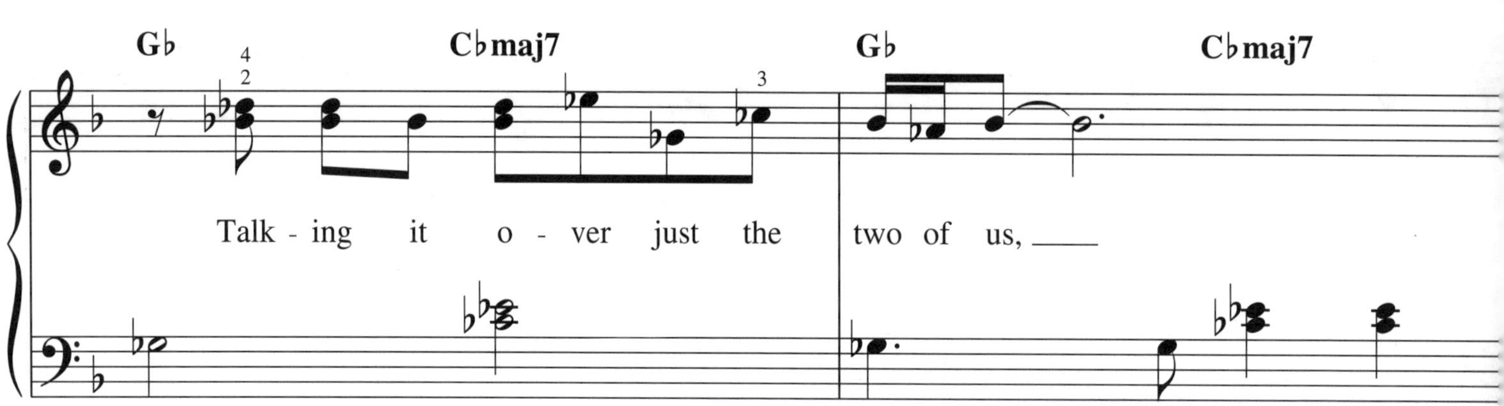
G♭
C♭maj7
G♭
C♭maj7
Talk - ing it o - ver just the
two of us,

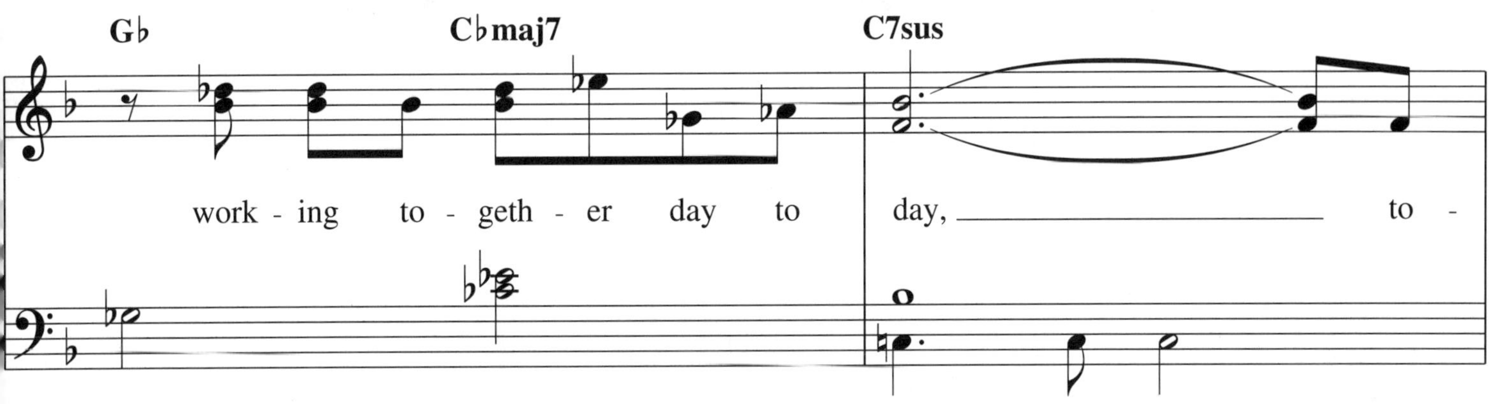

G♭
C♭maj7
C7sus
work - ing to - geth - er day to
day, ___ to -

1.
C9sus
2.
C9sus
C7sus
D.S. al Coda
geth - er. ___
geth - er, ___ to -
geth - er. ___

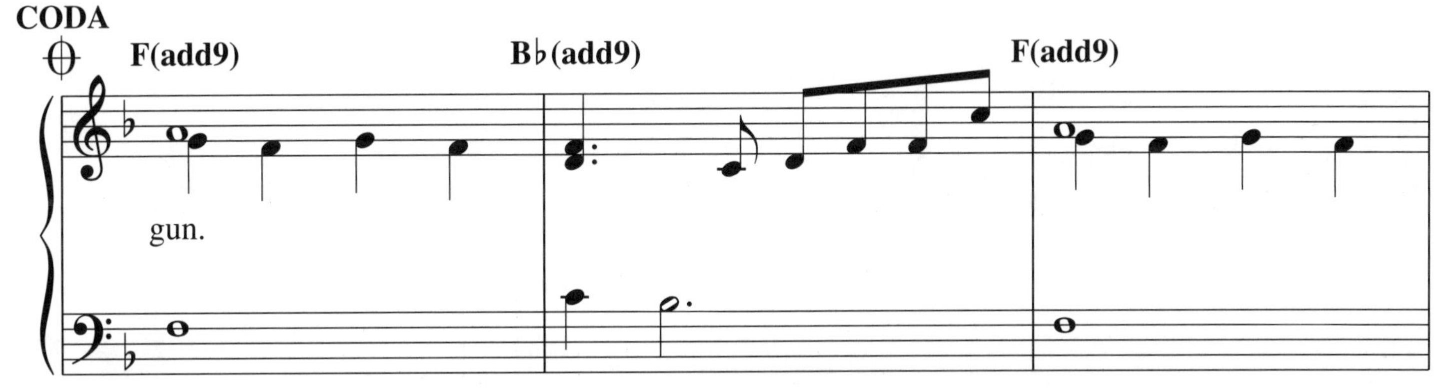

CODA
F(add9)
B♭(add9)
F(add9)
gun.

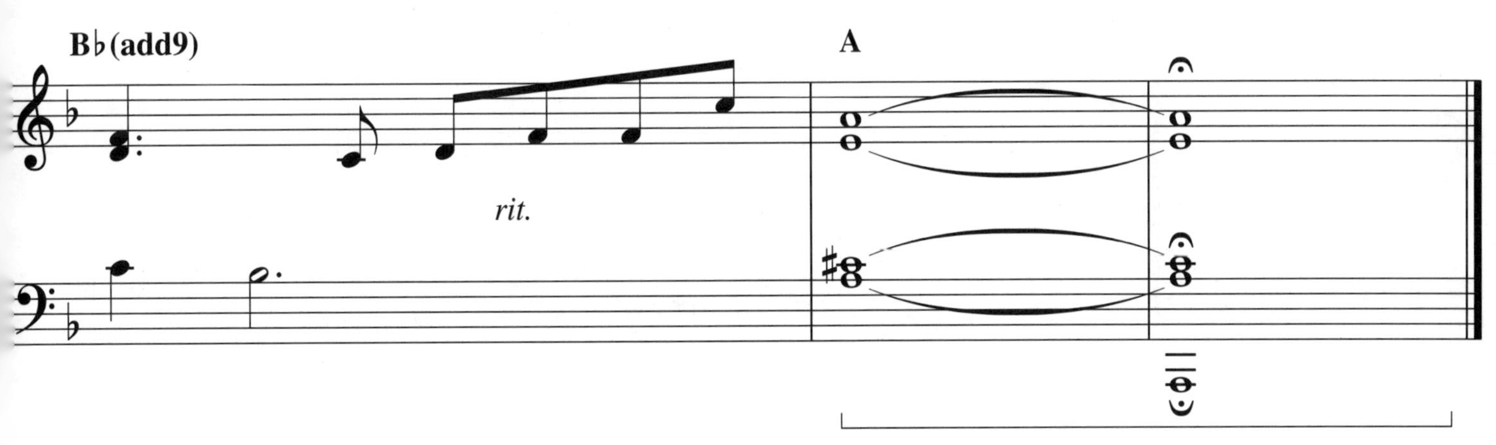

B♭(add9)
A
rit.

WHEN WILL I BE LOVED

Words and Music by
PHIL EVERLY

Copyright © 1960 (Renewed 1988) by Acuff-Rose Music, Inc.
All Rights Reserved Used by Permission

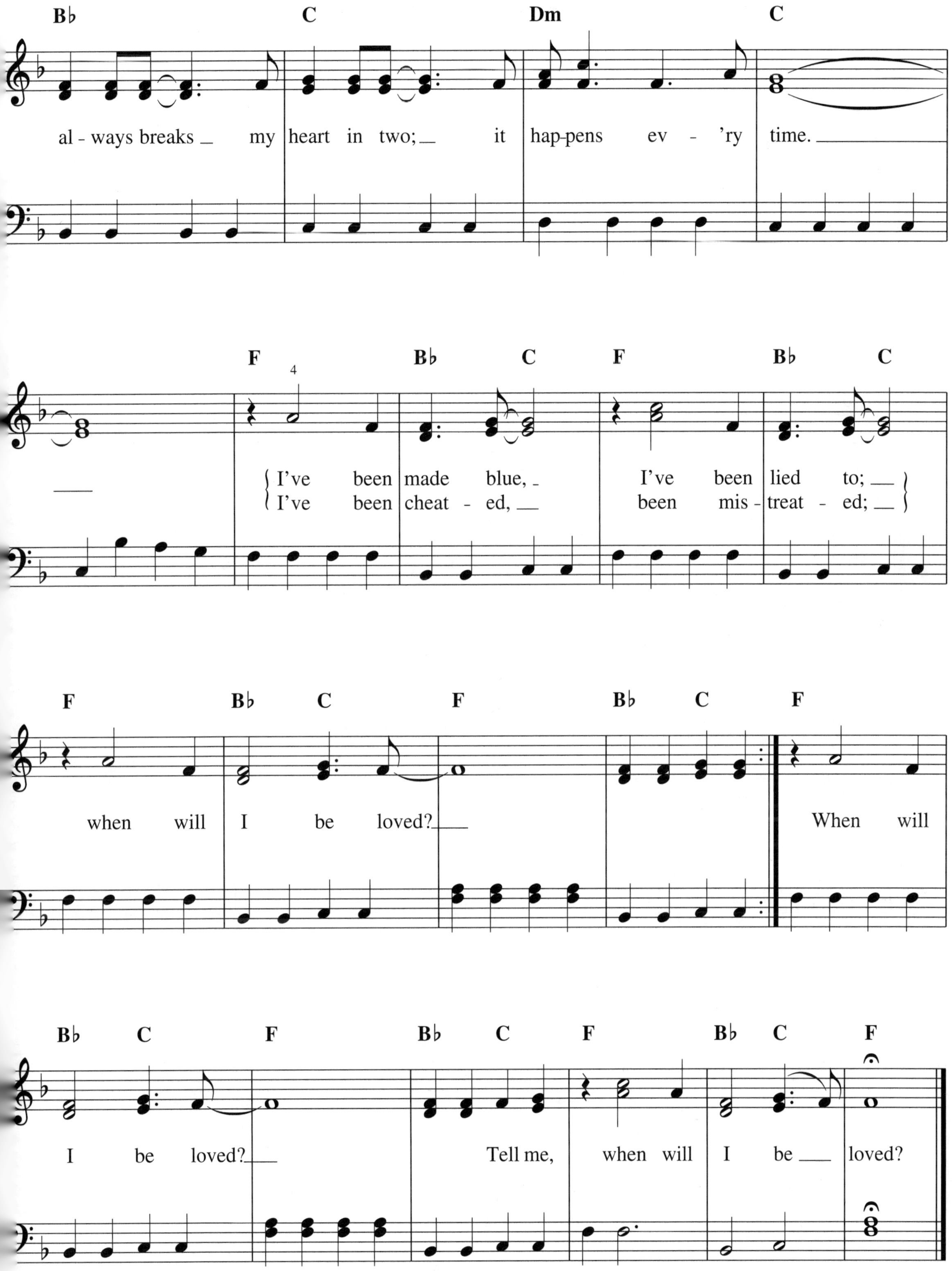

B♭ C Dm C

al - ways breaks __ my heart in two; __ it hap-pens ev - 'ry time. ____

F B♭ C F B♭ C

I've been made blue, __ I've been lied to; __
I've been cheat - ed, __ been mis - treat - ed; __

WHERE DO I BEGIN

(Love Theme)

from the Paramount Picture LOVE STORY

Words by CARL SIGMA
Music by FRANCIS LA

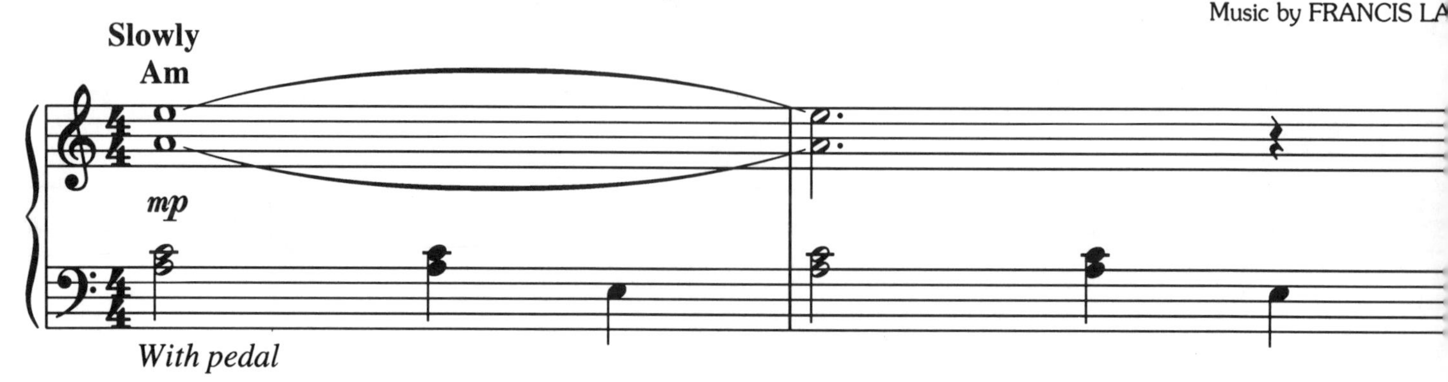

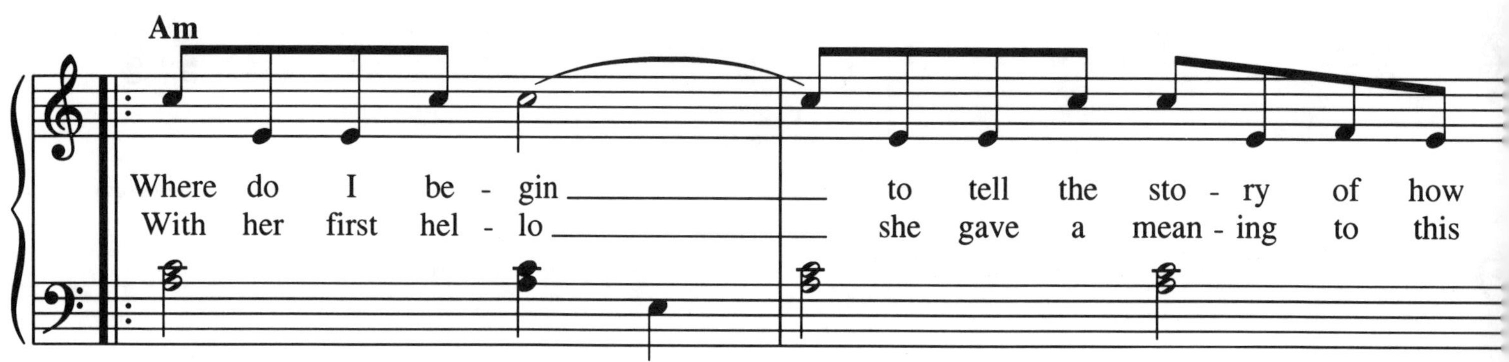

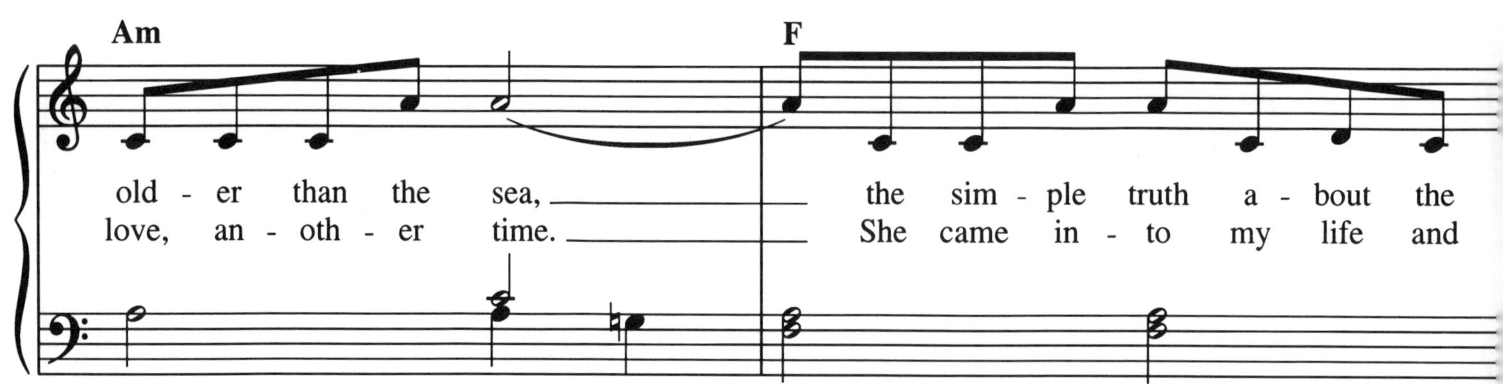

Copyright © 1970, 1971 by Famous Music Corporation
Copyright Renewed 1998, 1999 and Assigned to Famous Music Corporation and Major Songs Company
All Rights for the world excluding the U.S.A. Controlled and Administered by Famous Music Corporation
International Copyright Secured All Rights Reserved

E
1.
E7
Am
love she brings to me?
made the liv - ing fine.
Where do I
start?

2.
E7
Amaj7
She fills my
heart.
mf

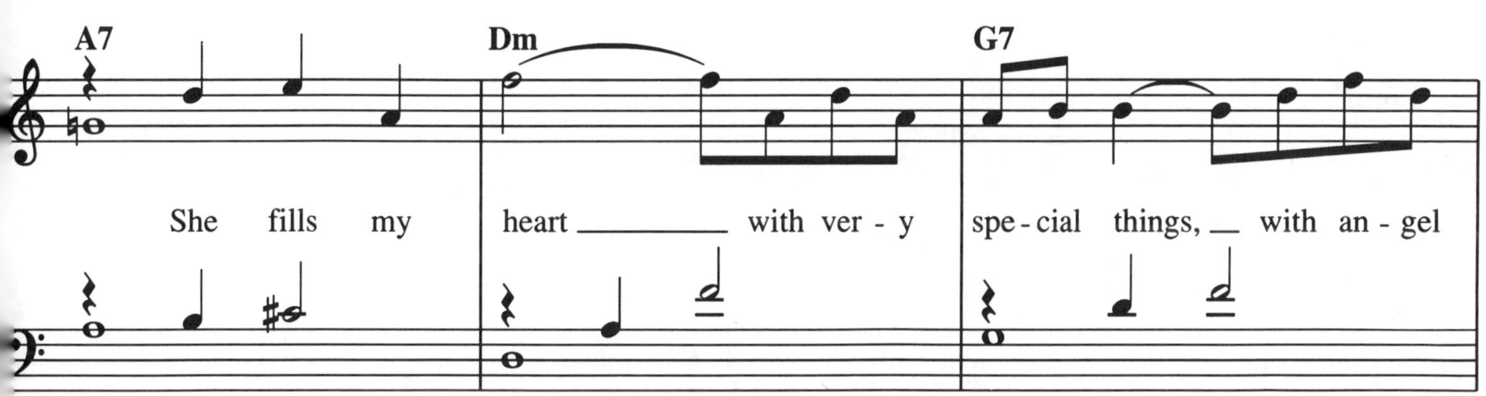
A7
Dm
G7
She fills my
heart with ver - y
spe - cial things, with an - gel

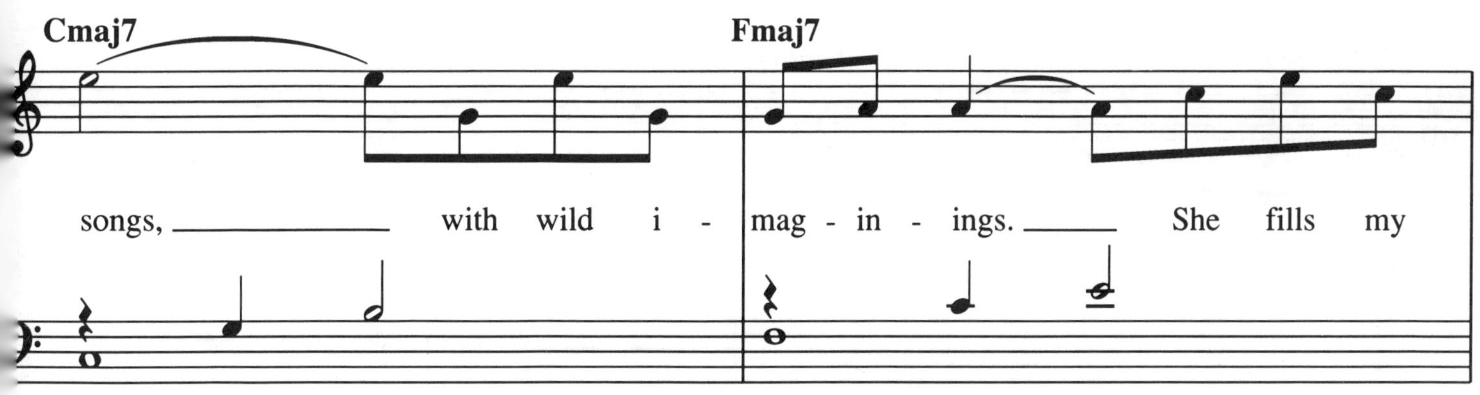
Cmaj7
Fmaj7
songs, with wild i -
mag - in - ings. She fills my

Bm7♭5
E7
Am
soul ___ with so much love that an - y - where I

Dm
G7
go ___ I'm nev - er lone - ly. ___ With her a -

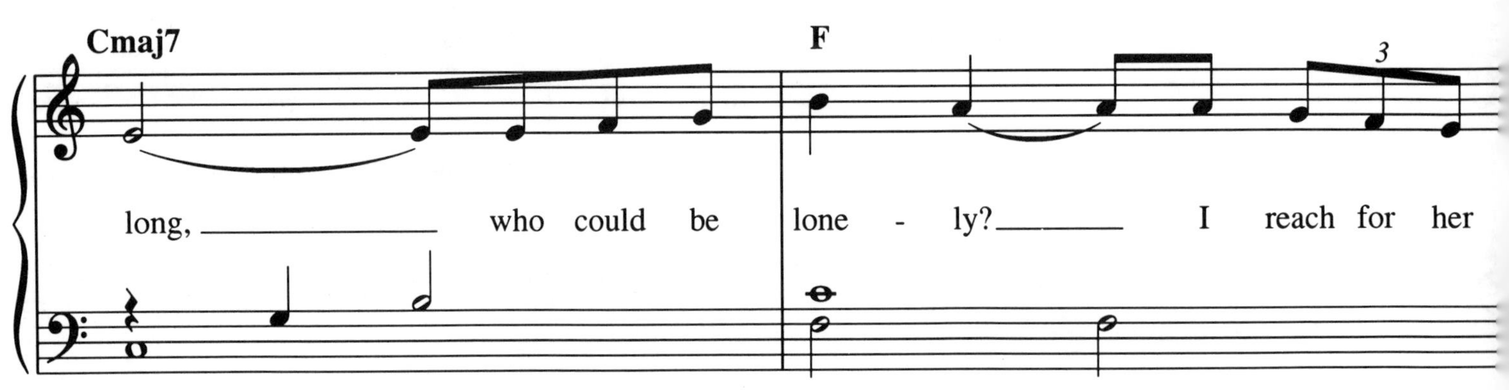
Cmaj7
F
3
long, ___ who could be lone - ly? ___ I reach for her

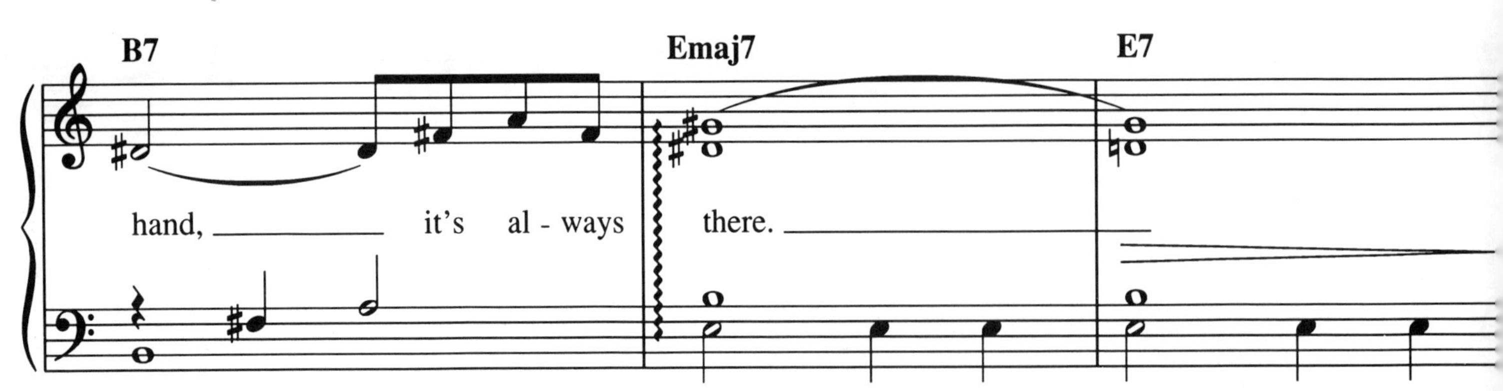
B7
Emaj7
E7
hand, ___ it's al - ways there. ___

Am
How long does it last?
mp
Can love be meas - ured by the

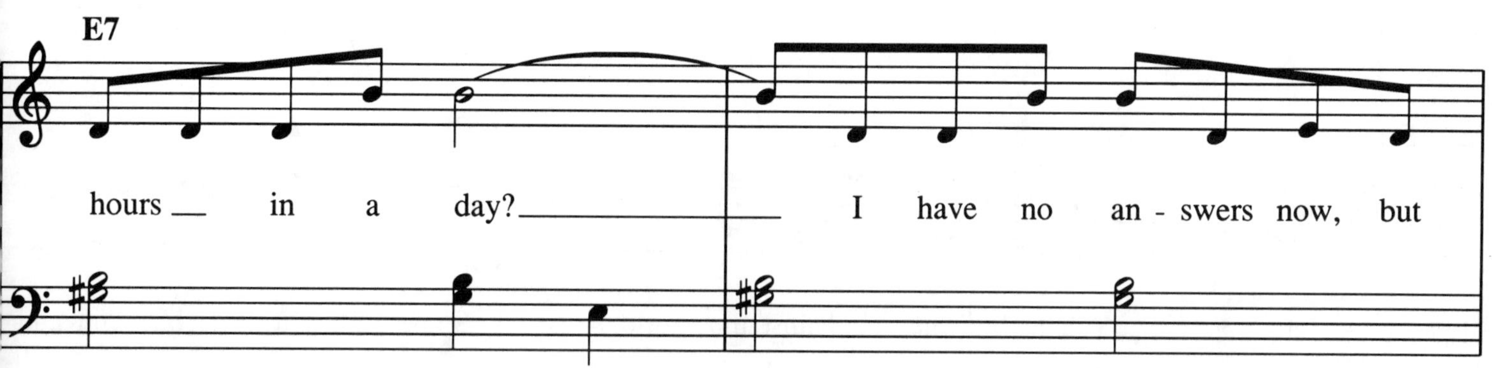
E7
hours in a day?
I have no an - swers now, but

Am
F
E
this much I can say:
I know I'll need her 'til the
stars all burn a - way,

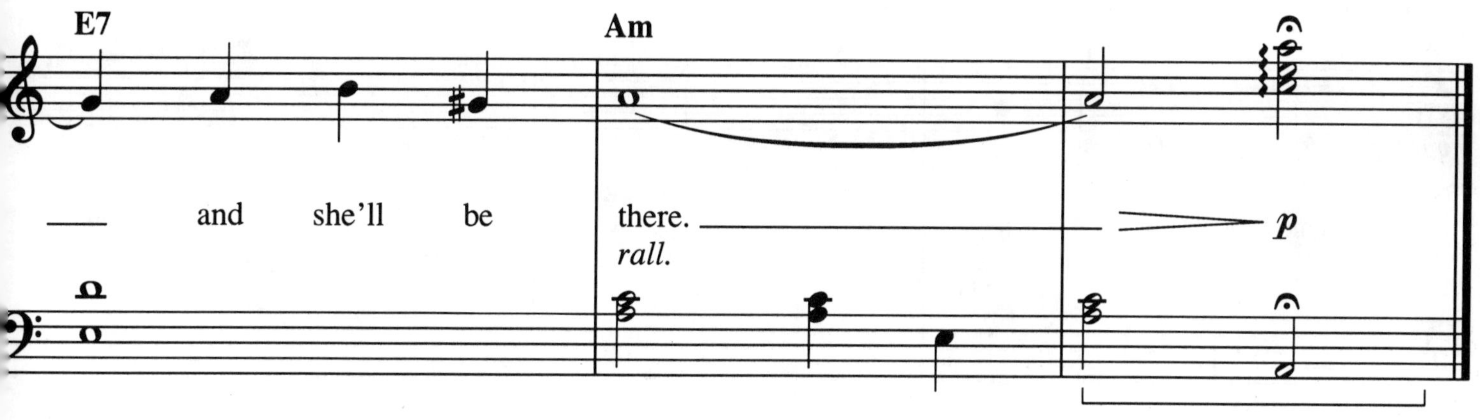
E7
Am
and she'll be
there.
rall.
p

YOU AND ME AGAINST THE WORLD

Words and Music by PAUL WILLIAMS
and KEN ASCHER

Copyright © 1974 ALMO MUSIC CORP.
All Rights Reserved Used by Permission

Em
B7
cir - cus came to town
and you were
fright - ened by the clown?

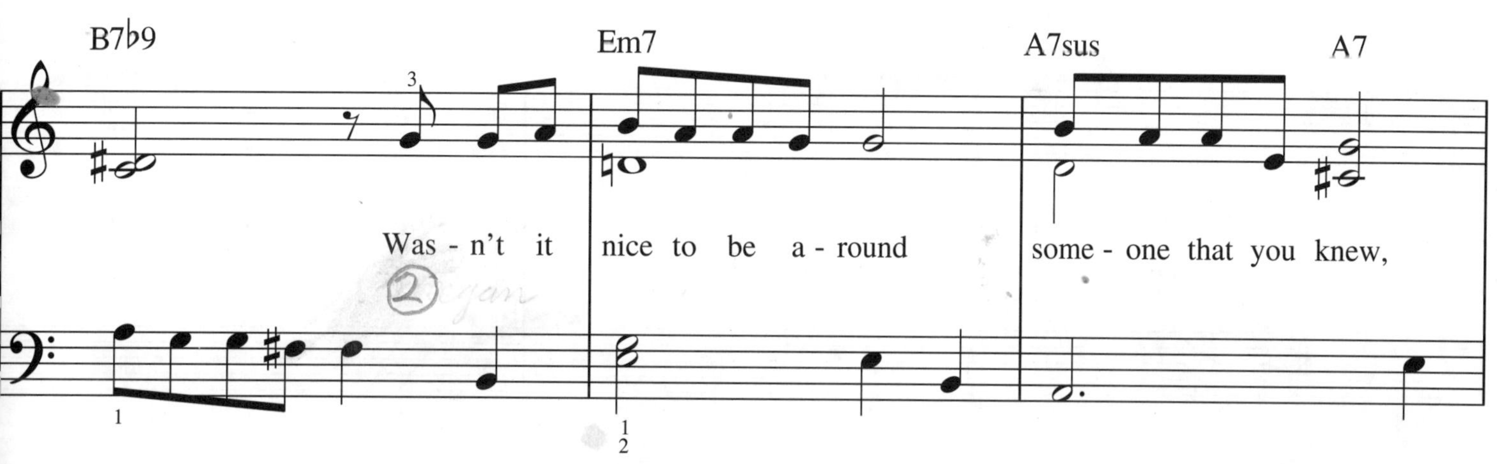
B7♭9
Em7
A7sus
A7
Was - n't it
nice to be a - round
some - one that you knew,

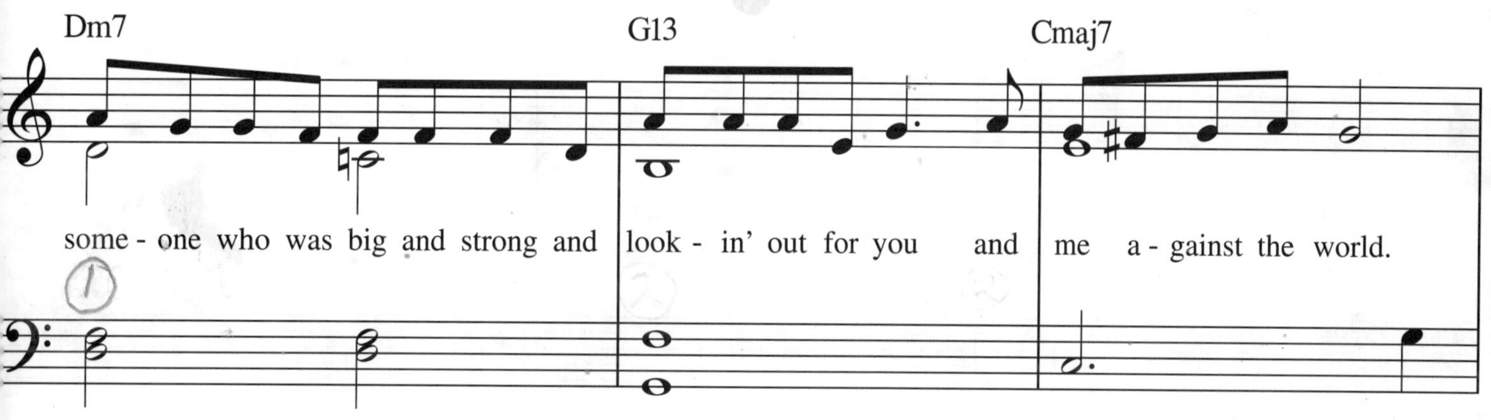
Dm7
G13
Cmaj7
some - one who was big and strong and
look - in' out for you and
me a - gainst the world.

Fmaj7
Cmaj7
B7sus
E7
Some - times it feels like you and
me a - gainst the world
and for all

Am9
C7/G
F♯dim
the times we've cried, I
al - ways felt the odds were on our
side.

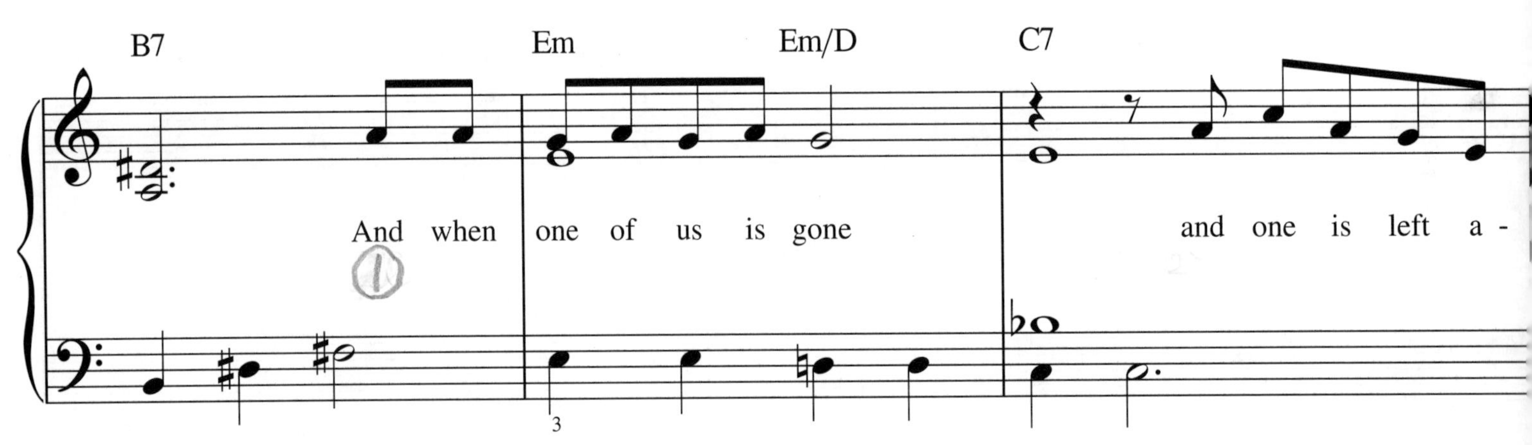
B7
Em
Em/D
C7
And when
one of us is gone
and one is left a -

F6
Fm6
Em7
lone to car - ry on,
well, then re -
mem - ber - ing will have to do;

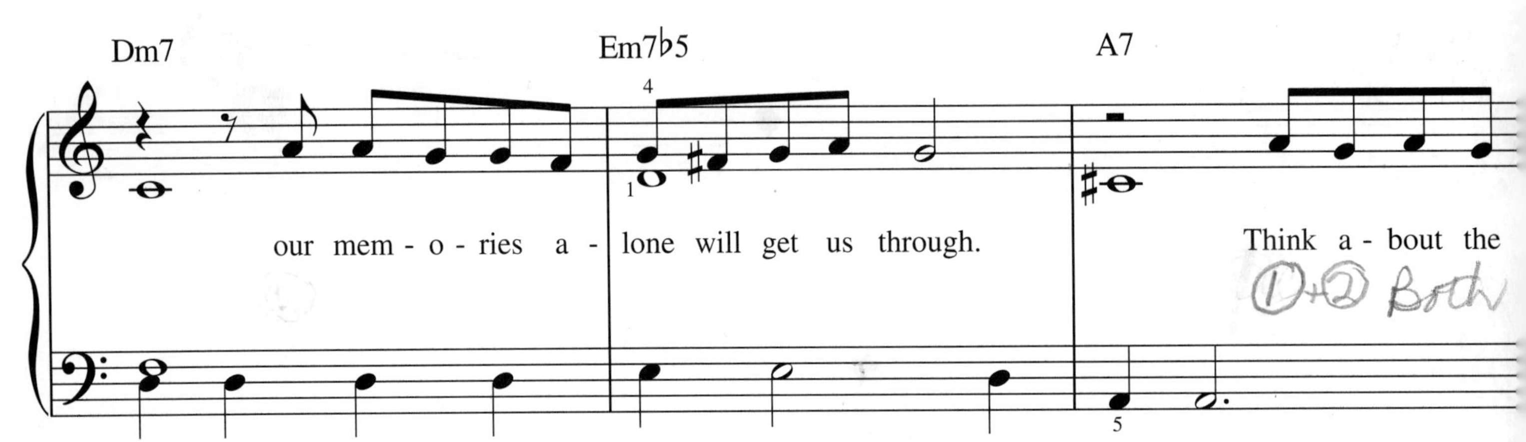
Dm7
Em7♭5
A7
our mem - o - ries a -
lone will get us through.
Think a - bout the

Dm7
G7
Cmaj7
days of me and you,
of you and me a - gainst the
world.
END
Keep same note
go down

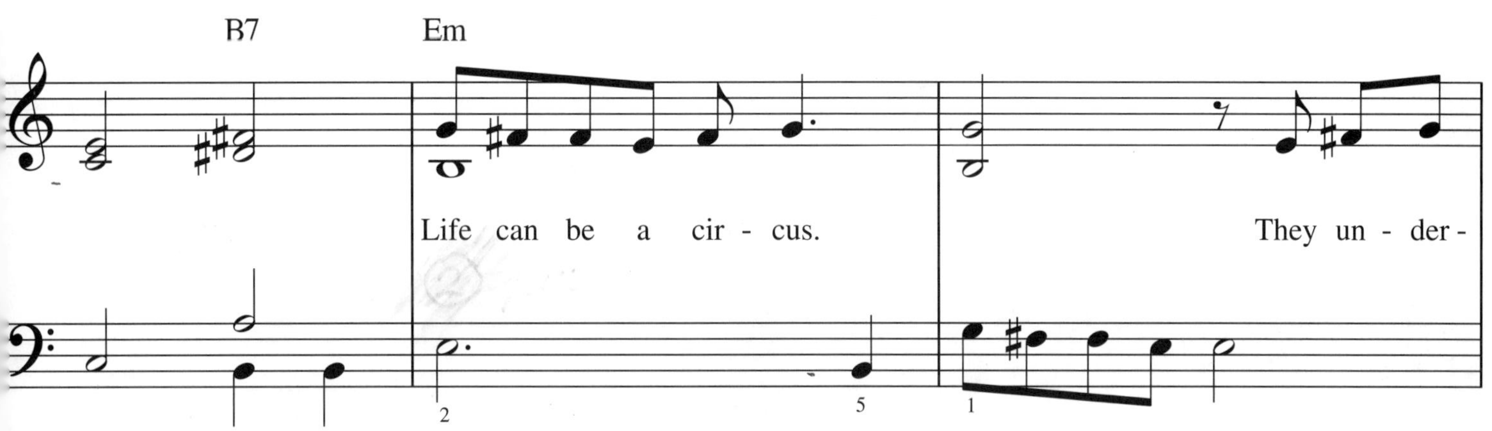
B7
Em
Life can be a cir - cus.
They un - der -

B7
Em7
pay and o - ver - work us
and though we
sel - dom get our due

A7sus
A7
Dm7
G13
when each day is through
I
bring my tir - ed bod - y home and
look a - round for me
and

Cmaj7
Fmaj7
Cmaj7
you a - gainst the world
Some - times it feels like you and
me a - gainst the world.

B7sus
Am9
C7/G
And for all
the times we've cried I
al - ways felt that God was on our

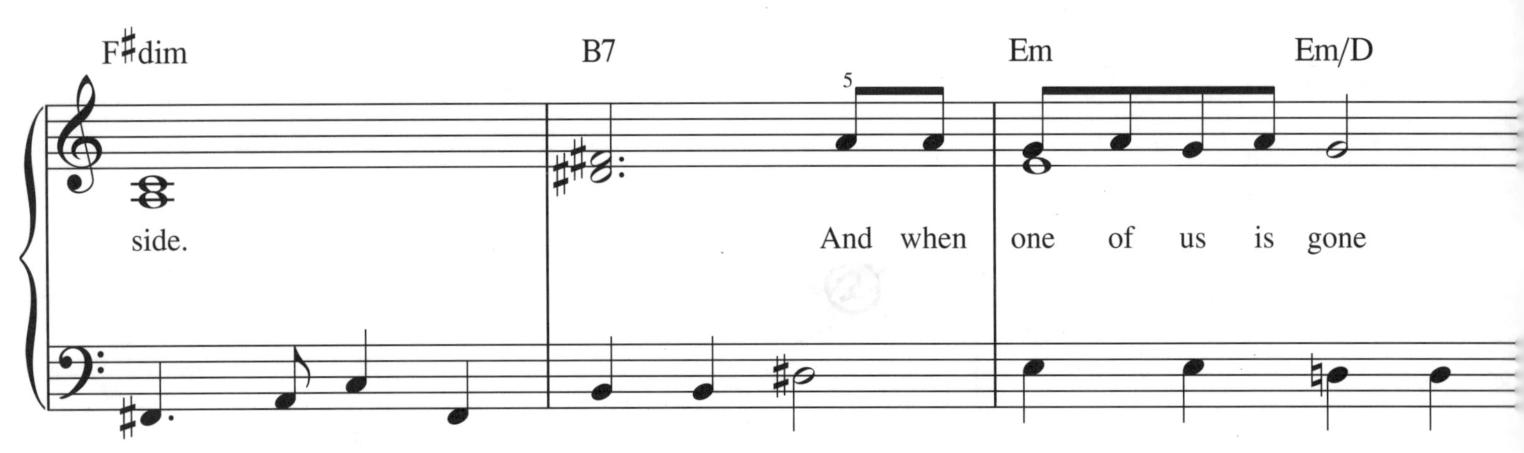
F♯dim
B7
Em
Em/D
side.
And when
one of us is gone

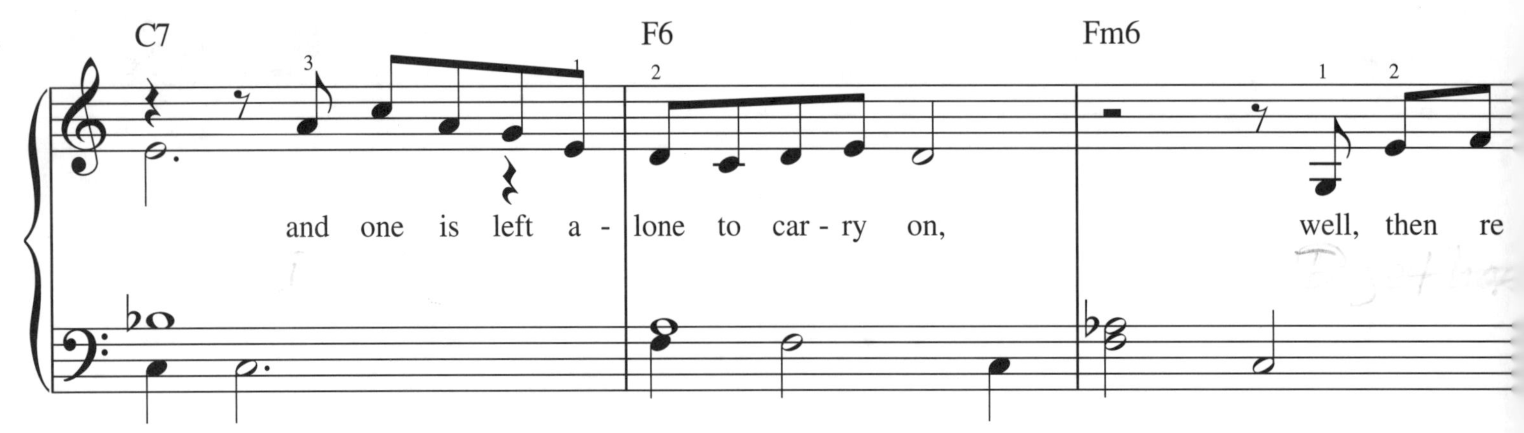
C7
F6
Fm6
and one is left a -
lone to car - ry on,
well, then re

Em7
Dm7
Em7♭5
mem - ber - ing will have to do;
our mem - o - ries a - lone will get us through.
A7
Dm7
Think a - bout the days of me and you,
G7
Cmaj7
Fmaj9
of you and me a - gainst the world.
Cmaj7
Fmaj9
Amaj7

YOU'VE GOT A FRIEND

Words and Music by
CAROLE KING

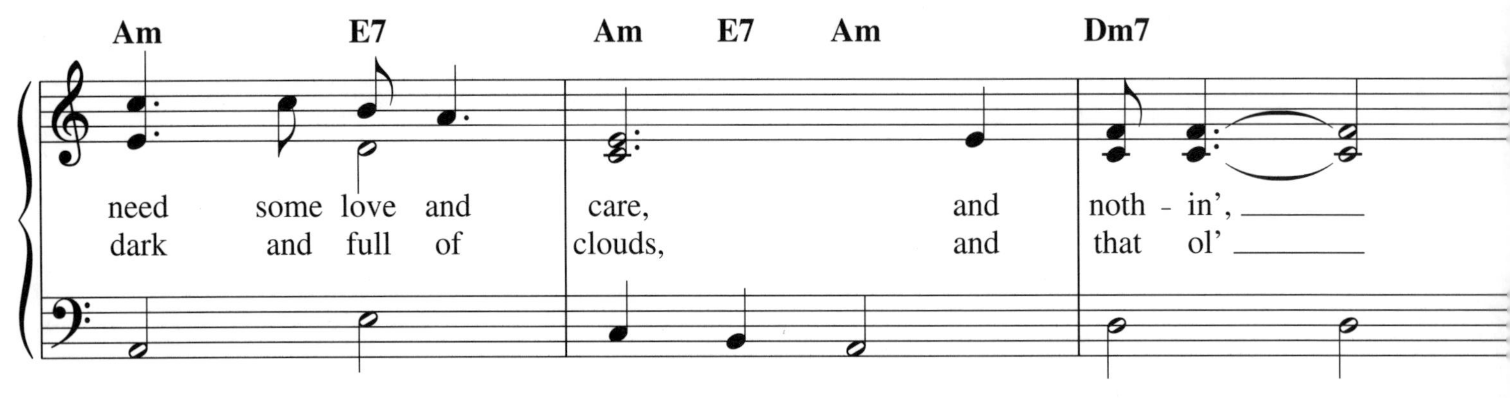

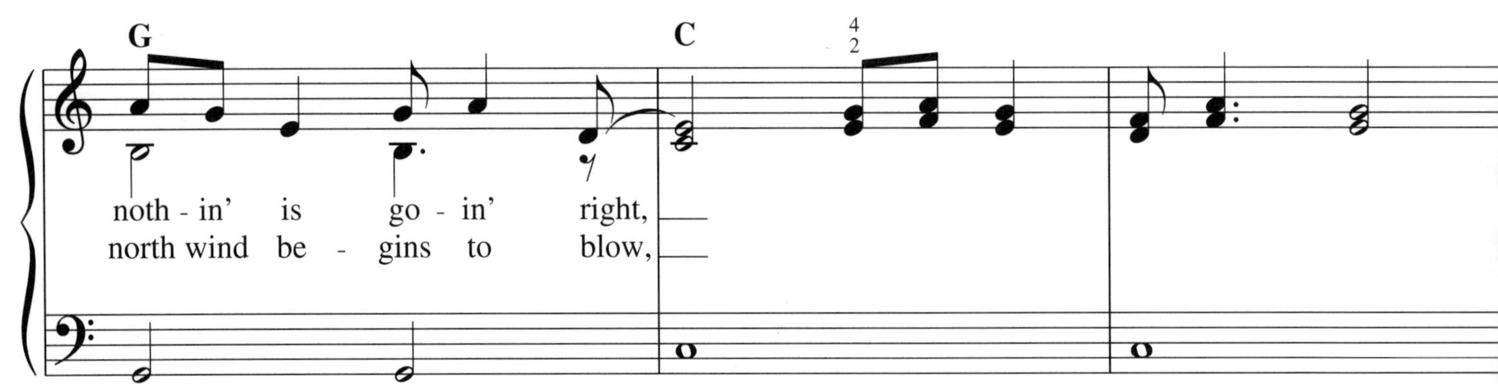

© 1971 (Renewed 1999) COLGEMS-EMI MUSIC INC.
All Rights Reserved International Copyright Secured Used by Permission

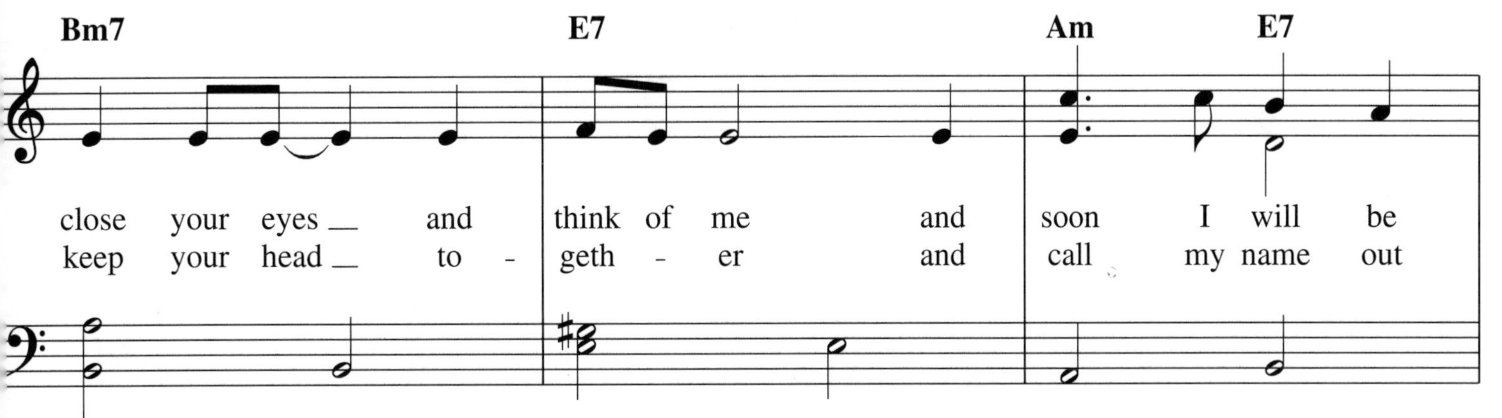
Bm7
E7
Am
E7
close your eyes and think of me and soon I will be
keep your head to - geth - er and call my name out

Am
E7
Am
Dm7
Em7
there to bright - en up e - ven your dark - est nights.
loud; soon you'll hear me knock - in' at your door.

F/G
G
F/G
C
You just call out my name

F
and you know wher - ev - er I am I'll come run -

C
F/G
3
- nin'
to see you a - gain.

C
Cmaj7
2
1
Win - ter, spring, sum - mer and fall,

F
2
C7
To Coda
all you have to do is call
and I'll

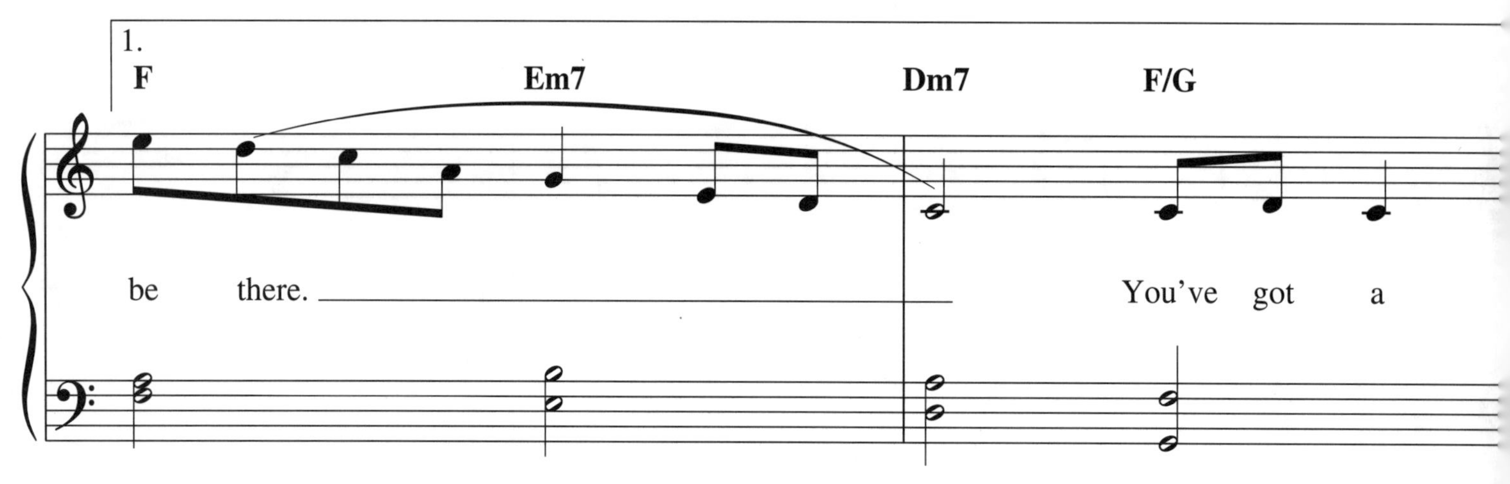
1.
F
Em7
Dm7
F/G
be there.
You've got a

C
F/C
C
friend.

Bm7
E7
2.
F
Em7
Dm7
G7
If the
be there,
yes, I will.
Now

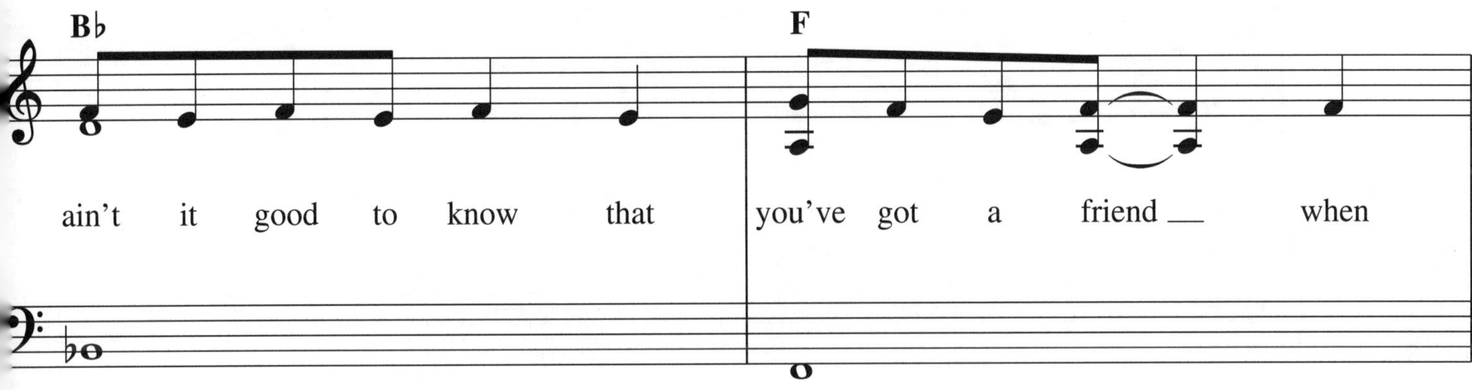
B♭
F
ain't it good to know that
you've got a friend
when

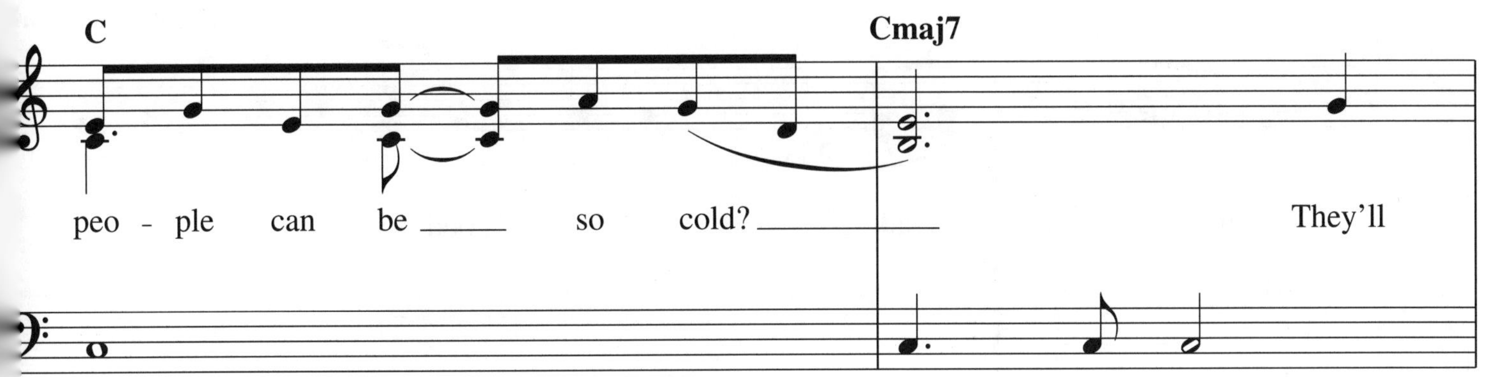
C
Cmaj7
peo - ple can be
so cold?
They'll

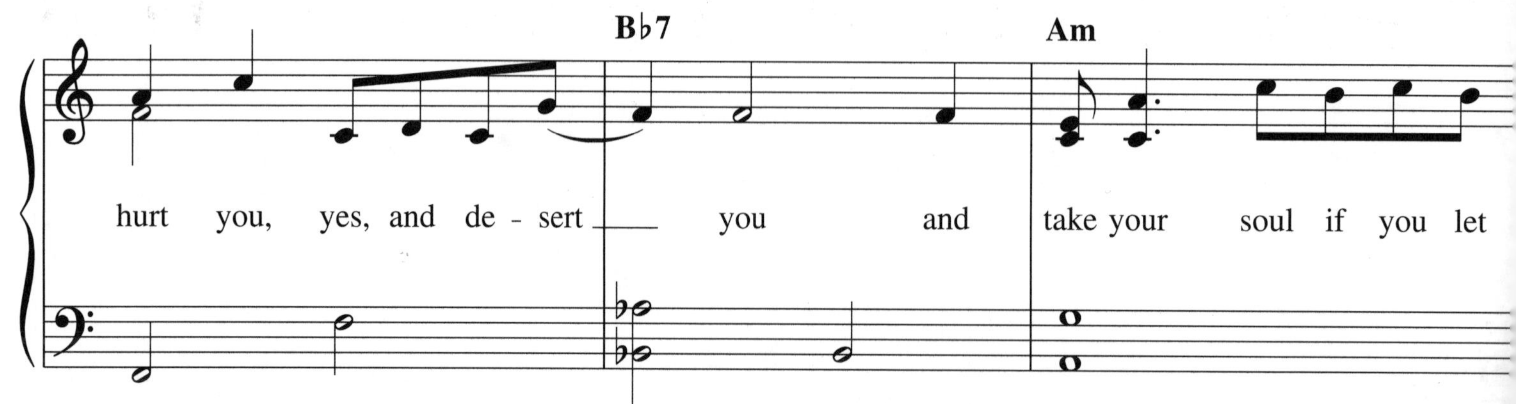

B♭7
Am
hurt you, yes, and de - sert ___ you and take your soul if you let

D7
D9
Dm7/G
D.S. al Cod
3
them. Oh, but don't you let ___ them. You just

CODA
F
Em
Dm7
Dm7/G
C
be there _ yes I will. ___ You've got a friend. ___

F
C
F
Repeat and Fa
You've got a friend. ___ Ain't it good to know you've got a

THE DECADE SERIES

for Easy Piano

The Decade Series explores the music of the 1920s to the 1990s through each era's major events and personalities. Each volume features text and photos and over 40 of the decade's top songs arranged for easy piano, so readers can see how music has acted as a mirror or a catalyst for current events and trends.

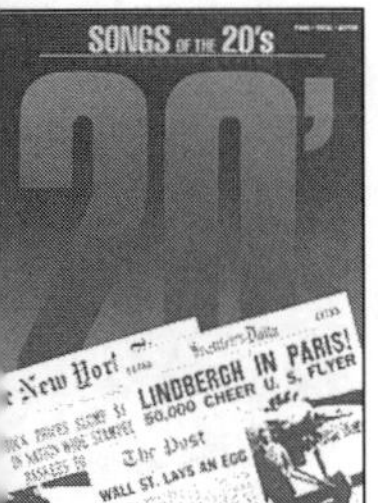

SONGS OF THE '20s

58 songs, featuring: Ain't Misbehavin' • April Showers • Baby Face • California Here I Come • Five Foot Two, Eyes of Blue • I Can't Give You Anything But Love • Manhattan • Stardust • The Varsity Drag • Who's Sorry Now • and more.

_____00110023...$14.95

SONGS OF THE '30s

61 songs, featuring: All of Me • The Continental • I Can't Get Started • I'm Getting Sentimental Over You • In the Mood • The Lady Is a Tramp • Love Letters in the Sand • My Funny Valentine • Smoke Gets in Your Eyes • What a Diff'rence a Day Made.

_____00110022...$14.95

SONGS OF THE '40s

61 songs, featuring: Come Rain or Come Shine • God Bless the Child • How High the Moon • The Last Time I Saw Paris • Moonlight in Vermont • A Nightingale Sang in Berkeley Square • A String of Pearls • Swinging on a Star • Tuxedo Junction • You'll Never Walk Alone.

_____00110021...$14.95

SONGS OF THE '50s

59 songs, featuring: Blue Suede Shoes • Blue Velvet • Here's That Rainy Day • Love Me Tender • Misty • Rock Around the Clock • Satin Doll • Tammy • Three Coins in the Fountain • Young at Heart.

_____00110020...$14.95

SONGS OF THE '60s

60 songs, featuring: By the Time I Get to Phoenix • California Dreamin' • Can't Help Falling in Love • Downtown • Green Green Grass of Home • Happy Together • I Want to Hold Your Hand • Love Is Blue • More • Strangers in the Night.

_____00110019...$14.95

SONGS OF THE '70s

More than 45 songs including: Don't Cry for Me Argentina • Feelings • The First Time Ever I Saw Your Face • How Deep Is Your Love • Imagine • Let It Be • Me and Bobby McGee • Piano Man • Reunited • Send in the Clowns • Sometimes When We Touch • Tomorrow • You Don't Bring Me Flowers • You Needed Me.

_____00110018...$14.95

SONGS OF THE '80s

Over 40 of this decade's biggest hits, including: Candle in the Wind • Don't Worry, Be Happy • Ebony and Ivory • Endless Love • Every Breath You Take • Flashdance ... What a Feeling • Islands in the Stream • Kokomo • Memory • Sailing • Somewhere Out There • We Built This City • What's Love Got to Do With It • With or Without You.

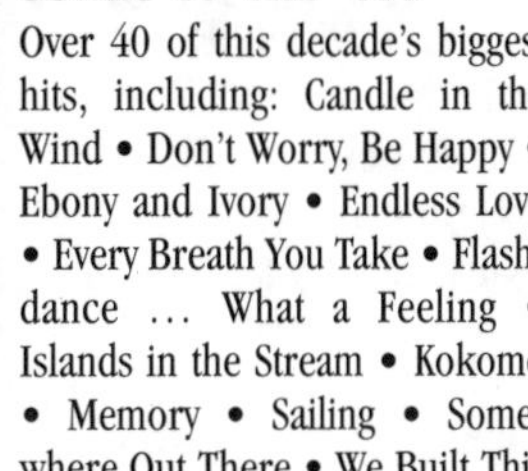

_____00110015...$14.95

SONGS OF THE '90s

39 great songs from the '90s plus a summary and pictorial review of the events and special people who made this decade so memorable. Songs include: Achy Breaky Heart • All for Love • Always • Beautiful in My Eyes • Friends in Low Places • Have I Told You Lately • Here and Now • Hero • Hold My Hand • Losing My Religion • The Power of Love • Save the Best for Last • Theme from "Schindler's List" • Tears in Heaven • Vision of Love • A Whole New World (Aladdin's Theme) • With One Look • and more.

_____00310160...$14.95

MORE SONGS OF THE DECADE

Due to popular demand, we are pleased to present these new collections with even more great songs from the 1920s through 1980s. Perfect for practicing musicians, educators, collectros, and music hobbyists.

MORE SONGS OF THE '50S

Over 50 songs, including: Book of Love • Chantilly Lace • Hey, Good Lookin' • Hound Dog • I Could Have Danced All Night • Lonely Teardrops • Luck Be a Lady • Mister Sandman • Mona Lisa • Sixteen Tons • Splish Splash • Unchained Melody • Why Do Fools Fall in Love? • and more.

_____00310871...$14.95

MORE SONGS OF THE '60S

60 songs, including: Are You Lonesome Tonight? • Breaking up Is Hard to Do • Crazy • Eleanor Rigby • Fun, Fun, Fun • Good Vibrations • Hey Jude • I Get Around • The Impossible Dream (The Quest) • Leaving on a Jet Plane • Moon River • (You Make Me Feel Like) a Natural Woman • Oh, Pretty Woman • Respect • Soul Man • Stand by Me • What the World Needs Now Is Love • and more.

_____00310872...$14.95

MORE SONGS OF THE '70S

50 songs, including: Annie's Song • Copacabana (At the Copa) • Happy Days • I Honestly Love You • I Write the Songs • It's Too Late • Joy to the World • Nadia's Theme • Precious and Few • She's Always a Woman • So Far Away • Summer Nights • Top of the World • The Way We Were • When Will I Be Loved • You've Got a Friend • and more.

_____00310873...$14.95

MORE SONGS OF THE '80S

Over 35 songs, including: Almost Paradise • Bring Him Home • Chariots of Fire • Elvira • Eternal Flame • Footloose • Lady in Red • Livin' on a Prayer • The Longest Time • On the Road Again • Saving All My Love for You • Under the Sea • Up Where We Belong • You're the Inspiration • and more.

_____00310874...$14.95

MORE SONGS OF THE '90S

40 songs, including: Adia • Blue • Change the World • Circle of Life • Fields of Gold • From a Distance • Give Me One Reason • I Can't Make You Love Me • I Don't Want to Wait • I Will Remember You • More Than Words • My Heart Will Go on (Love Theme from 'Titanic') • Save the Best for Last • Something to Talk About (Let's Give Them Something to Talk About) • You'll Be in My Heart (Pop Version) • Zoot Suit Riot • and more.

_____00310875...$14.95

FOR MORE INFORMATION, SEE YOUR LOCAL MUSIC DEALER, OR WRITE TO:

7777 W. BLUEMOUND RD. P.O. BOX 13819 MILWAUKEE, WI 53213

Visit Hal Leonard Online at
www.halleonard.com

Prices, contents and availability subject to change without notice

It's Easy to Play Your Favorite Songs with Hal Leonard Easy Piano Books

The Best of Today's Movie Hits

16 contemporary film favorites: Change the World • Colors of the Wind • I Believe in You and Me • I Finally Found Someone • If I Had Words • Mission: Impossible Theme • When I Fall in Love • You Must Love Me • more.

00310248 ....$9.95

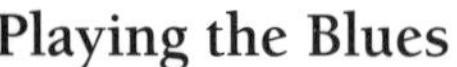

Playing the Blues

Over 30 great blues tunes arranged for easy piano: Baby, Won't You Please Come Home • Chicago Blues • Fine and Mellow • Heartbreak Hotel • Pinetop's Blues • St. Louis Blues • The Thrill Is Gone • more.

00310102..$12.95

The Best Songs Ever

Over 70 all-time favorite songs, featuring: All I Ask of You • Body and Soul • Call Me Irresponsible • Crazy • Edelweiss • Fly Me to the Moon • The Girl From Ipanema • Here's That Rainy Day • Imagine • Let It Be • Longer • Moon River • Moonlight in Vermont • People • Satin Doll • Save the Best for Last • Somewhere Out There • Stormy Weather • Strangers in the Night • Tears in Heaven • Unchained Melody • Unforgettable • The Way We Were • What a Wonderful World • When I Fall in Love • and more

00359223 ....$19.95

Country Love Songs

34 classic and contemporary country favorites, including: The Dance • A Few Good Things Remain • Forever and Ever Amen • I Never Knew Love • Love Can Build a Bridge • Love Without End, Amen • She Believes in Me • She Is His Only Need • Where've You Been • and more.

00110030 ....$12.95

R&B Love Songs

27 songs, including: Ain't Nothing Like the Real Thing • Easy • Exhale (Shoop Shoop) • The First Time Ever I Saw Your Face • Here and Now • I'm Your Baby Tonight • My Girl • Never Can Say Goodbye • Ooo Baby Baby • Save the Best for Last • Someday • Still • and more.

00310181 ....$12.95

Rock N Roll for Easy Piano

40 rock favorites for the piano, including: All Shook Up • At the Hop • Chantilly Lace • Great Balls of Fire • Lady Madonna • The Shoop Shoop Song (It's in His Kiss) • The Twist • Wooly Bully • and more.

00222544...$12.95

I'll Be Seeing You

50 Songs of World War II

A salute to the music and memories of WWII, including a chronology of events on the homefront, dozens of photos, and 50 radio favorites of the GIs and their families back home. Includes: Boogie Woogie Bugle Boy • Don't Sit Under the Apple Tree (With Anyone Else But Me) • I Don't Want to Walk Without You • Moonlight in Vermont • and more.

00310147...$18.95

The Really Big Book of Children's Songs

63 kids' hits: Alley Cat Song • Any Dream Will Do • Circle of Life • The Grouch Song • Hakuna Matata • I Won't Grow Up • Kum-Ba-Yah • Monster Mash • My Favorite Things • Sesame Street Theme • Winnie the Pooh • You've Got a Friend in Me • and more.

00310372...$15.95

Broadway Jazz Standards

34 super songs from the stage: All the Things You Are • Bewitched • Come Rain or Come Shine • I Could Write a Book • Just in Time • The Lady Is a Tramp • Mood Indigo • My Funny Valentine • Old Devil Moon • Satin Doll • Small World • and more.

00310428...$11.95

Best of Cole Porter

Over 30 songs, including: Be a Clown • Begin the Beguine • Easy to Love • From This Moment On • In the Still of the Night • Night and Day • So in Love • Too Darn Hot • You Do Something to Me • You'd Be So Nice to Come Home To • and more

00311576...$14.95

FOR MORE INFORMATION, SEE YOUR LOCAL MUSIC DEALER, OR WRITE TO:

7777 W. BLUEMOUND RD. P.O. BOX 13819 MILWAUKEE, WI 53213

www.halleonard.com

Prices, book contents, and availability subject to change without notice